Library of
Davidson College

An Uncomfortable Authority

Portrait of Maria Edgeworth by Alonzo Chappel. Courtesy of the National Gallery of Ireland.

An Uncomfortable Authority

Maria Edgeworth and Her Contexts

Edited by
Heidi Kaufman and Chris Fauske

Newark: University of Delaware Press

© 2004 by Rosemont Publishing & Printing Corp.

All rights reserved. Authorization to photocopy items for internal or personal use, or the internal or personal use of specific clients, is granted by the copyright owner, provided that a base fee of $10.00, plus eight cents per page, per copy is paid directly to the Copyright Clearance Center, 222 Rosewood Drive, Danvers, Massachusetts 01923. [0-87413-878-7/04 $10.00 + 8¢ pp, pc.]

Other than as indicated in the foregoing, this book may not be reproduced, in whole or in part, in any form (except as permitted by Sections 107 and 108 of the U.S. Copyright Law), and except for brief quotes appearing in reviews in the public press.

Associated University Presses
2010 Eastpark Boulevard
Cranbury, NJ 08512

The paper used in this publication meets the requirements of the American National Standard for Permanence of Paper for Printed Library Materials Z39.48-1984.

Library of Congress Cataloging-in-Publication Data

An uncomfortable authority : Maria Edgeworth and her contexts / edited by Heidi Kaufman and Chris Fauske.
    p. cm.
    Includes bibliographical references and index.
    ISBN 0-87413-878-7 (alk. paper)
    1. Edgeworth, Maria, 1767–1849—Criticism and interpretation. 2. Women and literature—Ireland—History—19th century. 3. Ireland—In literature. I. Kaufman, Heidi, 1969– II. Fauske, Christopher J., 1963–
PR4647.U53   2004
823'.7—dc22
                                                                                                 2004002844

PRINTED IN THE UNITED STATES OF AMERICA

For Michael DePorte and Janet Aikins

Contents

A Note on the Text 9

Introduction 11
    CHRIS FAUSKE AND HEIDI KAUFMAN

Part I: History, Mythology, and Edgeworth's Ireland

Edgeworth, the United Irishmen, and "More Intelligent Treason" 33
    MARILYN BUTLER

History and Utopia in *Ormond* 62
    PETER COSGROVE

The Keener's Cry in *Castle Rackrent:* The Death of Irish Culture? 84
    FRANCES R. BOTKIN

Part II: Representing Ireland: Fiction, Realism, and Authority

"Le vrai n'est pas toujours vraisemblable": The Evaluation of Realism in Edgeworth's Irish Tales 105
    JACQUELINE BELANGER

"Distorted Nature in a Fever": *Irish Bulls,* Irish Novels, the 1798 Rebellion, and their Gothic Contexts 127
    DARRYL JONES

National Character and Foreclosed Irishness: A Reconsideration of *Ennui* 146
    KATHLEEN COSTELLO-SULLIVAN

Part III: Education, Empire, and the Anglo-Irish Dilemma

"The Fashion Not To Be an Absentee": Fashion and Moral Authority in Edgeworth's Tales   165
   HEIDI THOMSON

"Games of Chance": *Belinda,* Education, and Empire   192
   JESSICA RICHARD

Control Experiment: Edgeworth's Critique of Rousseau's Educational Theory   212
   CATHERINE TOAL

Part IV: Edgeworth's Influences

Harrington and Anti-Semitism: Mendelssohn's Invisible Agency   235
   SUSAN MANLY

A Whillaluh for Ireland: *Castle Rackrent* and Edgeworth's Influence on Sir Walter Scott   250
   KIT KINCADE

Bibliography   270
Notes on Contributors   283
Index   286

A Note on the Text

MARIA EDGEWORTH WAS NOT CONSISTENT IN THE APPLICATION OF initial capitals to aristocratic titles in her work. The essays in this collection follow her practice according to the novel(s) they are discussing

Introduction

Chris Fauske and Heidi Kaufman

In recent years, Maria Edgeworth (1768–1849) has been the subject of increasing interest. A woman, a member of the landholding elite, an educator, and a daughter who lived under the historical shadow of her father, Edgeworth's life and writing are difficult to categorize. Ironically, these very aspects of Edgeworth's identity that once excluded her from literary and historical discussions now form the basis of current interest in her life and her writing. Precisely because she is a woman writer, authorizing herself from under her father's shadow, and because she chose to depict Ireland from the position of both a Protestant landholder and as one who maintained sensitivity to the dispossessed Catholic Irish throughout her life, Edgeworth and her works have been the subject of much debate. Throughout her career, Maria Edgeworth used her fiction to address the inherent problems of acts delineated by religious, national, racial, class-based, sexual, and gendered identities. In many ways, Edgeworth's entire adult life was an attempt to reconcile the irreconcilable, an attempt to justify and preserve her own privileged position even as she acknowledged the tenuousness of that position and as she sought to claim other privileges denied her. Edgeworth's writing continues to challenge readers to understand her historical contexts as much as it obliged her to confront the politics of her literary authority.

In her famous letter to her half brother M. Pakenham Edgeworth, begun on 14 February 1834, Edgeworth alludes to the difficulty of representing Ireland in her writing:

> It is impossible to draw Ireland as she now is in a book of fiction—realities are too strong, party passions too violent to bear to see, or care to look at their faces in the looking-glass. The people would only break the glass, and curse the fool who held the mirror up to nature—distorted nature, in a fever.[1]

Although this statement is ostensibly about early nineteenth-century Irish identity and the cultural work of "a book of fiction," it also speaks to Edgeworth's anxiety about her position of authority and her effectiveness in addressing national and narrative concerns in her writing. If Ireland is unavailable as a looking-glass image, the same might be said of Maria Edgeworth herself, whose ambitious attempts to present "distorted nature" in her novels expose the manner in which her own identity was distorted by her uneasy position as one who supported and identified Irish causes, thereby disassociating herself from the English, while maintaining her position on the estate her family took from the Irish years before. Even as Maria Edgeworth writes from this hard-to-pin-down place, she constantly invokes questions about place itself and about the contested lines and politics of establishment rule in Ireland. Thus, our readings of Edgeworth are very much bound up with questions of place—her sense of her place, her contemporaries' various senses of place, and our historical sense of her place.

Reading Edgeworth is complicated in part because her depictions of Ireland and England suggest that these are not simply geographic locations. Indeed, the places we encounter in Edgeworth's work are neither physically nor emotionally the same as those that she occupied. As Richard Mabey rightly notes, "Landscape [is] a vernacular production, made in a rather haphazard way by us, nature and the weather,"[2] but once made it is often subject to being viewed as if it were the consequence of deliberate design. Edgeworth's landscape was incapable of being described in a single vernacular when she wrote, and now our vernaculars of description applied to her work must compete with conflicting notions of "official landscape[s]."[3] Edgeworth looked out from Ireland's landscape. The descendant of colonists, she also looked at the landscape aware that, as Mabey continues,

> There is another, more anciently rooted sense of place, which has no satisfactory English word to describe it. This is landscape as the home ground, the native patch which becomes familiar by being experienced from ground level, landscape as something you look out from, not at.[4]

With hindsight, we may understand that "between [the] historical and [the] personal there exists an exactly derived cartography of the reclamation of the language,"[5] but it fell to Edgeworth to survey the terrain whereon such reclamation could be undertaken. As with pioneers of cartography, we may now find some of Edgeworth's representations oddly discomforting for being both so familiar and yet so strange, but we can see in the peninsulas and promontories of her work the fundamental contours of a discourse that is always evolving and always difficult to situate.

Edgeworth's role as holder of a cracked looking glass exposes not only "distorted nature" but also her uncomfortable authorization of that nature. In her continuation of the letter to M. Pakenham Edgeworth, Maria Edgeworth includes an anecdote that provides a place to begin to understand the historical and political locale from which she writes:

> Sir Walter Scott once said to me "Do explain to the public why Pat, who gets forward so well in other countries, is so miserable in his own." A very difficult question: I fear above my power. But I shall think of it continually, and listen, and look, and read.[6]

If this passage points to Edgeworth's uncertainty about her own position, it also offers us advice on how to understand Edgeworth's authority from our position, as listeners, observers, and readers. Edgeworth was not alone in having this sense of heaviness: "in regard to the union [with Britain]," Martha McTier had written in a letter postmarked on 30 January 1800 to her brother William Drennan, a founder of the United Irishmen, "I care not a straw, except for the malicious satisfaction of seeing rogues forced to appear as they are."[7] Drennan's own doubts about the likely consequences of the new union are clear:

> A people in losing their Country lose that cementing principle which gives them the character and courage of a nation . . . They become a mere number, not a nation, without any inherent principle or motive of common action, unattached to each other, degraded in their own eyes, contemptible and condemned, they degenerate.[8]

Maria Edgeworth, like her father, had opposed the Act of Union. She had lost a country that had never been wholly hers and lived among those who thought themselves to have lost more than she had, writing for those who assumed her loss in fact to be a gain.

Maria Edgeworth's career was in one sense a lifelong struggle to prevent that degeneration of which Drennan had warned. Her fictional depictions of Ireland and her efforts to redeem and valorize Irish culture often subvert her contemporary contexts by her invention of a nostalgic past, not the past as it was, but the past as it was becoming. For Edgeworth, the present was increasingly judged against a historical narrative she was creating alongside and through the fictional world of her novels. If, as many scholars have noted, the novel itself is a distinctly British or imperial cultural trope, then depictions of Ireland produced in this medium always necessarily reassert British cultural hegemony at some level even when, or especially when, Ireland is produced and imagined for the edification of British audiences. Edgeworth's position of authority comes not simply from her role as advocate for the Irish, but from her identity as an Irish fictionalizer, as one who produced Ireland by way of a distinctly fictional British medium. As Edgeworth chronicled the subsumation of Irish society into British cultural tropes, she became caught in, and representative of, a nexus of political concerns and elisions. As a later literary scion of a distinct Anglo-Irish identity, Louis MacNeice, put it:

> A house can be haunted by those who were never there
> If there was where they were missed.
> . . . .
> A life can be haunted by what it never was
> If that life were merely glimpsed.⁹

In either case, "The haunting anyway is too much."¹⁰ Along these lines we see an image of Edgeworth as she attempts to get out from under the very power structure she critiques, but that, oddly enough, enables her to speak from a position of power. Her earnest efforts to reconstitute and celebrate Irish culture while simultaneously admonishing the effects of British imperialism have the apparition-like effect of identifying a kind of disembodied Ireland she both claims personally and reclaims culturally as valid. When we think of Edgeworth as uncomfortable—as uncomfortably situated historically, politically, and culturally—we recognize that she herself was haunted by a past which had never been and yet which very much existed in her mind. In creating viable myths for one Irish type, she had to do so while being careful not to validate other increasingly recognizable claims to identity, claims that seriously challenged her own authority to speak on behalf of "Ireland," but claims that nonetheless provided her with a historical context for her own explorations of culture. As a result, Edgeworth's political position evolved over the years as she revised earlier ideas or became more forthright in her assertions. When, for example, *Castle Rackrent* did not have the appeal she had hoped for, Edgeworth responded with her *Essay on Irish Bulls*. We begin to understand the significance of Edgeworth's evolution as a writer, and the hauntings she inevitably depicts, as her awareness of the contradictions of her own position develops throughout her life. Yet, if Maria Edgeworth's own position as an author of native Irish culture was drawn by contested political lines, the same might be said of her imagined national identities and the fictional voices that appropriate those identities. Indeed, the chronology of Edgeworth's novels trace what Suvendrini Perera calls "the gradual anglicanization of feudal Irish society."[11] Accordingly, if *Castle Rackrent* is the "first significant English novel to speak in the voice of the colonized," *The Absentee* "records the completion of that process."[12] Tracing this process illuminates as much about "the voice of the colonized" as it does about the problem of representing "the voice of the colonized" when one is both affiliated with and alienated from colonial and colonizing factions.

Perhaps it is not surprising that, as Heidi Thomson notes elsewhere, Edgeworth's "claim of interest in [Irish] 'merits' often reveals [her] desire for distance and control, her wish for authority on the subject of Irishness and her own ingrained sense of English superiority."[13] In a tradition dating back to William Molyneaux and expressed not so long before her by Charles Lucas, Edgeworth writes, Marilyn Butler explains, with the "goal [of] gaining for her Irish characters, regardless of their religion, the rights enjoyed by their English counterparts. Thus, her strategy is not to prove that the Irish are unique, and therefore worthy of nationhood, but to show them in essence the same [as the English], and therefore worthy of equality."[14] This mind-set placed her in opposition not only to much Catholic sentiment in Ireland but also undermined her potential sympathies for the Grattan-era parliament. Her father's obvious sympathies for the United Irishmen's agenda also troubled her, for her justification of "Irish" rights came from a political analysis that was not theirs. As she grew to understand the contradictions of her allegiance both to her cultural definition of Ireland and to her defense of Irish rights as essentially English, Edgeworth's novels were increasingly informed by her own paradoxical position that Irish culture ought to be valorized because it is *as* complex and *as* interesting as English culture.

One facet of Edgeworth's uncomfortable authority, and of our discomfort in reading that authority, comes from her contingent identity as at once and alternately Anglican and Irish, Protestant landholder and sympathizer of the Catholic situation in Ireland. Criticism in this arena has focused on novels such as *Castle Rackrent, The Absentee,* or *Belinda* in an effort to understand Edgeworth not only as a regional and/or national novelist, but also to explore the uses of postcolonial theory to "recover," as Mary Jean Corbett explains, "the heterogeneity that has been suppressed within British studies itself."[15] What do we mean, though, when we label Edgeworth as Anglo-Irish? One reading, according to Julian Moynahan, is that Anglo-Irish means "the doubled or split consciousness of a unique situation, this situation entailing, on the one hand, a link with, yet removal from, English origins and English society; and on the other, a closeness to, and yet a removal or isolation from, the native Irish community."[16] However, the Anglo-Irish themselves understood the relative merit of the two parts of the phrase quite differently and were often surprised and discomforted to discover how others viewed them. When Irish identity was established as essentially Catholic and in opposition to English culture, it came as a genuine shock to many to learn that, as Stephen Gwynn explains of his own experiences, "the new nationalism prefer[red] to describe me and the like of, as Anglo-Irish . . . So all my life I [had] been spiritually hyphenated without knowing it."[17] Edgeworth's own indistinct appreciation of these various nuances, many of which would be identified and defined only after her own life had ended, results in significant variant readings of, for example, her choice of Thady Quirk as narrator in *Castle Rackrent.* While Corbett asserts that "Thady Quirk and his masters are laughable only to the extent that we persist in seeing them as beneath or below us,"[18] the possibility remains, as Butler reminds us, that

> however seductive the appearances we have to test further [*Castle Rackrent*'s] typing as a colonial novel . . . The strongest historical objection to interpreting Thady as archetypal colonial man is the fact that his literal role, that of serving man, is more generally familiar and has stronger ideological connotations in the eighteenth century.[19]

Even in a text such as *The Absentee,* which apparently espouses the success of landlordism in Ireland by the English, the narrative remains, W. J. McCormack maintains, "undermined by contradictions, evasions, and reservations . . . The pressures of these conflicts, and maybe a subconscious recognition of their intractability in the circumstances of the time, brought Maria Edgeworth in contact with (literally) the grounds of her experience."[20]

Well aware of the differences between perception and reality, Maria Edgeworth understood that landscape, in both its vernacular and its formal sense, mattered very much, for she was of the generation that urgently had to define for itself what it meant to have a stake in Ireland. Edgeworth lived on her land and depended upon it, and yet she was aware that she and her family did not simply own that land. Others were aware of that, too, aware of it for the reason that the land had recently belonged to them and had been taken from them through no legitimate means.[21] However, once Edgeworth's family sided with those who would claim the rights and privileges of freeholders in a free Ireland, they had by necessity to reject their dependence upon British force of arms. Risking and seeking separation from the forces that had heretofore defined and defended them, landowners who now identified themselves as Irish had to shape a new legitimacy. Where they were and why they were there became charged questions. These are the questions of the settler, "less perplexed," as Northrop Frye maintained of Canadians, "by the question 'Who am I?' than by some such riddles as 'Where is here?'"[22]—a concern that resonates with Edgeworth's depictions of Ireland. However, once you begin to think about place, you begin also to think about your relation to that place, and the question turns back to one of "Who am I" or, for our purposes here, of who is Maria Edgeworth?

Without a sense of place, political and economic relations are about power; once the contested terrain matters, relations get even more complicated. As early as 1697 William King, representative of the privileged Irish elite, observed that

> Ireland is a province and, generally speaking, it has been the fate of all provinces to be under governors who had no interest or concern to seek their welfare ... hence the wise man tells us, Eccl[esiastes] 5,8: "If thou seest oppression of the poor and violent perverting of judgement and Justice in a province marvell not at the matter," for this is generally the case of all provinces and particularly of Ireland.[23]

Edgeworth's scrupulously fictitious explorations of the causes and consequences of such "oppression of the poor and [the] violent perverting of judgement" serve to complicate her and her work. Often concentrating on domestic issues, matters of the home, of the land, and of the family, Edgeworth explicitly and implicitly uses the domestic sphere as an allegory for national home space.

Yet for a writer so rooted in her immediate surroundings, and so concerned with identity, Edgeworth includes very little scenic description of Ireland. Her interest is, rather, one of an eighteenth-century patriot, focused not on national identity but on what Joep Leerssen describes as the "economic improvement and the relations between [the] public and authority,"[24] a patriotism "characterized by its tendency towards heteronomy: the constitutional acceptance of local particularisms and of legal diversity between the state's different regions."[25] However, even as she explores the relationship between, and strains within, family, community, and place, Edgeworth is well aware of the "one momentous, immediate and disruptive effect of the Union: it pulled the parliamentary rug from under the ideological feet of Irish patriotism."[26] For Edgeworth and others with her political and cultural sympathies, even as the question of "where is here?" becomes important there is a recognition that the answer to that question mattered only in a very local context. At the same time, Edgeworth's writing is informed by a nostalgic yearning for a time when it had been possible to believe that, as William Drennan had written in 1791,

> men who differ in their creed may form a sound part of the same civil constitution, and we do wish from the bottom of our hearts that the time may be accelerated when the rights of men and the rights of citizens may meet together in the name of Irishmen—for—until that time we shall seem to act merely from self-interest, *ourselves*, a dictating and domineering party—*ourselves* a monopolising aristocracy.[27]

Part of that "monopolising aristocracy," albeit a dissenting part, Edgeworth was also obliged to acknowledge other presuppositions of the "dictating and domineering party" that shaped not Irish but English cultural hegemony. Her response to those prejudices was no less uncomfortable than her consideration of Irish affairs. Writing in the aftermath of Mary Wollstonecraft's contested *A Vindication of the Rights of Women*, Edgeworth also faced the daunting task of writing in a culture alternately hostile to and fascinated by women writers. Was Edgeworth complicit in perpetuating a patriarchal culture from which she was excluded as a woman and a woman writer, so that her identification with, as Elizabeth Kowaleski-Wallace maintains, "masculine literary discourse . . . at best, creates a female subject according to its own bias and interests"?[28] Or did Edgeworth, "like many Romantic women novelists, endorse Edmund Burke's concept of the family as the paradigm for a successful system of government—[even as] she insisted on the equal rights of the mother and the father to guide and control those children who need to be governed," as Anne Mellor has suggested.[29] Whatever domestic sphere her writing is read as a commentary upon or product of, Edgeworth appears to be closely focused on the events unfolding around her. Thus, Edgeworth's representations of "outsiders" and "insiders," of the cultural elite, and of the politics of racial and class exclusion, reveal both her commentary on boundaries and boundary crossings, and her place as author within such categories.

An Uncomfortable Authority begins in two places at once. Some of the following essays analyze Edgeworth's writing in an effort to make sense of and illuminate her political, historical, and cultural contexts. These essays view her novels as cultural productions that reflect and produce political and social ideologies. Other essays in this collection begin instead with the political and historical contexts and move on to read and understand Edgeworth as a historical subject and novelist.

The essays themselves are gathered in four groups. The first section, "History, Mythology and Edgeworth's Ireland," considers Edgeworth's place in, and understanding of, the Ireland wherein she lived and wrote. Mythology, as much as history, had its place in defining Ireland, as Edgeworth well knew and sought to use in her writings. Marilyn Butler's essay, "Edgeworth, the United Irishmen, and 'More Intelligent Treason,'" demonstrates the multiple uses that Edgeworth (and, at times, her more radical father) made of the various contemporary tropes of Irish "history." Tracing links between the Edgeworths' Irish writing and the United Irishmen movement, Butler reads the *Essay on Irish Bulls* as "a gesture of intellectual solidarity with the United Irishmen cause." Butler's analysis examines literary and journalistic writing alongside one another to understand the Edgeworths' work within the political contexts that shaped and were shaped by their literary texts. "Is it true," Butler asks of the *Essay on Irish Bulls*, that:

> as certain critics maintain . . . Edgeworth in her thoughtful nation-construction failed to make use of history . . . ? The *Essay* proves otherwise, by its crowded use of real historical extracts and citations from print cul-

ture in its ephemeral and more disreputable forms—propaganda, libel, perjured evidence, fanaticism, intolerance, rumor, sensation-mongering, and incitement to violence and to national or sectarian hatred.

Edgeworth, in fact, draws from "documentary material," both the history and the myth of her fictionalized "real" Ireland, to play competing myths against each other. Butler's reading suggests that Edgeworth enables us to challenge the certainties of various factions whose combined power make it "impossible to draw Ireland as she now is."

Edgeworth cannot be understood outside of the contexts into which the recent history of the United Irishmen was already being placed by commentators on Ireland. Just as Butler's essay here explores the *Essay on Irish Bulls* in its contemporary contexts, so Peter Cosgrove's "History and Utopia in *Ormond*" examines Edgeworth's choice to set her novels in the past as a means to challenge nationalist myths, myths that had very recently once again been variously reconstituted by all parties in Ireland. Cosgrove maintains that "while it is possible that Edgeworth casts her novel in the past as a fantasy wish that the two ruling classes [Gaelic and Anglican Irish] had cast their lot with each other before the 1798 rebellion and that the United Irishmen had changed forever the political history of Ireland, there is strong evidence that the Black Islands," home of an almost mystical Gaelic and clan-based kingdom, "exists outside of time . . . the true thing, [which had] never changed," as one of Sir Ulick's servants puts it. This "changelessness," Cosgrove argues, "is a sign that . . . truth is not in history but in a utopia that is unchangeable because it is non-existent."

The inherent strains between and within plots, inevitable in a writer such as Edgeworth with her investment in various disparate analyses of Ireland's past, present, and future, is a fault line Frances Botkin explores from a different perspective in "The Keener's Cry in *Castle Rackrent*: The Death of Irish Culture?" in which she argues that "the depiction of Irish funerary customs in *Castle Rackrent* brings into sharp relief issues of cultural loss and rebirth." Botkin reads Irish women's funeral wails within the context of a "governing class that threatened" Ireland for centuries. In addition, depictions of the keeners illuminate not just an important cultural tradition but also an image of women's roles in a country more often depicted in terms of patriarchal traditions. One question Edgeworth seems always to raise without offering an answer, or perhaps without being able to provide an answer, is what "culture" means in an Irish sense, and in the language of English-Irish relations. Certainly, there are some deaths, some expiring "cultures" that should be mourned, but where, then, does that leave a present that can only be secured when its various pasts are understood and reconciled?

Except that Edgeworth's past was often not one that her contemporaries, on either side of the Irish Sea, wished to recognize. One reason for this was the difficulty of agreeing on terms. Who, in Edgeworth's time, were the "Irish"? This question, and its related concerns, occupies the attention of the essays gathered in the second section of this collection, "Representing Ireland: Fiction, Realism, and Authority." Edgeworth's writing offered an opportunity for those outside Ireland to give their opinions on the subject, whether informed only through a reading of Edgeworth herself, or whether influenced by a broader grasp of national, cultural, and, increasingly, colonial issues. Maria Edgeworth knew this, and was both able and obliged to accept this fact of her writing. She was Irish but no more so than she was also not Irish, and her work is redolent with the resentment of someone being observed against her will as equally as it delights in claiming to be nothing more than objective observation offered in rebuttal of others' claims of objectivity. Jacqueline Belanger defines

> Edgeworth's relationship with her contemporary British critics [as] not a case of mere reception, one in which reviewers simply evaluate the realism of Edgeworth's descriptions of Ireland by measuring them against a "pre-constituted reality"; rather, critics struggle to define the parameters of what is seen to be realistically Irish for their British readers *through* their reviews of Edgeworth's work.

Belanger's essay, "'*Le vrai n'est pas toujours vraisemblable*': The Evaluation of Realism in Edgeworth's Irish Tales," opens up the series of potential readings available to Edgeworth as she continued to write and publish. Belanger examines acts of seeing and representing Ireland by Edgeworth, by writers about Edgeworth, and by readers of Edgeworth, all of whose various politicized positions are brought to bear on their (mis)understanding of Irish culture.

Clearly, the act of reading itself inevitably raises questions of what is fiction, what is realism, and what authority exists in depictions of one or both. Edgeworth's discomfort in representing Ireland as it is, might be why, as Darryl Jones explains, Edgeworth's work serves to demonstrate that the conventional wisdom about "Irish" Gothic literature, that is, Gothic literature written by Irish residents rather than about Ireland, is probably wrong. Jones's essay, "'Distorted Nature in a Fever': *Irish Bulls*, Irish Novels, the 1798 Rebellion, and their Gothic Contexts," examines why conventional wisdom holds that realism is only possible when created from a position of stability and that Gothic writing is the mode of the troubled extremities of the political state. The problem with this argument, according to Jones, is that "much of what is now recognized as the most notable Irish Gothic was not really the product of the disenfranchised community within Ireland, but of the remnants of the colonizing class," such as Edgeworth. To be successful, the Gothic also requires an agreed upon vocabulary of "distorted vision," the phrase Maria Edgeworth used in her letter to M. Pakenham Edgeworth, a distorted vision of which Edgeworth made use freely not only to describe Ireland as she saw it, aware that it might not be how others saw it. In doing so, she denied the existence of easy solutions as she raised questions of representation that complicate assertions she had made elsewhere.

It is these attempts to balance competing descriptions that Kathleen Costello-Sullivan maintains in "National Character and Foreclosed Irishness: A Reconsideration of *Ennui*," offer a way to understand Edgeworth's contemporary critics who often "differ[ed] in their conceptualization of how Irishness functions in the text . . . [although they] accept[ed] the role of education as a *catalyst*, a device whereby a negotiation or a reconciliation takes place." In contrast to this view, Costello-Sullivan maintains of *Ennui* that "Irishness exists either as an origin to be negotiated or a stage through which to pass, via the enlightened path of education, on the evolutionary trail to Anglo-Irishness." Costello-Sullivan illuminates the ways in which Maria Edgeworth's educational reform in *Ennui* ultimately endorses the anti-Irish views against which Edgeworth attempted to position herself.

The third section of this collection, "Education, Empire, and the Anglo-Irish Dilemma," explores how for Edgeworth, perhaps because of her own family's problematic relationship to its estate, education was the touchstone upon which to judge society and manners, and the whetstone upon which to seek to create a society where at least the most violent of the cultural strains could be obviated. After all, Edgeworth was, among her other roles, a self-appointed didact, as Heidi Thomson discusses in "'The Fashion Not

To Be an Absentee': Fashion and Moral Authority in Edgeworth's Tales." While "Edgeworth's professed admiration in her tales for characters who pay off debts honorably, and who are literally and morally not indebted to anybody" might seem to "jar with her equally strongly held belief that the landowning aristocracy is essentially superior to the trading classes," there is an added twist in Edgeworth's depictions of the struggle of the Irish landowner to conduct him or herself appropriately. If English culture is the epitome of Enlightenment progress, England is, presumably, where someone of education and standing should be seen, but

> in their efforts to socialize with the group they aspired to identify with ... the absentees ruined themselves by their absence from the estate. In order to keep up with fashionable life in London, an endless supply of funds was needed, derived from the estate in Ireland by the middleman. Those middlemen or agents, so feared in both [Richard Lovell Edgeworth's] *Memoirs* and [Maria Edgeworth's] tales, ran the estate for their own profit while the landlord in London was blissfully ignorant of the state of his finances. As a result, the landowner lost his grip over the estate and got embroiled in an intricate system of debts largely incurred by an expensive lifestyle, which superficially equated him with the English aristocracy.

If not capable of holding their own in England, then what claim did Irish landowners have to being equal in any sense with the English? What price to Ireland if England were to remain the epicenter of Irish cultural aspirations?[30]

Jessica Richard's evaluation of *Belinda* builds on these problems as she examines Edgeworth's analyses of British efforts to legitimize their position in Ireland in light of their acts of legitimization in colonial settings. In "'Games of Chance': *Belinda*, Education, and Empire," Richard makes it plain that Edgeworth was not alone in examining gambling and the perceived West Indian plantation owners' propensity to squander their capital in such pursuits. This squandering of opportunity Edgeworth explicitly identifies as an even greater vice than Irish landholders' proclivities to mismanagement and ill-considered expenditures, suggesting, perhaps, a greater claim to legitimacy for Protestant Irish landholders than for other representatives of the emerging Empire, claims for legitimacy that distinguished Ireland from the "colonies." Edgeworth was interested in moral and practical education and while gambling was obviously a vice it was also an appropriate way of learning about ideas of chance; moreover, it had connotations that differed from place to place. In general, for Edgeworth, gambling was bad but exposure to it was good, at least as a means of providing moral instruction. Even here, however, Edgeworth's sensitivity to nuance, her recognition of her own class's tenuous claims of legitimacy, and her awareness of the contradictions of English ideals of civil society and English practices in Ireland and other colonial spaces raised uneasy questions. In *Belinda,* as Richard demonstrates, "it is difficult to determine . . . [whether] Edgeworth's novel is covertly condemning the speculative imperialist enterprise of the colonies and the slave labor on which they depend, or whether it is hoping to avoid taking a stand on the controversial topic of slavery by vilifying Vincent as a gamester, rather than as a slave-owner."

These are exactly the ideas Catherine Toal explores in "Control Experiment: Edgeworth's Critique of Rousseau's Educational Theory." Edgeworth was not just an Irish writer, as she was certainly not simply an Irish writer either. Education, however, was no easy alternative to contemplating her status in society, for it required the balance of desire and practicality, of idealism and realism. Jean-Jacques Rousseau and her father's friend Thomas Day were wrong in crucial respects when it came to educating children, as Edgeworth and her father pointed out in *Practical Education* and as Maria alone demonstrated in *Belinda.* Toal suggests that "an examination of the relation between elements of *Émile* and the Edgeworth texts which respond to it . . . outlines an explanation for the apparently outlandish and extravagant features of *Belinda,* showing the reasons for their largely untroubled co-existence with a comfortable scheme of domestic order and romantic wish-fulfillment." Ultimately, Maria Edgeworth's "wish-fulfillment" involves a fairly conventional sense of order, no easy wish to fulfill for a writer as aware of contexts as was Edgeworth.

This desire for order, perhaps unexpectedly, can also be found on both frontiers of Edgeworth's work as an author and social critic, frontiers explored in the final section of this collection, "Edgeworth's Influences." Authors are influenced not just by the time and place in which they live and write but by the ideas to which they are exposed. Susan Manly's analysis of the title character's journey toward overcoming his anti-Semitism in *Harrington* reveals not only the novel's criticism of "English ruling-class complacency," rather than of Protestant bigotry, but also traces Moses Mendelssohn's influence on *Harrington,* maintaining that Edgeworth is, in fact, aligned with "European, non-Protestant opponents of the idea of state religion." Manly's argument is rooted in the gap between the myths about and reality of late eighteenth-century political reform that managed its "liberal" changes in such a way that ultimately endorsed xenophobia and antagonism toward those who were not considered to be English.

These myths flourished well enough for later writers to employ them as easy tropes to establish their own imagined realities. Not long after Edgeworth had established herself as an "Irish" writer for the English, Sir Walter Scott took up his pen and offered a series of novels and mythic creations in work he claimed was at least, in part, devised in the spirit of Edgeworth. In one particular sense, Scott was probably a better exemplar of Edgeworth's own authorial problems than he had intended, for his romanticized Scottish past was very much a part of his quest for a stable, secure, in some sense far more conservative society than even Edgeworth yearned for. Scott recognized that Edgeworth's interest in the ever-shifting Irish present assumed a place for a past open to competing claims. Scott seized on the possibilities of historical fiction identified by Kit Kincade in her essay "A Whillaluh for Ireland: *Castle Rackrent* and Edgeworth's influence on Scott." Kincade argues that Edgeworth's awareness that her "anti-history, [such as *Castle Rackrent* is] told by a narrator with so little understanding of the events he recalls, and with no ability at all to see any perspective but the narrowly defined, ill-informed viewpoint from which he interprets these events," is not simply an ironic tool. That Thady Quirk "cannot fathom the irony the reader elicits from the text his words create," might seem to require a level of sophistication from the reader on which most authors do not typically rely.

In giving voice to such overlooked characters, Kincade maintains, Edgeworth also highlights the chasm that had developed between groups, between those with access to the means of self-promotion and those denied those opportunities. It is not always clear that Edgeworth was comfortable with this role she took upon herself, even while showing the way to later writers such as Scott. Edgeworth was all too aware of the risks of either acknowledging or denying a troublesome past and of the impossibility of simply ignoring it.

Which brings us right back to where we began; for Maria Edgeworth this seems particularly appropriate. Determined to identify and to name behaviors and aspects of culture, she also understood that each act of identification was subject to interpretation and so was always in need of revision and reiteration. She managed, however, to shape a life and a literature out of these acts of willful creation, and perhaps the best testament to her creative powers comes not from her work but from the two barrels of flour sent from Boston to Ireland during the height of the famine and addressed only, "To Miss Edgeworth, for her poor." There are a variety of readings possible in that message. Maria would have happily provided several of them.

Notes

1. A[ugustus] J. C. Hare, ed., *The Life and Letters of Maria Edgeworth* (London, 1894), 1:55.
2. Richard Mabey, "Landscape: Terra Firma?" in *Towards a New Landscape*, ed. Bernard Jacobson (London: Bernard Jacobson, 1993), 62–68, 65.
3. Mabey, "Landscape," 65.
4. Ibid.
5. Ian Wedde, "Introduction," in *The Penguin Book of New Zealand Verse*, eds. Ian Wedde and Harvey McQueen (Auckland: Penguin, 1985), 43.
6. Hare, *Life*, 550.
7. In Jean Agnew, ed., *The Drennan-McTier Letters: 1776–1819*, 3 vols. (Dublin: The Women's History Project / Irish Manuscripts Commission, 1998–1999), 2: 571.
8. William Drennan, "Protest against an Union with Great Britain," *The Microscope; or Minute Observe*, 1800, 133.
9. Louis MacNeice, "Selva Oscura," in *The Collected Poems of Louis MacNeice*, ed. E. R. Dodds (Rev. ed. London: Faber, 1979), 512–13.
10. Ibid., 512.
11. Suvendrini Perera, *Reaches of Empire: The English Novel from Edgeworth to Dickens* (New York: Columbia University Press, 1991), 15.
12. Ibid.
13. Heidi Thomson, "Introduction," in Maria Edgeworth, *The Absentee*, ed. Heidi Thomson and Kim Walker (London: Penguin, 1999), xiii.
14. Marilyn Butler, *Maria Edgeworth: A Literary Biography* (Oxford: Clarendon, 1972), 391.
15. Mary Jean Corbett, "Another Tale To Tell: Postcolonial Theory And The Case of *Castle Rackrent*," *Criticism* 36, no. 3 (Summer 1994): 384.
16. Julian Moynahan, *Anglo-Irish: The Literary Imagination in a Hyphenated Culture* (Princeton: Princeton University Press, 1995), 13.
17. Stephen Gwynn, *Experiences of a Literary Man* (London: Butterworth, 1926), 11.
18. Corbett, "Another Tale," 383.
19. Marilyn Butler, "Introduction," in Maria Edgeworth, *Castle Rackrent* and *Ennui*, ed. Marilyn Butler (London: Penguin, 1992), 9–10.
20. W. J. McCormack, *Ascendancy and Tradition in Anglo-Irish Literary History from 1789–1939* (Oxford: Clarendon, 1985), 168.

21. The final great land grab of the Protestants had come after the Williamite campaign, and what legal authority there was for the dispossession of the vast majority of remaining Catholic landholders who did not convert to the Church of Ireland was to be found in the Treaty of Limerick as finally ratified by the Irish Parliament in 1697. The bill submitted to ratify the treaty differed so significantly from the terms of surrender agreed with James II's generals, and revoked so many of the concessions granted nonparticipant Catholics, that William King, bishop of Derry, one of seven Church of Ireland bishops to oppose the bill, argued in the House of Lords that the bill could have neither legal nor moral authority. He felt so strongly he wrote a remarkably moving letter to perhaps his oldest friend in the Church of Ireland, Nathaniel Foy, bishop of Waterford, who had stayed away from the session, pairing his vote with "one who has made use of it to establish inequity ... and to break the public faith of the Kingdom in the Articles of Limerick. I much confess I do not know how you will answer it to God." In Francis Godwin James, "The Church of Ireland in the Early 18th Century," *Historical Magazine of the Protestant Episcopal Church* 48, no. 4 (Dec. 1979): 446. See also James, *Lords of the Ascendancy: The Irish House of Lords and its Members, 1600–1800* (Washington, D.C.: The Catholic University of America Press, 1995), especially 60–61; and Philip O'Regan, *Archbishop William King of Dublin (1650–1729) and the Constitution in Church and State* (Dublin: Four Courts Press, 2000), 86–87.

22. Northrop Frye, "Conclusion to *A Literary History of Canada*," in *The Stubborn Structure: Essays on Criticism and Society* (London: Methuen, 1970), 284.

23. William King, bishop of Derry, to Gilbert Burnet, bishop of Salisbury, 29 Jan. 1697, in Joseph Johnston, ed. "Archbishop King's Diagnosis," in *Bishop Berkeley's Querist in Historical Perspective* (Dundalk: Dundalgan, 1970), 23.

24. Joep Leerssen, *Remembrance and Imagination: Patterns in the Historical and Literary Representation of Ireland in the Nineteenth Century* (South Bend: University of Notre Dame Press, 1997), 16.

25. Ibid., 19.

26. Ibid., 20.

27. William Drennan to Sam McTier, 11 July 1791, in Jean Agnew, ed., *The Drennan-McTier Letters, 1776–1793*, 1: 364–65.

28. Elizabeth Kowaleski-Wallace, *Their Fathers' Daughters: Hannah More, Maria Edgeworth, and Patriarchal Complicity* (New York: Oxford University Press, 1991), 12.

29. Anne K. Mellor, "A Novel Of Their Own: Romantic Women's Fiction, 1790–1830," in John Richetti, ed., *The Columbia History of the British Novel* (New York: Columbia University Press, 1994), 333.

30. One of the strongest arguments against absenteeism made by the landowning Irish themselves, at least by those who did engage in such analyses, had been made as early as 1729 by Thomas Prior in his publication *A List of the Absentees of Ireland, and the Yearly Value of their Estates and Incomes spent abroad. With Observations on the Present State and Condition of that Kingdom* (Dublin). Prior "drew from [William] Petty [1623–87] the notion of placing the payments to absentee landlords on the debit side of the balance of Irish trade," but, unlike Petty, instead of relying on guesswork he made exhaustive personal enquiries as to the amounts involved. He calculated a net drain from Ireland in 1729 of the enormous sum of £621,499. (*Books and Periodicals of Irish Interest* . . . Catalogue 56: Part B, Belfast: P & B Rowan [2002]).

An Uncomfortable Authority

Part I
History, Mythology, and Edgeworth's Ireland

Edgeworth, the United Irishmen, and "More Intelligent Treason"

Marilyn Butler

IN THE LAST TWO DECADES OF THE TWENTIETH CENTURY WE SAW FROM Irish historians a fine collective effort to describe and assess the politics, local and national, of late eighteenth-century Ireland. Beginning before 1980 and continuing through to the late 1990s, a body of detailed research helped put together the elements of Norman Vance's "finest hour of culturally pluralistic Ireland" between 1780 and 1800.[1] The 1990s also saw some important literary studies, such as those of Joep Leerssen and Katie Trumpener.[2] But thus far neither the historians' strong generic theme—late eighteenth-century popular and local Ireland and its culture—nor their acknowledgment of the self-conscious and imaginative adoption of this local and popular culture by the United Irishmen, has been picked up to the degree one might expect by literary scholars, with honorable exceptions such as Vance and Mary Helen Thuente's pathbreaking overview of United Irish newspapers and song, *The Harp Restrung*.[3]

There is a (long-belated) new tendency to examine the United Irish poet Tom Moore and his origins. So far, however, there has been no effort to recruit Maria Edgeworth to a similar status, but both these writers must be considered if we are to focus on what was said, thought, and published by conscious participants in the United Irish movement, especially in its "culturally pluralist" phase, at its peak in the short era 1795–99. Edgeworth was already immersed in those years preparing two of her five works about Ireland—*Castle Rackrent* (1800) and the *Essay on Irish Bulls* (1802).

I do not propose that either Edgeworth, father or daughter, belonged to the United Irish Society or to one of its cells in the literal sense of taking an oath. I do seek to show the Edgeworths' jointly authored *Essay on Irish Bulls* (1802) came into being as a gesture of intellectual solidarity with the United Irish cause, probably in response to the Dublin government's shutting down of the main United Irish newspaper, Samuel Neilson's *Northern Star*, in May 1797; that the themes of the *Essay*, highbrow and popular, echo the diverse publications of the *Northern Star*, and that radical miscellaneous journalism constitutes a model for the *Essay*, and thus a cornerstone for tales that in due course built, in words and symbols, the portrait of a hybrid but coherent Ireland.

I shall, to some degree, play down one cultural pursuit that has already received attention from Vance, Trumpener, and Leerssen— the late eighteenth-century revival of an interest in "cultural antiquities" by scholars of the Irish language and of its poetry and myths. Maria Edgeworth knew the work of the historian Sylvester O'Halloran and the translator Charlotte Brooke, as we shall see, but she used this knowledge in any depth only later, as Sydney Owenson also did in *The Wild Irish Girl* (1806). Neilson, the owner-publisher-editor of the *Northern Star* (2 Jan. 1792–13 May 1797) was sufficiently sympathetic to employ Patrick Lynch to edit an Irish-language anthology, *Bolg an Tsolar*, in 1795. That lengthy and seriously meant anthology did not continue, though described as volume 1. This limited the Gaelic content of United Irish publications prior to 1798.

There are other gaps in the cultural theories and activities of the United Irishmen, or in our knowledge of them. Were any of the leaders students of the Gaelic-Irish language or indeed of Hibernian English, or real enthusiasts for song and ballads, in the serious sense of, say, James Macpherson and Robert Burns in Scotland and Bishop Thomas Percy, Joseph Ritson, and Francis Grose in England? If so, did any of them communicate with other popular culturalists in Britain or France? Did they establish working relationships and social camaraderie with the urban lower orders in Dublin, Ulster, or Wexford, or actually join the peasant-based Defenders? Or was the motivation for expressions of interest in Gaelic Irish essentially practical—the need to recruit men for an armed struggle to come?

William Drennan, Belfast Presbyterian, physician, and poet, had a position of seniority in the movement, and it was he who, in October 1791, called together a group of Belfast friends and colleagues willing to bind themselves together by oath in the first Society of United Irishmen. Drennan's father, a clergyman, was a friend and intellectual follower of another Ulsterman, Francis Hutcheson, a founder of the "Inner Light" or liberal, self-examining, and independent tendency in eighteenth-century Presbyterianism, and an important force in the Scottish as well as the glimmering Ulster Enlightenment. Drennan first made his name as an eloquent writer for the volunteer movement in 1784. In the following year, at a last congress, he mingled with like-minded volunteers and would-be parliamentary reformers mostly from Belfast and Dublin, and with a new acquaintance from the Irish Midlands: Richard Lovell Edgeworth, who had returned from England in June 1782 in order to set up a country retreat, in effect a miniature republic, much as Monsieur de Wolmar seeks to do in Jean-Jacques Rousseau's *Julie ou la Nouvelle Héloise* (1761). In 1785 Drennan, a fine eloquent writer in both prose and verse, caused a stir with his caustic *Letters from an Irish Helot*, in which he berates himself and his fellow Irish as "willing slaves." It was probably after reading this pamphlet by Drennan that R. L. Edgeworth told Drennan he "would become the Irish Rousseau."[4] Drennan remembered the expression and a letter in which R. L. Edgeworth told him that a fifteen-year-old Edgeworth daughter was his great admirer.[5] Indeed, nine years later Drennan wrote a most interesting self-analysis comparing himself to Rousseau as a man capable of flashes of great power, even genius, who was also tormented—"social yet solitary" and "hurt in his pride for being taken for what he appears."[6]

R. L. Edgeworth was drawn to Drennan by his Rousseauism, which Edgeworth was well qualified to recognize since he belonged to an influential English group of early Rousseau admirers. In 1763 Edgeworth had left Trinity College, Dublin for Oxford. By the age of twenty, in 1764, he was married to an unintellectual Oxfordshire woman (Anna Maria Elers), only to find home life with her insupportable. After an interlude in raffish London high society Edgeworth encountered the Midlands physician and polymath Erasmus Darwin, who introduced him into the Lunar Society of Birmingham. The members of this informal think tank for the English Enlightenment were inventors, entrepreneurs, chemists, doctors—James Watt, Matthew Boulton, James Keir, Josiah Wedgwood, his partner Thomas Bentley, Joseph Priestley, and, following Edgeworth, Thomas Day. Among the main topics being discussed when Edgeworth joined the Lunar group in the mid-1760s, Rousseau and especially his educational treatise *Émile* (1762) were to the fore.

In the mid-1770s the most radical members of the Lunar group, who certainly included R. L. Edgworth's close friends Darwin, Wedgwood, and Day, attempted to set up a "religion of nature" based on the proposition of their friend Benjamin Franklin that religious observance should not require belief.[7] But although he dismisses institutional religion and priestly teaching, Rousseau's vicar refers pupils to the simple faith observable in rural communities, and also, importantly, to the similarity between the central tenets of the world's great religions. He boldly speaks of "the clear and universal agreement of all peoples [in favor of religious belief] ... the striking unanimity in the judgment of mankind."[8] This is wording that echoes, perhaps accidentally, the proposition of the English diplomat and philosopher Edward Herbert, Lord Cherbury (1583–1648), who implicitly advocated universal toleration in his Latin treatise, *De Veritate* (1624), and in subsequent religious works, several of which were picked up and developed by the controversial Irish radical and deist John Toland (1670–1722). Herbert argued that there is a universal religious instinct by which individuals at different times and in unrelated cultures have arrived at a similar account of a just and beneficent deity who cares for mankind and whom it is proper to worship. Although as individuals we are unable to prove either God's existence or the immortality of the soul, it is fitting that we should respect what the world's peoples have acquiesced to. This common sense of mankind is a grand concept, democratizing on a truly universal scale. That, no doubt, is why Tom Paine deployed the phrase as the title of his first political tract in 1776, and why Herbert, undergoing a revival in the eighteenth century despite or because he had been dubbed "the father of English deism," was, like Rousseau, a cult figure for the Lunar Society of Birmingham. On concepts such as "the common sense of mankind," universalism over patriotism, and democracy over aristocracy, the deists among the "Lunatics," as they referred to themselves, could, and at times did, run these two thinkers together.[9]

It looks likely to have been a Rousseauist decision; it could have been a United Irish one. For whatever reason, the Edgeworths brought out *Practical Education* without a chapter most commentators declared was obligatory, that on religious education. The initial outcry was renewed more loudly when a second, revised, edition appeared in 1801, still without religion, but with the explanation, most unlikely to pacify orthodox critics, that parents could call in the help of their own pastor.[10]

Mary Wollstonecraft complained bitterly of Rousseau's far-from-universal approach to the education of girls. She proposes in *A Vindication of the Rights of Woman* (1792) that Sophie should be brought up as a mere complement and companion for Émile. The Edgeworths dismissed such an idea and in their handbook *Practical Educa-*

tion (1798) urged parents to educate girls and boys together, using the same syllabus and teaching all children to think, so that anyone might qualify for citizenship. The girls in the Edgeworths' tales and lessons for children and Maria's sympathetic women in fiction for adults are all thinkers; her work reclaims Rousseau's inspirational educational system for women. It was for the progressive social messages disseminated by book 4 that the Lunar Group became part of Rousseau's support system when he came to England to escape further persecution in France in 1766–77. By changing the hearts and minds of the young of the upper and middle orders and opening them to the impulses of nature,[11] Rousseau implies that as adults they will be minded to reshape society:

> The people are mankind; those who do not belong to the people are so few in number that they are not worth counting . . . All distinctions of rank fade away before the eyes of a thoughtful person; he sees the same passions, the same feelings in the noble and the guttersnipe; there is merely a slight difference in speech, and more or less artificiality of tone . . .[12]

Through this utopian dream of a restored, egalitarian humankind, he encourages liberals to become, for practical purposes, democrats and radicals. Equally telling, the Savoyard Vicar urges everyone to put aside authority, both secular and religious, and to identify the "active force" within, regardless of social status or gender: "It is not easy for a man to begin to think; but when once he has begun he will never leave off . . . the understanding when once practised in reflection will never rest."[13]

It has become common to describe some of the most committed United Irishmen as "social radicals" and, perhaps, less common to examine the nature or sources of such a position. The aims and rhetoric of the best-known young United Irishmen were not so different from those of their British, French, and American contemporaries. They criticized monarchy and aristocracy as corrupt and believed the future would be simpler, more natural, more humane, and democratic. The United Irish Volunteer movement certainly seems to have had a more internationalist than nationalist intellectual underpinning at the outset. That being so, we should look for a wider cultural range, and more expressive writing in the United Irish output of the 1790s than the often sectarian emphasis of recent historical work has so far reported.

Hybrid Texts and Intertextuality: The *Northern Star*, *The Press*, and the *Essay on Irish Bulls*

There are almost no direct discussions of popular culture in the *Northern Star* or its associated publications. There is, however, one most intriguing item in 1796, Robert Burns's friendly salutation, written 1791, to the radical English antiquary, Captain Francis Grose. The decision to present Irish readers with a poem in Scots dialect suggests that someone on the newspaper's staff was an enthusiast for the poem's content, and presumably for the role of the vernacular in forming notions of national identity, community, and solidarity. Burns, the so-called plowman poet, was a cult figure for liberals of the American/French revolutionary era because of his articulacy and power as a spokesman for the common man. His one slim volume of poetry, *Poems* (1786), written mostly in Lowland-Scots or Lallans dialect, boldly featured the vigorous, undisciplined youth of rural Ayrshire, made up of erring village lovers, drinking companions, hostile Presbyterians, and freemasons. Burns's engaging and open world lightly epitomized a new egalitarian ethos, a village republicanism realized with intelligence and humor, warmly illustrated in his informal poetic epistles to friends:

> Hear, Land o' Cakes, and brither Scots,
> Frae Maidenkirk to Johnie Groat's;—
> If there's a hole in a' your coats,
> I rede you tent it:
> A chield's amang you takin notes,
> And, faith, he'll prent it:
>
> If in your bounds ye chance to light
> Upon a fine, fat fodgel wight,
> O' stature short, but genius bright,
> That's he, mark weel;
> And wow! he has an unco sleight
> O' cauk and keel.
>
> By some auld, houlet-haunted biggin,
> Or kirk deserted by its riggin,
> It's ten to ane ye'll find him snug in
> Some eldritch part,
> Wi' deils, they say, Lord save's! colleaguin
> At some black art.

> It's tauld he was a sodger bred,
> And ane wad rather fa'n than fled;
> But now he's quat the spurtle-blade,
> And dog-skin wallet,
> And taen the-Antiquarian trade,
> I think they call it.[14]

The *Northern Star*'s choice of Burns, and of this poem in particular, might well have seemed obscure to some, to others inspired. Burns was a sophisticated poet, who, against the advice of the Edinburgh literati, used the vernacular for poetry. Increasingly, he turned into an editor of traditional Scottish ballads. Many of the hundreds of songs, ballads, and tunes he handled were political, often Jacobite. Both the Jacobitism and the tunes were shared with Ireland and gave Burns an ongoing significance there as Britain's leading cultural nationalist of the day.

Though the Falstaffian Grose was in Scotland to complete an expensive two-volume work on the *Antiquities of Scotland*, his general reputation was, and is, as a pathbreaking collector and commentator on vernacular English. His longest-lasting work, in print through the nineteenth century and still a resource for Eric Partridge in the twentieth century, was *A Classical Dictionary of the Vulgar Tongue* (1785), a three-thousand-word compilation of contemporary slang and obscene or otherwise offensive euphemism. Grose's use in his title of the word "classical" positively invited impudent comparison with England's Great Lexicographer and Tory, Samuel Johnson, who had died in 1784. Grose also referred in his preface to a disreputable source, the *Satyrical and Burlesque Dictionary of M Le Roux* (banned in Bourbon France), and he jeered at France's despotic old régime. Grose was, in short, a pioneer of cultural anthropology within the British Isles, openly political, and indebted to French models. His focus took in language and song—hence the visit to Burns. In 1787 he had brought out *A Provincial Dictionary*, a compilation of English regional dialects, along with sections on proverbs and local superstitions, and on the historical roots in, for example, the Old Norse of some dialect words.

After a pleasant meeting in Ayrshire, during which they talked of Burns's as yet unwritten Gothic poem "Tam o' Shanter," Grose went on to Dublin. In the 1780s in his own capital, London, Grose liked to go on midnight rambles accompanied by his manservant to the notorious cellars and stews of St Giles. He may have had such plans for Dublin, and, who knows, to make a start on the Hibernian-English tongue. Whom he met and what he learnt we can only guess at since, still in 1791, the captain collapsed and died in a Dublin street, leaving unanswered the obvious question: Was Dublin already a milieu where linguistic phrase collecting and cross-class socialization of Grose's kind was developing?

Two or three years later Grose would, once he had made the right contacts, almost certainly have been passed on from place to place, especially in the culturally rich areas still partly or largely Gaelic-speaking. In the period after 1795, professed specialists in local antiquities moved through the four Irish provinces and were offered hospitality thanks to the grapevine afforded by membership of the secret societies, and even of the Royal Irish Academy, which had a number of United Irishmen among its members. Where published writings are concerned, the nearest approach to Grose's democratized linguistics in 1790s Ireland does not come from the United Irishmen movement proper but from two purposeful experiments using Hibernian English, the Edgeworths' *Essay on Irish Bulls* and Maria Edgeworth's *Castle Rackrent.*

Throughout much of the 1790s an exceptionally high standard of writing about the public sphere was maintained by the *Northern Star.* For more than five years it delivered a simplified, concentrated political agenda directed at two main aims. The first target was to reduce the corruption of the Dublin parliament and widen the franchise, thus reducing the power of a very small Anglican political élite. The second was to establish cooperation across the sectarian divisions, so that opposition Anglicans, Catholics, and Presbyterians could achieve civic rights on the same terms as the Anglican establishment. Each of these aims was to be sought by peaceful means, the pressure of public opinion. In addition, Irish readers were given well-documented accounts in the *Northern Star* of the key French-revolutionary reforms—in 1792, the new Constitution, male suffrage, and a state education system (for boys); in 1796, social legislation to help support the poor.[15] English state trials were also covered, and maneuvers by the Whig opposition, such as the Duke of Bedford's success in 1795 in protesting against the French war on behalf of all the inhabitants of Bedfordshire, not merely the freeholders. [16]

After 1795, however, these objectives, delivered often quite formally in an educated style, were supplemented, and in some ways undercut, by diverse "entertainments" designed to attract the lower orders and achieve a mass circulation of print materials. These included a single sheet, or broadside, containing a political song, poems in fashionable styles, sentimental, satirical, and political, and longer, book-length prose and verse burlesques. Above all, within the paper there was now a greater concentration on popular song. Outside it, collections of songs were issued as separate publications, a rich contribution to the multistranded and politicized tradition of Irish song set to already familiar tunes from the British Isles, France, and, from the 1780s, America.

Like English newspapers, the *Northern Star* and its successor *The Press* (28 Sept. 1797–14 Mar. 1798), edited by Arthur O'Connor and Thomas Addis Emmet, were miscellanies which from the start carried individual short poems of a reasonably popular, accessible, middlebrow kind, usually political but occasionally sentimental. The poems continued, but from early in 1795 Neilson ran a much more diverse publishing operation, going out of his way to re-publish and further distribute two main types of populist items. The first group, broad political burleques of a type popular in Dublin throughout the eighteenth century, were first serialized (anonymously) in the *Star* from 1793, then issued independently and still anonymously as books for sale. These went down well from the outset and were occasionally reissued as popular humorous classics up to the middle of the nineteenth century.[17] The burlesques could hit quite hard, but they belonged to an established comic genre and were relatively unlikely to be prosecuted.

This was not true of the second innovation—the publication, similarly anonymous, of four songbooks entitled *Paddy's Resource*, the first two appearing in Belfast (1795, 1796), the remaining two in Dublin (1798, 1803?). There were 161 different songs in these four volumes; about a quarter of them had previously appeared in the *Northern Star* or *The Press*. The songs, whether in the newspapers or the songbook, were provided with a title, and, under it, the name of the tune it was to be sung to. The boldest songs were run off as single broadsheets and if these were located in house searches the owner was liable to be prosecuted.

Since the songs were anonymous it is impossible to differentiate a United Irish song with certainty, except where it emphasizes the word United, as the songs of 1795 and 1796 often dutifully did. Henry Joy McCracken, in "The Thistle and the Shamrock," celebrated the "union" of Catholics and Presbyterians, though at a time when such camaraderie was far from universal. It was subtler to deliver cultural unity by stealth, for example by teaching singers and their audiences a poetic and musical name for Ireland as a whole. Already a visual persona existed, a youthful goddess seen above the titles of the *Northern Star* and in a frontispiece to the *Transactions of the Royal Irish Academy* she wore a warrior's helmet or even a democratic Phrygian cap, carried arms—a sword or a pike—and was accompanied by a harp. These icons were now given a name, Erin or Ierne, and could therefore be constantly reiterated in poems and songs.

Since Ierne, in particular, appealed to the classically educated, more homely substitutes began to appear, using traditional names from oral Gaelic culture. "Granu" or "Granuweal" is the name of an unlearned, unaesthetic old woman, signifying Mother Ireland. She probably derives from the aristocratic Gaelic woman whom the English called Grace O'Malley, a chieftain in late sixteenth-century Connaught who fought Gaelic neighbors and the governors Elizabeth I sent to pacify the province. From 1796 Granu seems to have been the favorite popular figure for Ireland in the songs. In the songbook of 1798 she appears in an opening line, rallying her sons to take up arms and if need be to die.

Drennan, in particular, was adept at evoking Ireland as a loved landscape and a larger, national unit, as in the phrase "Emerald Isle." He was also one of several writers to make structural use of history. Typically, such songs begin with a reference to a golden age, followed by an invasion by cruel strangers who settled on the land and remained there as alien rulers. Wars caused by these Danes or English are then introduced with harsh landlords of the present day, along with high rents, taxes, tithes, insecurity of tenure, eviction, perhaps exile.

R. L. Edgeworth maintained some contact during the 1790s with acquaintances in the United Irishmen movement through their common membership of the Royal Irish Academy. His paper to that body on the telegraph (1795) placed an emphasis on secrecy and encryption that was evidently considered suspicious by some of his neighbors in Co. Longford, and perhaps by the authorities. Otherwise, R. L. Edgeworth's criticisms of the repressive policies of Pitt and the Irish administration, especially regarding the freedom of the press, were mainly shared with family connections and with his English friends, including Darwin and Edgeworth's son-in-law, Thomas Beddoes.[18] Maria Edgeworth's play *Whim for Whim* (written November 1798), a comedy about a secret society, signals her sympathy with Beddoes and with the idealistic reformer and United Irishman, Lord Edward Fitzgerald. In *Whim for Whim*, set unspecifically in London, Edgeworth's youthful, impetuous leading man, Opal, combines publicly identifiable traits of Beddoes (*viz*, his keen discipleship of Kant) and of Lord Edward Fitzgerald (his having a freed slave as a servant).

Early in 1797, Lord Chancellor Fitzgibbon, by now Lord Clare, was giving an ominous description of the present state of popular opinion in Leinster and Ulster, writing of "an ignorant and deluded populace, misled by more intelligent treason."[19] At Edgeworthstown, R. L. Edgeworth learned that the government had rejected his offer of his own telegraph and codebook. He was looking for a new project to work on with his daughter. The breaking-up of the *Northern Star*'s presses may have been the incentive he needed. The chosen project was impeccably *patriot*, in precisely the style in use by the United-Irish poets and burlesque writers: it was a scheme of Jonathan Swift's as sketched by Swift himself in October 1730 to his friend Lord Bathurst in London:

> a certain wag, one of my followers, is collecting materials for a tolerable volume of English Bulls in revenge of the reproaches You throw on us upon that article . . . all these are to be gathered, others invented, and many transplanted from hence to England . . . And there must be a long Introduction proving the native Irish rabble to have a better tast for Wit than the English, for which philosophical causes shall be assigned, and many instances produced.[20]

Each of these aims is accurately delivered in the Edgeworths' *Essay on Irish Bulls*, along with a vastly extended agenda concerned with the spoken language, print culture, and genre—especially the comic and low, the symbolic or literal expression of the people.

The *Essay on Irish Bulls* openly realizes Swift's "revenge" on the English while, unannounced, it also effectively imitates, echoes and extends the two United Irish newspapers and miscellaneous radical publications, some of which emanated from Neilson's printing house. The mimicry self-consciously focuses on newspaper stories, satires, and pamphlet propaganda not only from the 1790s, but from history, particularly Charles II's reign. That age is elaborately recreated from its scandals, lies, and journalism, as if to enforce a comparison with the Ireland of 1798. Provocative journalism of the Stuart period is slotted together with French-revolutionary-style tracts for the masses, a collage that again emphasizes continuities in radical print culture.[21] Coupled with the dense references to printed ephemera, the spoken "bulls" recorded in the opening chapters of the *Essay* create the effect of a heteroglossia, a confusion of tongues. In due course, overheard examples of more sustained Irish wit and eloquence take over as a more natural record of the Hibernian-English voices of the street, of villages, of witnesses and defendants in court.

Drawing on midcentury Scottish critics' established interest in popular culture and the vernacular, the Edgeworths put together an analytical and philosophic case for folk tradition, low comedy, and regional dialect—the terms on which the spoken language deserves respect and equal status with other vernaculars. It is the former Jesuit, James Adams, who argues that an inventive metaphorical vernacular can be used as a literary language.[22] The approval accorded to these implicitly democratic "one nation" Scottish intellectuals echoes the "good news" stories carried by the *Northern Star* on mainland British liberals, and serves as a reminder that the United Irish policy of unity across classes and religions was largely driven by "Scottish" Ulster Presbyterians.

In order to defend the Irish as a nation, the *Essay* gives us the common people in conversation, interaction, and movement, and in their specific social locales, whether town or country. Rejecting the existing stage stereotypes of the Irish as an English calumny, it provides a body of utterances and speech acts by the largely unidentified poor, in streets, villages, or courtrooms, as actually heard. Had the authors declared soon after 1798 that their book was a description of the Irish people, they would have met with resistance from readers of the English press particularly. As the book was being written, newspapers of the day carried the horrors of the 1798 uprising, the underground cells, the caches of pikes and guns, an almost inconceivable death toll of thirty thousand. By linking the *Essay* to Swift's anti-English but jocular proposal, and by engaging readers in a seemingly nonpolitical discussion of a dialect rather than a people, the Edgeworths deliver an indirect, unforced portrait of the Irish poor in daily life and times of peace. Rousseau's eloquent passage quoted earlier, "the people are Mankind," is a key context for the *Essay on Irish Bulls*,[23] but Maria Edgeworth had meanwhile discovered, in her distinctive method as a fiction writer, how neutrally to represent the people of her own time and of the past by making a collage, sometimes misread as an uncomfortable neglect of her historical contexts, of what they said or (more usually in her work) what they wrote.

Is it true, then, as certain critics maintain, that Maria Edgeworth in her thoughtful nation-construction failed to make use of history, leaving that dimension to be developed by Sir Walter Scott? The *Essay* proves otherwise by its crowded use of real historical extracts and citations from print culture in its ephemeral and more disreputable forms—propaganda, libel, perjured evidence, fanaticism, intolerance, rumor, sensation mongering, and incitement to violence and to national or sectarian hatred. Much of this documentary material derives from prose writing of the seventeenth century, particularly the Commonwealth era and Charles II's and James II's reigns. This midcentury period covers not only the English Civil War and interregnum, but also the two Irish civil wars, beginning in 1641 and 1688. One striking feature of that period is the hysteria and sectarian hatred generated in England by Titus Oates, English Puritan fanatic and liar, who by forgery and perjury sent twenty-four Catholic gentlemen and priests to their deaths in the 1680s. Why did the Edgeworths choose this episode to revive?

Because, following the 1798 rising and the Act of Union, a new polemicist had appeared in Ireland, a near equivalent for modern times of Oates himself. Richard Musgrave, a former Irish MP from Munster and a violent anti-Catholic, wrote a polemical *History of the Irish Rebellions of 1641, 1688 and 1798* (1801), in which he alleged that the blame for all these insurgencies rested with the Catholic masses and their priests. The Edgeworths take more than a leaf from Musgrave's book. By following him into the topic of the English-Irish seventeenth-century wars they can portray Titus Oates's England in a manner that implicates Protestant bigots and an idle monarch in the anarchy, intolerance, and violence of that era, along with its harsh Williamite sequel, the Penal Laws.[24]

Another datable event—the revival during 1797 of the issue of a parliamentary Union—produced a flurry of satirical verse of good quality over the next two years, carried in several new journals that ran only as long as the issue did. The Edgeworths had shrewdly turned to Swift for their project. A new, talented United Irish poet now did the same. Robert Emmet, brother of T. A. Emmet, under the pseudonym Trebor (Robert backward) wrote two neat poetical allegories, "London Pride and the Shamrock" (*The Press*, 21 Oct. 1797) and "The Two Ships" (*The Anti-Union*, 10 Jan. 1798). These were national allegories, a subgenre associated with Swift, especially for his classic satire on Scotland's forced Union with England in 1707, "The Injured Lady," which became an Irish classic after its posthumous publication in 1748. Trebor's immediate source is not "The Injured Lady," a domestic allegory in which a faithless man (England) jilts a naïve young Ireland for an older woman (Scotland). Instead, Emmet makes ingenious use of Swift's more economical poem in eleven couplets, "Verses said to be written on the Union," which includes two condensed metaphorical narratives, one botanical ("As if a Man, in making Posies / Should bundle Thistles up with Roses"), the other naval:

> Henceforward let no Statesman dare
> A Kingdom to a ship compare;
> Lest he should call our Commonweal
> A Vessel with a double keel.[25]

Maria Edgeworth apparently followed a contemporary trend when she inserted three chapter-length prose national allegories in the *Essay on Irish Bulls*. "Little Dominick," "The Hibernian Mendicant," and "The Irish Incognito" are not such strict examples of the genre as Swift's and Emmet's, though they do observe the basic rules of introducing personifications of each of the three kingdoms, who act out the resentments of England's two partners. Edgeworth appears to play down and weaken the political allegory by introducing other genres that serve to naturalize her three stories—a child's experience of boarding school; a tragic ballad, in which two lovers (England and Ireland) fight over the same Irish girl, and kill her; and, in "The Irish Incognito," a cross-fertilization of sentimental stage comedy and Lucianic fantasy.

A few examples cannot do justice to the effect of the packed literary, political, and historical allusions in an *Essay* such as this. It is a seventeenth-century form, a miscellany or anatomy; such books were usually well-indexed and annotated; Edgeworth from the outset needed an annotated edition for this career-forming book more than all the rest. Annotation reveals how the *Essay* as a whole sweeps across a single hybrid society, the Irish nation in real time and place. It is both a history and a map, locating the Irish of the day among their British and Atlantic neighbors, especially the French. Each anecdote, even if set in Herodotus's Greece or on the moon, serves as a metaphor or analogue, a piece which, when other pieces are assembled, will constitute a coherent, readable picture of the Irish in or just after 1798.

Edgeworth's Fiction and Catholic Gaelic Ireland

In the nineteenth century, Edgeworth came to be regarded in Ireland as an Ascendancy writer. It was a century in which the word *patriot*, which previously signified a Protestant, was replaced with the word *nationalist*, meaning a Catholic. Most of the well-known recent commentators who have written substantially on Edgeworth have seemed content to categorize her as a writer living in Ireland but not qualifying for the term Irish writer. A trawl of 1990s books and articles by Tom Dunne, Seamus Deane, Catherine Gallagher, Terry Eagleton, Kevin Whelan, even the more exact Katie Trumpener and Ina Ferris, yields the following nouns and adjectives that serve as her affiliations: Colonist, Anglicizer, Anglo-Irish, Ascendancy, Protestant, Unionist, Big House, decorous, conservative, didactic, political economist, utilitarian, improver, landlord class.[26] The first seven terms in this list have particularly negative connotations in Ireland; each of them presupposes a commitment to Britain or to England as an occupying power. Application of these terms to Edgeworth is based on assumptions, rather than on a close reading of either Edgeworth's texts or the cultural and political contexts for her work. Thus, they flatly contradict the carefully considered opinions of two contemporaries whose views on this topic should carry weight: the evangelical English dissenter John Foster, and the Irish Anglican John Wilson Croker, both of whom concluded that Edgeworth was not a Protestant or indeed a Christian writer.[27] The Edgeworths were regarded as reformers and radicals of a rather older provenance and with an international rather than a nationalist agenda. Their vocabulary was closer to Rousseau's than to Paine's, and they were tolerant in respect of religion. Maria Edgeworth's register was hardly aristocratic; her distinctive feature was her detailed, focused attention to the language, manners, and daily lives of the Irish masses.

As a national novelist, Edgeworth's contribution is to recover, by allusion and citation, an impression of the Irish both in present and past time, together with the European and British early modern historical context: the world of Europe's old régimes, élitist nation states ruled on monarchical and aristocratic principles, hierarchical, and religiously intolerant. Edgeworth's consistent return to the seventeenth century in four of her five Irish works (not *The Absentee*) is not handled in Scott's direct manner, by transporting the reader into the past, but echoes and old names still current in talk, and the garrulity and mind-set of Ellinor in *Ennui*, sketch the historical underlying causes of Ireland's Rebellion in 1798. Place is more specific in her fiction than is time. *Ennui*, like *Castle Rackrent*, is focused on a single estate and its numerous people. Edgeworth consistently avoids identifying the (Irish) nation with its own or any nation-state, or its institutions, including state religion, by representing it instead as a cultural formation with very strong local roots, the village and land, surrounded by the region (Annaly) or province (Leinster or Munster). Her symbolic plots lead her characters toward the locality where they belong, and leave them with the task of building a community.

Edgeworth's allegorical plots and her use of symbol and myth were criticized and failed to catch on. The opposite is true of her empirical, positivist style of writing. After the slackness and gush of sentimental-novel prose, Edgeworth's hard-edged, worldly wise, and reflective narratorial manner was rapidly incorporated into nineteenth-century novel writing, the underrated prior condition for the coming more "masculine" genres, the regional novel and the historical novel, with their overlapping subject matter and shared reliance on fact.

Castle Rackrent is based on a real-life family history that chronicles and archives the history of four Edgeworth seventeenth-century landlords, the last of whom, Edgeworth's great-grandfather, was dispossessed of his house and estate and immediately died, as his wife also did, in 1709. In essence, *Rackrent* has claims to be a true story of the chaotic eighty years that incorporated two Irish civil wars (1641, 1688) and culminated, around 1700, in the Penal Laws, designed to separate the Catholic aristocracy and gentry from the land and its people. Though closely local, *Castle Rackrent*'s account of seventeenth-century Longford family histories accords well with Raymond Gillespie's fine article on this matter, largely focused on the Gaelic family of O'Farrell, once dominant in Annaly, and on the terminal decline of its northern branch.[28] There is another more obvious analogy: a story of four landlords of the same dynasty, their fortunes and their fall, neatly allegorizes the demise of the Stuart dynasty, on whose behalf many of the Catholic Irish gentry had fought, died, or gone into exile by 1700.

But the manner of the story's telling takes precedence over the national allegory. Thady M'Quirk, the narrator, was deliberately chosen, according to the ironic preface, as a "village gossip," too simple to tell lies or flatter the great (his masters). The preface itself partly lies—the Quirk family, and perhaps Thady himself, are cunning, not simple, and hereditarily so, as "enslaved" Irish helots, figures borrowed from Drennan and Sir John Davies.[29] But the preface also gets things right—Thady's narration from below allows us to see the effect of the spendthrift and negligent Rackrents on their servants and tenants. So, although *Castle Rackrent* stands apart formally from Edgeworth's later tales, it too tells a village, not a "Big House" story. Moreover it tells it, uniquely, in Hibernian English, and in quotidian estate-life detail. The story of the Rackrents, formerly O'Shaughlins, also draws on the family histories of the proliferating Edgeworths along with those of Catholic neighbors—the nearby Nugents and O'Farrells. *The Absentee* (1810) takes readers back openly and by place-name to the very same locale, at most six miles across, between Edgeworthstown and Granard. In its overall mission to write popular rather than aristocratic history, and in occasionally provocative allusions in the glossary notes and footnotes, *Castle Rackrent* expresses the crisis years of its writing, even as it remains largely silent on Gaelic Ireland.

In Edgeworth's fiction of high life, set in England and France, the conversation of both English and French characters reveal their élite culture's debts to France's hegemonic seventeenth century under the Sun King, Louis XIV. The French literary allusions (to Jean de la Fontaine, Molière, Adélaïde Marie Thérèse de Lascaris de la Rochefoucault, the Marquis de Sévigné, and Voltaire) convey to the reader who picks them up the aristocratic and hierarchical mind-set of the English upper classes as well as the French. Edgeworth wrote two full-dress political novels strongly critical of English eighteenth-century governance under the Whig aristocracy, *Vivian, Tales of Fashionable Life,* (1812), and *Patronage* (1814). Great landed proprietors and the borough-mongers are the main agents and hence the author's targets in her assault on a corrupt and unrepresentative system. Jeremy Bentham, leading philosophical radical, saluted *Patronage* and saw the new Edgeworthian political novel as an admirable lever for influencing public opinion.[30]

Class animus against the proprietors was already a commonplace in rural Ulster in the first half of the 1790s. For its share of this, *Castle Rackrent* can be seen as an original addition to the genre of Billy Bluff and the Squire. *Ennui* (1809) and *The Absentee* each satirize their landed families, anticipating the themes of Edgeworth's later English writings. In two opening sections, each of five chapters, they portray aristocratic system, in *Ennui*'s case from the Roman empire on. The ideal reader for this framing device would be politically informed and theoretical, at home with, say, William Godwin's *Political Justice* (1793), and with the French physiocrats and Scottish political economists. For *Ennui*, as it unfolds, is a consistent satire on the systemic incompetence of great proprietors such as Glenthorn. It marks a shift into novels that critique society as a whole rather than the more restricted eighteenth-century high-society field covered by *Belinda* (1801).

The conventional appearance of *Ennui* as the travels of an upper-class Englishman is complicated by a second, undercover plot, implicitly allegorical in its nature, which represents the people of a hidden Ireland. A first indication of this new Gaelic-Irish subplot is that the Anglicized hero hears a "rousing" call to go to Ireland and play an active part there. In a variety of ways, uninstructed heroes in *Ennui*, in *The Absentee*, and in *Ormond* (1817) each gradually familiarize themselves with the people of a remote estate, and so deliver the appropriate closure, the prospect of a localized, hybrid, and ideal society, mutually tolerant and harmonious within itself. It is the Irish future as prophesied in Gaelic writing, in Sir John Davies, the seventeenth-century plantation builder, and in the typical United Irishmen song of 1797–98.

Though most recent critics of these new national novels now interpret their finales collectively as "a mystical marriage" representing the Union with Britain, this reading is at best speculative and barely if at all supported in Edgeworth's texts. These are more strongly and decidedly focused on the deep historical and religious cultural differences within Ireland, and on the overriding need for a miscegenated factional population to find ways of cohabiting in their localities than are Owenson's finales to similarly themed texts. This clearly signaled difference (if indeed Edgeworth's contemporaries and successors were really so preoccupied with the Union), is one of Edgeworth's most readily identifiable gestures of solidarity with the United Irish cause as first announced in 1792.

Ennui goes even further than Edgeworth's other tales by introducing a striking innovation: Gaelic legend, myth, and ritual play an exotic role at the heart of its plot. What is the rousing call that Glenthorn hears—and, in his sluggish, almost drugged state, acts on?—to go to his castle in Ireland, a strikingly alien late bastion of feudalism. He hears the call from an old woman, his foster nurse, Ellinor O'Donohoe; she does not say, but could be supposed to know, that the rebellion of 1798 is about to break out, Ellinor is a very political village woman, who passes on to the sick Glenthorn in chapter three a whole history of Irish insurgencies, heroes, deliverers, double agents, and martyrs. Or she could be the *bean si* [banshee], the crone that comes to prophesy the fall of a house. Her effect is that of Granuweal—"You sons of old Granu, give ear to your mother . . ."—the warlike personification of Ireland who from 1796 occurs in song, calling her sons to battle.

There are, however, no fewer than three supernatural women in *Ennui*, the others being the aristocrat, Lady Geraldine, and the heir-at-law to the estate, Cecilia Delamere. It seems easiest to think of all three as different realizations of a medieval conception, the Sovereignty Queen. According to medieval records, referred to in preliminary chapters of Catholic histories of Ireland, such as Sylvester O'Halloran's and Francis Plowden's, when a male claimant for chieftainship or more likely kingship appeared, a ritual was invoked for which there is documentary evidence. The mortal claimant's election or coronation took the form of his symbolic marriage with a supernatural woman representing the land to be ruled. While this marriage prospered (that is as long as he was credible as the legitimate ruler), the land prospered. If he failed, or if a usurper succeeded him, putting the Sovereignty Queen metaphorically in thrall or driving her out, misery and poverty followed for the Queen and the inhabitants.

Ennui, begun in the autumn following Robert Emmet's rebellion of June 1803, is then the first and most elaborate of Edgeworth's Gaelicized allegories. A candidate for "Kingship" in a locality seemingly in southwest Munster emerges in the unlikely figure of an idle, degenerate English great proprietor, Lord Glenthorn, who is to be the novel's narrator and protagonist. Each of the three significant women he encounters is a figure of personal power and authority, and in different ways suggestive of the Sovereignty Queen. When Ellinor tells Glenthorn in an aside that the O'Donohoes, her family, were once High Kings, he dismisses her pretensions; but his name derived from her wholly alters his status and significance when, in the finale, he returns to the estate as Christy O'Donohoe, an Irish commoner.

As for the other Queens, the aristocratic Lady Geraldine has a name evoking the Fitzgerald family, headed by the Duke of Leinster and contemporaneously in the public eye for the exploits of Lord Edward Fitzgerald. Geraldine's firm refusal of Glenthorn's proposal—because she has found a suitor of more merit—fits neatly into the allegory of the goddess's power to choose. So does Cecilia Delamere's demand that Glenthorn work for seven years at his legal articles before she will agree to marry him. In general, Edgeworth works hard to give her supernatural women, especially the first two, a human, normal-life presence and activities. Ellinor ends the most complex of the three, for she also acts the explicitly Irish role of the canny foster nurse who bonds an Irish sept by bearing messages, creating alliances, and above all by spying.[31] Ellinor is for that reason the plausible mother of a son and foster son (who is the blacksmith and the legitimate earl), both suspected of being United Irishmen.

The folkloric plot of *Ennui* was detested by some critics, including Francis Jeffrey in the *Edinburgh Review*. Ellinor's confession that she had changed her own son, Glenthorn himself, whilst at nurse for the earl's son (now the blacksmith) is condemned as a "stale contrivance."[32] So are other convenient coincidences, such as the outgoing earl's successful courtship of the heir to his estate. Allegorically, however, the plot of *Ennui* delivers a resounding climax. The former earl, now named O'Donohoe, adds his wife's name Delamere to his own name to become Donohoe-de-la-mer or de-la-mere. The medieval O'Donohoe, a hero in the Killarney region, according to legend walked out over the lake and under it when he felt ready to die, but not before he had told his people that if needed he would return. Though deliverers in Irish legend habitually came from across the sea, it would have been equally appropriate for the O'Donohoe to have come from the "mere," or Lake Killarney. In addition, a further pun may have been intended—"from the mother": for the compelling Ellinor, as Granuweal, is the mother of all Irish sons at this time.

All three of Edgeworth's later Irish tales have a crytographic subtext made up of an ingenious range of popular elements—placenames, family names, allusions to mythology, song, and story. To the three sovereignty goddesses of *Ennui* are added Grace Nugent, heroine of *The Absentee* and Florence Annaly of *Ormond*. It is the marriage of the Anglicized hero to this heroine that in each tale brings happiness and improved prospects to a remote part of traditional village Ireland.

Grace Nugent, for example, has a difficult career, quite naturalistically developed, as an impoverished ward of Lady Clonbrony. She accompanies the family to England, but is from the start homesick for Ireland, and the main advocate in the plot for returning the Irish absentee family to their Irish home. It is Grace, then, who delivers the "rousing" call and who is appropriately named Grace, in Irish Grainne (or Granu), who was both a historical woman chieftain and a semisupernatural figure.

Edgeworth appears to have known something of the checkered history of the forlorn woman in Irish song. She evidently knew that in seventeenth-century vision or "aisling" poetry and song such a woman could be depicted as traduced and even degraded by her experiences. This was not at all the case for the real Grace Nugent, who lived four miles north of Edgeworthstown when Maria Edgeworth's grandfather Richard was growing up. Grace was not only a member of the distinguished Catholic family of Nugent; she was the niece of Richard Talbot, Earl of Tyrconnell, James II's Lord-Lieutenant of Ireland. The blind Gaelic-Irish harper Carolan was a visitor to her house, Castle Nugent, and it was he who wrote a song, "Gracey Nugent," that routinely praises the beautiful daughter of his host.

For her own purposes Edgeworth borrows from the aisling tradition the seventeenth-century tragic plot. She gives Colambre an active hero's role, by seeking out the Gaelic-Irish soldier and nobleman Count O'Halloran, who assists him in tracing the sole survivor of Grace's immediate family—her grandfather, who has the unexpectedly English name of Reynolds. It was another O'Halloran, a brain surgeon, who helped the hero of *Ennui* to confirm that he was not the legitimate earl, because he did not have the scar on his head from the wound sustained by the Earl's baby. In both *Ennui* and *The Absentee*, then, the Gaelic and Catholic historian and brain surgeon, Sylvester O'Halloran, acts as an interpreter and wisdom figure for the Gaelic-Irish plot.

"Gracey Nugent," though sung to the tune of "The British Grenadiers," had strong Jacobite associations. The Nugents were an eminent Catholic military family; and Tyrconnell's brother, Peter, was the Catholic Archbishop of Dublin. This meant that the family was known to Protestants by an even more famous song, the triumphalist Protestant "Lillibulero" that celebrates the Catholic defeats in the 1688–91 civil war, at the Battles of the Boyne and of Aughrim, and ends by mocking the Talbot brothers.[33]

Grace's names all have Gaelic and Catholic resonance, going back to Grainne. Her mother's maiden name is symbolic, Miss St Omer: this was the name of the French seminary where many Irish Catholic boys, especially those intended for the priesthood, were educated. She has a village name and namesake, Grace Nugent II—an acknowledgment of the democratization of the aisling format. Since she is called Nugent, presumably her husband's name, we take it he had followed his family's military tradition of serving one of the Catholic monarchs, usually in France or in Austria. A civilian, Robert Nugent, was, however, also a notable late eighteenth-century figure and could be included in the compliments the novel pays to the family. With Edmund Burke and others in 1778 he had lobbied in the Westminster parliament for better trade concessions for Ireland and for repeal of its anti-Catholic legislation.

Where then in all of this does a Reynolds fit in? The answer is an ingenious extension of *The Absentee*'s language of song. A young songwriter of the late 1780s and 1790s was known to some by initials that appeared in various forms, eg G-e R-s, G-e R-n-lds, not in *The Northern Star* or *The Press*, but in miscellaneous Dublin magazines of the radical kind, the *Sentimental and Masonic Magazine, Carey's Evening Star,* and *Watty Cox's Irish Magazine*. Eventually George Nugent Reynolds, a Protestant gentleman from South Leitrim, became well-known for one song in particular, known variously as "The Exiled Irishman's Lamentation," "Green were the fields where my forefathers dwelt-O" or, after its rousing Irish language chorus, "Erin go brah." The song adroitly combined both sentiment and compulsion:

> But hark! I hear sounds, and my heart strong is beating
> ... Erin go brah!
> Friendship advancing—delusion retreating ...
> We have numbers—and numbers do constitute power:
> Let's will to be free—and we're free from that hour: ...

First published in the last number of the *Northern Star*, Nugent Reynolds's song claims to be the most evocative and universally known of all United Irish contributions to popular culture. So there is some significance in the near-identical fit, when given in compressed form, of Grace/Granu's name with George's.

How many readers, and which readers, would follow the clue of the surname Reynolds to a rousing Irish song never quoted in the novel or mentioned by name? Even Irish readers in 1812, when *The Absentee* appeared, could have been excused for not doing so. And yet, in the tense, distressing year of 1798–99, when magistrates and judges were committing many rebels or suspected rebels to hanging or transportation, George Nugent Reynolds had his hour of fame.

He was a magistrate in South Leitrim, only a few miles from the battlefield of Ballinamuck. Lord Clare removed him from the bench, on the strength presumably of his authorship of "The Exiled Irishman's Lamentation" in particular. Reynolds published an open letter of remonstrance, in which he brought up Clare's Catholic antecedents. He would have "known more decency and good manners" Reynolds suggested, if, as his father once intended, he had been educated at the College of St Omer.[34]

George Nugent Reynolds died suddenly in 1801 at Stowe, the great house and garden which was then the home of a Nugent scion, Robert, Earl of Buckinghamshire. After his death George's property rights in his most successful song became obscured because the poet Thomas Campbell in effect appropriated the song, by publishing on 28 January 1801 a less political, still more sentimental version of it as his own, and renaming it "The Exile of Erin."

There is a curious little episode in *Patronage* between the two sisters of the Percy family, Rosamund and Caroline, in which both nominate a favorite national song. The heroine, Caroline, names Thomas Campbell's "Ye Mariners of England" subtitled "A Naval Ode." Her elder sister, Rosamund, names Campbell's "Exile of Erin." The sisters speak as though Campbell wrote both poems, although two years earlier, as she worked on *The Absentee*, Maria Edgeworth was plainly ascribing the earlier version to George Nugent Reynolds.

From the time of the children's story, "The Purple Jar" (1800), the name of Rosamund was associated with Maria Edgeworth herself, who had a family reputation for being impulsive and mercurial, where her much-admired stepsister, Honora (the model for *Patronage*'s Caroline) who had died in 1790, was rational and calm. In at last identifying herself as a national writer, Edgeworth gives the episode in *Patronage* some weight—but it is less weight than George Nugent Reynolds brings to the heroine Grace as a personification of Ireland in the years 1798–99.

If *The Absentee* is the most modern in feel of Edgeworth's Irish tales, *Ormond* seems the most literary, poetic, and, in some sense, abstracted. It is partly set on an island in, presumably, Lough Ree, largest of the Shannon lakes. The Black Islands are a location in the *Arabian Nights*, already a land of fantasy. Remote Irish islands are typically the location of the ruined abbeys and round towers of Ireland's rich medieval church culture. A strong romance and literary link is with Edmund Spenser, associated in real life with Munster's fertile Blackwater valley. Equally important seventeenth-century names are those of other Annaly and Munster landowners, planters, and intellectuals, such as the O'Farrells in Annaly and William Herbert of Castleisland, along with his son-in-law Edward Herbert, Lord Herbert of Cherbury, and also Lord Castleisland, who between them account for the name Edgeworth bestows on the novel's model landlord, Herbert Annaly. Edgeworth's national tale, always a highly conscious and flexible literary-historical subgenre, appears at its most surreal and magical-realist in *Ormond*, where Edgeworth multiplies her protagonist into a host of idealistic (Irish) questers by drawing evocatively on late Renaissance seventeenth-century quest romances such as Sir Philip Sidney's *Arcadia*, Spenser's *Faerie Queene*, Edward Herbert's fictionalized *Arcadian Autobiography* (first published by Horace Walpole in 1754) and François de la Salignac de la Mothe Fénelon's *Télémaque*.

In all three homecomings the focus is as much on the community as on the homecomer. Arguably both Utopia and the plantation express "English" and Protestant dreams, associated in Ireland with the Plantation policy of Elizabeth and James I. But in *Ormond* especially, Edgeworth avoids giving an impression of Anglicization by bringing out the range of Ormond's Catholic friendships—with Corny, Dora, Moriarty, Peggy, Shelagh, and Tommy. Equally, some of the Irish characters, Dora, Black Connal, Mlle O'Faley, however remote and rural their home, make a career for themselves at the court of the greatest Catholic nation, France. In marrying a woman called Annaly, Ormond associates himself with the medieval and Gaelic name of the Edgeworths' region; but, by bearing the name Florence, his wife can also be thought of as a republican, or as a nonsectarian wisdom figure associated with the neo-Platonist Catholic mysticism of the sixteenth and early seventeenth centuries.

Edgeworth had moved by 1817, as Owenson did still later in *The O'Briens and the O'Flaherties* (1827), to a position Katie Trumpener sees in Swift, but is thus far unable to detect consistently in the Swiftian Edgeworth: what Trumpener perceives imaginatively as Swift's "call for new political solidarities across ethnic and religious divides."[35] Ormond's future home on the Black Islands has features of a transnational Utopia, but on resonantly Irish terms: a mixed community; industry, employment, and children at school; and the Gaelic-Catholic dream, a restitution of the land.

Terry Eagleton finds little to praise in Edgeworth's novelistic technique, largely because a more prosaic realist novel is the only novel he recognizes, but he does grant her primacy, for her work is "the place where a whole distinctive *object* known as Ireland makes its first fictional appearance."[36] It would be more exact to say that two contemporaneous attempts or "assays" at this act of realization, *Castle Rackrent* and the *Essay on Irish Bulls*, had the effect of transforming the scope and possibilities of the whole range of national tales and novels they helped to generate. From April 1802, when the *Essay on Irish Bulls* appeared, Edgeworth had a template for her own later *Tales*, a way of constructing a single organic entity, a nation, out of the uses real Irish people had made of language: Irish stories, mentalities, speech acts, testimonies, records, prophecies, and memories.

In one key respect, however, the later tales differ from the *Essay*. Because it echoed the United Irish press, *Irish Bulls* drew widely on Dublin wit and satire, literary or vulgar, and omitted distinctive Gaelic-Irish materials, though not the speech of the village Irish. The striking innovation in Edgeworth's three later tales is the introduction of traditional Gaelic-Irish allegorical plots, incorporating a distinct body of story, of myths, heroes, symbols, and prophecies. Allusively, via the medium of song, *Ennui* and *The Absentee* enact the mass rebellion and its aftermath. Since other plotlines introduce Anglicized Irish characters, the resulting collage captures a hybrid, divided Irish people at the point in their history when they heard a dynamic call—that of the United Irish movement for unification into a single organic nation.

Notes

1. Norman Vance, *Irish Literature: A Social History* (Dublin: Four Courts Press, 1990), 66. Among the works I have in mind are, Marianne Elliott, *Partners in Revolution: The United Irishmen and France* (New Haven: Yale University Press, 1982) and *Wolfe Tone, Prophet of Irish Independence* (New Haven: Yale University Press, 1989); Jim Smyth, *The Men of No Property: Irish Radicals and Popular Politics in the Late 18th Century* (London, Macmillan, 1992); Thomas Bartlett, "An End to Moral Economy: The Irish Militia Disturbances of 1793," *Past and Present* 99 (1983), 41–64; "Defenders and Defenderism in 1795," in *Irish Historical Studies* 24 (1984–85), 373–94; Nancy Curtin, *The United Irishmen: Popular Politics in Ulster and Dublin, 1791–1798* (Oxford: Oxford University Press, 1994); Kevin Whelan, *The Tree of Liberty: Radicalism, Catholicism and the Construction of Irish Identity, 1760–1830* (Cork: Cork University Press, 1996) and "Politicisation in Co Wexford," in Gough, Hugh, and D. Dickson, eds. *Ireland and the French Revolution* (Dublin: Dublin University Press, 1990), 156–70; I. R. McBride, *Scripture Politics* (Oxford: Oxford University Press, 1998).

2. Joep Leerssen, *Mere Irish and Fior-Ghael: Studies in the Idea of Irish Nationality, Its Development and Literary Expression Prior to the Nineteenth Century* (Cork: Cork University Press, 1996); "Anglo-Irish Patriotism and its European Context: Notes Towards a Reassessment," *Eighteenth-Century Ireland* 3 (1988): 7–24; *Remembrance and Imagination: Patterns in the Historical and Literary Representation of Ireland in the Nineteenth Century* (Cork: Cork University Press, 1996). Katie Trumpener, *Bardic Nationalism: the Romantic Novel and the British Empire* (Princeton: Princeton University Press, 1997).

3. Mary Helen Thuente, *The Harp Restrung* (Syracuse: Syracuse University Press, 1994).

4. William Drennan to Martha McTeir, *Drennan/McTeir Letters* n.d. [1794], ed. Jean Agnew, 2 vols. (Dublin:Women's History Project / Irish MSS Commission, 1998–99), 2: 103: "I have been reading . . . the *Confessions* of Rousseau . . . though I did not at all like it the first time, I was exceedingly captivated . . . on a second perusal. I think the chief reason was . . . that I found some resemblance to myself in the portrait—in the reserve of countenance—the awkward timidity—the shortsightedness—the voice—(Edgeworth told me the first time he saw me, you have the voice of Rousseau)—really frank and open, apparently sullen and shut up . . . hating vulgarity, loving the vulgar."

5. William Drennan to Martha McTeir, *Drennan/McTeir Letters* n.d. [1794], 1: 193. If the letter's date is correct, the daughter concerned would have to be Emmeline, b. 1769. Maria however, b. 1768, seems the more likely candidate.

6. William Drennan to Martha McTeir, *Drennan/McTeir Letters* n.d. [1794], 2: 103. See note 4.

7. The interesting story of Benjamin Franklin's project, c. 1775, of "a society for philosophical religion" from which "matters of faith were to be omitted" for which a liturgy was commissioned from the deist David Williams, has been established in two editions by Peter France, to which my account is indebted. After the appearance of Williams's *Liturgy on the Universal Principles of Religion and Morality* (1776), a group of about a dozen, including Wedgwood, Bentley, and Day met first in a hired chapel in Margaret Street, London. R. L. Edgeworth does not mention a liturgy when recalling his membership during the period the group met in Slaughter's Coffee House. See Peter France, ed., *Thomas Bentley, Journal of a Visit to Paris (1776)* (Falmer, Brighton: University of Sussex Library, 1977), 13–17, and David Williams, *Incidents in my Own Life* (Brighton: University of Sussex Press, 1980), 4–5.

8. Jean-Jacques Rousseau, *Émile*, trans. Barbara Foxley, Everyman's Library (London: Dent, 1974), 251–52.

9. cf Joseph Wright of Derby's celebrated painting of Sir Brooke Boothby, friend of Darwin and Wedgwood and a leading patron of Rousseau in England. Wright paints Boothby lying beside a stream in a wood and reading a work by Rousseau. The design is copied from Isaac Oliver's odd narrative portrait of Edward Herbert, future Lord Cherbury; that painting, c 1616, appears as a frontispiece to Herbert's *Autobiography*, first published by Horace Walpole c. 1764.

10. See Butler,"Irish Culture and Scottish Enlightenment," in S. Colloni, R. Whatmore, and B. Young, eds. *Economy, Polity and Society* (Cambridge: Cambridge University Press), 165.

11. Rousseau, *Émile*, 187.

12. Rousseau, *Émile*, 186. *Émile* is partly a work of fiction, in which Rousseau casts himself as the teacher of the boy Émile, partly of educational thinking from Michel

de Montaigne, René Descartes, John Locke, François de Salignac de la Mothe Fénelon, and the deist tradition more generally. In *Émile* Rousseau brings his own qualities to the topic of education: he is observant, intuitive, and psychological, and his lessons are child-centered. The boy should run free like farm boys, endure cold, recover from hard knocks, come to feel at home in a primitive, simpler world or just a natural physical environment, anything rather than be shown off as a mannequin in a salon. Rousseau denounces society for corrupting the child by teaching artificial objectives such as vanity, greed, status, and power. Books play a part in the conspiracy to deform children. By teaching the child understanding and self-reliance through attentive one-to-one conversations, Rousseau introduces a new aim, to educate children to be citizens as well as individuals. The citizen is a mature, reflective thinker of whatever class or background. Though Émile is a rich boy in the book, Rousseau's system is easily interpretable as a universal one, as subsequent educational reformers, including Adam Smith, Marie Jean Antoine Nicolas de Caritat Condorcet, and the Edgeworths, picked up. For more on this see Emma Rothschild's "Condorcet and Adam Smith on Education and Instruction" in *Philosophers on Education: Historical Perspectives* ed. Amélie Oksenberg Rorty (London: Routledge, 1998), 209–26. For the Edgeworths' indebtedness to Smith on education, see M. Butler, "Irish Culture and Scottish Enlightenment," 160–66.

13. Rousseau, *Émile*, 217.

14. Robert Burns, "On The Late Captain Grose's Peregrinations Thro' Scotland Collecting The Antiquities Of That Kingdom," *Collected Poems*, The Official Robert Burns Site, 22 May 02 http://www.robertburns.org/works/275.html ll 1–30.

15. "The Rights of Men and Citizens and the Duties of Men and Citizens" appeared in the *Northern Star* (no. 5, Jan. 1792, preceded by a clarificatory "Catechism of the French Constitution" which began in no. 4). A new "Constitution and new Declaration of the Rights and Duties" was again translated in full in no. 441, 21–24 Mar. 1796.

16. *Northern Star*, no 441 (21–24 Mar. 1796).

17. William Sampson and Thomas Russell, *Review of the Lion of Old England* (serialized NS, Sept.–Dec. 1793); William Sampson, *A Faithful Report on the Trial of Hurdy Gurdy* (serialized NS July–Aug. 1794), and, most successful and enduring, the Rev James Porter's *Billy Bluff and the Squire* (NS May–Nov. 1796).

18. For R. L. Edgeworth's letters to Darwin on Ireland see *Memoirs*, vol 2, especially 155–61. Thomas Beddoes published a pamphlet in response to the English naval mutiny at the Nore in May 1797, "Alternatives Compared: or what shall the Rich Do in Order to be Safe?" (1797). This was targeted at the Prime Minister, Pitt, for his repressive legislation of 1795 directed at the English press and at rights of assembly. Beddoes reissued the pamphlet (1798/99) with a new Preface referring this time to Ireland and demanding the impeachment of Pitt and of the Administration in Dublin for their failure to prevent the 1798 rebellion.

19. *Dublin Evening Post*, 21 March 1797; quoted in Whelan, *The Tree of Liberty*, 73.

20. Jonathan Swift to Lord Bathurst, October 1730; ed. David Woolley, *The Correspondence of Jonathan Swift, D.D.*, 4 vols (Frankfurt: Peter Lang, 1999–), 3:327. The Edgeworths' acknowledgement to Swift in *Irish Bulls*, ch 2, was cut in 3rd and subsequent editions: see *Works*, 1: 374.

21. For example, into a paragraph concerned with seventeenth-century party warfare, the Edgeworths casually insert the name of the *Children's Catechism*, a noto-

riously virulent Belfast handbill of 1794. The modern document mentioned and not quoted resembles the propaganda issued in revolutionary France, and the question-and-answer format is typical of Irish secret societies:

> Q. What are the common curses of mankind?
> A. The habit of affixing great Ideas to little Things—hence the phrase as great as a King, (although a German Bastard) . . .
> Q. When will happiness attend mankind?
> A. At the extirpation of SLAVERY, Priestcraft, kingcraft, and Aristocracy—thence spring fair Liberty and Equality, that Men may enjoy the BLESSINGS of GOD in an earthly Paradise.

from Handbill, *The Children's Catechism* (1794), Linenhall Library, Belfast, Joy MSS, quoted in McBride, *Scripture Politics*, 180.

22. James Adams, *The Pronunciation of the English Language . . . with an Appendix on Dialect . . . and Vindication of the Dialect of Scotland* (Edinburgh, 1799), 157.

23. Rousseau, *Émile*, 186.

24. Boldly imitating Musgrave's method of historical cross-reference, the Edgeworths, in a historically suggestive passage in chapter 3 (rev 3rd ed., 1808), lampoon the English General Lake for "calming" the Ulster countryside in the style recommended to him by Chancellor Fitzgibbon:

> we read the following article of country intelligence in a Dublin newspaper:— "General [Lake] scoured the country yesterday but had not the good fortune to meet with a single rebel." The author of this passage seems to have been a keen sportsman; he regrets the not meeting with a single rebel, as he would the not meeting with a single partridge; and he justly considers the human biped as fair game, to be hunted down by all who are properly qualified and licensed by government. (*Essay on Irish Bulls*, chap. 2, 85.)

Maria Edgeworth and Richard Lovell Edgeworth, *An Essay on Irish Bulls*, in *Caslte Rackerent, Irish Bulls and Ennui*, ed. Jane Desmarais, Tim McLoughlin, and Marilyn Butler (London: Pickering and Chatto, 1999).

25. Jonathan Swift, "Verses said to be written on the Union," *Poems of Swift* ed. Harold Williams, 3 vols (Oxford: Oxford University Press, 1958); *Field Day Anthology*, ed. Deane, 1: 477. Swift was alluding in these lines to a humiliating episode in Dublin Bay in which an experiment with a catamaran got out of control when the wind changed. In his development of the theme Emmet represents the English ship as battered and unsound compared with the smaller, trimmer Irish vessel. Contemporaries might have suspected a reference to the failure of the English navy the previous year to prevent a French fleet from entering and afterward leaving Bantry Bay without let or hindrance. For an account of the "Injured Lady" national allegory type from Swift to its revival, 1797–1800, see Trumpener, *Bardic Nationalism*, 133–37.

26. For example, Tom Dunne, "Haunted by History: Irish Romantic Writing, 1800–1850" in *Romanticism in a National Context* eds. Roy Porter and Miklas Teich (Cambridge: Cambridge University Press, 1988), 80; Seamus Deane, *Strange Country* (Oxford: Clarendon, 1997) 30–40; Catherine Gallagher, "The Changeling's Debt: Maria Edgeworth's Productive Fictions" in *Nobody's Story* (Oxford: Clarendon, 1994) 257–327; Terry Eagleton, *Heathcliff and the Great Hunger* (London: Verso, 1995) especially 161–67; Kevin Whelan, foreword: "Writing Ireland, Reading En-

gland" in *Wild Irish Girl: a National Tale* eds. Claire Connolly and Stephen Copley (London: Pickering and Chatto, 2000), ix–xxiv.

27. Foster reviewed the 2d series, *Tales of Fashionable Life*, vols 4–6, which includes *The Absentee* (1812), for the *Eclectic Review* 8 (1812): 979–1000. His criticisms of her religious position appear on 998–1000. Croker admired *The Absentee* (*Quarterly Review* 7, June 1812]: 329–42, but wrote a harsh exposé of her father's deism as given away in his *Memoirs* (*Quarterly Review* 23 [1820]: 510–49, esp. 528, 544–49).

28. Raymond Gillespie, "A Question of Survival: the O'Farrells and Longford in the seventeenth century" eds., *Longford: Essays in County History* eds. Gillespie and Moran (Dublin: Lilliput, 1991), 13–29.

29. William Drennan, *Orellana* or *Letters of an Irish Helot* (Dublin, 1785) and Sir John Davies, "A Discoverie of the True Causes why Ireland was never entirely subdued" [1612] in *Complete Works in Verse and Prose of Sir John Davies*, ed. Chertsy Worthies Library, Alexander B. Grosart, 3 vols (London, 1878): "such as are oppressed and live in slavery, are ever put to their shifts" (2: 107).

30. See J. R. Dinwiddy, "Bentham as a Pupil of Miss Edgeworth's" *Notes and Queries* 29 (June 1982): 208–10.

31. Davies, "Discoverie": "Fostering . . . being the cause of many strong combinations and factions do[th] tend to the utter ruine of a Commonwealth . . . Fostering hath always been a stronger alliance than Bloud" (1: 109).

32. [F. Jeffrey], "Tales of Fashionable Life," *Edinburgh Review* 14 (July 1809): 379.

33. The last two verses of "Lillibullero," believed to have been written in 1687 by a future Whig Lord Lieutenant of Ireland, Thomas Wharton, and set to a quickstep by Henry Purcell, are the best remembered: "There was an old prophecy found in a bog / Lilli burlero bullen a la / That Ireland should be ruled by an ass and a dog: / Lilli etc / And now this prophecy is come to pass, / Lilli etc / For Talbot's the dog, and Tyrconnell's the ass, / Lilli etc." See Deane, *Field Day*, 1: 475–76: "the refrain, which is a garbled version of Irish, means 'Lilly will be manifest: the day will be ours'" (1: 475n).

34. J. Roderick O'Flanagan, *Lives of the Lord Chancellors of Ireland* (London, 1875), 2: 250–51.

35. Trumpener, *Bardic Nationalism*, 50.

36. Eagleton, *Heathcliff*, 175.

History and Utopia in *Ormond*

PETER COSGROVE

LESS INNOVATIVE THAN *CASTLE RACKRENT*, LESS FANTASTIC THAN *ENNUI*, less didactic than *The Absentee*, *Ormond* is the most sophisticated of Maria Edgeworth's four Irish novels in addressing her concerns about the place of history and myth in Ireland. Gaelic clan life receives a more generous acknowledgment than in her other novels, and hybrid identities abound, thereby further complicating the classifications of Irishness and Englishness. The educational ideals Edgeworth and her father had been developing for the previous quarter century come in for serious reconsideration: innate moral strength and autodidacticism now appear to take pride of place over a proper education. *Ormond* also offers a re-evaluation of how this autodidacticism and innate moral strength mediate questions of national identity. All the Irish characters of *Ormond*, except for King Corny, seem mostly hybrid, as if hybridity were the condition of Irishness; and their hybridity is a result of the historical and material conditions prevailing in Ireland at the end of the eighteenth century. The protagonist, proposed as an essentially moral subject who transcends history, can only find his proper place in a zone composed of overlapping reminiscences of texts from the history of utopia. This conclusion is offered in a novel where notably literary form takes on a more active role than in Edgeworth's earlier work. Overt allusion and generic frameworks subsidize characters and events but also accumulate a surplus of signification.

Edgeworth's use of contrasting characters is certainly an important part of *Ormond*: contrasts between Dora and Florence, Ormond and Marcus, Corny and Sir Ulick, the two Connals, Black and White, all perform important functions.[1] Yet, additional characters turn these pairs into more complex units: Lady Millicent and the young women at Castle Hermitage enlarge the simple opposition between Dora and Florence: Sir Herbert and Black Connal, King Corny and Sir Ulick stake out a variable framework beyond simple dichotomies.

Many of the characters define their positions with allusions to prior texts. Sir Ulick quotes Alexander Pope, Black Connal quotes Emmerich de Vattel, the natural law theorist. Harry Ormond's own reading is intrinsic to the drama of his becoming; in pursuit of her hero's education, Edgeworth resuscitates the quarrel between Henry Fielding and Samuel Richardson and cites Chesterfield's *Letters.* Additionally, the novel evokes two overlapping genres, the bildungsroman and the apologue, forms which reinforce and contradict each other. Neither the reader of *Ormond,* nor the protagonist, confront comfortable choices but rather negotiate a multidimensional puzzle as to the appropriate courses of behavior advocated by the novel—a negotiation that mirrors the acts of adjustment and re-adjustment engaged in by those living in early nineteenth-century Ireland and looking to competing histories and utopias for justification.

Doubling and intertextuality are complex forms that ultimately lead a literary work toward the positing of multiple meanings unresolvable into a single message. They are therefore the opposite of the kind of form we expect from an educator and didactic novelist. Indeed, many of Edgeworth's most cherished notions, if not exactly scrutinized, are discussed in *Ormond* with at least a sense of indeterminability. The commitment to education dissolves into the goal of a self-originating moral will. The practical guide to the landlord's role in Ireland retreats into an impossible utopia. Edgeworth had not been guiltless of interpretative opacity before. Indeed, *Castle Rackrent* remains foremost in the canon of her writing partly because of its polysemousness. A similar effect occurs in *Ormond* because, through various devices, Edgeworth articulates the codes of writing. In John Mowitt's words, Edgeworth's work discloses "the infrastructure of language . . . through whose functioning linguistic meaning takes place."[2]

These codes are the semantic oppositions on which meaning is constructed: to take a familiar example, individual will and social convention. This group comes as a unit from which meanings or, perhaps more precisely, authorial positions, are generated. Whichever side the author gives a positive charge to the other receives a negative charge. Other such thematic doublets in *Ormond* are self-construction versus learned behavior and history versus utopia. Such topoi are so broad that they give little indication as to what the actualized text will ultimately produce. Readers cannot decipher the codes until they are embodied in the images, characters, and situations of the book. In *Ormond*, however, the formal structures—doubling and intertextuality—reproduce the base unit over and over again as if the actual process of discourse refuses to generate the appropriate position. The importance of education sits uneasily with notions of self-origination, moral exceptionalism oscillates with sociability, the integrity of the subject with dualistic hybridity, history with utopia. The modern reader's recognition of these counterpointed units is due not to a postmodern creative reflexivity but to Edgeworth's anxiety about the ineluctability of historical determination, which ultimately drives her to the literary consolations of a utopia of whose fantasy elements she is preternaturally aware.

Commentators attuned to the nuances of language and genre have long found more complex patterns in Edgeworth's texts than the conflict of realism and didacticism. Mark Hawthorne perceives a double structure that allows the novelist's "doubts" to counteract her father's "dogma": "Her father's ideas everywhere struck the unsuspecting reader, but her plots, her imagery, her characterization were at odds with this surface. The resulting tension gives her mature fiction a depth that is not at all like the usual didactic novel."[3] More recently, Mitzi Myers has proposed that Edgeworth's technique in her educational works for women amounts to a female bildungsroman articulated through "double-voiced narratives."[4] For Brian Hollingworth, "it is clear that the *Ormond* text operates as a highly intricate linguistic construct, referencing and cross-referencing a significant number of other texts, literary, historical, classical and vernacular."[5] Hollingworth, moreover, notes that the competing genres in *Ormond* are not realism and romance, but the bildungsroman and the moral tale, or apologue. The bildungsroman is the novel of the growth of the self and the apologue, in Sheldon Sacks's definition, is "a work organized as a fictional example of the truth of a formulable statement or a series of such statements."[6] Bildungsroman and apologue double and occlude each other in *Ormond*, two intertwined genres as much contradicting as reinforcing each other. These forms activate two moral plots: the plot of the public education of the ruler, which takes the protagonist through four different examples of good and bad forms of government, and the plot of personal development, without which the ruler traditionally is thought to lack legitimacy. This doubling develops an opposition of interior and exterior, public and private—through a consideration of ideals of government. The apologue introduces history, while, outside the constraints of history, the bildungsroman raises the issue of the struggle for interiority. *Ormond* acknowledges, by refusing to resolve, the question of whose history is public and whose private.

Two of *Ormond*'s intertexts noted by Hollingworth are William Shakespeare's *Henry IV* and François de la Salignac de la Mothe Fénelon's *Les Aventures de Télémaque*. Both evoke the moral advancement of the ruler. In the Black Islands, Harry Ormond is figured as a young prince Hal among the revelers at the Boar's Head Tavern. He must cast off the "base contagious clouds" to come fully into his own royal powers (*I Henry IV*, I.ii.186), though King Corny, the leader of the revelers, is a morally sounder role model for Ormond than Falstaff was for Prince Hal. The parallel with Fénelon's *Télémaque*, however, structures the plot of *Ormond* from beginning to end. This famous educational novel is indirectly alluded to through the name of one of Ormond's mentors, Dr. Combray. Combray is the title of Fénelon, the archbishop of Combrai under Louis XIV, who was also an educator and the tutor of Louis's grandson, the duc de Bourgogne, and, most notably, the author of the very successful moral guide for princes, *Les Aventures de Télémaque*. (Amusingly, the Combray of *Ormond*, far from being a Catholic prelate, is a Church of Ireland pastor of Huguenot descent.) Curiously, Fénelon's work, although cast in the strange form of the heroic romance of the seventeenth-century moral tale, is an entirely appropriate framework for the probationary travels of a young prince such as Harry seems to be. The parallels between the two works are not exact: Dr. Combray does not keep a permanent station by Ormond's side as Mentor does in Fénelon's work, but there are sufficient allusions to prove that the French book influenced Edgeworth. Sir Ulick, one of Harry's substitute fathers, is satirized for his political corruption in a poem entitled *Ulysseana*. *Télémaque* plots a kind of circular progress in which Ithaca is the beginning and end point of the hero's journey. Harry Ormond's circular journey is from his own Irish Ithaca, the Black Islands, through the surrounding estates of Ireland to the great nation of France, and back to the idealized poverty whence he started. Télémaque wanders around the Mediterranean viewing forms of administration in imaginative versions of Egypt, Phoenicia, Crete, and Salente, not to mention that darling of the *fêtes galantes*, Cythera; Ormond travels through domains on the North Atlantic seaboard: King Corny's folk community in the Black Islands, Sir Ulick's realm at Castle Hermitage, Herbert Annaly's virtuous rule over his coastal estates, and the order of the old regime in France before the revolution. The four realms, as have been frequently noted, stand for different forms of government: Corny's island, traditional native Irish clans; Sir Ulick's, corrupt party politics in the British system; and Sir Herbert's, moral but not communitarian rule—his people desert to Sir Ulick when they can do better even by immoral means. Of Paris, we might say that life is social but not political, as befits the English view of an absolute monarchy, whose subjects, denied full participation in government, are confined to a life of the senses.

As with *Télémaque*, history in *Ormond* is overtly emplotted as romance. This is not to say that *Ormond* is merely a romance; Edgeworth astutely uses the antique form to thematize the limits on historicality. She indicates that the various historical societies through which Harry Ormond wanders are illusions, illusions with only a tenuous hold on existence and all of which have vanished by the end of the novel, mirroring the illusion that Irish history had in some sense ended with the Act of Union. Castle Hermitage is a "magic lantern" (169) in which figures magically appear and disappear, and the vice-regal visit to Sir Ulick's home is "a raree show" (172). By the end of the book, the show has closed forever with only the lamentations of its servants to remember it: "and after all, where is the great friends now?—the quality that used to be entertaining at the castle above? Where is all the favour promised him now? What is it come to?" (290). The pre-Revolutionary French society Harry visits is on the point of total dissolution: "Nor would it have been possible to convince half at least of the crowd, who assisted at the king's supper that night, that . . . all the attachment, *le devouement*, professed habitually, perhaps felt habitually—for the reigning monarch . . . should in a few years pass away and be no more seen" (253–54). Sir Herbert Annaly's just administration has no stability except that conferred by his personal existence—on his death it will pass by entail to a distant relative. The same glamorous illusions that characterize Castle Hermitage and the Paris of Louis XV are inscribed directly on Sir Herbert's body with as little assurance of permanence as the others: "The hectic colour, the brilliant eye, the vividness of fancy, the superiority of intellectual powers, the warmth of the affections, and the amiable gentleness of the disposition of this young man, were, alas! but so many fatal indications of his disease" (223). All the historical conditions revealed to Harry are "evanescent fancies . . . [which] though they left scarce any individual traces they made a general and useful impression" (169). In *Ormond*, the mind of the observer has a more solid existence than any of the worldly phenomena reflected in it.

This aspect of Edgeworth's technique has not gone unnoticed by historians. L. M. Cullen, committed presumably to history writing as the inscription of a real past, complains about the value of Edgeworth's books as historical evidence, arguing that they "are a parody in which a sense of reality is created by the accuracy of everyday details and of speech, but where the novelist enjoys a wide freedom of imagination by putting the scene safely, as in *Castle Rackrent*, in an irrevocable past."[7] Similarly, Joseph Kestner, discussing the historicity of the regional novel at this period, points to a feature notable in *Ormond*: "The regional novelists use the subject matter of the eighteenth century actually to confront nineteenth-century problems. Their works are palimpsests of two temporal levels: one, the eighteenth century, whether 1707, 1715, 1745, or 1750; the other, the nineteenth century, the time of composition."[8] In *Ormond*, superimposed historical eras create a stereographic illusion. The old regime in France, supposedly contemporary with Ormond's action, receives a retrospective cast through a famous quotation from Edmund Burke's *Reflections on the Revolution in France* about Marie Antoinette, "then Dauphiness—at that time full of life, and splendour, and joy, adorning and cheering the elevated sphere she just began to move in" (259). The precise historical moment of Sir Ulick's financial operations is also hard to pin down, it could be either eighteenth or nineteenth century. Another example of overlapping temporalities is evident when Moriarty meets Ormond in the Paris of Louis XV after his escape from Kilmainham Jail in Dublin, not built until 1792. This kind of confusion can only belong to representation, not to the ineluctable modality of temporal succession. Cullen's "parody" is not perhaps quite right; he has noticed the same technique as Kestner. The double structure can only belong to fiction. *Ormond* articulates the historical context in a way that makes it difficult to employ as a grounding for the oscillating meanings of the text.

Violation of the boundaries between fiction and history receives another kind of dramatization in *Ormond*. Fictional asseveration triumphs over historical interpretation of evidence. Paradoxically, while fiction is polysemous it is also absolute. Interpretations are endlessly debatable but the events are indisputable. If the narrator tells us that Ormond did not "seduce Peggy Moriarty, and by deserting Dora had thrown her into the arms of a French adventurer," and that he had by no means "renounced the Protestant religion, and . . . turned Catholic for the sake of absolution" (188), these are truths beyond historical narrative. At one point in the novel, however, these libels against Ormond are circulated by newspaper reports and by rumors that follow Harry's duel in defense of Sir Ulick against the satirical *Ulysseana* mentioned above. These forms of communication, preserved in archives, diaries, and memoirs, are the very stuff of history, adequately sifted, of course, for their reliability. Chapter twenty-one's astonishing synopsis of the first half of Edgeworth's novel, in the voice of malicious slander, besides creating further difficulties between Harry and Lady Annaly, seems to address directly the issue of distorting the record.

History does not deal in facts, the author suggests, but in opinions—opinions, indeed, that are unfair and inaccurate. The absolute narrator who steps in to correct the misapprehensions leaves both fiction and history in some turmoil; history because it stands convicted of fictionalizing and fiction because its authority is incontestable but only within the limits of a nonhistorical form of representation. History in *Ormond*, then, submits to the double-structure of fictional form, possesses less sure representational power than fiction, and is transient with regard to the mental faculties of representation.

Initially, it might seem that against this evanescent historicity Edgeworth proposes the contrary value of the interior self. The bildungsroman model lends itself to this alternate theme. In this mode the novel contrasts interiority with the evanescence of historical societies. The two genres economically rely on the same set of circumstances to urge their different claims on the reader. While Harry ponders the nature of the governments of King Corny, Sir Ulick, Herbert Annaly, and Louis XV, the societies over which they rule are also the scene of his confrontations with himself. The bildungsroman, in the view of one of its most influential interpreters, is the novel of the struggle of an interior subject against the meaningless patterns of the world around it. For Georg Lukács, the bildungsroman is a quest narrative of the interior life: "The novel tells of the adventure of interiority; the content of the novel is the story of the soul that goes forth to find itself, that seeks adventures in order to be proved and tested by them, and by proving itself, to find its own essence."[9] The probation period consists largely of a threat to the individual consciousness from forces external to it: "such a threat arises only when the outside world is no longer adapted to the individual's ideas and the ideas become objective facts—ideals—in his soul."[10] Lukács calls this soul the "problematic individual" because it is disaffected with the social world in which it finds itself.[11] While Lukács's theory of pure interiorities confronting the rigidity of conventions might seem outdated today, his scheme usefully differentiates between the developing novel and those predecessors to which *Ormond* is also indebted, the picaresque and the moral tale, or the apologue. Harry Ormond is certainly problematic in his eighteenth-century society: of obscure birth, with no patrilineal estate to secure his title among the Irish gentry, his status depends on the kindness of his father's army friend, Sir Ulick. And the world of the novel, the site of Harry's testing, is also a fallen world of "a reality that is heterogeneous in itself and meaningless to the individual."[12] Liberated from a predetermined role, Ormond struggles to understand and to differentiate himself from a role defined by social convention. Harry Ormond must come to terms with the category difference between his search for himself and the inability to find any objective order that can satisfy his longings. It is a narrative search for self through the constraints of categorical differences which employs the tropes of divergent Irish histories no less than it draws upon more stable English understandings of acceptable convention.

Edgeworth signifies Harry's independence of convention by recurrent references to his innate characteristics of resolution and independence. "Resolution," remarks the narrator, "is a quality or power of mind totally independent of knowledge of the world. The habit of self-control can be acquired by any individual, in any situation. Ormond had practised and strengthened it even in the retirement of the Black Islands" (171). The Black Islands are home to the folk monarchy of King Corny, the ruler of a traditional Irish Catholic clan, a holdover from a disappearing past. This community specifically evokes the notion of independence in contrast to the accommodations with bad social norms accompanying more conventional notions of success, represented by Corny's cousin and Ormond's guardian. Sir Ulick is the pattern of "old corruption," involved in the parliamentary system of bribery and placeholding, whose deepest betrayal of principle is his mercenary conversion from Catholicism to Protestantism. He is at one with the false society that he represents. Corny by contrast, despite some innocent faults, is a paragon of self-sufficiency, his own man, isolated from the corrupting and debilitated historical norms:

> The one living in the world, and mixing continually with men of all ranks and characters, had, by bending easily, and being all things to all

men, won his courtier way onwards and upwards to the possession of a seat in Parliament, and the prospect of a peerage.

The other, inhabiting a remote island, secluded from all men but those over whom he reigned, caring for no earthly consideration, and for no human opinion but his own—had for himself and by himself, hewed out his way to his own objects—and then rested satisfied—Lord of himself, and all his (*little*) world his own. (45)

Harry's independence and resolution are also fostered by an "ideal," transcribed into the text in Lady Annaly and her daughter, Florence, simultaneously the least realistic and the most central characters of the novel.[13] Lady Annaly functions as another mentor who offers the protagonist help, encouragement, and advice. Florence is the nuptial reward for Harry's success. Their initial appearance is in conjunction with the first evidence of Harry's worst tendencies, a hasty temper that descends to violence. The novel begins with Ormond's shooting of a laborer and suspected rebel, Moriarty Carroll. But the protagonist's promise shows itself almost immediately, when, after tending Moriarty's wound all night, Ormond takes him the next day to the Black Islands to complete his recovery. Lady Annaly appears to him at one of their rest stops, a schoolhouse, and reprimands and encourages him. Harry is suffused with a new feeling: "Since there exists a being, interested for me, I must be worth something—and I will make myself worth something more—I will begin from this moment, I am resolved to improve—and who knows in the end I may become everything that is good" (32). Lady Annaly's encouragement, however, consists of no more than the observation that "fate is an unmeaning commonplace . . . [By] far the greatest part of our happiness or misery in life depends upon ourselves" (31). Her exhortation has no explicit moral context, though happiness and misery have a long ethical tradition in western thought as implying good and evil respectively. The neo-stoical resonance of self-dependence, however, seems to reinforce the expectation that Harry Ormond will stand outside dependence on worldly customs.

Harry's transcendence of bad social patterns rests on his achievement of two tasks: controlling his temper and overcoming the temptation to adultery, and on these two tasks the bulk of the novel relies for its plot. *Ormond* begins, as we have seen, with the almost fatal consequences of Harry's violence. Other examples of his rashness occur throughout the book, notably the duel in defense of Sir

Ulick's political reputation mentioned already. Harry's most dangerous deviation from the path of self-control follows on his misinterpretation of the scene between Florence Annaly and his rival Colonel Albemarle when he spies on them through the window. Believing that she is accepting rather than rejecting Albemarle's hand, he rushes off to Paris to bury his woes without waiting for an explanation. His triumph over this character defect comes when he returns to Ireland and apologizes to Florence and Lady Annaly for his intemperateness.

The task of avoiding adultery is not an inner difficulty but one imposed by the conventions of the society and does not arise for the protagonist until nearly the end of the novel; by then all circumstances conspire to tempt Harry. The woman is his earliest flame, Dora, daughter of Corny of the Black Islands, who was wooed away from him by the French-Irishman, Black Connal, and taken to live in Paris. When Harry meets her again she is dissatisfied with her life as the wife of a society gambler; she still shows some fondness for her old companion, and "les usages—les convenances—les nuances—enfin la mode de Paris" are supremely conducive to their relationship (252). This mode is elucidated by Mme. de Foley, Dora's chaperone, when after pointing out a number of married women at cards with their *cavaliere sirvente*, she "explained all these arrangements with the most perfect sang-froid, as things of course, that everybody knew and spoke of, except just before the husbands" (248).

This convention is given some authority by the *Letters* of Lord Chesterfield, not coincidentally perhaps an erstwhile Lord Lieutenant of Ireland. These notorious lessons in correct behavior gave the imprimatur of the noble lord to what Samuel Johnson called "the manners of a dancing master and the morals of a whore."[14] In a tightly wrought scene, Edgeworth places the cynical Sir Ulick, the quasi-adulterous Lady Millicent, and the naive Harry together under the auspices of Lord Chesterfield's advice on fornication: "You are shocked," says Sir Ulick, "at the idea of Lord Chesterfield's advising his pupil at Paris to prefer a reputable affair with a married woman to a disreputable intrigue with an opera girl" (176). Lady Millicent blushes at this remark, not, as Sir Ulick disingenuously implies, because of her virtuousness, but because she would have had an adulterous affair in Dublin, had not her husband's death scared off the lover, "who thought Lady Millicent no longer worthy of his pursuit, when he might have her for life" (180). Edgeworth, moreover, punishes Sir Ulick for his approbation of these false norms and issues a warning to Harry on the eve of his departure to Paris, when Marcus, Sir Ulick's son, precipitates through an adulterous liaison the financial crisis that brings down his father's banking empire. When Harry, then, at the last moment prevents himself from taking Dora in his arms, it is a triumph over the social model provided by Chesterfield—"a manual of education" that holds out "the vain hope of getting cheaply second-hand knowledge of the world" (176), dangerous knowledge that Harry is better off not having.

"Patterns" is Edgeworth's term for these unsavory conventions that confront Harry with the face of dead interiority. The world through which the protagonist must make his way is a world of patterns, illusory patterns, Edgeworth implies, lacking substance. Lady O'Shane is "a strict pattern lady, severe on the times, and not infrequently lecturing young men gratis" (5). Her pattern of traditional moral values is satirized as an interfering prudishness and later revealed to be of the shallowest when Edgeworth remarks on her "frippery appearance" (9). The implications of pattern as social hypocrisy recur in some of the events in the Black Islands. Corny contravenes all the proprieties of Betty the housekeeper by offering Sir Ulick last night's leftovers instead of "when strangers come to dine . . . mak[ing] a bit of an exertion, if one could" (46). Betty goes off in some dudgeon at this breach of the proprieties, and "for an hour afterwards she reasoned against the obstinacy and folly of man, and the chorus in the kitchen moralized, in conformity and commiseration—in vain" (47). What Betty fails to understand is that Corny expects the visit to be a hostile one and prefers to express his feelings openly rather than pretend a hospitableness he does not feel. Another sense of "pattern," the opposition of form and content, is taken up through the traditional imagery of clothing to signify appearance without substance. At Castle Hermitage, Mr. Darrell values "a famous *invaluable receipt* he has for polishing those boot-tops, which is to make quite another man of him" (166). Later, in Paris, clothing imagery dominates the rules of society, transforming even accidence into essence: "It was essential to the appearance of a gentleman . . . that he should, from the moment he is dressed, *be* or at least *seem* above his dress. In this as in most cases the shortest and safest way to *seem* is to *be*" (251). Harry Ormond, of course, does not need to seem; he carries within himself the substratum of essence denied to the societies through which he moves.

The role of pattern in *Ormond* takes on a different twist when viewed as "original without originality" (168). The Annalys themselves represent a moral force outside social norms. They are as committed to independence as Harry comes to be in the course of the novel. One of Sir Ulick's young female guests designates them "flats"—people who are gulled through their own innocence of the world.[15] They are "good for nothing in society, except to be torn to pieces" (168). Yet these implicit critiques of a world that could treat so maliciously the virtuous and the good are modified somewhat by the recurrence of the word pattern among these contemptuous remarks: Lady Annaly and her daughter are "Patterns of perfection" (168). While Edgeworth works to differentiate between true and false patterns, she raises sufficient ambiguity to cast doubts on the comfortableness of the fit between social patterning and personal independence. King Corny, perhaps a more important moral guide than Harry's female mentor, views Lady Annaly as coming precariously close to the Lady O'Shane pattern of "lecturing young men gratis" (59). Angry with Harry for constricting his "passionate" nature according to Lady Annaly's dictates, Corny fulminates: "What business had she, because she's an old woman and you a young man, to set up preaching" (57). And the social butterfly, Miss Lardner, is given a striking phrase that seems to put patterns of goodness at odds with independence: "[Lady Annaly] is stiff and tiresome and original as ever was seen or was heard of—and the worst of it is she is an original without originality" (168). "Original" for the speaker carries the pejorative eighteenth-century connotation of antisocial eccentricity, though Edgeworth presumably intends the reader to apply the recent ameliorative connotations of Edward Young's *Conjectures on Original Composition*. Lady Annaly's unoriginality, however, must reside in a timeless pattern of goodness and virtue. If so, Edgeworth has given us reason to put the two themes of Harry's education in conflict. Lady Annaly and her daughter are confusing models because they warn of the dangers of patterns while at the same time being themselves patterns. Does the rigidity of convention affect even timeless patterns? Are resolution and independence stifled by even virtuous regulations? It seems that Edgeworth perceives the incomensurability of individual becoming and social norms, even good ones.

Lady Annaly's unoriginal originality, moreover, must lead us also to reflect on the character of the book. The novel itself is patterned, and since the sketchy characterization of Lady Annaly and Florence does not afford the screen of realism, their portrayal is most likely to draw our attention to the narrative functions they perform. Indeed, they are patterned on exceedingly traditional models. Lady Annaly and Florence are characters not from the world of realism, but from folklore and myth. Their narrative function is kin to similar figures in romance, that which Northrop Frye calls "the sybilline wise mother-figure, often a potential bride . . . who sits quietly at home waiting for the hero to finish his wanderings and come back to her . . . [she is] often the lady for whose sake or at whose bidding the quest is performed."[16] Their real force in this text is drawn from archaic elements. Their ambiguous inseparability makes an almost Oedipal conjunction of mother and bride. The last sentence of *Ormond* delineates this figure exactly: "Lady Annaly . . . gloried in the full accomplishment of her prophecies, and was rewarded . . . by seeing the perfect felicity which subsisted between her daughter and Ormond" (297–98). Mother and daughter are shadowy representatives of the helper function in fairy tales. So rarely does this couple appear in the novel that this function is almost all we have of them. The conflict between ideals of originality and the rigidity of pattern extend into the construction of the novel; the problem of patterns also becomes a problem of textual originality.

Harry Ormond himself is original without originality: at the level of character he is a composite of his reading; at the level of the novel's codes, he is a construct of inescapable generic devices. Edgeworth indeed has slyly acknowledged from the beginning of the book that it is impossible to struggle against generic patterns without also including them. When Harry first bursts romantically upon the scene at the ball with which the book opens, "pale as death, and stained with blood" (14), attracting Florence Annaly's attention as well as the reader's, Edgeworth poses the question: "at the moment when covered with the blood of an innocent man he stood before her, an object of disgust and horror, could any sentiment like love exist or arise in a well-principled mind?" The answer, somewhat surprisingly is, "Certainly not" (25), but the knowing reader deduces correctly from many other scenes of this nature in many other novels that Florence will marry Harry Ormond. Edgeworth's problem with genre then arises almost immediately in trying both to honor the contract of romance while suggesting that this writerly contract will be fulfilled under completely variant auspices, that of moral regulation. The initial scene of *Ormond* illustrates the paradoxes of trying to contravene literary patterns. The true significance of the scene, however, is that Edgeworth herself openly perceives the problem. Even as her moral succumbs to the irresistible force of genre, the writing itself becomes one of the subjects of the book.

The problem of patterns returns with a vengeance through the hybridity that seems to be a characteristic of almost everyone in the novel. Dora, Mme. de Foley, and Black Connal are all French-Irish, whose allegiance is more to France than to Ireland. To some degree they represent the fate of the dispossessed Catholic gentry who fled to France at the end of the Williamite wars. Sir Ulick is a hybrid of Catholic origins and Protestant conformism. White Connal is a hybrid of gentleman and entrepreneur. Harry Ormond, however, is the most succinctly hybrid. His heritage is not clear to the reader. His father was a captain in the British army, one supposes. Captain Ormond leaves his family in Ireland to go to India. Ormond's mother's heritage is not given, but we know that she is "without a fortune" (10). After her death, Ormond is rescued by Sir Ulick O'Shane at the age of four from his place "at nurse in an Irish cabin" (10). Whether or not his mother was Irish, Ormond subsequently straddles the two cultures by moving back and forth between Sir Ulick's Protestant estate and the Catholic King Corny's traditional domain on the Black Islands, and becomes Gaelicized to such an extent that he is accused of having become a Catholic. In addition, Ormond has strong links to the other great augmentation to the British empire, India. The fortune that rescues him from poverty after Corny's death comes from a reversion of his father's property in India "to his European son" on the demise of all members of the family Captain Ormond established there. Sir Ulick explains: "You know your father's second wife, the Indian woman, the governor's mahogany-coloured daughter—she had a prodigious fortune, which my poor friend, your father, chose, when dying, to settle upon her and her Indian son" (157). The Indian property is expropriated and transferred to Ireland by an authority simultaneously patriarchal and imperial. Harry, however, must bear a hereditary taint more complex than that of being the beneficiary of unjust exploitation. Rescued from an Irish cabin and heir to a "mahogany-coloured step-mother," his birth and fortune are both products of hybrid alliances. From the outset, then, Ormond is either a product of all the constituent parts of the British empire, combining disparate geographic entities as well as being the colonized as much as the colonialist, or he is profoundly deracinated, not that these are necessarily exclusive. In either case, his situation is far from that of Colambre in *The Absentee*, expounded by Mary Jean Corbett as fulfilling Burke's goal of "familial order" as a buttress against "innovation, revolution, and the hybridity they breed."[17] While no revolutionary, Ormond does not in any way represent the kind of hereditary stability provided by the settled continuance of property and aristocratic family ties for which Burke stood. Edgeworth tries a different model in *Ormond* from the model she applied in *The Absentee*. While Colambre represents the enlightened utilitarian landlord, Ormond, landless and uprooted, must find his proper self through his own exertions.

The issue of the hybrid comes closer to articulation through an allusion by Sir Ulick to Alexander Pope's character of Sporus. Sir Ulick quotes Pope almost at every turn, whether because of Pope's own standing as a Catholic among Whig lords or to give additional personality to Sir Ulick, who despite his shortcomings is one of the most likeable characters in the book. In an attractive little vignette, after Sir Ulick with great good humor settles the problem of Peggy Moriarty's trespassing cow, he reflects on the inept haughtiness of his son Marcus, just returned from England with all the prejudices against his Irish heritage never possessed by his father: "Your pride—'pride that licks the dust'" (199). The quotation from the "Epistle to Dr. Arbuthnot" evokes the most notorious satiric portrait of a hybrid in English literature up to this time. In Lord Hervey, the original of Sporus, Pope targets hybridity as such. He castigates Hervey as a "vile antithesis, an "amphibious thing" and uses contrasts—"now trips a Lady, now struts a Lord" and "a Cherub's face, a Reptile all the rest"—to illustrate and reinforce the unprincipled moral character, sexual indeterminacy, and political deviousness of his victim.[18] Pope's work stands as a precursor of Edgeworth's theme of virtuous withdrawal from courtly corruption. Sporus might, then, seem to be a straightforward thematic signal supporting the ideal of personal integrity. But like other variant moral patterns in *Ormond* the allusion to Sporus is quite confusing. It is odd that the accusation should come from the mouth of Sir Ulick, the most likely comparison to Hervey in terms of political chicanery. Pope's portrait of Sporus, furthermore, makes an association between hybridity and lack of inner self-worth. The contrasting portrait of the good man in the same epistle makes it clear that only a person who is whole, unified, and singular can have any moral integrity. This viewpoint can only create problems for the thematic coherence of *Ormond*.

Granted that the issues of hybridity in Edgeworth's novel revolve round national identity, nevertheless, national characteristics are endowed with plentiful moral associations. But it is not only the morally suspect characters such as Black Connal and Marcus O'Shane who are hybrids; as we have seen, the most hybrid of all the characters is Harry Ormond, the bearer of the banner of integrity. Nor does the conclusion of the plot offer any relief from this dilemma. Harry is no less hybrid when he returns to the Black Islands at the end of his journey than he was at the beginning. Pope himself failed to resolve the problem of moral behavior and the consistency of the self. Sporus is a "vile antithesis," but so is Man, as the famous antitheses of the opening of *An Essay on Man, Epistle II* reminds us, or, more forcefully, the lines from the "Epistle to Cobham": "That each from other differs, first confess; / Next, that he varies from himself no less."[19] The theme of the moral integrity of the hybrid in *Ormond* has just as many irreconcilable dimensions as there are confusing national attributes.

The antitheses that are certainly one of the defining features of any kind of hybridity are most marked in Harry Ormond. But Edgeworth raises collateral questions about the inner workings of antitheses by complicating the supposedly inalienable states that comprise them, in this case the integrity of national characteristics. French/Irish and English/Irish presumably combine essences to make up the secondary category, but what is French and, especially, what is English is not clear. The book hardly presents any English people typifying the best of their race. The two most prominent English characters are Lady O'Shane and her housekeeper, Miss Black—curious the association with Corny's islands, as if Edgeworth is reluctant to distinguish at the level of race. The latter after marrying Sir Ulick's steward becomes Mrs. M'Crule, an aptronym expressing her obsessive bigotry in preventing the Catholic boy, Tommy Dunshaughlin, from attending a charity school. Lady O'Shane's maiden name is Scraggs, a sign of class condescension on the part of the author that indicates the preference among the cultivated English of the time for names of French rather than of Anglo-Saxon extraction. And Edgeworth has no truck with the urban/peasant distinction between Ireland and England, slyly indicating with italics the grammatical offenses of an English serving-man: "We *bees* from England" (233).

The paradoxes of settling the values of an original race become acute during Ormond's sojourn in Paris. The Parisians he meets, despite being acquaintances of the Connals, refer to Harry as "le bel anglais," perhaps from the same ignorance of Great Britain that Barrington records when he mentions a Frenchman who believed that "Ireland was a large house where the English were wont to send their idle vagabonds, and from whence they were drawn out again as they were wanted to fill the ranks of the army."[20] Dora herself corrects this into "mon bel irlandois" (255). But we are never sure about Harry. Dora presents him to M. de Jarillac as "'Anglois—Irlandois—an English, an Irish gentleman'" (244). We can infer some characteristics of his Irishness from his "conscious[ness] of having talked away at a great rate" in response to Dora's sneer that a Parisian hostess may have "nothing better to say of an English guest than that "'Ce monsieur là a un grand talent pour le silence'" (250): and of his Englishness from the French attributing his unwillingness to have an affair to "English bizarrerie" (257). To outsiders, then, Harry's nationality seems indeterminate; his hybridity only causes confusion.

It could be said that in her creation of Harry Ormond Edgeworth is not so much confessing that he differs from himself as constructing a third type out of two national characters. This view would be more convincing were it not for two notable moments. Edgeworth separates herself from any suggestion of hybridity, despite her own background, when she steps out of the fiction and addresses a graceful tribute to the Abbé Morellet, who is both a character in the book and an acquaintance of her father's whom she met in Paris in 1802: "May he live to receive among all the other tributes . . . this record of the impression his kindness left on grateful English hearts!" (260). Her claim to an indisputable English birth, true of herself (though not of her father, also included in the English hearts), emphasizes even more completely the hybrid condition of her protagonist. More significantly, Ormond's salvation from the threat of adultery ultimately comes from the most thoroughly Irish of the communities invoked by the book, King Corny's. The Irish nature of Ormond's salvation is independent of reference to English bizarrerie quoted above, of the reference to Dora's "English prejudices" in bolting her dressing room door against Harry, and of Harry's in approving of those prejudices (252). Earlier, Chesterfield's *Letters*, whose advice on adultery was so fatally followed by Marcus O'Shane, had been repudiated with acknowledgment of "the good sense of England [which] soon cast into disrepute" the book "which . . . has since sunk, fortunately for the nation, almost into oblivion" (176); yet, despite this apparent preparation for Ormond's faithfulness to Florence to be contingent on his "English" moral fiber, when push comes to shove, it is the memory of Corny that saves him: ultimately the old Gael is more powerful a moral guide than Lady Annaly. The occasion for Harry refusing the last temptation, the entering with Dora into the conventional but morally illicit adulterous compact, is the sight of a lock of Corny's hair in Dora's ring:

> Harry found himself at her feet. But while he held and kissed in transport the beautiful hand, which was but feebly withdrawn, he seemed to be suddenly shocked by the sight of one of the rings on her finger.
> "My wedding ring," said Dora with a sigh, "Unfortunate marriage!"
> This was not the ring on which Ormond's eyes were fixed.
> "Dora, whose grey hair is this?"
> "My father's," said Dora, in a tremulous voice.
> "Your father!" cried Ormond starting up.
> "And is this return I make!—Oh, if he could see us at this instant!" (270–71).

Ormond's final moral triumph comes at the instigation of the dead father rather than of Lady Annaly, whom we might call the living mother. Harry's moral quest seems to be fulfilled through the forceful recurrence to, not to mention the uncanny return of the dead from, the site of originality and perhaps of national authenticity, the Black Islands. Harry is saved from his uncomfortable stranding between two worlds by a ghostly emanation from the uncontaminated unity of his isolated Irish realm.

In *Ormond*, then, if history is corrupt and transient, and originality is impregnated with the hybrid patterns that prevent the central character from achieving independence, the only place to turn to or return to is the utopia where the dreams of escape from history began. It comes as no surprise that the Black Islands should return as the apparent moral center of the novel. Even as a social realm they have been preemptively designated as a rebuke to the great societies that Harry visits in his telemachiad. The doomed French society of the pre-Revolutionary era stands in contrast to the organic folk community of the Black Islands. Edgeworth compares the two kingdoms through state suppers held at Versailles and at Corny's court. In France, Ormond is obliged to keep "his Irish risible muscles in order" as "he looked around and considered all these magnificently decorated personages, assembled for the purpose of standing at a certain distance to see one man eat his supper" (253). Long before his travels begin, however, while he was still a young princeling at

Corny's court, Harry had observed a far different king's supper in the Black Island: "the crowd . . . was admitted into the dining room, where they stood round the king, prince, and father Jos, as the courtiers during the king's supper at Versailles, surrounded the king of France. But these poor people were treated with more hospitality than were the courtiers of the French king; for as soon as the dishes were removed, their contents were generously distributed among the attendant multitude" (36). For Edgeworth, Marie Antoinette's good deed celebrated in Dagote's painting (259) may be singular in France but represents the permanent state of affairs at Castle Corny.[21]

The concatenation of the moral and political ideals in the Black Islands, however, ought not be mistaken for some yearning for a political solution for Ireland. The Black Islands are wholly utopian—a dream where history can be suspended. The depiction of Corny has attracted attention because of Edgeworth's apparent willingness to give some sort of Ascendancy approval to the old Gaelic families her class supplanted. Corny's island is taken for a representation of that decayed Irish aristocracy that Kevin Whelan has so remarkably brought to our notice.[22] In these views, Harry Ormond's return to the Black Islands with the Annaly governorship as a model for his future rule achieves a fantasy reconciliation between the conquered and the conquerors. While it is possible that Edgeworth casts her novel in the past as a fantasy wish that the two ruling classes had cast their lot with each other before the 1798 rebellion and that the United Irishmen had changed forever the political history of Ireland, there is strong evidence that the Black Islands exist outside of time: Corny's kingdom, as one of Sir Ulick's servants says, "was the true thing, and never changed" (290).

The changelessness is a sign that Corny is not historical; he does not belong to the sublunary realm of ceaseless transformation. Truth is not in history but in a utopia that is unchangeable because it is nonexistent. The Black Islands are a utopian fantasy; even more they are an intertextual fantasy because the history of utopia has no artifacts. The utopias of a ruling race are often fabricated out of their fantasies of the conquered. And in the century following the publication of *Ormond* more than sufficient numbers of Anglo-Irish gentry produced versions of the national myth that in Joep Leerssen's words evoked "The Irish countryside as an idyllic, timeless, traditional, community with a hint of faery uncanniness."[23] But the Black Islands, Irish though they may seem, are partly a vessel for confiding versions of utopia familiar in eighteenth-century literature. In particular, they perform another of the attacks on luxury and preference for virtuous simplicity in public life prevalent from the Restoration to the French Revolution. Not the least of the attacks on luxury is found in *Les Aventures de Télémaque*. When Télémaque tells the Cretans who want to make him king of their powerful and wealthy country, "For my part, I prefer my country, the poor, petty island of Ithaca, to the hundred cities of Crete, and all the glory and opulence of this kingdom," he has already explained how a good king fosters the value of poverty over luxury: "he will restrain luxury and effeminacy, and all those arts that serve only to foster and promote vice: but he will cherish and encourage those that are useful and necessary in life; particularly he will make his subjects apply themselves vigorously to agriculture, and thereby procure them plenty of all necessaries. The people being laborious, simple in their manners, plain and frugal in their way of living, will multiply prodigiously."[24] Corny's island fits into a vision of virtuous frugality, not the vision that would inspire the French revolutionaries but the aristocratic vision of Fénelon that sought to counteract the dangers of distance between the rulers and the people.

Ormond hints that the author knows that this island is an island of signs. Edgeworth seems to adopt a humorous attitude toward the struggle to go beyond the comforts of traditional genres and patterns through a utopian vision constructed out of a colonized people for whom her respect is at best a wavering one. Yet the utopia of the Black Islands is both outside textuality and deeply involved in it. Finally, utopia is the most inscribed of all representations. History can perhaps claim some stimulus from the real world. Utopias, especially those uncomfortable utopias that grow from a colonizer's idealized depiction of a subdued people whom she wishes to keep in a dependent condition, make for a profoundly generic model, one that imposes a pattern not to be seen in the original, because it exists only in written forms, and in this case in previously written forms, the various intertexts that go into its construction. At the end of the book, then, Edgeworth returns to the problems of escaping genre that she evokes at the beginning. The romance pattern she tried to grapple with in the first meeting of Harry and Florence is fulfilled in the utopian pattern. Strikingly, the site of the theme of originality is also the site where the conventionality of literary structure is most apparent.

In bringing to our attention these complications in the problems of writing, Edgeworth has constructed her most interesting and unusual work. The themes of *Ormond* are not the dominant element in the work; rather, they are articulated uncomfortably, without resolution. To grasp the complexities of Edgeworth's compositional process we need to follow her hyperawareness of the way that themes are patterned in representation. The dominant theme of *Ormond* is the variety of genres that structure the book. Moreover, *Ormond* closes off the back door escape that history, by stilling the unruly polysemousness of the literary artifact, often provides for problems of representation. Edgeworth questions history also as a literary artifact and undermines the naïve empiricism that historical analysis tries to foster by embedding any historical allusions in the utopian Black Islands, a utopia that dominates the first half of the book and that comes full circle at the end. *Ormond*, her last Irish novel, reverts to the complexity of the first and demonstrates that with the passage of time Maria Edgeworth only deepened her understanding of her art.

Notes

1. All references are to *Ormond*, Maria Edgeworth, ed. Claire Connolly (London: Penguin, 2000).

2. John Mowittt, *Text: The Genealogy of an Antidisciplinary Object* (Durham: Duke University Press, 1992), 107.

3. Mark Hawthorne, *Doubt and Dogma in Maria Edgeworth* (Gainesville: University of Florida Press, 1967), 25.

4. Mitzi Myers, "The Dilemmas of Gender as Double-Voiced Narrative; or Maria Edgeworth Mothers the Bildungsroman," in *The Idea of the Novel in the Eighteenth Century*, ed. Robert W. Uphaus (East Lansing: Colleagues Press, 1988), 67–96, 74.

5. Brian Hollingworth, *Maria Edgeworth's Irish Writing: Language, Politics, History* (London: St. Martin's Press, 1997), 199–200.

6. Sheldon Sacks, *Fiction and the Shape of Belief: A Study of Fielding with Glances at Swift, Johnson and Richardson* (Berkeley: University of California Press, 1964), 26.

7. L. M. Cullen, *The Emergence of Modern Ireland, 1600–1900* (New York: Holmes and Meier, 1981), 242–43.

8. Joseph Kestner, "Defamiliarization in the Romantic Regional Novel: Maria Edgeworth, Walter Scott, John Gibson Lockhart, Susan Ferrier, and John Galt," *The Wordsworth Circle* 10, no. 4 (Autumn 1979): 326–31, 328.

9. Georg Lukács, *The Theory of the Novel*, trans. Anna Bostock (Cambridge, Mass.: MIT Press, repr. 1973), 89.

10. Ibid., 78.

11. Ibid., 14.

12. Ibid., 80.

13. It is possible that Edgeworth was acquainted with a Lady Annaly. There were two Baron Annalys of Tenelick in County Longford. The first died in 1784 in Dub-

lin; his widow died in 1794. The second Baron Annaly was brother to the first, created Baron in 1789, sheriff of County Longford, and died in 1793. His widow, however, lived until 1812.

14. James Boswell, *Boswell's Life of Johnson*, ed. R. W. Chapman (Oxford: Oxford University Press, 1904), 188.

15. In the 1817 edition "*flatts.*" Grose has both "flat" and "flatt": "A bubble, gull, or silly fellow," Francis Grose, *A Classical Dictionary of the Vulgar Tongue*, ed. Eric Partridge (New York: Barnes and Noble, 1963).

16. Northrop Frye, *Anatomy of Criticism* (Princeton: Princeton University Press, 1957, repr. 1971), 195.

17. Mary Jean Corbett, "Public Affections and Familial Politics: Burke, Edgeworth, and the 'Common Naturalization' of Great Britain," *ELH* 61, no. 4 (Winter 1994): 877–99, 878.

18. For the portrait of Lord John Hervey, see Alexander Pope, "Epistle to Dr. Arbuthnot," in *Poetry and Prose of Alexander Pope*, ed. Aubrey Williams (Boston: Houghton Mifflin, 1969), 197–211, esp. lines 305–33.

19. Alexander Pope, *Epistles to Several Persons [Moral Essays]*, "Epistle I to Richard Temple, Viscount Cobham," in *Poetry*, ed. Williams, 158–66, lines 19–20.

20. Jonah Barrington, *Personal Sketches and Reminiscences of His Own Time* (Dublin: Ashfield Press, 1997), 241.

21. The artist is Jean Baptiste André Gautier Gagoty. The painting is the *La Benfaisance de la Dauphine* and, after Marie Antoinette became queen, "*de la Reine.*" It illustrates the Incident of Achères. While still Dauphiness Maria Antoinette stopped to comfort a peasant gored by a stag that the royal party had been chasing. She also gave his wife a purse of money. The painting was exhibited at the Salon du Colisée in 1776. See Vuaflart, Albert, and Henri Bourin, *Les Portraits de Marie-Antoinette: Étude d'Iconographie Critique* (Paris: André Maty, 1910), 2: 91–92.

22. See, Kevin Whelan, "An Underground Gentry," in *The Tree of Liberty: Radicalism, Catholicism, and the Construction of Irish Identity, 1760–1830* (Cork: Cork University Press, 1996).

23. Joep Leerssen, *Remembrance and Imagination: Patterns in the Historical and Literary Representation of Ireland in the Nineteenth Century* (South Bend: University of Notre Dame Press, 1997), 187.

24. "Pour moi, je préfère ma patrie, la pouvre, la petite île d'Ithaque." Fénelon, *Les Aventures de Télémaque*, ed. J. L. Goré (Paris: Éditions Garnier, 1987), 212. "Il retranche le faste, la mollesse et tous les arts qui ne servent qu'à flatter les vices; il faut fleurir les autres arts, qui sont utiles aux véritables besoins de la vie: surtout il applique ses sujects à l'agriculture. Par là, il les met l'abondance des choses necessaries. Ce peuple laborieux, simple dans ses moeurs, accoutumé à vivre de peu, gagnant facilement sa vie par la culture de ses terres, se multiplie à l'infini" (Fénelon, 209). Trans: Tobias Smollett, *The Adventures of Telemachus, the Son of Ulysses*," intro. Leslie A. Chilton, ed. O. M. Brack, Jr. (Athens: The University of Georgia Press, 1997), 63, 61.

The Keener's Cry in *Castle Rackrent*: The Death of Irish Culture?

FRANCES R. BOTKIN

WHEN MARIA EDGEWORTH SETTLED WITH HER FATHER IN IRELAND IN 1782, the year of Irish parliamentary independence, she encountered a country in the throes of change and with a relatively cosmopolitan capital. However, Edgeworth came to realize she had returned to a country fraught with social, political, and cultural conflict, which she documented in her depictions of Anglo-Irish absorption of Irish culture. Marginalized herself as a woman writing from within the ascendancy class, Edgeworth empathized (perhaps even sympathized) with the Irish element of her split national identity. Consequently, she penned novels that expressed profound concern for native Irish conditions, calling into question the ways in which her Anglo-Irish compatriots governed.

Edgeworth published *Castle Rackrent,* one of the very first regional novels written in a dialect of English, anonymously in 1800. Her slim novel underscores the tenacity of an Irish culture surviving despite a governing class that had threatened its existence for centuries. The depiction of Irish funerary customs in *Castle Rackrent* brings into sharp relief issues of cultural loss and rebirth; the funeral wail—performed specifically by Irish women—represents a lamentation for, and effort to preserve, Irish culture. This essay identifies Edgeworth with the figure of the funeral keener, suggesting that she carves out a space where alternative voices may be heard; these voices challenge the picture of Ireland represented by a male-dominated, English literary history. Edgeworth introduces Irish funerary practices, in part, as rituals through which an English outsider can read and understand the history of Ireland. At the same time, she foregrounds women's voices and Irish customs unknown to her English and Anglo-Irish audiences. Thus, ironically, it is the keener's cry that works to preserve an Irish national consciousness in the face of English efforts to reconstitute that culture.

Irish funerary customs have long been understood to embody Irish political, cultural, spiritual, and, more recently, national identity. Sympathizers and critics alike have carefully documented rituals such as keening and waking the dead, indicating their centrality to understanding Irish culture. Nineteenth-century English and Anglo-Irish literary representations of Irish funerals often emphasize the cultural significance of these practices, frequently attended by scathing censure. Edgeworth's depictions of these practices in *Castle Rackrent* and the well-documented correlation between women and Irish funerary traditions calls particular attention to her problematic status as an Anglo-Irish woman writer.

Castle Rackent anticipated the Irish national tale, a genre often associated with women writers such as Sydney Owenson (Lady Morgan), Mrs. Hamilton, and Mrs. Ferrier.[1] The first published national tale, Lady Morgan's *The Wild Irish Girl* (1806), for example, recalls elements of Edgeworth's *Castle Rackrent* and looks forward to *The Absentee* (1812). Yet Edgeworth was not, like her fervent contemporary Lady Morgan, preoccupied with "nationalism"; instead, she endeavored to address and to legitimize the cultural and national hybridity that had come to characterize those aspects of the country that she loved. As Esther Wohlgemut succinctly states, Edgeworth attempted to "reconstitute 'Anglo-Irish' less as a category than as an ongoing mediation between borders."[2]

Influenced by her father, Edgeworth came to understand Ireland's myriad problems as the responsibility of the Anglo-Irish class. Thus, her later Irish tales (*Ennui* in 1809, *The Absentee* in 1812, and *Ormond* in 1817) directly and optimistically engage the relationships between the Anglo-Irish and native Irish classes after the Union. However, Edgeworth wrote *Castle Rackrent* on the eve of the Union, and she situated it, according to her title page, "before the year 1782," the very year, significantly, that she had returned to Edgeworthstown; it therefore functions more as a requiem for the old order rather than as a celebration of the new.

In *Castle Rackrent*, Thady Quirk, the illiterate family retainer, tells the story of "his" family: the downfall of four generations of Irish landlords. Death plays a central thematic as well as symbolic role in *Castle Rackrent*. Edgeworth's regional tale concludes with the dissolution of the Rackrent lineage, accomplished by Thady's son, whose purchase of the estate represents the emergence of an Irish Catholic middle class and the subsequent need for a reformed ascendancy order that could accommodate these social shifts.

While the many deaths in *Castle Rackrent* symbolize the end of a way of life and of a family line, they also provide a link in the chain of Irish history, a history marked by usurpation, domination, assimilation, and intermarriage. In Edgeworth's novel, the existing Anglo-Irish hegemony is not only critiqued but also is transformed by Irish culture, even as (or because) it modifies Irish culture. In a discussion of Lady Morgan's *The Wild Irish Girl,* Joep Leerssen designates the national tale as a "type of clearing-house through which most pre-romantic appreciations of Ireland . . . passed from out-of-date modes of discourse into the realm of literature, where they were given a new lease of life."[3] The "death" of Ireland around the Act of Union can thus be understood as part of a historical and mythological process by which Ireland both lost and claimed identities.

In *Dying Acts: Death in Ancient Greek and Modern Irish Tragic Drama,* Fiona Macintosh explains that, to the Irish, death is a process that links the living and the dead. Further, she argues that Irish funerals and wakes are public rather than private events, suggesting that funerary customs affirm group identity, ensuring that group's survival.[4] The funeral lamentations sung by women, then, portray family (or private) deaths while celebrating the continuity of Irish national (or public) history. This process evokes the Anglo-Irish Edmund Burke's famous vision of society as an organic connection between "those who are living, those who are dead, and those who are to be born."[5]

Although Burke finds women's roles in this continuity purely reproductive, the figure of the old woman keener intimates that women also play a significant—and perhaps even subversive—role in documenting Ireland's genealogical history. Macintosh points out that the death process begins with the cry of the banshee: the female death messenger and the believed archetype of the keener. Then, after women prepare the corpse for the wake, female mourners and relatives (usually led by keeners) sing personal songs accompanied by a repertoire of highly ritualized gestures. The semi-professional keeners engage in murmuring, singing, swaying, rubbing their eyes, and beating the ground. Macintosh describes beating the ground as a gesture that establishes connections between the living and the dead as well as between the women and the earth; uniting the women in their grief, this gesture also universalizes their complaints.[6]

Castle Rackrent introduces the figure of the keener as a curiosity, a relic of the past who nonetheless keeps the past alive. These old Irish women may be seen as rebellious figures who uphold ancient Celtic traditions in an Anglo-Irish culture that tries to suppress them. By disseminating Irish culture through song, they threaten to undermine Anglo-Irish authority by reminding the Anglo-Irish of the cultural foundations upon which their own power has been constructed. For this reason, *Castle Rackrent* mediates the keener's songs with an editorial voice that distances them from their English readers. The relationship between the keener and the editor—like the relationship between Thady and the editor—parallels the engagement and mediation of Celtic traditions required by Anglo-Irish aspirations at the turn of the nineteenth century.

Edgeworth's text reveals the difficulties that Irish natives encounter in telling their own stories to an ignorant audience. In addition to Thady's Irish narrative and the footnotes that attend it, *Castle Rackrent* includes a preface, a postscript, and substantial glossary notes, all in the voice of a male, English editor. Edgeworth added the glossary in 1800 after the text proper (Thady's narrative, footnotes, and the preface) had already gone to press, and with it she included an apologetic advertisement. This advertisement explains that "friends" had suggested to the editor that Thady's history would not be "intelligible" to English readers without further explanation. Yet, the editorial paratext does not always complement but, rather, competes with the narrative, thereby complicating issues of authority and prioritization. The plethora of voices contributes to a cacophony of ideologies resonating within the text that represent their author's own sense of her Anglo-Irishness.[7] The complex editorial commentary on the vociferous *whillaluh* (funeral lamentation) demonstrates particularly well how a primarily oral Gaelic culture is at once reanimated and distorted by the texts that represent it.

Edgeworth employs two long glossary notes and a footnote on funerary procedures. The first glossary note consists of three full pages of information on the *whillaluh*, deriving its material from a wide variety of sources. In addition to a fair amount of editorial commentary, it includes quotations in Latin from Virgil and from Ovid, a thorough history of the Caoinan, and several passages transcribed from the fourth edition of *Transactions of the Royal Irish Academy*. Generously quoting from *Transactions*, the editor painstakingly distinguishes between the lamentation over the dead (the Gol or Ullaloo) and the participatory funeral song (Caoinan) with its first semichorus, second semichorus, and full chorus of groans, sighs, words, and music. The editorial commentary also delineates the complex nature of funerary customs, including variations in region and in tone, based on the keener's conflation of template and extempore art.[8] In addition, the editor systematically relates English criticisms of these practices. True to Edgeworth's detail-oriented practice, the editor offers a sociologically accurate account which, Marilyn Butler claims, determines Edgeworth as the "founder" of the national tale in her depictions of "a modern society with all its parts functioning in their real-life relation to one another."[9]

Castle Rackrent's description of these customs closely resembles other written accounts of nineteenth-century oral culture. For example, folklorist Thomas Crofton Croker similarly documents the history and censure of the Irish howl.[10] Neil Hultin employs Croker's research to delineate different modes of keening such as memorization and composition, emphasizing Croker's distinction between "the keener's carefully wrought nature in contrast with the spontaneous shriek, which constituted the chorus."[11] Moreover, Hultin stresses Croker's awareness that English critics charged the keeners with hypocrisy and transgression, and that women in particular comprised the "guilty" party. Hultin suggests that Croker intended to make his English readers aware of the keen, "not merely as an expression of grief created by 'folk artists' of considerable talent . . . but also to show that . . . the keen is a powerful political weapon to preserve the oral history of a culture which has survived despite centuries long oppression."[12] Hultin's analysis of Croker's study reveals, like Edgeworth's *Castle Rackrent*, the highly controversial and complex nature of the keen, while also demonstrating its centrality to an understanding of Irish culture and politics.

Significantly, *Castle Rackrent*'s editor appears both critical and admiring of funeral rites: the lower Irish are "wonderfully eager" to attend funerals and a crowded funeral attests to one's popularity in life, yet the description of "profligacy and drunkenness" simultaneously undermines the sympathetic tenor of comments in the very same glossary note (102). Similarly, the funerals in *Castle Rackrent* allow critics to question Thady's intentions and loyalties, pointing to the ambiguity of his textual positioning.[13] For Thady, the Rackrent funerals measure the worth of the men who are mourned, but his darkly humorous commentary, like the editor's more serious one, calls such sympathy into question.

"Loyal" Thady unintentionally introduces the deaths themselves as symptoms of social and moral mayhem as he lovingly recounts the story of his beloved masters. Sir Patrick drinks himself to death after a toast to his health; Sir Murtagh bursts a blood vessel arguing with his wife; the dueling Sir Kit receives a "ball in a vital part" (33) and is "brought home speechless on a hand-barrow" (34), and, coming full circle, Sir Condy drinks himself into a lethal fit. Thady ignores the irony surrounding these deaths; instead, he focuses on the festivities that celebrate (or do not celebrate) them.

Thady's story begins with Sir Patrick's inheritance of the Rackrent estate on the death of a cousin-german, Sir Tallyhoo Rackrent. He explains that by an act of parliament Sir Patrick's inheritance was contingent upon bearing the Rackrent surname and arms (and presumably their religion as well). Thady carefully points out that the original O'Shaughlins (now Rackrents) were related to the kings of Ireland, and his inclusion of this information suggests the longevity and honor of the family history, reminding contemporary readers of the intertwining of Celtic and English traditions, an intertwining whose final shape had still to be determined. The symbolic "death" of the O'Shaughlins impels the birth of the Rackrent line. Occasionally (in the 1800 edition) Thady refers to Castle Rackrent as Castle Stopgap, further suggesting gaps or ruptures in the family lineage. Despite Sir Patrick's seemingly traitorous capitulation, people adored him for his parties, dances, and generosity, and a memorial erected in his honor reads, "Sir Patrick lived and died a monument of Old Irish hospitality" (84).

Since a well-attended wake signifies a well-loved individual, Thady's preoccupation with the Rackrent funerals is not surprising. The wake serves the important purpose of keeping the deceased incorporated within the community. Ilana Harlow explains that the wake marks a "liminal moment" in the community: "In the period between death and burial, a person being waked is physically still part of the community and is present at the social gathering, yet is unable to participate . . . Wake activities are a creative response to death and its disruption of social life."[14] Thady's narrative also links his own generation to Sir Patrick's, keeping the family alive despite the original disruption of Sir Patrick's death.

Thady proudly narrates his grandfather's description of Sir Patrick's successful funeral: "to see all the women even in their red cloaks, you would have taken them for the army drawn out.—Then such a fine whillaluh! you might have heard it to the farthest end of the country" (11). Thady's reiteration of his grandfather's story suggests the extent to which the Irish funeral constitutes an important part of Irish culture, conflating personal and national histories.

Thady, however, also relates how the creditors interrupted the festivities by seizing the body for debt and that the new heir, Sir Murtagh, expressed himself obliged to let the law to take its course (even as it is rumored that Sir Murtagh had planned the seizure to avoid paying his debts). Irish funerary customs depended upon the proper disposal of the body: some Irish believed that those not buried and waked honorably would return to haunt those left behind.[15] By allowing the creditors to seize the body, Sir Murtagh allows dishonor to taint the family name, foreshadowing his own pathetic demise, and perhaps hinting at an Anglo-Irish inability either to bury the old "Celtic" Ireland or to incorporate it, ending, instead, haunted by a body politic neither buried nor waked honorably.

Thady's rendering of Sir Murtagh's death suggests that one who ignores Irish culture will die a lonely death. The irreverent Sir Murtagh, for example, thoughtlessly runs over a fairy mount despite Irish beliefs that such destruction merely borrows trouble. Moreover, Sir Murtagh disregards the wail of the banshee, even though Thady recognizes the banshee as the very spirit who foretold Sir Patrick's death.[16] In addition, unlike the Rackrents before and after him, Sir Murtagh does not host fabulous parties, sharing his wealth and liquor. Sir Murtagh's disrespect for both familial and cultural traditions (moreso, in Thady's view, than his litigiousness or stinginess) results in a pitiful death, and Thady makes no mention of any funerary festivities.

In contrast, Sir Kit—though a negligent landlord, brutal husband, and careless womanizer—inspires, in Thady's verion of events, the adoration of his tenants. Once he finally returns from Dublin and locks up his Jewish wife, Sir Kit gallantly resumes the Rackrent tradition of hosting balls and dinners, restoring Castle Rackrent to its previous glory. Thus, when Sir Kit dies his loss is greatly bemoaned. Thady recounts, "there was a song made upon my master's untimely death in the newspapers, which was in every body's mouth, singing up and down through the country, even down to the mountains, only three days after his unhappy exit" (34–35). This song, a rendition of a keen, underscores the continuing role of song in memorializing the passing of popular Irish role models.

Thady's accounts of Sir Patrick's, Sir Murtagh's, and Sir Kit's deaths constitute a relatively small component of the novel. He devotes the most time and space to Sir Condy, the very last Rackrent. Although reportedly well loved, Sir Condy dies a solitary death after losing the estate, and Thady alone laments the passing of the man and the family line. Yet, Sir Condy's death and funeral unfold in a much more symbolically loaded manner than those of his predecessors. Condy feigns his own death so that he can hear what his friends and family have to say about his passing.[17] His wake, however, proves anticlimactic: Thady recounts that "to my mind Sir Condy was rather upon the sad order in the midst of it all, not finding there had been such a great talk about himself after his death as he had always expected to hear" (83). In fact, Sir Condy and Thady find that the throngs of people attending the wake had come to drink and smoke rather than to mourn the dead. But Sir Condy's next and real death proves worse still. Depressed because he has lost his estate to Jason, Condy essentially drinks himself to death and nobody attends the wake. Thady harbors no illusions here:

> —"I'm in burning pain all within side of me, Thady,"— . . . and he gave a terrible screech with the torture he was in— . . . "brought to this by drink (says he)—where are all the friends?—where's Judy?—Gone, hey?—Aye, Sir Condy has been a fool all his days"—said he, and there was the last word he spoke, and died. He had but a very poor funeral, after all. (95–96)

Thady's narrative ends shortly after this episode. Condy's downfall and wake puncture his death to such an extent that even loquacious Thady has very little to add.

A strange and uncustomary keener, Thady details and laments Rackrent family history in a lively, uncritical manner. Drawing from his grandfather's repertoire, Thady employs Quirk family gossip to reconstruct the Rackrent genealogy at the domestic level; alternately, the paratextual matter provides at the public level a more scholarly reconstruction of Thady's narrative.[18] The preface reads:

> Several years ago [Thady] related to the editor the history of the Rackrent family, and it was with some difficulty that he was persuaded to have it committed to writing; however, his feelings for "*the honor of the family*," as he expressed himself, prevailed over his habitual laziness, and he at length completed the narrative which is now laid before the public. (4)

Here, the editor reveals a cultural bias toward "lazy" Thady, echoing common English perceptions of the native Irish. But if Thady reluctantly permits the editor to commit his story to print, the editor similarly "permits" Thady to complete his narrative. Despite the editor's apparent patronizing, Thady's Irish voice prevails.

Edgeworth places the keener at the center of this paratextual matter, where the old woman's song endures the scrutiny of an educated, male, English editor. Despite his initial objectivity, the editor's increasingly critical analysis of keening reflects English concerns about the perpetuation of Irish culture, especially through rowdy and mysterious rituals perceived as threats to English authority. Kirkpatrick suggests that the glossary notes to the earlier part of the text more overtly support Thady's narrative voice, but the voice of the later notes disassociates itself from the Irishness it describes.[19] The note on the willaluh, for example, appears earlier in the text, and it offers a more objective—though ambivalent—commentary. The glossary note and the footnote on the wake, however, come much later, and here the editor's tone is more critical.

The footnote on the wake reads: "A wake in England is a meeting avowedly for merriment—in Ireland, it is a nocturnal meeting avowedly for the purpose of watching and bewailing the dead; but in reality, for gossiping and debauchery" (81). Primarily women and lazy peasants, the editor suggests, generate this kind of behavior. Mistaking current practice for an older, more noble tradition poses a threat to a social and moral order that had absorbed what it considered appropriate traditions while rejecting other practices. Criticizing the practice on the grounds of cultural degeneration, the editor reduces the keeners to an almost prelinguistic status, highlighting their supposed brutishness:

> It is curious to observe how customs and ceremonies degenerate. The present Irish cry or howl cannot boast of much melody, nor is the funeral procession conducted with much dignity . . . [The mourners] begin to cry . . . raising their notes from the first Oh! to the last Agh! in a kind of a mournful howl. (101)

Moreover, the editor describes how the custom has lost its status and charm, becoming a mercenary and insincere practice:

> Those who value customs in proportion to their antiquity, and nations in proportion to their adherence to antient customs, will doubtless admire the Irish *Ullaloo*, and the Irish nation, for persevering in this usage from time immemorial. The Editor, however, has observed some alarming symptoms, which seem to prognosticate the declining taste for the Ullaloo in Ireland. In a comic theatrical entertainment represented not long since on the Dublin stage, a chorus of old women was introduced, who set up the Irish howl . . . After the old women have continued their

Ullaloo for a decent time, with all the necessary accompaniments of wringing their hands, wiping or rubbing their eyes ... one of the mourners suddenly suspends her lamentable cries, and turning to her neighbour, asks—"Arrah now, honey, who is it we're crying for?" (102–3)

The editor thus targets those who have taken advantage of the custom more than the custom itself, and he also condemns those who sentimentally hang on to old traditions that have lost their validity. This impatience parallels his introductory remarks to *Castle Rackrent* where he suggests that in an ideal world individuals would accept the new habits of their nation and discard attachment to their old identity.[20]

Most importantly, the editor criticizes the particular contributions of women to both the decline and the perpetuation of the keen, stating, "We are told that formerly . . . (the metrical feet) of the Caoinan were much attended to, but on the decline of the Irish bards these feet were gradually neglected, the Caoinan fell into a sort of slip-shod metre amongst women" (101). Although the transmission of Irish culture through the "slip-shod metre" of women appears to have diminished its legitimacy, the so-called "decline" of the bards in fact opened up a space for women to contribute to the making of Irish history.[21] The association of both women and peasants with the funeral song contributes to the sense that those with the least cultural authority are also those who uphold Irish culture. The important task of cultural continuity falls to the old women who keen.

The keener's song documents the history of Ireland through the lives of individual persons and families. Edgeworth's editor reports that the funeral song and chorus detail the genealogical and personal history of the deceased:

The genealogy, rank, possessions, the virtues and vices of the dead were rehearsed, and a number of interrogations were addressed to the deceased: as, Why did he die? If married, whether his wife was faithful to him, his sons dutiful, or good hunters or warriors? If a woman, whether her daughters were fair or chaste? (100–01)

In keeping Irish tradition and history alive, the keeners also undermine forces that seek to repress them. The oral transmission of Irish history challenges the (textual) history of Ireland that the Anglo-Irish claim as their own. Moreover, the festivities of the wake, including drinking, singing, and dancing, additionally preserve older traditions that threaten to unleash chaos and depravity.

A footnote and a later glossary note to Sir Condy's wake (following his feigned death) demonstrate how the wake comes to represent a breakdown in, or complete absence of, any kind of social, linguistic, or moral order. The page-long glossary note explains that the "wake is a midnight meeting, held professedly for the indulgence of holy sorrow, but usually it is converted into orgies of unholy joy" (113). Once the adults fall asleep, the "lads and lasses romp with one another," and "[i]t is said that more matches are made at wakes than at weddings" (114). These unhallowed sex orgies may thus result in the continuation of the Irish race and religion, undercutting the ruling class's desire to replace what it considers a questionable and depraved genealogy with its own, more cultured one.

In another glossary note the editor discusses the custom of a "raking pot of tea" which may be compared to the custom of the wake. The raking pot of tea, the editor explains, holds mysteries "sacred to females," although these "orgies" have also included men. After a festive event, such as Sir Condy's election to parliament or a ball, a "few chosen female spirits" call upon a favorite maid to make a pot of tea, and they settle around the tea table for "gossip, raillery, and sexual confidences" (112). The editor emphasizes that the custom originated with washerwomen and laundry maids, suggesting that these lower-class women have negatively influenced their upper-class sisters. It is precisely this creeping spread of maimed remnants of traditional Irish culture into the homes of the new ruling class that threatens the stability of Anglo-Irish culture and society.

Edgeworth's depictions of keeners, banshees, and washerwomen come to embody aspects of Irish culture that persist despite their perceived threat to Anglo-Irish domination. Their rituals and their songs demonstrate the limitations of Anglo-Irish written, legal, or moral codes that may censure but fail to suppress articulations of grief or joy. The editorial authority about Irish customs implies a need to circumscribe, control, or translate elements that appear threatening. However, at the same time the glossary notes also may be seen as legitimizing the customs they describe and as censuring Anglo-Irish attitudes toward them. Against the lively descriptions of festive parties, the editor's authoritative antiquarianism appears dry—a literal interruption of the patient reader's good time.

The editor—whose attitude toward the Irish shifts even within glossary notes—proves equally critical of his "*lazy*," presumably English, readers who "would rather read a page than walk a yard" to learn about Ireland (100). Although Irish customs such as the funeral and wake may have "degenerated" from their previous status, discerning readers might recognize that English attitudes set the stage for this decline: the English drove out the bards, leaving the tradition to keeners and priests. That the funerary customs remained attests to their strength rather than to their weakness. Edgeworth's novel documents the apparent decline of Irish culture for "ignorant" (and lazy) English readers who should—but do not—recognize their own role in the demise of their sister country. The Rackrentses' faults are the faults of an English-inflected system that brought the landlords to dissipation. Rackrenting, absenteeism, and a system of credit leads the Rackrents to their ultimate habits and follies. More important still, the problematic Anglo-Irish (mis)rule stems from England's colonization of Ireland over hundreds of years.

The relationship between the English editor and the Irish calls attention to the problematic position of the Anglo-Irish in Ireland; as an Anglo-Irish author writing an Irish text for English readers, Edgeworth's uncomfortable authorial position embodies the conflict her novel evokes. The Anglo-Irish class endured its own struggle for identity: after all, they were neither English nor Irish. The Act of Union of 1800 further complicated these issues by politically uniting a country torn apart by internal conflicts with a country which was itself a union of competing national identities. Though many Anglo-Irish opposed the Union, many others assumed that aligning themselves politically with the Protestant British parliament would enable them to maintain control over the native Irish Catholics. Over the course of the nineteenth century, the Anglo-Irish in fact lost power; the Union enforced a form of direct rule by the British government over the Irish and Anglo-Irish alike. Displaced from power in Ireland, the Anglo-Irish, as Julian Moynahan notes, "far from becoming fully British became unfortunately Irish, in the old brooding unhappy sense of the term."[22] The Anglo-Irish, as Edgeworth's *Absentee* underscores, were equally out of place in England and Ireland; they were "at home" nowhere.

Edgeworth's own family chronicles, *The Black Book of Edgeworthstown*, document the Edgeworth family saga in Ireland, beginning in 1595, and some of her ancestors even serve as models for the Rackrents.[23] Edgeworth's father, Richard Lovell Edgeworth, devoted his life to social and political reform, focusing especially on estate management and education. His commitment to the native Irish and to Catholic emancipation earned him enemies among other Anglo-Irish, but as a member of the ascendancy class he was equally suspect in the eyes of Irish nationalists. The bitter debate over the Act of Union reinforced these divisions, aggravating national, cultural, and religious ruptures between the nations. Richard Lovell Edgeworth confused issues still more by voting against the Union for political reasons even though he supported it on economic grounds.[24]

The Edgeworths' experience as members of the Anglo-Irish gentry, especially in the pre-Union decade, cannot be separated from the composition of *Castle Rackrent*. According to Butler, Maria Edgeworth wrote Sir Patrick's, Sir Kit's, and Sir Murtagh's narratives in the tranquil period of 1794–95, but Sir Condy's would have been composed in 1796–98, during local unrest that caused the Edgeworths to flee their home. Thus, in the midst of political chaos and on the eve of the much-debated Union, Maria Edgeworth's friends and family recommended a glossary to temper the potentially radical narrative.[25] The glossary, however, cannot mask the political and cultural tensions to which the story alludes. In fact, the glossary calls particular attention to these very tensions.

Edgeworth's belated addition of the glossary to the first text she had written without her father's supervision calls its role further into question. Whatever her personal, political, and authorial reasons for their inclusion, the glossary notes were literally an afterthought and perhaps one not entirely to her liking. Kathryn Kirkpatrick, for example, believes that Edgeworth never fully agreed to the revisions the glossary made to her work.[26] Interestingly, Richard Lovell Edgeworth supposedly wrote the glossary note to the wake (a particularly condescending note), adding yet another textual layer to the novel. However, this note, like the entire glossary, constitutes a subordinate voice in a predominantly Irish story.[27] The notes on the wake and the funeral do very little to contain the hilarity and grief related in *Castle Rackrent*, much as the English and Anglo-Irish themselves never succeeded in thwarting Irish funerary customs.

Edgeworth's representations of funeral procedures, however, do not necessarily suggest her unmitigated approval of them.[28] Indeed, she harbored suspicions about the unruly nature of Irish wakes and funerals, as she did about all undisciplined, chaotic activities. Elizabeth Kowaleski-Wallace suggests that Edgeworth was simultaneously attracted to and repulsed by the Irish poor, asserting that she was fascinated by the "grotesque Irish body that she found displayed in the undisciplined practices... of the indigenous population."[29] Certainly Edgeworth perceived certain elements of Irish customs as potentially dangerous to the Anglo-Irish hegemony, and she saw herself as one who could help direct their improvement. However, despite Edgeworth's possible uneasiness with the Irish lower classes, *Castle Rackrent* may also be viewed as a means of facilitating rather than objectifying or disciplining the Irishness it represents. *Castle Rackrent,* like Edgeworth's later novels, demonstrates an ongoing concern for the Irish poor as well as a censure of Anglo-Irish neglect, attesting to her belief that Irish and Anglo-Irish alike owe it to themselves and to each other to regulate their behavior.

Edgeworth's status as a woman writer, like her Anglo-Irishness, advances these uncomfortable contradictions. Kirkpatrick asserts that Edgworth shares Thady's status of limited power and claims that "the Anglo-European woman and the native Other share a significant legal, social, and economic invisibility during this period."[30] Nonetheless, Edgeworth's female voice controls the Irish-identified text. Edgeworth—as a woman author—is more akin to the keener than to Thady. The keener's marginal positioning in the text of *Castle Rackrent* does not detract from her symbolic importance; she represents a history of Ireland that cannot be diluted by the editor's notes nor by Thady's "loyalty." Despite the presence of a male narrator and editor, a particularly feminine element thus marks *Castle Rackrent.*[31] The keener's song subversively resuscitates Irish culture despite the (male) forces that have suffocated it for centuries; *Castle Rackrent* particularly emphasizes this figure that must lurk in the margins of the text. Butler has observed that Edgeworth generally favors male narrators and male heroes, but she remarks that Edgeworth's Irishwomen deserve particular attention because "their symbolic roles have to do directly or implicitly with national consciousness."[32] The keener, though not the kind of Irishwoman Butler has in mind, clearly occupies this very symbolic space.

In *Castle Rackrent,* the notable absence of a keener for Sir Condy reminds us that some deaths should not be mourned, or at least not be celebrated. The fissure separating Sir Condy from Jason and the conclusion to *Castle Rackrent*—foreshadowing the Act of Union—illustrates the difficulties surrounding Ireland's death and rebirth process. Edgeworth's later Irish novels pick up where *Castle Rackent* leaves off, and they address Ireland's problems after the Act of Union. Although she opted in later novels to exclude Irish dialect as a central narrative mode, Edgeworth still incorporated overt emblems of Irish culture, such as the wake and funerary procedures, suggesting the consistency of their significance.[33] The keener, too, recurs in these novels, singing a mournful tune for a lost Ireland while also connecting a heroic past to a hopeful future when Irish identity will have successfully incorporated the various aspects of its history in a single, vital, historically rooted culture.

Notes

1. For background on the intersection of gender and genre in the national tale, see Marilyn Butler, Introduction. *Castle Rackrent and Ennui* (London: Penguin, 1992), 50–54; Ina Ferris, *The Achievement of Literary Authority: Gender, History, and the Waverley Novels* (Ithaca: Cornell University Press, 1991); and Katie Trumpener, *Bardic Nationalism: The Romantic Novel and the British Empire* (Princeton: Princeton University Press, 1997).

2. Esther Wohlgemut, "Maria Edgeworth and the Question of National Identity," *SEL: Studies in English Literature* 39, no. 4 (Autumn 1999): 645–58.

3. Joep Leersen, *Remembrance and Imagination: Patterns in the Historical and Literary Representation of Ireland in the Nineteenth Century* (South Bend: University of Notre Dame Press, 1997), 65.

4. Fiona Macintosh, *Dying Acts: Death in Ancient Greek and Modern Tragic Drama* (Cork: Cork University Press, 1994), 30.

5. Edmund Burke, *Reflections on the Revolution in France* ed. L. G. Mitchell (Oxford: Oxford University Press, 1999), 195. See Esther Wohlgemut's "Maria Edgeworth and the Question of National Identity" for a thorough discussion of Edgeworth's intersection with and departure from Burke's idea of an organic, inherited nation. Wohlgemut identifies an anti-Burkean figure of "international crossover" in Edgeworth's writing, arguing that education links her rewriting of Burke with cosmopolitanism (647).

6. Macintosh, *Dying Acts*, 30.

7. Critics have extensively discussed the heteroglossic nature of *Castle Rackrent*, especially the dialogic within the paratextual matter and between the paratext (the editor) and text proper (Thady). Subsequently, both Thady's and the editor's positionality may not be easily determined. Most critics agree that the complex narrative structure of *Castle Rackrent* underscores the ambiguity of Edgeworth's authorial intention, calling for a wide range of possible textual interpretations. Many conversations are available on this topic, among them are: Frances Botkin, "Edgeworth and Wordsworth: Plain Unvarnished Tales," in *Ireland in the Nineteenth Century: Regional Identity*, ed. Leon Litvack and Glenn Hooper (Dublin: Four Courts Press, 1999); Marilyn Butler, introduction to *Castle Rackrent* and *Ennui*; Kathryn Kirkpatrick, "Putting Down the Rebellion: Notes and Glosses on *Castle Rackrent*," *Eire-Ireland* 30, no. 1 (Spring 1995): 77–90. Also, see below, note 14.

8. Maria Edgeworth, *Castle Rackrent*, ed. George Watson (Oxford: Oxford University Press, 1984), 99–103. Further references to this text are cited parenthetically.

9. Marilyn Butler, *Maria Edgeworth: A Literary Biography* (Oxford: Clarendon Press, 1972), 394.

10. Neil C. Hultin, "Mrs. Harrington, Mrs. Leary, Mr. Croker, and the 'Irish Howl,'" *Eire-Ireland* 20, no. 4 (Winter 1985): 43–64. Hultin analyzes Croker's *The Keen of South Ireland as Illustrative of Irish Political and Domestic History, Manners, Music, and Superstitions* (London, 1844) as well as Croker's earlier writings on Irish cultural history and folklore. Interestingly, the Irish-born Croker worked as a civil servant for the Anglo-Irish ascendancy, and his arguably split loyalties place him in a similar position as Edgeworth's. Hultin argues that although Croker's editorial role and conservative political stance rendered him suspect in Irish nationalist eyes, he sincerely believed in defending the Irish against English injustices (61–62). Hultin writes that Croker's study of the keen was "intended to educate an English audience, to make them aware of the culture which was Irish, with the hope that understanding would produce a change" (62). In this sense particularly, Croker's account parallels Edgeworth's.

11. Hultin, "Mrs. Harrington," 48.

12. Ibid., 64.

13. Critics have long debated whether Thady innocently describes a beloved family or whether he knows how negatively he portrays them while secretly supporting his own son's usurpation of the estate. For Thady's textual positioning, see James Newcomer, "The Disingenuous Thady Quirk," and Elizabeth Harden, "Transparent Thady Quirk," both in *Family Chronicles: Maria Edgeworth's Castle Rackrent*, ed. Cóilín Owens (Dublin: Wolfhound, 1987), 79–96. See also Elizabeth Kowaleski-Wallace, *Their Father's Daughters: Hannah More, Maria Edgeworth, and Patriarchal Complicity* (Oxford: Oxford University Press, 1991), 138–72, and Kirkpatrick's "Putting Down the Rebellion."

14. Ilana Harlow, "Creating Situations: Practical Jokes and the Revival of the Dead in Irish Tradition," *Journal of American Folklore* 110, no. 436 (spring 1997): 140–68.

15. Ibid., 152.

16. A footnote to this passage informs the reader that every "great" family possesses a banshee but laments the discontinuation of such visits in recent years. Edgeworth, *Castle Rackrent*, 17.

17. Dáithí Ó hÓgáin parallels Condy's prank to a popular legend of a man who pretended to be dead to see if his wife was faithful, a legend retold in John Synge's *The Shadow of the Glen*. See "'Said an Elderly Man . . .': Maria Edgeworth's use of Folklore" in Owens, *Family Chronicles*, 68. Harlow discusses similar joke-stories and pranks associated with wakes, such as pretending to animate the corpse ("Creating Situations," 152).

18. Edgeworth constructed the character of Thady from Edgeworth family "gossip." She transcribed Thady's dialect from the speech of the Edgeworth family retainer, John Langan. In addition, the Edgeworth family documented their family history in a document called *The Black Book of Edgeworthstown*. This text, too, comes as much from family gossip as from written documents; ultimately, the Edgeworth family genealogy is constructed in a manner similar to that of *Castle Rackrent*. See Butler, *Literary Biography*, 240–42.

19. Kirkpatrick, "Putting Down the Rebellion," 78.

20. The preface to *Castle Rackrent* concludes: "There is a time when individuals

can bear to be rallied for their past follies and absurdities, after they have acquired new habits and a new consciousness. Nations as well as individuals gradually lose attachment to their identity, and the present generation is amused rather than offended by the ridicule that is thrown upon their ancestors" (5).

21. This trajectory follows the path of the novel, a form that had belonged to men (i.e., Samuel Richardson and Henry Fielding). Once the novel "declined," women writers took over, and for a period (in the 1790s especially) the genre endured a lapse in status. Ultimately, Sir Walter Scott transformed the female-authored national tale into the masculine historical novel. For a thorough discussion on this topic see Ferris, *Literary Authority*.

22. Julian Moynahan, *Anglo-Irish: The Literary Imagination in a Hyphenated Culture* (Princeton: Princeton University Press, 1995), 9.

23. See Butler, *Literary Biography*, 13–16, for the Edgeworth family history.

24. Ibid., 182.

25. See Butler, Introduction, 5; and Kirkpatrick, "Putting Down the Rebellion," 78.

26. Kirkpatrick, "Putting Down the Rebellion," 87.

27. Conversely, Kowaleski-Wallace suggests that the editor's commentary on the funeral practice works as a strategy of containment, providing a means for exposing Thady's limitations as a narrator. See Kowaleski-Wallace, *Their Father's Daughters*, 159.

28. In 1810, Edgeworth wrote the preface and notes for *Cottage Dialogues Among the Irish Peasantry* by Mrs. Leadbeater, a protégée of an Edgeworth family friend. One of the footnotes to *Cottage Dialogues*, recalling the notes to *Castle Rackrent*, explains how the custom of the wake has declined, becoming "parties of pleasure for the living instead of mournings for the dead." But her note also marks improvement in the manners and customs of wake-goers: "[W]e are happy to state of late years it has become disreputable, in some counties of Ireland, for young women to attend wakes by night . . . This is a great improvement." Mary Leadbeater, *Cottage Dialogues Among the Irish Peasantry*, ed. Maria Edgeworth (London, 1811), 30.

29. Kowaleski-Wallace, *Their Father's Daughters*, 159. Kowaleski-Wallace suggests that Edgeworth uses the Irish peasant as a symbolic body onto which she displaced her own bodily anxiety while she helped to promote her father's "New-Style Patriarchy." See Kowaleski-Wallace, 159–67.

30. Kirkpatrick, "Putting Down the Rebellion," 80.

31. Many feminist critics have evoked the story of Sir Kit's Jewish wife locked in the attic. For a seminal discussion of the this topic, see Sandra Gilbert and Susan Gubar's *The Madwoman in the Attic: The Woman Writer and the Nineteenth-Century Literary Imagination* (New Haven: Yale University Press, 1979). See also Kowaleski-Wallace, *Their Father's Daughters*.

32. Butler, Introduction, 50.

33. In *Ennui*, for example, Lord Glenthorn's old Irish nurse, Ellinor, represents the figure of the keener, singing him homey tales of his ancient Irish family, the O'Shaunessys. Her funeral is well attended, and while mildly disgusted by the wake procedures (he perceives the numbers who "habitually" attend funerals as indicative of insincerity), Glenthorn respects the memory of his nursemaid and loyally pays his respects. Similarly, *Ormond* relates the death rituals of the eponymous hero's guardians, King Corny and Lord Ulick O'Shane. The popular King Corny

(who staunchly upheld old Irish traditions on the Black Islands) receives a grand funeral, crowded with mourners and keeners; like Lord Glenthorn, Ormond finds the wake festivities offensive, but he appreciates the gesture for his dear friend. Conversely, Lord Ulick, a politicking and greedy friend to the ascendancy culture, dies almost unmourned, his corpse hunted by creditors and with mobs of people cursing his name. Ormond's and Lord Glenthorn's response to the funerary procedures echoes the editor's voice in *Castle Rackrent*, and they reflect English attitudes toward Irish customs. However, all three suggest that one's value in the world may be gauged by one's funeral and wake.

Part II
Representing Ireland: Fiction, Realism, and Authority

Part II

"Le vrai n'est pas toujours vraisemblable": The Evaluation of Realism in Edgeworth's Irish Tales

Jacqueline Belanger

> The traits of Irish character with which Miss E. presents us are not only interesting, but are in themselves often highly humourous, and *may be trusted for their truth and accuracy.*
> —Review of *Tales of Fashionable Life*, 1810[1]

THE EVALUATION OF THE "ACCURACY" AND PLAUSIBILITY OF MARIA EDGE-worth's representations of Ireland was one of the primary areas of interest for Edgeworth's early nineteenth-century British reviewers. The all-pervasiveness of British reviewers' concern with Edgeworth's realistic representations of Ireland is signaled by a continual return to this subject in reviews of her work—even in reviews of novels such as *Patronage*, where the inauthenticity of Edgeworth's portrayals of English life are compared unfavorably with what are considered to be her more accurate depictions of Ireland. Edgeworth's relationship with her contemporary British critics, however, is not a case of mere reception, one in which reviewers simply evaluate the realism of Edgeworth's descriptions of Ireland by measuring them against a "pre-constituted reality";[2] rather, critics struggle to define for their British readers the parameters of what is seen to be realistically Irish *through* their reviews of Edgeworth's work. Seamus Deane notes that for British readers, "It was hard to believe what passed for reality in Ireland, especially if the reporter was Irish and therefore untrustworthy. The untrustworthiness was often confirmed for the English reader by any attempt to blame or even cast in a disobliging light the vagaries of English misrule or cruelty."[3] It is precisely this question of "what passed for reality in Ireland"—and, indeed, if it was at all possible to define that reality through the mediums of fiction and critical discourse—that exercised both Edgeworth and her critics.

Whether Edgeworth's (or indeed any) representations of Ireland were entirely trustworthy and accurate was a central issue for the many reviewers who freely admitted their initial lack of knowledge on Ireland. In an 1814 review of *Patronage,* John Ward, the critic for the *Quarterly Review,* wrote that Edgeworth's Irish fiction "enabled her at once to delight and instruct the public, to which, generally speaking, the peculiar manners of Ireland were less known than those of Otaheite."[4] A similar remark is made, again highlighting the parallels between Ireland and other "exotic" locales, in a survey article entitled "Irish novels" in the *Edinburgh Review.* "The advantage of being a *terra incognita,* at least to English statesmen, Ireland has, til lately, possessed almost as fully as the interior of Africa."[5] If reviewers highlighted this previous ignorance of Ireland, it was to emphasize that this lack of knowledge was no longer characteristic of the British reading public. This, the reviewers admit, is largely due to the educational value of Edgeworth's Irish tales, which have enabled reviewers to feel as if they "know . . . the Irish nation" thoroughly.[6] In confidently asserting their newfound knowledge of Ireland, the uncomfortable question is inevitably raised about how Edgeworth's own representations were judged as accurate in the first instance, given this initial lack of knowledge. In part, the invocation of Edgeworth's personal experience of Ireland validated her works as reliable sources of information. This circular approach to defining accurate representations of Ireland was not without its problems, however, as revealed in the consistent interrogation by both author and reviewers of the links between experience and the production of reliable and realistic portrayals of Ireland.

Given that many, if not most, of Edgeworth's British readers were not going to have personal experiences of Ireland against which to judge representations of it, both Edgeworth and her reviewers attempted to produce the kinds of readers who could be equipped through reading to "judge for themselves" the increasing range and diversity of texts on Ireland available to them in the post-Union period. It is in part through the interpolation of the "*ignorant* English reader"[7]—the reader explicitly addressed in *Castle Rackrent* (but also more generally in *Ennui* and *The Absentee*) and in the reviews of Edgeworth's work—that Edgeworth and her reviewers attempted to educate their readers about what and how they should read. While a historical assessment of the true "ignorance" of this "ignorant English reader" is difficult, the reviewers' claims of a lack of knowledge about Ireland were certainly echoed in a range of texts well into the nineteenth century.⁸ However, the uncomfortable and insistent refrain of "ignorance" is difficult to reconcile with the intensity of the production of literature (in the broadest sense of the term) about Ireland after the Union. I would suggest that if the lack of knowledge about Ireland was often seen as problematic by Edgeworth, her reviewers and, indeed, by numerous other travelers and writers, it was also the enabling factor in their own attempts to produce knowledge about Ireland. In telling readers that they had little knowledge of the "real" Ireland, or that the knowledge they did possess was inadequate, a space was created for both author and reviewer to advance their own views on what was authentically Irish—this is "the *advantage* of being a terra incognita" identified by the *Edinburgh* reviewer.

Addressing the "ignorant" English reader may have made possible the (re)education of this reader, but there is also an ambivalence in Edgeworth's work about the extent to which her fiction (or any fiction) should be relied upon for accurate information on Ireland. The critical and popular reception of Edgeworth's first Irish tale, *Castle Rackrent*, almost immediately highlighted the possibility that undiscriminating British readers would accept certain fictional representations as truth. Many British reviewers and readers (including George III)⁹ seemed to read the "tale of other times" as an accurate up-to-date reflection of Irish manners, one which, according to reviewers, obviously pointed to the wisdom of the Union between the two nations:

> In these Hibernian Memoirs, we have been highly entertained with the exhibition of some admirable pictures, delineated (as we conceive) with perfect accuracy and truth of character; and we apprehend that, from a due contemplation of these portraits, many striking conclusions may be drawn, and applications made, respecting the necessity and probable consequences of an union between the two kingdoms.¹⁰

Edgeworth was not only faced with the prospect of British readers being unable or unwilling to tell the difference between fact and fiction in relation to Ireland, but she also had to contemplate the disturbing notion that reading works such as *Castle Rackrent* might actually distort firsthand experiences of Ireland. The suspicion that British readers, travelers, and politicians could filter their actual views of Ireland through the lens of Edgeworth's fictional representations was confirmed by a comment made in 1801 by Chief Secretary Charles Abbot to the lord lieutenant, Philip Yorke, third Earl of Hardwicke, that he had "dined one day at a thorough Castle Rackrent, but pray never say so."[11]

Perhaps British readers were not to be blamed for their seeming confusion, however; not only did *Castle Rackrent* send conflicting signals about its status as fiction (with the use of the fictional editor and glossary explaining aspects of Irish life that would be unfamiliar to British readers), but British reviewers also struggled with their assessment of the regional novel both as a particular subgenre and as a potential source of information. The contemporary reception of *Castle Rackrent* vividly illustrates the difficulties faced by reviewers and readers alike who attempted in vain to categorize Edgeworth's work. The use of the fictional editor in *Castle Rackrent* perhaps made recourse to Edgeworth's own experience more difficult in gauging what was "fact" in this work; in response, reviewers sought alternative methods of enabling their readers to judge what was truly Irish—methods that did not require actual experience of Ireland. The critic in the *Imperial Review* notice of *Castle Rackrent* commented that:

> In this ingenious Hibernian tale there is much *local* interest, which is unavoidably lost to the mere English reader: such, however, is the humorous delineation of character in the family portraits exhibited in *Castle Rackrent*, that though incompetent to decide on the accuracy of the likeness, we hesitate not to pronounce on the merits of execution which displays the hand of a master.[12]

In highlighting the inability of the "mere English" to judge the truth-value of Edgeworth's descriptions of Ireland, the reviewer points the way to mastery over Irish subject material through formal categories of textual judgment, shifting the focus from questions of accuracy to the evaluation of plausibility and realism. This was an approach to Edgeworth's works that was to be even more fully developed in the reviewing of her subsequent Irish tales *Ennui* and *The Absentee*.

In response to the unanticipated reception of *Castle Rackrent*, *An Essay on Irish Bulls* speaks directly to some of the problems posed by readers uncritically taking textual representations as truth rather than seeing or judging the subject matter for themselves. The Edgeworths' caution to British readers about the dangers of trusting books that may provide outdated or inaccurate information is articulated in the "Bath Coach Conversation" chapter of *An Essay on Irish Bulls*, where the Englishman states:

> What little knowledge I have of Ireland has been drawn more from observation than from books. I remember when I first went over there, I did not expect to see twenty trees in the whole island: I imagined that I should have nothing to drink but whiskey, that I should have nothing to eat but potatoes, that I should sleep in mud-walled cabins . . . But experience taught me better things: I found that the stories I had heard were *tales of other times*.[13]

The direct and pointed quotation from the preface to *Castle Rackrent*—in which the editor states that he "hopes his readers will observe that these are 'tales of other times'"—is significant: in incorporating the text of *Castle Rackrent* into this warning, Edgeworth highlights the possibility that using even her own fiction as a reliable source of facts about Ireland may handicap British readers and travelers in their endeavors to see the "real" Ireland.

Thirteen years after its initial appearance, *Castle Rackrent* was still a common point of reference in discussions about how the British public read and interpreted Irish fiction. In fact, references to Edgeworth's first Irish novel seem to have functioned in both the British and the Irish periodical press as a sort of cultural shorthand for debates about how knowledge of Ireland was acquired in the post-Union period. In a brief commentary on the Dublin journal *The Anonymous*, the reviewer in the *British Critic* takes issue with the assertion in the Irish periodical that British readers derived information about Ireland from *Castle Rackrent*:

> The author is evidently an Hibernian, partial to his countrymen, and not quite free from prejudices against the English. He accuses us of taking our chief notions of Ireland from castle Rackrent, of which, to our utter surprise, he speaks in the following terms: "Towards attaining a consummate ignorance of Irish manners, no better means can be adopted, than the study of castle rackrent; which accordingly many English seem to have perused with great attention and effect." If this be true, we are certainly very much in the dark on this side of the water, where a very contrary idea is universally prevalent.[14]

Regardless of which reviewer is correct, the extraordinary nature of the exchange itself should not be underestimated. *The Anonymous* was a short-lived Dublin review that appeared in 1806–7 and ran to only two volumes. Reprinted in England in 1810, the brief notice of it did not appear in the *British Critic* until November 1813. A degree of defensiveness about any imputation of British inability to see (more than ten years after the Union) that *Castle Rackrent* was not a reliable guide to "Irish manners" is evident in the reviewer's need to refute a three-year-old accusation made in a rather obscure Dublin journal. Perhaps disturbingly for Edgeworth, just as *Castle Rackrent* may have prevented Chief Secretary Abbott from seeing the "real" Ireland, the controversy over British reading and reception of her text similarly enabled reviewers to evade any discussion of the "real" Ireland as well.

Edgeworth's later Irish tales continued the interrogation of the links between experience and representations of Ireland that began with works such as *An Essay on Irish Bulls*. The focus in both *Ennui* and *The Absentee*—as it was in the "Bath Coach Conversation" in *Irish Bulls*—is on the reliability of texts purporting to describe Ireland accurately and on how a British audience might be taught, through reading, to judge any such descriptions of Ireland. In the use of a narrative focalizer who learns about Ireland through actual experience, Edgeworth provides her readers with a character whom they could follow and identify with in his educational journey through Ireland. Perhaps like many of her British readers, the protagonist of *Ennui*, Lord Glenthorn, admits to having strong prejudices against Ireland. Before he has traveled to Ireland, Lord Glenthorn's only conception of his Irish estate is through a representation: he claims his castle is "placed in a bold romantic situation; at least as far as I could judge of it by a picture, said to be a striking likeness, which hung in my hall at Sherwood park in England" (145). As Brian Hollingworth notes, "There is some irony in the phrase 'said to be a striking likeness,' since this reflects Edgeworth's view that English attitudes to Ireland are formed by misleading artistic stereotypes rather than by firsthand knowledge."[15]

However, even firsthand experience does not always guarantee a complete understanding of Ireland. The preconceptions observers bring to Ireland affect how they see the facts presented to them, as is the case with *Ennui*'s Lord Craiglethorpe who, like Glenthorn, comes to Ireland "full of English prejudices against Ireland and everything Irish," intending to "publish a Tour through Ireland, or a View of Ireland" (211), the titles alluding to Arthur Young's *Tour of Ireland* (1771) and Edmund Spenser's *View of the Present State of Ire-*

land (1633). In response to the idea of Craiglethorpe writing such a book, the Anglo-Irish aristocrat Lady Geraldine states:

> "He! With his means of acquiring information!" exclaimed Lady Geraldine. "Posting from one great man's house to another, what can he see or know of the manners of any rank of people but of the class of gentry, which in England and Ireland is much the same? As to the lower classes, I don't think he ever speaks to them; or, if he does, what good can it do him? for he can't understand their modes of expression, nor they his: if he inquire about a matter of fact, I defy him to get the truth out of them, if they don't wish to tell it; and, for some reason or other, nine times out of ten, they do not wish to tell it to an Englishman. There is not a man, woman, or child, in any cabin in Ireland, who would not have wit and *cuteness* enough to make *my lard* believe just what they please. So, after posting from Dublin to Cork, and from the Giants' causeway to Killarney; after traveling east, west, north, and south, my wise cousin Craiglethorpe will know just as much of the lower Irish as the cockney who has never been out of London, and who has never, *in all his born days,* seen an Irishman but on the English stage; where the representations are usually as like the originals, as the Chinese pictures of lions, drawn from description, are to the real animal." (211)[16]

In this passage, the circularity of the colonial encounter is deconstructed: those, like Craiglethorpe, who arrive in Ireland filled with prejudices and expectations of what they will find (based largely on earlier reportings and textual representations of Ireland), will only see their own preconceived notions reflected back at them by those "lower Irish" who have mastered colonial discourse. This encounter is then written as the truth, which in turn guides the opinions of the British reading public and perpetuates a false understanding of Ireland. As Lady Geraldine later remarks: "imagine a set of sober English readers studying my cousin Craiglethorpe's New View of Ireland, and swallowing all the nonsense it will contain!" (212). In viewing a reality already predetermined by previous representations, any possibility of seeing a truthful picture of Irish life is made virtually impossible, even with firsthand experience.

The reproduction in *Ennui* of arguments used both in *An Essay on Irish Bulls,* as well as in the Edgeworths' joint 1806 *Edinburgh* review of John Carr's *The Stranger in Ireland,* also permits these critiques of Craiglethorpe to be read in terms of their political implications for Ireland. In a comment that will be reiterated almost verbatim in *Ennui,* the Edgeworths' claimed in their review that Carr's text is "a book of stale jests . . . All the old stories of bulls and blunders, which, as we are informed, have for years past been regularly brought forward for the recreation of every new lord-lieutenant and his secretary, are here collected for the edification of the public."[17] The textual echoes between *Ennui* and the review not only register the consistency in Edgeworth's thinking on the subject of misrepresentations of Ireland but also take on a particular resonance and urgency when we remember how Chief Secretary Abbot filtered his experience of Ireland through *Castle Rackrent* and subsequently reported it to Lord Lieutenant Hardwicke. It is not just the case that the "stale jests . . . and blunders" that are "brought forward" to amuse successive lord lieutenants may undermine the governance of Ireland by confirming prejudices against the Irish, but also that these prejudices may actually be enabled by an uncritical attitude toward Edgeworth's own texts.

Even with his own newfound experience of Ireland and with the salutary lesson of Lady Geraldine's raillery against Craiglethorpe, Glenthorn himself persists in mediating his views of Ireland through texts, still preferring artistic representations to thinking and observing for himself. During his tour of the Giant's Causeway he describes his "experience" of the location as conforming to representations of it he has previously encountered. Rather than describing the scene himself, he quotes a description of it from a travelogue.[18] It is only his own laziness that prevents him from writing his own travel account of Ireland, and while this account—like Craiglethorpe's—would merely perpetuate inaccuracies about Ireland, it would carry with it the supposed legitimacy of being based on firsthand experience. If *Ennui* explores how false representations of Ireland can mediate actual experiences—and how these experiences are in turn recouped in texts that propagate incorrect impressions of Ireland among the British public—it suggests that the way to break this vicious and politically damaging cycle is to make British readers aware of their own complicity in this process in their very consuming ("swallowing," in Lady Geraldine's phrase) of such texts.

Unlike *Ennui*, *The Absentee* does not offer any direct addresses to its "sober English readers" to make them conscious of their own reading practices. However, in enabling readers to identify more closely with lord Colambre than they had perhaps been able to with either the ridiculous Craiglethorpe or the dissipated Glenthorn, *The Absentee* allows British readers to participate more fully in Colambre's attempts to negotiate a variety of representations of Ireland.

Both before and during his trip to Ireland, Colambre is vulnerable to others' misrepresentations of Ireland as a result of his inexperience and reliance on others to understand the country and its people. Despite the lesson from the English officer Sir James Brooke about "not deducing general conclusions from a few particular cases, or arguing from exceptions, as if they were rules,"[19] Colambre's experience of Ireland is manipulated by the mercenary lady Dashfort. During her campaign of "misrepresentations" designed to turn Colambre against Ireland, Dashfort claims to show Colambre the "real" Ireland but in fact shows him the worst part of it: "No one could, with more ease and knowledge of her ground, than Lady Dashfort, do the *dishonours* of a country" (104). The scenes involving lady Dashfort dramatize the dangers of taking the most extreme or unusual aspects of Irish life as the general rule, but—just as importantly—they also illustrate how even the most seemingly authentic firsthand experience of Ireland can be mediated and manipulated.

Narrowly escaping Dashfort's skillful manipulation of his views of Ireland (itself made possible by her intimate knowledge of the country), Colambre is reminded of the value of "seeing with his own eyes, and judging with his own understanding . . . the country and its inhabitants" (124). Colambre then travels incognito so that "he might see and hear more than he could as heir apparent to the estate" (124), thereby removing himself from the trap of the circular colonial encounter anticipated by Craiglethorpe, in which travelers are told only what it is believed they want to hear. Edgeworth's protagonists are equipped to "read" critically through experience, against which they can judge the truthfulness of various representations of Ireland, and of Irish representations of themselves. In the imaginative identification between reader and focalizer made possible by Edgeworth's text, readers have access to the sort of experience necessary to get at the truth, thus making "judging for oneself" in actual experience analogous to critical reading of texts.

Although Colambre's experiences in Ireland enable him to return to England in order to dispel the "misrepresentations" of Ireland to which Lord and Lady Clonbrony are vulnerable, and which they themselves have perpetuated in London, Edgeworth's texts also interrogate both what it means to be a trustworthy authority on Ireland and the nature of the experience that underpins such authority. At the same time as Edgeworth's texts make claims for themselves as authoritative sources of factual information on Ireland, they also function to caution readers about taking such seemingly authoritative representations on faith. Even those supposedly trustworthy authorities named by Sir James Brooke in *The Absentee* are not beyond question. Brooke speaks to Colambre of "different representations and misrepresentations of Ireland" (78) and endorses Spenser, Sir John Davies, Young, and Daniel Beaufort as those authors who have written the fullest and (for their time) most accurate factual and statistical accounts and surveys of Irish life. However, the echoes of Young's and Spenser's work in Craiglethorpe's proposed title for his own study of Ireland draw even these supposedly trustworthy authorities into an uncomfortable proximity to those very representations Edgeworth works to discredit. Sir James also speaks highly about the pamphlet "An intercepted Letter from China," which W. J. McCormack and Kim Walker have identified as a pamphlet attributed to John Wilson Croker entitled *An Intercepted Letter from J——T—— Esq.: Written at Canton to His Friend in Dublin, Ireland*. Croker's pamphlet, as McCormack and Walker point out, is not a "slight, playful" work but is instead a "heavy-handed piece of satire" that actually contradicts Brooke's own praise of post-Union Dublin society,[20] thus suggesting that Brooke's comments should perhaps be treated with some caution.

The source of Brooke's knowledge about Ireland is also not entirely unproblematic. It is Brooke's military service that has enabled him to travel extensively through Ireland—because he has been garrisoned in a number of places throughout the country, Brooke has thus had the wide-ranging experience of a large cross-section of Irish life that he recommends to Colambre as the best method for truly understanding Ireland. That Sir James's knowledge directly results from his affiliation with an instrument of British state power in Ireland exposes how the accumulation of knowledge about the colonized nation is implicated in the functioning of more overt forms of colonial power. Like *Ennui*'s Lady Geraldine (who herself becomes part of the British colonial enterprise in India), Edgeworth's own intimate knowledge of Ireland is derived from her experiences as the daughter of an Anglo-Irish landowner. Ultimately, Edgeworth's fictions suggest that the circumstances by which experience is gained reflect back on knowledge itself, and that even firsthand experience unaffected by prejudice is not free of the tainted influence of colonial power relations. In thus problematizing the basis for any knowledge about Ireland, Edgeworth's texts raise a disturbing prospect for those British readers and reviewers who are already largely, and perhaps uncomfortably, dependent on texts for information about their "sister kingdom." In opening up questions about the experience that underpins any representation of Ireland, and about whether any text can be entirely trustworthy, both *Ennui* and *The Absentee* disrupt attempts to read them as potential sources of accurate information, thereby challenging the pattern established by some of the readings of *Castle Rackrent.*

Edgeworth's works placed reviewers in the unenviable position of relying on texts that cautioned them against relying on texts, and which encouraged the need for critical reading while asserting sometimes contradictory claims to their own authoritative representations of Ireland. If Edgeworth's own warnings about the dangers of trusting to any representation of Ireland (no matter how experience-based) and her questioning of the mediated nature of experience introduced the potentially radical possibility that there was simply no way to get at the "real" Ireland, reviewers attempted to resolve this dilemma by basing their judgment of descriptions of Ireland on something over which they (and their readers) would have complete authority and certainty—the assessment of realism. In order to produce and reinforce their own readings of Ireland, reviewers asserted the value of aesthetic and formal standards of realism over experience, a move that had been signaled as early as 1804 in the *Imperial Review* notice of *Castle Rackrent.*

Reviewers' definitions of what was realistically and plausibly Irish in Edgeworth's national tales were often determined by the political agendas of the reviews themselves. For many reviewers, Edgeworth's "trustworthiness" lies in the seemingly unthreatening political sentiments offered in *Ennui* and *The Absentee,* and the explicit focus on reform of the Anglo-Irish ruling class in *Ennui* and *The Absentee* made her Irish tales automatically more realistic for those reviewers who were sensitive to any hint of direct criticism of British rule in Ireland. Reviewers' assumptions of a shared view with Edgeworth on the issue of Catholic emancipation in particular led many critics to endorse the verisimilitude of Edgeworth's depictions of Irish life. The reviewer in the evangelical journal *The Christian Observer* believes *The Absentee* should "stand forth as a species of map, or authentic document, pourtraying the real 'case' between Irish grievances and Irish discontents."[21] Perhaps unsurprisingly, for this reviewer the root of all Irish grievances is absenteeism, not the disenfranchisement of the majority of the population. In spite of the fact that Edgeworth, in collaboration with her father, expressed support for emancipation in an 1806 review of John Carr's *The Stranger in Ireland*,[22] the reviewer in the *Christian Observer* expresses his opinion confident of being "in accordance with Miss Edgeworth." Although later consistently criticized by both British and Irish journals for failing to advocate emancipation in her novels, this perceived gap in her Irish tales clearly enabled reviewers to overlook Edgeworth's own opinions in order to read her works in a way that validated their opinions. That her works are presented as "authentic documents" and "maps" not only obscures how Edgeworth's texts are used by reviewers to support their own political views, but also how reviewers are actually constructing the "real" and the authentic based on the extent to which the representations accord with their particular political agendas.

Edgeworth's realism was not affirmed solely on the basis of her critics' views of Irish politics—her realism was also a politics in and of itself, in that it confirmed for reviewers a shared ideological commitment to "society as it is."[23] Just as the *Edinburgh Review*'s Francis Jeffrey had praised Edgeworth's realism in *Popular Tales* for its ability to save impressionable British readers from the "pernicious absurdities" of Wordsworth and Paine,[24] the realism of Edgeworth's Irish tales was deemed politically acceptable specifically in light of the alternative: the romantic proto-nationalism of Sydney Owenson (Lady Morgan). For the reviewer of *Harrington* and *Ormond* in *Blackwood's Magazine*, the verisimilitude of Edgeworth's portrayals of the Irish lies in her willingness to show "their virtues and their vices alike undisguised," unlike other authors who "exhibit only the bright side of their character."[25] The reviewer's point is not that Edgeworth's "mixed" characterizations are inherently realistic (although this general issue did occupy early nineteenth-century reviewers to a large degree), but rather that they are comparatively so when placed alongside those of Morgan.

John Wilson Croker (Lady Morgan's own critical *bête noir*), reviewing the second series of *Tales of Fashionable Life* for the Tory *Quarterly Review*, also stresses that Edgeworth's claims to accuracy rest on presenting nuanced views of Ireland and the Irish in her tales, in particular on her ability to differentiate Irish society into its various social strata:

> Other writers have caught nothing but the general feature, and in their description, every thing that is Irish is pretty much alike, lords, peasants, ladies, and nurses: to Miss Edgeworth's keen observation and vivid pen-

cil, it was reserved to separate the genus into its species and individuals, and to exhibit the most accurate and yet the most diversified views that have ever been drawn of a national character.[26]

The reviewer in the *Christian Observer*, however, advances nearly the opposite view: "The great difficulty in the conception and delineation of national character is, that they should be not individual, but generic."[27] That the two reviewers could suggest such opposing standards of realism in relation to Irish national character again suggests the contentiousness of the *process* of developing these standards, rather than a simple application of set criteria to a given text.

That there were *competing* definitions of what constituted a realistic description of Irish national character is itself evidence of reviewers' seeming inability to attach representations securely to any recognizably "real" Ireland. In praising Edgeworth's fictional renderings of fashionable life, the critic in the *British Review* makes a comment that might also apply to Edgeworth's descriptions of Irish life: "One of her most obvious causes of advantage is her habitual acquaintance with those modes of life which others are *compelled to take upon trust*, and to copy from report."[28]

The lack of knowledge of Ireland expressed by a number of reviewers is perhaps a source of concern in and of itself, but even more so when reviewers and readers are "compelled" to rely upon fictional representations of Ireland. Reviewers responded to this challenge to their own authority by declaring that not even Edgeworth's own experience could guarantee the plausibility of her representations of Ireland:

> Of the manners and characters of the Irish peasantry, we cannot venture to hold up our own conjectures in opposition to Miss Edgeworth's experience . . . [But] we should not have believed (had not Miss Edgeworth assured us of it), that my Lord Colambre could, without the interposition of a miracle in his favour, have met in one day with so many honest, brave, disinterested, affectionate, kind, good, sensible, well-educated, refined, sentimental, moral, and religious poor people, as he has the good fortune to find on his progress through his father's estate at Clonbrony.[29]

Universally positive representations of the Irish strained against the bounds of plausibility and undermined the very aim of the fictions themselves: "we think her obnoxious" writes one reviewer of the second series of *Tales of Fashionable Life* "to the charge of over-colouring her picture and caricaturing her subject to an extent which may, we fear, essentially detract from the utility of her labours."[30] The reviewer's sarcastically deferential attitude to Edgeworth's "experience" points to the limits of Edgeworth's status as an authority on all matters Irish, undermining the claims to superior powers of observation and the privilege of actual experience that bulwarked the accuracy of her representations of Ireland. Where before Edgeworth had seemed an "authority that cannot be questioned,"[31] her assurances to readers are now shown to be untrustworthy, undone by the falling away from standards of realism that results from attempting to represent the Irish both sympathetically and accurately. [32] Rather than defer to Edgeworth's own authority, British reviewers were beginning to forge a critical language of realism through which they could assert their control over descriptions of the foreign and unfamiliar in the national tale. The shift to the aesthetic evaluation of realism is succinctly put in John Wilson Croker's oft-quoted comment in his review of the second series of *Tales of Fashionable Life*: "we are prepared to insist that, while the '*vrai*' is the highest recommendation of the historian of real life, the '*vraisemblable*' is the only legitimate province of the novelist."[33] Thus, the truth-like is given precedence over the "truth" in any representation of Ireland, clearing the way for reviewers themselves to privilege their interpretations on the actualities of Irish life over Edgeworth's.

In judging the "merits of execution" rather than the "accuracy of the likeness"—to return to the distinction made in the *Imperial Review* notice of *Castle Rackrent*—reviewers employed a variety of strategies, not least of which was the assertion of the difference between Edgeworth's representations of Ireland and any hitherto available to British audiences. As Jeffrey notes in his review of *Ennui*, Edgeworth's "Irish characters are inimitable—not the coarse caricatures of modern playwrights."[34] According to a reviewer in the *Quarterly*, Edgeworth's "merit was not that of describing what had never been described before—it was greater, it was that of describing well what had been described ill—of substituting accurate finished resemblances, for clumsy confused daubings by the sign-post artists of modern comedy."[35] These kinds of comments enable us to see that criticism was not simply measuring Edgeworth's representations of Ireland against a "pre-constituted reality," but instead highlight how, in Homi Bhabha's phrase, such representations are "constructed in a process of reference and difference in relation to other ideological and historical discourses which constitute its conditions of existence and intervention."[36] Just as Edgeworth implicitly asserts the difference between her own writings and inaccurate works such as that proposed by the fictional Craiglethorpe, reviewers assert the difference between her Irish characters and eighteenth-century stage-Irish figures. In both cases, the accuracy of the representation is guaranteed by no inherent qualities of its own, merely by its relation to another representation.

This mode of establishing accuracy is not without its pitfalls, however, as one reviewer recognizes in his assessment of Edgeworth's depictions of her Jewish characters in *Harrington*:

> If Miss Edgeworth really wished to serve the cause of the children of Israel, we apprehend the best mode would have been, to have searched out and fairly laid before the public, evidences of their disinterestedness, generosity, and benevolent feeling, from their actual history and living characters: short of this, all efforts are merely appeals to the imagination: it is purely opposing the Shylock of Shakespeare to the Sheva of Cumberland, leaving the public completely ignorant which original sat for the picture thus arbitrarily drawn from the imagination . . . Imaginary characters thus played off against imaginary characters neutralize each other's effect on the minds of the spectators.[37]

Fiction, then, merely replaces one equally plausible representation with another, and it is only through recourse to history or biography that truth can ultimately be established. The use of "imaginary characters" to counter other imaginative creations simply confuses the public, thus revealing the potentially disconcerting arbitrariness underlying any endorsement of accuracy in fiction. All these imaginative representations bear an uncertain relationship to an "original," but the reviewer's complaint of not knowing "which original" to compare with the description opens up the further possibility that there simply might not be *an* original at all. The prospect of there being no single "original" radically levels any attempts to establish hierarchies of accuracy in representations of Ireland, as any representation may be as accurate as any other. This prospect is both problematic and liberating for Edgeworth's British critics struggling to assess the realism of her Irish tales: on the one hand, it echoes the anxious questions raised in Edgeworth's work about the implications of being unable to achieve any unmediated experience of Ireland; on the other hand, if it is impossible for reviewers to compare the representation to the original, then reviewers are free to concentrate on assessing the formal qualities of the representation itself, which of course requires no experience of Ireland at all.

In only one case—that of Irish reviewer and MP for Downpatrick, John Wilson Croker—is the experience of the reviewer explicitly brought into play: "We wish that our limits permitted us to introduce our readers to be better acquaintance with Larry, the postillion . . . and to give them some specimens of Irish posting which (we speak from experience) is most accurately described."[38] However, even while asserting his insider knowledge of "Irish posting," Croker withdraws from any claim of Irishness in his discussion of Edgeworth's portrayals of the English in Ireland: "we own that we have been almost as much pleased with Miss Edgeworth's portraiture of our own countrymen (if we may venture to make the distinction) in Ireland, as with that of the Irish themselves."[39] In placing himself in alliance with British readers while claiming the authority of personal experience, Croker affirms the validity of British judgments of the accuracy of Edgeworth's descriptions of Ireland. However, reviewers generally did not choose this particular method of evaluating Edgeworth's Irish tales, perhaps because it held the potential to demonstrate how little reviewers knew about Ireland.

In light of the debates about the links between experience of Ireland and the constitution of fictional realism, it is perhaps no surprise that Edgeworth's final Irish tale, *Ormond*, attempts in some ways to bypass these vexed issues. As a historical fiction whose central character and narrative focalizer is—unlike Glenthorn and Colambre—perfectly "at home" in the various strata of Irish society, *Ormond* seems to offer fewer claims to educate British readers about ways of reading and understanding Ireland than her earlier works. While Edgeworth thus circumvents some of the more contentious issues involved in offering factual evidence about contemporary Ireland, she does reiterate the need for critical reading in terms remarkably similar to those used by the reviewers of *Ennui* and *The Absentee*. During Harry Ormond's novel-reading phase, Cornelius O'Shane puts the young and impressionable reader on his guard: "'No cramming anything down his throat,' he said. This daring temper of mind, though it sometimes led him wrong, was advantageous to his young friend. It wakened Ormond's powers, and prevented his taking upon trust the assertions, or the reputations, even of great writers" (72). It is significant that the lesson teaching Harry not to "trust" even "great writers" comes from O'Shane—his warning not only points back to the general question of trusting even the most seemingly authoritative depictions of Ireland, but it also acts as a submerged interrogation of the possibility that even "great" Anglo-Irish writers could have access to the native Irish culture he represents. Just as *Irish Bulls* responded to the reception of *Castle Rackrent* by warning against taking "tales of other times" as sources of accurate information about Ireland, O'Shane's warning to Harry Ormond suggests an awareness of the pitfalls of being taken "on trust."

Long after Edgeworth published her final Irish tale, the question of experience and its role in underpinning accurate representations of Ireland remained central to both British and Irish criticism of Edgeworth's works, and indeed to the evaluation of realism in the Irish novel generally. Perhaps ironically, given her own ambivalence about the value of artistic representations in understanding Ireland, British reviewers used Edgeworth's own fiction as a benchmark against which they assessed the mimetic power of authors such as William Carleton and John and Michael Banim. Just as Edgeworth's work was evaluated on the basis of its difference from eighteenth-century drama, the novels of the Banims and Carleton seemed more realistic when compared with Edgeworth's "genteel" fiction that centered largely around the Anglo-Irish gentry. Reviews that had once praised the verisimilitude of Edgeworth's delineations of Irish life now distanced themselves from these earlier judgments. One particularly striking instance of this is John Wilson Croker's revised opinion of the realism of Edgeworth's representations of Irish life. In 1812 he had praised Edgeworth's ability to individualize her portrayals of Irish characters; in 1820 he saw Edgeworth's mode of "drawing from the life" as faulty: "This mode, of sketching after individual nature, has a strong tendency to caricature, and ... accordingly, the portraits which Mr. and Miss Edgeworth compose ... by collecting into one canvass the features of many individuals, are often exaggerated, and tend to give us an amusing rather than a just representation of the Irish character."[40] While his opinion of the representations had changed, this later view is still consistent with that expressed in 1812 in its underlying emphasis on the *vraisemblable* over the *vrai*—it was simply the case that what had seemed comparatively realistic before now seemed more like "caricature."

Reviewers obscured the ever-shifting nature of their standards surrounding fictional realism in the Irish novel by asserting that it was not the case that the reviewers themselves had misjudged the relative accuracy of Edgeworth's work, but that Edgeworth's own lack of experience had prevented her from seeing—much less representing—certain aspects of Irish life now made visible by the fiction of the Banims and Carleton:

> [W]hen Miss Edgeworth quits genteel society, of which she seizes and exposes all the foibles so inimitably, and extends her views of life beyond the circle she has moved in, her ideas of the actual state of and temper of the people are somewhat superficial and lady-like. She seems to have some notion that her poorer fellow-country-men are deficient in sundry articles of clothing and cleanliness—that the pig is an admitted parlour-boarder, and the middleman an occasional visitor of their cabins.[41]

Denying Edgeworth access to a newly defined "real" (centered on the Catholic peasantry) that emerged in later fiction thus enabled reviewers to disentangle themselves from the earlier critical struggles to define realism and the "real" that had surrounded the initial reviews of her work, thus obscuring the origins of such definitions in aesthetic standards. What the ever-changing and often arbitrary definitions of realistic representations of Ireland reveals is that the questions asked by some recent critics about "the success or otherwise of Irish attempts at literary realism" may indeed be "secondary or subsidiary questions"[42] that mask how the initial reviewing of Irish fiction helped to form those very standards of plausibility and representativeness by which Irish fiction is now judged.

Seamus Deane has argued that the increased number of publications that sought to map and explain Ireland after the Act of Union functioned to make Ireland "recognizably part of the United Kingdom."[43] Knowledge did not only move in one direction to bring Ireland closer to British readers, however; both Edgeworth's works and the reviews of these works brought British readers closer to Ireland. An 1831 survey of Irish fiction in the *Edinburgh Review* remarks of Edgeworth's achievements as a novelist:

> We never saw the Irish grouped—we never trode with them on Irish ground—we never viewed them as natives of a kindred soil, surrounded by the atmosphere of home, and all those powerful accessaries which made *them* natural, and *us* comparatively strange and foreign. We had seen them alone in English crowds—solitary foreigners, brought over to amuse us with their peculiarities; but we had never been carried to Ireland, and made familiar with them by their own hearths, till, for the first time, they were shown to us by Miss Edgeworth.[44]

The shifting of narrative ground[45] to Ireland accomplished by Edgeworth's texts seems to make the descriptions of the Irish in these works more presentation than re-presentation (the Irish are "shown" by Edgeworth), but it is precisely this issue of whether Ireland could in fact be represented without mediation, or if there was anything that could be unproblematically "shown" at all, that exercised both Edgeworth and her reviewers throughout the first two decades of the nineteenth century. While both Edgeworth and her reviewers worked to create a readership that could feel more confident about being educated by fictional texts—whether this was through a greater self-consciousness about their own reading practices or whether through the employment of aesthetic and formal criteria to judge realism—ultimately neither British reviewers nor Edgeworth could ever quite decide if her texts could indeed be "trusted for their truth and accuracy."

Notes

I am grateful to Claire Connolly and Lyn Innes for their helpful comments and suggestions on various drafts of this essay.

The quote in the title is from *Ennui*; Maria Edgeworth, *Castle Rackrent* and *Ennui*, ed. Marilyn Butler (London: Penguin, 1992), 273. With one exception all further references to this edition will be cited parenthetically.

1. [Review of first series of *Tales of Fashionable Life*], *Monthly Review* 62 (May 1810): 96–97. My emphasis.

2. Homi Bhabha, "Representation and the Colonial Text: A Critical Exploration of Some Forms of Mimeticism," in *The Theory of Reading*, ed. Frank Gloversmith (Sussex: Harvester, 1984), 99.

3. Seamus Deane, *A Short History of Irish Literature* (South Bend: University of Notre Dame Press, 1994), 94.

4. [John Ward, unsigned review of *Patronage*], *Quarterly Review* 11 (Jan. 1814): 309.

5. [Review of *To-Day in Ireland, Tales of the O'Hara Family, O'Hara, or 1798*, and *The Adventurers*], *Edinburgh Review* 43 (Feb. 1826): 358.

6. [Francis Jeffrey, unsigned review of second series of *Tales of Fashionable Life*], *Edinburgh Review* 20 (July 1812): 126.

7. Edgeworth, *Castle Rackrent*, 63.

8. Glenn Hooper discusses a number of post-Union travelogues that also emphasize the seeming lack of knowledge of Ireland on the part of the British public, many of which—like the British reviewers—frame the drive to accumulate knowledge about Ireland in terms of its status as a distant locale: "Ireland is a country that Englishmen in general know less about, than they do of Russia, Siberia or the Country of the Hottentots." From John Gough, *A Tour in Ireland, in 1813 and 1814; with an Appendix, Written in 1816, and Another Visit to that Island* (1817). Hooper reads the production of travel literature in the early nineteenth century in terms of the "connections between the availability of knowledge and political control" over

Ireland (36–37). Glenn Hooper, "Stranger in Ireland: The Problematics of the Post-Union Travelogue," *Mosaic* 28, no. 1 (Mar. 1995): 25–47.

9. "We hear from good authority that the king was much pleased with Castle Rack Rent—he rubbed his hands & said what what—I know something now of my Irish subjects." Letter from Richard Lovell Edgeworth to his father-in-law Daniel Beaufort, quoted in Marilyn Butler, *Maria Edgeworth: A Literary Biography* (Oxford: Clarendon, 1972), 359.

10. [Review of *Castle Rackrent*], *Monthly Review* 32 (May 1800): 91–92.

11. Quoted in Thomas Bartlett, *Acts of Union*, Inaugural lecture delivered at University College, Dublin (24 Feb. 2000), 8.

12. [Review of *Castle Rackrent*], *Imperial Review* 1 (Apr. 1804): 550.

13. Maria Edgeworth and Richard Lovell Edgeworth, *An Essay on Irish Bulls*, in *Castle Rackrent, Irish Bulls* and *Ennui*, eds. Jane Desmarais, Tim McLoughlin, and Marilyn Butler (London: Pickering and Chatto, 1999), 127.

14. [Review of *The Anonymous*], *British Critic* 42 (Nov. 1813): 534–35. The second series of *Tales of Fashionable Life* had been reviewed in the number just preceding this one, in Oct. 1813.

15. Brian Hollingworth, *Maria Edgeworth's Irish Writing: Language, History, Politics* (London: Macmillan, 1997), 124.

16. Lady Geraldine's speech reiterates the point made in *Irish Bulls* that: "Many foreign pictures of Irishmen are as grotesque and absurd as the Chinese pictures of lions: having never seen that animal, the Chinese can paint him only from the descriptions of the voyagers, which are sometimes ignorantly, sometimes wantonly exaggerated." Edgeworth and Edgeworth, *Irish Bulls*, 151–52.

17. [Maria Edgeworth and Richard Lovell Edgeworth, unsigned review of John Carr's *The Stranger in Ireland*], *Edinburgh Review* 10 (Apr. 1807): 42–43. *Ennui* reproduces these comments in the episode involving Lady Geraldine and Lord Craiglethorpe, when Geraldine supplies Craiglethorpe "with the most absurd anecdotes, incredible *facts*, stale jests, and blunders, such as were never made by true-born Irishmen" (212).

18. The irony of this criticism of Glenthorn's reliance on a travel narrative for his descriptions of Irish scenery is that Edgeworth herself actually traveled very little in Ireland, and often relied on travel books to provide her with descriptions of Irish scenery and landscape. In the case of Glenthorn's trip to the Giant's Causeway, the text that is quoted is Dr. William Hamilton's *Letters Concerning the Northern Coast of the County of Antrim* (1796). For Edgeworth's use of guidebooks for her descriptions of scenery, see Butler, *Biography*, 372.

19. Maria Edgeworth, *The Absentee*, ed. Heidi Thomson and Kim Walker (London: Penguin, 1999), 78. Further reference to this edition will be cited parenthetically.

20. Maria Edgeworth, *The Absentee*, ed. W. J. McCormack and Kim Walker (Oxford: Oxford University Press, 1988), 298.

21. [Review of second series of *Tales of Fashionable Life*], *Christian Observer* 11 (Dec. 1812): 793.

22. "Ireland never will be perfectly safe, till the causes of discontent among the great body of the people are removed. Complete *Catholic emancipation*, as it is called, should be granted to them; nothing less will do." [Maria Edgeworth and Richard Lovell Edgeworth], *Edinburgh Review* 10 (Apr. 1807): 58.

23. Marilyn Butler, *Romantics, Rebels and Reactionaries* (Oxford: Oxford University Press, 1981), 155.

24. [Francis Jeffrey, unsigned review of *Popular Tales*], *Edinburgh Review* 4 (July 1804): 330.

25. [Review of *Harrington* and *Ormond*], *Blackwood's Edinburgh Magazine* 1, no. 6 (Sept. 1817): 632. The reviewer does not actually name Morgan here, but the fairly standard nature of the comparison between the two Irish authors and *Blackwood's* own intense campaign against Morgan is enough to indicate clearly the author to whom the reviewer referred.

26. [John Wilson Croker, unsigned review of second series of *Tales of Fashionable Life*], *Quarterly Review* 7 (June 1812): 336.

27. [Review of first series of *Tales of Fashionable Life*], *Christian Observer* 8 (Dec. 1809): 786.

28. [Review of *Harrington* and *Ormond*], *British Review* 11 (Feb. 1818): 51–52. My emphasis.

29. [Review of second series of *Tales of Fashionable Life*], *Critical Review*, 4th series, 2 (Aug. 1812): 123.

30. Ibid., 122. The reviewer of *Harrington* in *Blackwood's* states that "by representing all her Jewish characters as too uniformly perfect, she has thrown a degree of suspicion over her whole defense," *Blackwood's Edinburgh Magazine* 1, no. 5 (Aug. 1817): 520. In her discussion of the tensions between reviewers' expectations of fictional realism and Edgeworth's own moral-didactic aims, Clíona Ó Gallchoir makes the point that the moral of Edgeworth's work was often undermined by her lack of realism: "The consensus seems to be that Edgeworth's moral purpose is both the source of her achievements in realism, and the stumbling block to a more fully naturalistic art" (88). "Maria Edgeworth's Revolutionary Morality and the Limits of Realism," *Colby Quarterly* 36, no. 2 (June 2000): 87–97.

31. [Francis Jeffrey] *Edinburgh Review* 20 (July 1812): 101.

32. As Marilyn Butler notes, there were often tensions in Edgeworth's work that resulted from Edgeworth being "nearly as much bent on improving Ireland's image with the English public as on serving the abstract interests of truth." Butler, *Maria Edgeworth*, 363.

33. [John Wilson Croker], *Quarterly Review* 7 (June 1812): 329.

34. [Francis Jeffrey, unsigned review of first series of *Tales of Fashionable Life*], *Edinburgh Review* 14 (July 1809): 380.

35. [John Ward], *Quarterly Review* 11 (Jan. 1814): 309.

36. Bhabha, "Representation and the Colonial Text," 102.

37. *British Review* 11 (Feb. 1818): 60.

38. [John Wilson Croker], *Quarterly Review* 7 (June 1812): 341.

39. Ibid., 337.

40. [John Wilson Croker, unsigned review of *Memoirs of Richard Lovell Edgeworth*], *Quarterly Review* 23 (May 1820): 511.

41. [Rev. of *To-day in Ireland, Tales by the O'Hara Family, The O'Briens and The O'Flahertys, Tales of the Munster Festivals,* and *The Croppy*], *Westminster Review* 9 (Apr. 1828): 423.

42. Both quotations are from Claire Connolly, "'I accuse Miss Owenson': *The Wild Irish Girl* as Media Event" (107). *Colby Quarterly* 36, no. 2 (June 2000): 98–115.

43. Seamus Deane, "The Production of Cultural Space in Irish Writing," *Boundary 2*, no. 21 (1994): 116.

44. [T. H. Lister, unsigned review of *The Croppy, The Denounced, Yesterday in Ireland, The Collegians,* and *The Rivals*], *Edinburgh Review* 52 (Jan. 1831): 411–12.

45. For a discussion of such attempts to shift the "site of enunciation" from Britain to Ireland in early nineteenth-century Irish fiction, see Ina Ferris, "Narrating Cultural Encounter: Lady Morgan and the Irish National Tale," *Nineteenth-Century Literature* 51, no. 3 (Dec. 1996): 287–303.

"Distorted Nature in a Fever": *Irish Bulls,* Irish Novels, the 1798 Rebellion, and Their Gothic Contexts

Darryl Jones

On St. Valentine's Day 1834, with O'Connellite agitation for repeal of the Union uppermost in her mind, Maria Edgeworth wrote to her half brother, M. Pakenham Edgeworth, explaining the provenance of her latest novel, *Helen*:

> I should tell you beforehand that there is no humour in it, and no Irish character. It is impossible to draw Ireland as she is now in a book of fiction—realities are too strong, party passions too violent to bear to see, or care to look at their faces in a looking-glass. The people would only break the glass, and curse the fool who held the mirror up to nature—distorted nature in a fever.[1]

Thirty-three years earlier, *Castle Rackrent* anticipates this scene when Thady Quirk, observing Sir Condy Rackrent shaving in a broken mirror, states "presently I had the glimpse of him at the cracked glass over the chimney-piece, standing up to shaving himself to please my lady."[2] *Ennui* (1809) also contains a description of Irish politics and identity in terms of a metaphor of distorted vision, this time with reference to the 1798 rebellion. The Earl of Glenthorn exclaims of this event, "this time all objects were so magnified and distorted by the mist of prejudice that no inexperienced eye could judge of their real proportions" (247). *Ennui* closes its account of its protagonist Lord Glenthorn's role in the politics of 1798 with a maxim from Nicolas Boileau's *Art Poetique*:

> "Le vrai n'est pas toujours vraisemblable," says an acute observer of human affairs. The romance of real life certainly goes beyond all other romances; and there are facts which few writers would dare to put into a book. (273)

Jacqueline Belanger in this collection discusses the useful critical distinction between "le vrai" and the "vraisemblable," especially as used by underinformed critics in evaluating Irish tales, that is tales both by writers resident in and presumably informed by Ireland and tales by nonresidents about, and presumably less informed by Ireland. Those Irish tales that are expressions of "distorted nature in a fever" and that were written by Maria Edgeworth and her contemporaries coincided not only with the emergence and prominence of the "gothic" tradition in British literature, but also with the first generation of retrospective analyses of the political turmoil at the end of the eighteenth century, turmoil that in Ireland culminated in the rising of 1798 and the passage of the Act of Union in 1800. This combination of factors, political upheaval, the emergence of the "gothic," and a flourishing critical interest in the truth and truthfulness of Irish novels has led not only too frequently to an elision of Edgeworth's work with novels with which it shares, at best, only superficial similarities, but also to a significant and still common misunderstanding of the relationship between Anglo-Irish and Gothic mimesis.

In each of the examples quoted above, Gothic nationhood, the representation of Ireland (and also, it has to be said, of Wales and of Scotland) as a marginal space, allows for the occurrence of bizarre gothic events that are nonrepresentable in realist terms (the mimetic "mirror up to nature" that is cracked and distorted).[3] This rhetoric also found employment in attempts to represent political ideas and actions to an audience distinctly separate from those involved in those political activities. One specific instance in which this trope for the understanding and inscribing of Ireland is transferred into political writing surrounding the 1798 rebellion appears in the series of open letters "To the Earl of Moira" (that is, Moira in County Down), which, as 1798 progresses, turn increasingly toward the gothic as a means of representing Irish politics. I use these articles to draw comparisons with Edgeworth's own novel about 1798, *Ennui*, and later to Edgeworth's writing more generally. The Edgeworths knew the Moiras well, particularly Lady Moira, mother of the neighbor Lady Granard, and "a leader of Dublin intellectual life" who, according to Marilyn Butler, "took kindly notice of Maria" in Edgeworthstown. The second Earl of Moira, Francis Rawdon-Hastings, is believed to have been the original for the character of Vivian in *Leonora*.[4]

One place to begin consideration of the distinction between Irish gothic and its British counterpart is a novel published in 1818, first submitted for publication in 1803, and started and set, tellingly, in 1798, Jane Austen's *Northanger Abbey*. It is a novel suffused with "disquisition[s] on the state of the nation," with the language and ideas of 1790s politics, from the mass-meetings of the London Corresponding Society in the early 1790s, and the use of the military to put them down, to the activities of John Reeves's *agent provocateur* organization, the Association for Preserving Liberty and Property against Republicans and Levellers.[5] In chapter 24, Henry Tilney famously admonishes Catherine Morland for her fantasizing:

> "Dear Miss Morland, consider the dreadful nature of the suspicions you have entertained. What have you been judging from? Remember the country and the age in which we live. Remember that we are English, that we are Christians. Consult your own understanding, your own sense of the probable, your own observation of what is passing around you— Does our education prepare us for such atrocities? Do our laws connive at them? Could they be perpetrated without being known, in a country like this, where social and literary intercourse is on such a footing; where every man is surrounded by a neighbourhood of voluntary spies, and where roads and newspapers lay everything open. Dearest Miss Morland, what ideas have you been admitting?"[6]

The next chapter opens:

> Her visions of romance were over . . . charming as were all Mrs Radcliffe's works . . . it was not in them, perhaps, that human nature, at least in the midland counties of England was to be looked for. Of the Alps and Pyrenees, with their pine forests and their vines, they might give a faithful delineation; and Italy, Switzerland and the South of France might be as in horrors as were there represented. Catherine dared not think beyond her own country, and even of that, if hard pressed, would have yielded the northern and western extremities.[7]

"The northern and western extremities" are what are still in some circles known as the "Celtic fringe," and Austen's implication figures the marginal as the locus of weirdness. Away from the home counties, moving metaphorically backward in time, strange things happen—think, for example, of Charles Maturin's *Melmoth the Wanderer*, which moves from Trinity College, Dublin (clearly imaged in this novel as an ascendancy or colonial center point) beyond the pale to County Wicklow, and from there to the dungeons of the

Spanish Inquisition, tropical islands, and finally, at the bottom of the slippery slope, to hell itself; of Eliza Fenwick's *Secresy, or The Ruin on the Rock*, set in a remote Cornish castle; or even of William Godwin's *Caleb Williams*, where Caleb flees Falkland's tentacles to the farthest margins of Britain, ending up as a teacher in a remote Welsh village.[8] In *Ennui*, the fashionably bored wastrel hero, Lord Glenthorn, having blown his money, returns to his family estate in Ireland and finds himself being driven westward across the country by a maniac coachman in a rickety coach, and is, for the first time in his life, not bored: "though I complained bitterly, and swore it was impractical for a gentleman to travel in Ireland; yet I never remember to have experienced, on any journey, less ennui . . . upon this principle I should recommend to wealthy hypochondriacs a journey in Ireland, *preferably to any country in the civilized world*" (175–76).[9] This is because Ireland, and most particularly the west of Ireland, is liminal to the "civilized world." Glenthorn Castle, his destination, is "insulated, in all the gloomy grandeur of ancient times" (177), and has Lord Glenthorn, like Catherine Morland at Northanger, anticipating nights of Gothic restlessness out of an Ann Radcliffe novel, in what is the transposition of a Catholic, continental European sublime onto a domestic setting:

> The state tower . . . was hung with magnificent, but ancient tapestry. It was so like a room in a haunted castle, that if I had not been too fatigued to think of any thing, I should certainly have thought of Mrs Radcliffe . . . when I awoke, I thought that I was on shipboard; for the first sound I heard was that of the sea booming against the castle walls. I arose, looked out of the window of my bedchamber, and saw that the whole prospect bore an air of savage wildness. As I contemplated the scene, my imagination was seized with the idea of remoteness from civilized society. (179)

Ormond (1817), the last of Edgeworth's Irish novels, offers an analogous geographical matrix, but this time moving *toward* centers of "civilization," tracking its hero, Harry Ormond, from the Black Islands of the quasi-feudal Catholic King Corny and the mainland estate of the Protestant Sir Ulick O'Shea to Dublin, and from there to London and to Paris.

Ennui and *Ormond*, with their ever-moving casts of characters, are among the novels upon which Terry Eagleton muses when he considers the question of why there appear to be so few instances of classic nineteenth-century realism in novels from Ireland:

> The realist novel is the form par excellence of settlement and stability, gathering individual lives into an integrated whole; and social conditions in Ireland hardly lent themselves to any such sanguine resolution. What resolutions the Irish novel does bring off have a notably factitious ring to them, fabular inventions or schematic devices which cut against the grain of the fiction itself.[10]

In this vein, there is much circumstantial evidence, and not only from Ireland, that political or cultural disenfranchisement leads to the production of nonrealistic, melodramatic, or even Gothic tropes. Often, as with Eagleton, such thinking draws on Raymond Williams's idea that the realist form presupposes a social stability commensurate with its narrative stability, and thus that it tends to be an ideologically centralizing form and is consequently reliant on conditions that simply did not obtain in Ireland.[11]

This argument is so persuasive that it has almost become accepted as received wisdom.[12] There are, however, a few problems here. Firstly, there is the fact that much of what is now recognized as the most notable Irish Gothic was not really the product of the disenfranchised community within Ireland, but of the remnants of the colonizing class; or, to put it another way, the argument would make more sense had Charles Maturin, William Maginn, Sheridan LeFanu, FitzJames O'Brien, Oscar Wilde, Bram Stoker *et al.* been students at Maynooth rather than at Trinity College, Dublin. Eagleton, like W. J. McCormack and Roy Foster, attempts to explain this "Protestant Gothic" (or in Foster's term, "Protestant Magic") in terms of kinds of political unconscious and collective fears, but this seems to be eliding the direct issue—Gothic becomes, by this reading, the representation of the fear by a landlord class of the potential for anarchy or violence from among its underlings—a very different matter than a manifestation of disenfranchisement.[13] This is not to argue that there is no connection between Protestantism and the Gothic; for, clearly there is, as *Melmoth the Wanderer* testifies. However, the connection is very complex. [14]

The more problematic aspect to Eagleton's dictum, and those like it, is that they are simply too close in sentiment, if not in tone, to the quotes from Edgeworth and Austen. All figure Ireland as a site of turbulence and, therefore, of the production of the fabulous: Ireland, as nonrepresentable in realist terms. We know this kind of thinking primarily from Matthew Arnold's lectures on Celtic literature, and we also know the Arnoldian ideological subtext (if it is even a subtext) to "Celtic Magic"—Eagleton and company, albeit with benign intention, seem to me to be repeating this paradigm (the same could be said of Declan Kiberd's now-famous suggestion that Ireland is "England's unconscious," athough Kiberd seems well aware of this).[15]

The situation at the time was more complex, as were the generative impulses behind the fiction that would evolve into "Irish gothic." If this term is even appropriate, it is not as easy to categorize as the assumptions outlined above would suggest. Take *Ennui*'s possible germinal idea, for example. Toward the end of 1797, Francis Rawdon-Hastings, the Earl of Moira, called in the British and Irish Houses of Lords for an investigation into the situation in Ireland, bringing to the Parliaments' attentions a series of atrocities and misdeeds committed against the Irish by the English and their hirelings. Moira's proposal was debated in College Green, Dublin, on 19 February 1798; an inquiry was refused, though at the cost of public embarrassment to Pitt's government. Lord Moira, a political liberal who went on to speak against the Union in 1799, was perceived, in Kevin Whelan's phrase, as a "fellow traveler" to United Irishmen sentiments—with some justification, as he got much of his information from the United Irishmen lawyer William Sampson, who had founded the Society for Obtaining Authentic Information of Outrages Committed on the People.[16]

For what we might call an official version of these events and the reaction to them, I shall turn to Sir Richard Musgrave's *Memoirs of the Different Rebellions in Ireland*. Musgrave's "instant history," first published in 1801, is generally reckoned to be the authentic voice of frothing Unionism, although Tom Dunne has recently suggested that his sources, at least, are generally sound:[17]

> In the month of February, the Earl of Moira came to Ireland, with a professed design of appeasing the disturbances which disgraced his native country, by recommending the government . . . discontinue the system of rigorous coercion which they had for some time adopted, and to which he attributed those evils; and by advising them to relax the penal laws recently enacted, and to use mild and conciliatory measures, as the only means of restoring peace and social order . . .
>
> Experience has since evinced how much his lordship was mistaken; the following incident proves how vain, how futile, and absurd it is, for any person of high birth and large fortune to expect to gain the affections of the populace by stooping to flatter their prejudices. His lordship had courted popularity in the county of Down, where he had

resided and his estate lay; and nobody can doubt but that he really merited it, for his humane and beneficent disposition: And yet, at a county meeting of united Irishmen held at Saintfield on the fourth of February 1798, the following paragraph appeared in the course of their proceedings on that day:

"Nothing particular was done, except that earl Moira's character was discussed at full length, to know, whether he was a man that could be depended on, or not, by the people? It was agreed that he was as great a tyrant as the lord lieutenant, and a deeper designing one!"[18]

Musgrave's account of Moira here is quite evenhanded: a recognition of a tolerant, humane landlord, but one who is also naïve and hopelessly out of his depth in the bloody world of Jacobin insurrection, an unwitting dupe of evil men.

Interestingly, *Ennui* seems to offer, in the person of Lord Glenthorn, a representation of a Moira-type landlord, potentially sympathetic to the rebel cause, and certainly perceived as being so: the rebels, Ellinor tells him, "would make Lord Glenthorn their captain, or have his life" (262). More broadly, what *Ennui* obviously does is to depict the position of Enlightenment-liberal Irish landlords such as Moira and, of course, Richard Lovell Edgeworth, faced with violent nationalist rebellion. While recognizing with some clarity a series of political injustices which lead to this violence, *Ennui* nevertheless stops far short of endorsing any radical social overhaul, resolving itself instead into a manifesto for land management and social status based on individual decency. Typically for Edgeworth—and perhaps this is inevitable given her position as an Irish ascendancy liberal—*Ennui* displays a considerable ideological ambiguity toward the rebellion. Mr. McLeod, the Adam Smith-reading land agent and the voice of Enlightenment rationality within the novel, begins an explanation of the sociology of rebellion: "My Lord, if we consider the condition of these poor people, and if we consider the causes—" (257). It is also worth noting that although the rebels attempt to kidnap and coerce Glenthorn it is the Protestant militia, led by McLeod's antitype, the corrupt agent Mr. Hardcastle, who are the instigators of violence and brutality in the novel: "I was more shocked," Lord Glenthorn's narrative records, "at the summary proceedings of my neighbours than alarmed at the symptoms of insurrection" (245). While McLeod puts his educational theories into practice in the schoolhouse he builds "on a little estate of his own in my neighbourhood" ("I almost thought myself in England," Lord

Glenthorn remarks) (215), Hardcastle expresses his belief that education leads to violence and rebellion:

> "Then, sir, in this country, where's the advantage of education, I humbly ask? No, sir, no, trust me—keep the Irish common people ignorant, and you keep 'em quiet; and that's the only way with them, for they are too quick and smart as it is, naturally. Teach them to read and write, and it's just adding fuel to fire—fire to gunpowder, sir. Teach them any thing, and directly you *set them up*: now it's our business to *keep them down*, unless, sir, you'd wish to have your throat cut." (193)

As early as January 1796, Edgeworth was writing of her own fears: "All that I crave for my own part is, that if I am to have my throat cut, it may not be by a man with his face blackened with charcoal."[19] The militia's raid on the cottage of Glenthorn's foster brother, the blacksmith Christy O'Donoghoe, which results in Christy being shot in the arm, leads directly to Glenthorn's involvement in the cause. It is this passage that closes with the metaphorical account of the turbulence of Irish politics in terms of distorted vision that I quoted above:

> *The rebels were up,* and *the rebels were down*—and Lord Glenthorn's spirited conduct in the chair, and indefatigable exertions in the field, were the theme of daily eulogium amongst my convivial companions and immediate dependants. But, unfortunately, my sudden activity gained me no credit amongst the violent party of my neighbours, who persisted in their suspicions; and my reputation was still more injured, by the alternate charge of being a trimmer or a traitor. Nay, I was further exposed to another danger, of which, from my ignorance of the country, I could not possibly be aware. The disaffected themselves, as I afterwards found, really believed, that, as I had not begun by persecuting the poor, I must be a favourer of the rebels; and all that I did to bring the guilty to justice, they thought was only to give a *colour to the thing,* till the proper moment should come for my declaring myself. (247)

Most directly, this is a fictionalized rendition of Richard Lovell Edgeworth's position in 1798 as one of a number of liberal landlords in County Longford (his neighbor the Earl of Granard was another) caught up in the crisis. Furthermore, Edgeworth himself *was* potentially sympathetic toward United Irishmen thinking. Although the *Memoirs of Richard Lovell Edgeworth* discusses his role in the events of 1798 in some depth, these events are recounted in the second volume, collated from her father's papers by Maria Edgeworth, and she tended to downplay or even excise her father's more overt radicalism. As Marilyn Butler notes:

> that winter, 1784–85 . . . [RLE] was one of the few representatives of the gentry to attend a . . . Congress on reform in Dublin. His fellow delegates included Napper Tandy, Todd Jones, Hamilton Rowan, William Drennan—all Dublin and Belfast radicals who in the 1790s were to belong to the revolutionary movement, the United Irishmen.[20]

Maria Edgeworth omits any mention of this in her section of the *Memoirs*, and, as Tom Dunne suggests, this is a tendency which recurs also in her fiction: "Maria never shared . . . [RLE's] libertarian ideology, and the reflection of her father's views in the novels had always been mediated through her innately conservative cast of mind."[21]

In *Ennui*, the account of the militia under "Mr. (now *Captain*) Hardcastle" (245) fictionalizes the activities of the ultra-Protestant "Granard rangers" in County Longford. The *Memoirs of Richard Lovell Edgeworth* also records their activities in the summer of 1798, and the suspicion with which they treated Edgeworth's liberalism:

> [F]or want of resident gentlemen, magistrates were made of men without education, experience, or hereditary respectability. During the war, and in consequence of what were called the *war-prices*, graziers, landjobbers, and middle-men had risen into comparative wealth; and instead of turning in due season, according to the natural order of things, into Buckeens and Squireens, they had been metamorphosed into justices of the peace and committee-men, or into yeoman lieutenants and captains . . . Upon slight suspicion, or vague information, they took up and imprisoned many who were innocent; the relations of the injured appealed to . . . [my father], who was known to be the friend of public justice . . . [and who] exerted himself upon all occasions, to keep the law in its due course, representing that, whether the accused were innocent or guilty, they were entitled to a fair trial . . . Those who were conscious of making themselves objects of dislike to the lower class of people . . . disregarded my father's representations, as far as they dared, and resented his interference; and were in unfeigned astonishment at his opposite course of conduct.[22]

Edgeworthstown itself was attacked by a rebel mob and the Edgeworths forced to flee. That their house was left untouched (the Edgeworths' housekeeper had once done a kindness to the rebel leader's wife) led to Richard Lovell Edgeworth's political sympathies being further scrutinized: he himself was attacked by Orangemen in Longford town and had to be rescued by the army.²³ Further suspicion greeted Edgeworth's attempt to raise a nonsectarian infantry corps:

> He raised a corps of infantry, into which he admitted Catholics as well as Protestants. This was so unusual, and thought so hazardous a degree of liberality, that by some of an opposite party it was attributed to the worst motives. Many who wished him well came privately, to let him know of the odium, to which he exposed himself—and the timid hinted fears and suspicions, that he was going to put arms into the hands of men, who would desert or betray him in the hour of trial.²⁴

Ennui, while depicting a violent rising, conceals a more profound social revolution: Lord Glenthorn, the returned Protestant absentee landlord, is discovered to have been switched in infancy with the man who is now the village blacksmith, Christy O'Donoghoe. The two switch places, the "rightful" (Catholic, Irish, peasant) Lord Glenthorn reluctantly sets himself up in the castle—the fake Lord Glenthorn, now a Protestant calling himself Mr. Christopher O'Donoghue, makes a career for himself as a Dublin lawyer. While the castle falls into disrepair and burns down, and the novel ends with a letter from the original Christy imploring the new Christy to become Lord Glenthorn once again, a kind of revolution has taken place, suggesting at the very least a social mechanics of the kind espoused throughout the novel by Mr. McLeod, based on merit and talent rather than on birth and blood.

The foundational text for Edgeworth here is obviously Edmund Spenser's *A View of the Present State of Ireland* (1633), a book that her father had given her shortly after their arrival in Ireland. Tom Dunne, though his view of Edgeworth and the Irish here lacks subtlety, has drawn out the parallels between Edgeworth's position in Anglo-Irish polity and Spenser's some two hundred years earlier:

> Like Spenser, she presented a stereotype of the native Irish, which suited her recipe for the Anglicization of all aspects of Irish life—in her case a benevolent, improving landlordism. This stereotype reflected the major Spenserian theme of the seductive as well as the hostile and degraded nature of native society together with her greater optimism about the possibility of exploiting its surviving mores in the interests of loyalism and social deference. It was what she perceived as the quasi-feudal na-

ture of that society which constituted for Maria 'its dangerous seductiveness' and its real potential.[25]

In *Ennui*, Cecil Devereux aspires to be a poet, and admires Spenser:

> He took Spenser's poems out of the book-case, and I actually rose from my seat to read the passage . . .
> "Very strong, indeed," said I, with a competent air, as if used to judge of poetry.
> "And it comes with still greater force, when we consider by whom it was written. A man, you know, my lord, who had been secretary to a lord lieutenant." (219)

Whether or not Devereux's poetic ambitions are fulfilled, he does exit the novel in Spenserian fashion, having secured a post as a colonial administrator in India. Clearly, this kind of colonial exoticism is in part here a figure for Ireland.[26]

In the same novel, Lady Geraldine amuses herself by fobbing off her cousin, Lord Craiglethorpe, who is writing a book on Ireland, with a series of fake bulls and phony Irishry. Lighthearted though the intention might be, Lady Geraldine is also making a serious political point about the essentially clichéd assumptions made by the English when it comes to defining the Irish:

> after posting from Dublin to Cork, and from the Giants' Causeway to Killarney; after travelling east, west, north and south, my wise cousin Craiglethorpe will know just as much of the lower Irish as the cockney who has never been out of London, and who has never, *in all his born days*, seen an Irishman but on the English stage; where the representations are usually as like the originals, as the Chinese pictures of lions, drawn from description, are to the real animal. (211–12)

Self-evidently, this passage derives much of its impetus and resonance from the Edgeworths' own *Essay on Irish Bulls*. Although Butler describes *Irish Bulls* as "not explicitly political at all," the opposite seems to me to be the case.[27] Published in the shadow of the Union in 1802 by the radical publisher Joseph Johnson (the Edgeworths' regular publisher), *Irish Bulls* is an unambiguously radical document. As Brian Hollingworth, one of the few commentators to have looked at *Irish Bulls* in any depth, suggests, "its timing and argument are strongly motivated by political intention. It reflects [the Edgeworths'] response to the rebellion and the Act of

Union."[28] Indeed, the Edgeworths' connection with Johnson came to be a concern, tainting them with accusations of Jacobinism, accusations which, on R. L. Edgeworth's part, were not without justification. As Butler notes, partly because of his connections with the radical scientists of the Birmingham Lunar Society, he was drawn to sympathy with the politics of revolutionary France: "In Ireland, among a landed gentry outnumbered ten to one by land-hungry peasants who were traditionally pro-foreign because they were Catholic, views like this increasingly laid a man open to being misunderstood."[29] Of the connection with Johnson, Maria Edgeworth's stepmother later wrote that "he became too much connected with [William] Godwin and [Thomas] Holcroft, and it was afterwards a disadvantage to Maria that her works were published by the printer of what were considered seditious and sectarian books."[30] Nevertheless, the connection persisted: R. Hunter, the publisher of *Memoirs of Richard Lovell Edgeworth*, advertises himself on the title page to that book as "Successor to Mr. Johnson."

Castle Rackrent's preface, written by R. L. Edgeworth and followed in all editions to 1815 by the "Advertisement to the English Reader," famously notes that "to those who are totally unacquainted with Ireland, the following Memoirs will perhaps be scarcely intelligible, or probably they may appear perfectly incredible. For the information of the *ignorant* English reader, a few notes have been subjoined by the editor."[31] *Irish Bulls*, also clearly directed at "the *ignorant* English reader," is a sustained refutation of the perception of the Irish as irrational, dismissing such prejudices as a violation of Enlightenment principles of employing "that admirable degree of scepticism which is necessary in judging a national cause with impartiality."[32] In drawing attention to English pre- and misconceptions about Ireland, *Irish Bulls* illuminates the attitudes and assumptions that would allow Irish fiction aimed at an English audience to assume, or be assumed to have assumed, the tropes of the gothic.

By beginning with an exegesis of the etymology of the bull, in Irish bulls, papal bulls, and John Bull, the Edgeworths connect and symbolically unite Ireland, Catholicism, and England, as if hitting upon an encapsulating symbol for the Irish problem, which, only half playfully, they redefine as an *English* problem, recalling that Jonathan Swift, "a man every way qualified to decide this matter, believed that bulls were of English origin, and therefore should properly be called ENGLISH bulls" (12). In a period of ferocious anti-French paranoia in England, and furthermore in the wake of the 1798 rebellion that saw French troops land on Irish soil to aid the cause of the rebels against the English, the Edgeworths in *Irish Bulls* also symbolically unite Ireland and France against England, as historic victims of English prejudice, in what can only be viewed as a direct reference to recent events:

> That species of monopolising pride, which inspires one nation with the belief that the rest of the world are barbarians, and speak barbarisms, is evidently a very useful prejudice, which the English, with their usual good sense, have condescended to adopt from the Greeks and Romans. They have applied it judiciously in the treatment of France and Ireland. The maxim, that one Englishman can beat ten Frenchman, has undoubtedly gained many a battle on sea and land. (19)

The examples adduced in *Irish Bulls* are often broadly political, drawing their substance from the contemporary Irish situation and attempting a rational explanation of Irish politics for "the *ignorant* English reader." Thus we have proclamations from Irish mayors, or from the Lord Lieutenant, about the consumption of grain and potatoes; disquisitions on the sale of estates containing woodland and turf-bogs; a dispute between a poor Irish widow and her landlord over the repossession and sale of a cow (the landlord, it transpires, is also poor and Irish).[33] The tale of the "Hibernian Mendicant" touches on the relationship between politics and religion, England and Ireland. The mendicant argues with an Englishman:

> "And the talk grew higher and higher; and from talking of blunders and such trifles, we got, I cannot myself tell you how, on to great party matters, and politics, and religion. And I was a catholic, and he a protestant; and there he had the thing against me." (153–54)

In a manner even more unambiguous than the account of English prejudice and its role in subjugating the Irish and defeating the French in battle, some of the bulls deal directly with the matter and events of 1798. There are many instances, such as this, on the trials and questioning of the United Irishmen: "When some *united man*, as they called themselves, were examined, they frequently answered to the questions, who, or what are you? I am a committee" (51–52).

The bulls themselves often reflect, foreshadow, or otherwise resemble events from Edgeworth's Irish novels, suggesting that the novels themselves might occupy broadly a similar ideological position as *Irish Bulls* and be part of a greater project for the definition and understanding of contemporary Irish politics and life. The very first bull analyzed in *Irish Bulls* turns on what is to be the narrative crux of *Ennui*, two children switched at birth by a nurse, and the issues of identity that this raises:

> Lord Orford, better known perhaps in the literary world by the name of Horace Walpole, records in his Walpoliana an irish bull, which he pronounces to be the best that he had ever heard—"I hate that woman," said a gentleman, looking at a person who had been his nurse, "I hate that woman; for she changed me at nurse." (21)

The Edgeworths go on to disprove the illogicality of this bull philosophically, with reference to John Locke, and to examine its antecedents in *Don Quixote* and Molière. But the novel which *Irish Bulls* most clearly anticipates is, of course, *The Absentee*. The notion that establishes the ideological position laid out in *Irish Bulls*, that "nobody in England may be somebody in Ireland," is a central contention of *The Absentee*: "lord Clonbrony, who was somebody in Ireland, who was a great person in Dublin, found himself nobody in England, a mere cipher in London."[34]

Visiting Ireland and his estate, Lord Colambre disguises himself as a Welshman, Mr. Evans, on a copper-mining expedition to Ireland. The Welsh identity here has clear narrative and ideological advantages for the novel. Not being Irish, Mr. Evans needs an education in Irish politics, and particularly in the politics of Irish landlordism, thus enabling Edgeworth to demonstrate a series of abuses to "the *ignorant* English reader," and in so doing to fulfill *The Absentee*'s political aim. But it is only because Mr. Evans is *not* English, but rather a citizen of a nation similarly colonized and disenfranchised *by* the English, that the Irish peasants and tenants are willing honestly to describe the specifics of their victimization to him.[35]

The Edgeworths, and later Maria alone, understood the opportunities offered by English assumptions about Ireland and Irishness to writers who might wish to refute one set of stereotypes while seeking to avoid having to take a limiting stance of their own. It was a position that was disconcerting, at best, to many of their contemporaries. Throughout 1797–98, the *Anti-Jacobin*, a journal whose ideological position needs no elucidation, ran a series of open letters to the Earl of Moira which it used as a springboard for its views on the Irish crisis. The first of the letters, published on 30 November 1797, is mild enough, its views anticipating the slightly later judgment of Musgrave:

Does your Lordship not know, that before the meeting of the Irish Parliament in November 1796, an alarming conspiracy was generally conceived to exist, which has since been detected; and that many Baronies throughout the North were in a state of the greatest insubordination and tumult? Is not your Lordship aware, that this Conspiracy had for its object the reduction of Rents, the division of Property, the abolition of Tythes, the absolute *destruction* of *Government,* and a *general massacre* of the principal Gentry throughout the Provinces? Was not the Constitution nearly put down, and the laws in general silenced, by a system of terror gradually extending itself over the Country, and threatening in its progress both a dissolution of Government and Society? Can any impartial spectator, then in the Country, deny this? At this period, your Lordship was in England; you are therefore entitled to call for proofs. Perhaps, if you had been upon the spot, the scandal of the scene would have impressed upon your Lordship's mind the necessity of being a little more cautious in relying so implicitly upon your channels of intelligence. You would have then seen a Country rich in population, soil and industry, in the wantonness of prosperity conspiring against its own happiness, and driven to the verge of Insurrection through the Diabolical machinations of traitors and demogogues.[36]

As the crisis deepened throughout 1798, so did the rhetoric of the *Anti-Jacobin* become more vitriolic, singling out Moira as a target. The journal, and others like it, were certainly not above conducting smear campaigns against individuals, but what is interesting about the attacks on Moira is their increasing fabulism, their representation of the Irish situation in a way which should, I hope, be familiar. As early as 8 January, the journal contained a letter dated "Dublin, December 29, 1798" and signed "An Irishman," smearing Moira by recourse to the apparent insanity of his father:

At a time when the Public attention in England has been very particularly called to the patriotic zeal, correctness, and propriety, with which a Noble Lord has given, in the Upper House of Parliament, his account of the Insurrection upon his estates, and in other parts of the North of Ireland; it must be highly interesting to your readers, to see the account given by the late Earl of Moira, in the Irish House of Lords, of the Insurrections upon his estates, and in other parts of the North of Ireland, in the year 1770. His Lordship's speech is not entered upon the Journals of the House of Lords; but it is given at length in a collection of essays called *The Batchelor,* printed in this City in 1772; from No. 29 of which, page 171, the following extract is taken *verbatim.*

It is recommended to public notice, as a most convincing proof of the abilities, veracity, and Patriotism of the Noble Speaker, and as a *model for such Narratives bequeathed by him to posterity.*

LORD MOIRA—"My Lords, I rise to return my thanks to the Noble Lord who spoke last. I can testify to the truth of all he has asserted. At the time of the insurrection in the North, I had frequent and intimate conversations with that celebrated Enchanter, *MOLL COGGIN.* I have often seen her riding on a black ram with a blue tail. Once I endeavoured to fire at her, but my gun melted in my hand into a clear jelly. This jelly I tasted, and had it been a little more acid, it would have been excellent . . . Once, I pursued this Fiend into my Ale Cellar: she rose instantly out of my sight into the bung hole of a Beer Barrel. She was at that time mounted on her black ram with a blue tail. Some time after, my servants were much surprized to find their Ale full of blue hairs . . . This MOLL COGGIN was the Fiend who raised the Oak-boys to Rebellion . . . I have known one of them tear up by the roots an Oak two hundred feet tall, and bear it upright in his head for four miles: his party were on that account called the Oak-boys. Noble Lords may laugh, but I speak from certain knowledge."[37]

Is this genuine? Insofar as it is a verbatim passage from the *Batchelor,* yes it is; insofar as it is an actual account of a parliamentary debate, no it is not. *The Batchelor: or Speculations of Jeoffry Wagstaffe, Esq.* was a satirical magazine, modelling itself upon the *Tatler,* which was published in Dublin between 1766 and 1773. The first edition has an engraving of "Jeoffry Wagstaffe, Esq." holding a quill pen, underneath which is an epigraph from Virgil that translates as "Trust not to My Face"; its manifesto states: "Two subjects I shall avoid, politics and scandal."[38] Politics and scandal are, in fact, *The Batchelor's* only subjects. The debate to which the *Anti-Jacobin* refers is a spoof, a debate between Lord Babeltongue (who recites a Pindaric Ode to himself mid-speech), Lord Verax ("Truthful"; that's Moira), Thomas Decorous Letriffle, Lord Forecastle and Will Spitfire—satirized versions of genuine Irish parliamentarians.[39] Lord Verax ends his speech on Moll Coggin by claiming that, for telling the truth to the Lord Lieutenant, he was kicked downstairs, and offers to show the assembly the bruises on his posterior; Letriffle suggests that a public viewing would be indecorous, and that his backside should be shown to a "secret committee."

That the *Anti-Jacobin* should offer such obvious nonsense as serious is largely, of course, because it was in its own political interests to do so. That it should be able to do this, I am suggesting, is because such an account partakes of a discourse that traditionally sought to figure Ireland as beyond realistic representation, and therefore available to Edgeworth for her purposes, as much as to others who attempt to document Ireland in its distorted gothicism.

Notes

1. Augustus J. C. Hare, ed. *Life and Letters of Maria Edgeworth* (London: Edward Arnold, 1894), 2: 202.

2. Maria Edgeworth, *Castle Rackrent* and *Ennui*, ed. Marilyn Butler (Hammondsworth: Penguin, 1992), 102. Though he does not make reference to the letter quoted above, Brian Caraher has recently shown how this image of the broken glass is a resonant one in Irish writing more generally as a political metaphor. The opening chapter of *Ulysses* contains the following famous exchange between Buck Mulligan and Stephen Dedalus, who is looking at his face in Mulligan's mirror, "cleft by a crooked crack":

> Laughing again, he brought the mirror away from Stephen's peering eyes.
> —The rage of Caliban at not seeing his face in a mirror, he said. If Wilde were only alive to see you!
> Drawing Back and pointing, Stephen said with bitterness:—It is a symbol of Irish Art. The cracked lookingglass of a servant. (James Joyce, *Ulysses: The Corrected Text* (New York: Vintage, 1986), 2: 135–36, 141–46).

Future references to *Ennui* are given parenthetically.

3. For accounts, some sceptical, of a "Gothic" Wales or Scotland, see C. W. Sullivan, "A Wizard Behind Every Bush," *Planet* 64 (Aug./Sept. 1987): 48–51; Tony Bianchi, "Aztecs in Troedrhiwgwair," in *Peripheral Visions: Images of Nationhood in Contemporary British Fiction*, ed. Ian A. Bell (Cardiff: University of Wales Press, 1995), 44–76; Dorothy McMillan, "Constructed Out of Bewilderment: Stories of Scotland," in Bell, 80–102.

4. Marilyn Butler, *Maria Edgeworth: A Literary Biography* (Oxford: Oxford University Press: 1972), 98, 258.

5. See Warren Roberts, *Jane Austen and the French Revolution* (Basingstoke: Macmillan, 1979), 22–31.

6. Jane Austen, *Northanger Abbey*, ed. Anne H. Ehrenpreis (Harmondsworth: Penguin, 1972), 199–200. For Henry Tilney's "disquisition on the state of the nation," see 126.

7. Austen, *Northanger Abbey*, 201.

8. My favorite example of this comes not from the Romantic period, but from H. P. Lovecraft's 1926 pulp horror story, "The Call of Cthulhu." A strange religious cult, characterized by barbarism, makes its presence felt simultaneously in many parts of the world; the cult strongly affects those of, in Lovecraft's terms, "backward" or "degenerate" races: "A dispatch from California describes a theosophist colony as donning white robes en masse for some 'glorious fulfillment' which never arrives, whilst items from India speak guardedly of serious native unrest towards the end of March. Voodoo orgies multiply in Haiti, and African outposts report ominous mutterings. American officers in the Philippines find certain tribes bothersome about this time, and New York policemen are mobbed by hysterical Levantines on the night of 22–23 March. The west of Ireland, too, is full of wild

rumour and legendry." Lovecraft, "The Call of Cthulhu," in *Omnibus 3: The Haunter in the Dark* (London: HarperCollins, 1994), 69–70. Lovecraft's views on race might charitably be described as unambiguous: On his arrival in New York in the 1920s, he wrote of the "loathsome Asiatic hordes who drag their dirty carcasses over streets where white men once moved": quoted in Colin Wilson, Introduction, in Lovecraft, *Crawling Chaos: Selected Works 1920–1935* (London: Creation, 1992), n. p.

9. Emphasis added.

10. Terry Eagleton, "Form and Ideology in the Anglo-Irish Novel," *Heathcliff and the Great Hunger: Studies in Irish Culture* (London: Verso, 1995), 146.

11. See Raymond Williams, *The County and the City* (London: Hogarth, 1993), 165–81, and *passim*, for the brilliant original of this argument about the ideology of realism.

12. For the classic version of this argument, analyzing the role of melodrama as a "substitute franchise," see Frank Rahill, *The World of Melodrama* (University Park: The Pennsylvania State University Press, 1967), xvi–xviii. See also Peter Brook, *The Melodramatic Imagination: Balzac, Henry James, Melodrama and the Mode of Excess* (New Haven: Yale University Press, 1976), xi and passim.

13. Eagleton, *Heathcliff and the Great Hunger*, 187–88. See also W. J. McCormack, Introduction to "Irish Gothic and After, 1820–1945," in *The Field Day Anthology of Irish Writing*, ed. Seamus Deane, vol. 2 (Derry: Field Day, 1991), 831–53; R. F. Foster, "Protestant Magic: W. B. Yeats and the Spell of History," *Proceedings of the British Academy* 75 (1989). See also Christopher Morash, "The Time is Out of Joint (O Cursèd Spite): Towards a Definition of Supernatural Narrative," in *That Other World: The Supernatural and Fantastic in Irish Literature and its Contexts*, ed. Bruce Stewart, 2 vols (Gerrards Cross: Colin Smythe, 1998), 123–42.

14. See Victor Sage, *Horror Fiction in the Protestant Tradition* (Basingstoke: Macmillan, 1988) for a lengthy analysis of the relationship between Gothic and Protestantism.

15. See Declan Kiberd, "Ireland—England's Unconscious," in *Inventing Ireland: The Literature of a Modern Nation* (London: Jonathan Cape, 1995), 29–32.

16. See Kevin Whelan, *The Liberty Tree: Radicalism, Catholicism and the Construction of Irish Identity 1760–1830*, Critical Conditions: Field Day Essays, no. 1 (Cork: Cork University Press, 1996), 137. For an account of Lord Moira's speech, upon which I draw heavily here, see Nancy J. Curtin, *The United Irishmen: Popular Politics in Ulster and Dublin 1791–1798* (Oxford: Clarendon, 1994), 216–17.

17. Tom Dunne, "The Scullabogue Massacre" (paper delivered at the Royal Irish Academy Conference, Dublin, April 1998).

18. Sir Richard Musgrave, Bart, *Memoirs of the Different Rebellions in Ireland*, ed. Steven W. Myers and Dolores E. McKnight (Fort Wayne, Ind.: Round Tower Books, 1995), 178–79.

19. Edgeworth, *Life and Letters*, 1: 42.

20. Butler, *Maria Edgeworth*, 96.

21. Tom Dunne, "'A gentleman's estate should be a moral school': Edgeworthstown in Fact and Fiction, 1760–1840," in *Longford: Essays in County History*, eds. Raymond Gillespie and Gerard Moran (Dublin: Lilliput, 1991), 104.

22. Richard Lovell Edgeworth and Maria Edgeworth, *Memoirs of Richard Lovell Edgeworth, Esq. Begun by Himself and Concluded by his Daughter, Maria Edgeworth* (London, 1820), 2: 205–7.

23. See Dunne, "A gentleman's estate," 105.
24. *Memoirs*, 2: 212.
25. Dunne, "A gentleman's estate," 98.
26. Edgeworth is fond of smuggling colonists, nabobs, or planters into her work, like the Creole slaver Mr. Vincent in *Belinda*, or, Dominick O'Reilly, also serving in India, in the *Essay on Irish Bulls*. It is also worth noting in passing here that Francis Rawdon-Hastings, the Earl of Moira, was made Governor-General of Bengal in 1813.
27. Butler, *Maria Edgeworth*, 364.
28. Brian Hollingworth, *Maria Edgeworth's Irish Writing: Language, History, Politics* (Basingstoke: Macmillan, 1997), 48.
29. Butler, *Maria Edgeworth*, 111–12.
30. Qtd in Butler, *Maria Edgeworth*, 124.
31. Edgeworth, *Castle Rackrent*, 63.
32. Richard Lovell Edgeworth and Maria Edgeworth, *An Essay on Irish Bulls*, 2d ed., corrected (London, 1803), 3.
33. Edgeworth and Edgeworth, *Irish Bulls*, 37, 38, 41–42, 174–78.
34. Maria Edgeworth, *The Absentee*, ed. W. J. McCormack and Kim Walker (Oxford: Oxford University Press, 1988), 21.
35. Similarly, it is a Scotsman, Mr. McLeod, who is most clear-sighted about the abuses in *Ennui*.
36. *The Anti-Jacobin; or, Weekly Examiner* 3 (Thursday, 30 Nov. 1797): 17.
37. *The Anti-Jacobin* 9 (Monday, 8 Jan. 1798): 70.
38. *The Batchelor: or Speculations of Jeoffry Wagstaffe, Esq.*, 3 vols. (Dublin, 1769–73), vol. 1 (1769): 3.
39. *The Bachelor* 3 (1773): 166–75.

National Character and Foreclosed Irishness: A Reconsideration of *Ennui*

Kathleen Costello-Sullivan

> The Irish national character is degraded, disordered; till this recover itself, nothing is yet recovered. Immethodic, headlong, violent, mendacious: what can you make of the wretched Irishman? . . . Such a people circulates not order but disorder through every vein of it;—and the cure, if it is to be a cure, must begin at the heart: not in his condition only *but in himself* must the Patient be all changed. Poor Ireland!
>
> —Thomas Carlyle, "Chartism"[1]

THOMAS CARLYLE'S ESSAY, "CHARTISM," REFLECTS THE LATE EIGHTEENTH- and early nineteenth-century British "obsession" with the question of national character and the debate over whether Ireland could be made a suitably civilized partner for its sister country, England.[2] Carlyle articulates a common English perception of this Irish national character, a source of frustration and concern for England in its hope to rehabilitate the wild and rebellious Irish.

Central to critical readings of Maria Edgeworth's 1809 novel *Ennui* are questions relating to how and why the Anglo-Irish sought to reform the Irish national character. Unlike Carlyle, who locates the defect of Irish character in the "heart," Edgeworth pinpoints the supposed flaw of the Irish in the mind. Her conclusion to the *Memoirs of Richard Lovell Edgeworth*, using her father's own words, signals her belief that the "problem" with the Irish is fundamentally one of education: "[T]he misfortunes of Ireland were owing not to the heart, but the head; and the defect was not from nature, but from want of culture."[3] Unlike Carlyle, who suggests the necessity for utter transformation of the Irish, Edgeworth suggests that the Irish national character can be reformed through education.

Reflecting Edgeworth's own emphasis on education, critics have generally concurred that *Ennui* is, at its core, didactic and concerned with reforming and educating Anglo-Irish landlords and Irish peasants alike.[4] Earlier interpretations often dismissed the text as transparently moralistic, pedagogical, and, consequently, even "boring."[5] However, recent criticism has produced more nuanced theoretical readings that engage questions of national character, cultural difference, and colonial negotiation.[6] Yet what is often elided in considering the difference between Carlyle's "cure" that "begin[s] at the heart" and Edgeworth's remedy to "misfortunes... owing not to the heart, but the head" is the fundamental similarity between the two proffered interpretations. In spite of their seeming disagreement, both Carlyle and Edgeworth accept the need for the Irish to undergo not just a perceptual or behavioral shift, but rather a *fundamental* alteration, as Carlyle suggests and as Edgeworth effects fictionally.

Although Edgeworth touts the rehabilitating effects of education, it is important to note that this education creates not evolution but utter transformation in her characters. Like Carlyle, then, Edgeworth believes that "*in himself* must the Patient be all changed." Thus, while critics have variously spoken of Lord Glenthorn's evolving relationship to Irishness in *Ennui* as one of "repression," of "nonblood kinship," of paternalistic evolution, or as reflective of the "interdependence of Irish identities,"[7] I will suggest that education functions not as a catalyst for identification or repression but, rather, as a process that exposes a prior rupture from Irish identity through the transmutation of Irishness into Anglo-Irishness. Rather than the cause of evolution, I argue that education in *Ennui* reflects a transformation that is, by the time Edgeworth writes this novel, already complete, and reflects Anglo-Irish desire for assimilation without colonial revolution or conflict.[8] Borrowing from Gayatri Spivak's discussion of that which is "crucial yet foreclosed—a necessarily 'lost' object"—I will suggest that Irishness in Maria Edgeworth's *Ennui* is not reformed, but constitutively foreclosed in the text.[9] Although Spivak uses the ethnographic concept of "foreclosure" in a different context, in arguing for the figure of what she calls the "native informant," I employ the term to capture both the constructional tone of her argument and the essential/ist nature of that foreclosure. In fact, *Ennui*'s emphasis on education exposes not the belief that Irishness can be reformed but, rather, the expectation that an essentialized Irishness must be *replaced*, through education, in Edgeworth's imagined reconstruction of the Irish nation.

Critics have repeatedly, and rightly, recognized that Edgeworth's

Ennui rejects the concept of blood-based privilege in favor of an educational program capable of rehabilitating the corrupt Irish national character. The novel follows the history of the Earl of Glenthorn, a jaded Anglo-Irish aristocrat who suffers from conniving advisers, bad judgment, a poor education, and, of course, ennui. A timely visit from his childhood Irish nurse/foster mother, Ellinor, prompts him to pay a visit to his Irish estates, where, after exercising his poor management skills and bad judgment, Glenthorn learns that his foster mother is in fact his *biological* mother and that his foster brother, Christy O'Donoghoe, is in fact the legitimate Lord Glenthorn.[10] After surrendering his title to its rightful owner and adopting his "real" identity, the erstwhile lord studies law and embarks on a modest yet respectable career, by virtue of which he wins the admiration and hand of Miss Delamere, the heir-at-law of the Glenthorn estate. When the castle, the heir, and most of the estate are destroyed by fire and by the mismanagement of the legitimate Lord Glenthorn and his retinue, the original lord is asked to resume governance of the estates and its people.

In recording Lord Glenthorn's experiences and encounters with the Irish before, during, and after the discovery of the nature of his birth, *Ennui* perpetuates many of the standard stereotypes of the Irish national character, illustrating the colonizer's paternalistic authority over the colonized.[11] The narrative chronicles stereotypical Irish traits and flaws: the narrator asserts, "I was struck with instances of grand beginnings and lamentable want of finish, with mixture of the magnificent and the paltry; of admirable and execrable taste."[12] The Irish are reproved for their poor work ethic (188–90); caricatured for their extreme hospitality (176) and pet-like servility (178); and, of course, held in disdain for their tolerance for squalor and filth (186). These traits are the target of the novel's didactic function. According to Seamus Deane, Edgeworth "was the first to realize that there was, within [Ireland], a missionary opportunity to convert it to Enlightenment faith" and that, therefore, "Irish national character was to be brought to school."[13] The paternalistic acceptance of the responsibility to "improve" the native is, of course, a standard colonialist trope, most fully realized in *Ennui* through the character McLeod.[14] The admirable Scottish steward oversees Glenthorn's Irish estate and establishes a school to train the native Irish children:

> We could not expect to do much with the old, whose habits were fixed; but we tried to give the young children better notions, and it was a long

time before we could bring that to bear. Twenty-six years we have been at this work; and in that time if we have done any thing, it was by beginning with the children: *a race of our own training* has now grown up. (215–16, emphasis added)

Through the improvements put into effect by McLeod, the reader understands that Irish national character can, indeed, be "schooled."[15]

Critics have generally agreed that Edgeworth's plot ultimately suggests that education trumps heredity—that "[d]espite an English inheritance, the Anglo-Irish can belong to Ireland, and, at the same time, they can continue to belong to England."[16] Edgeworth thus tacitly critiques the idea of a corrupt national character, for if blood is not the final determinant of behavior, then culture is:

As the babies-switched-at-nurse plot spotlights, Glenthorn's tale is about learning who he is: not an Anglo aristocrat but an Irish peasant . . . Locating Irish otherness not in defective genes but in a difficult environment, the story's symbolic action marks the self-making of the former earl as a narrative of national redefinition too.[17]

Education thus effects not just a reform of the Irish national character; it also facilitates a negotiation between Irish and Anglo-Irish identities. The return of the original Glenthorn to governance of the estate not only endows him with the legitimacy he originally lacked as an impostor, but, by having the legitimate Anglo-Irish lord, who was raised as an Irishman, destroy the ancestral estates, "[t]he plot calls into question certain assumptions about the role of the Anglo-Irish and their mandate to rule," suggesting that "[p]roperly educated, the Irish can rule."[18] Although these readings of *Ennui* differ in their conceptualization of how Irishness functions in the text, each accepts the role of education as a *catalyst*, a device whereby negotiation or reconciliation takes place. Irishness exists either as an origin to be negotiated or as a stage through which to pass, via the enlightened path of education, on the evolutionary trail to Anglo-Irishness.

Although Irishness may indeed serve a legitimizing function in validating Glenthorn's right to resume governance of the estate, this Irish legitimacy and/or greatness is not merely consigned to the past—as simple colonial greatness inevitably will be.[19] Rather, the Irish past is simultaneously claimed and rejected in a radical transformation that occurs at the moment of identification. In her assertion that Lord Glenthorn's "rebirth . . . effectively severs his ties both with Ellinor and with his Irish heritage," Elizabeth Kowaleski-Wallace's reading, with its emphasis on repression, intimates an awareness of the radical break Lord Glenthorn's identity represents.[20] But her argument also does not go far enough, for Glenthorn's Irishness is relevant precisely because it was *never really there*, save as an origin inaccessible to Glenthorn even in its very exposure. Via life-long education as an Anglo-Irish aristocrat, Glenthorn's very Irishness has been exorcised. In this way, his Irishness is relevant only in its *absence*. Education serves to cover over the constitutive absence it represents.

Critics usually identify Lord Glenthorn's ethnic identity as an interrogation of who—or what—he *is*,[21] noting that Glenthorn, in his ennui-ridden state, has many of those characteristics stereotypically attributed to the Irish.[22] Glenthorn's discovery of his "true" identity may, indeed, serve as a catalyst for the action—and by association, his moral and political education—that implements his narrative and constitutional betterment. Importantly, however, his Irishness is clearly represented as an *adopted* or *alien* identity, and not as a "natural" role for him. The erstwhile earl relates the sense that he is "traveling incognito" rather than assuming a new identity (291). Similarly, he describes his new life, and by association his true identity, as "new and rather strange" (292). Perhaps most telling is Glenthorn's response to his true name: "when I came to the signature, I felt a repugnance to signing myself, C. O'Donoghoe" (294). Problematically, the former earl's resistance to his "real" identity is replicated by the text, in that reference continues to be made to his prior state as earl, rather than to his *original* state as Christy O'Donoghoe: "Mrs Delamere—Miss Delamere—give me leave to introduce you to the late Earl of Glenthorn" (301). In introducing Glenthorn as the "late" earl, the narrative intimates a type of death for the erstwhile earl—a death that will be literalized by the text's conclusion. In the refusal of both the text and the character to employ the character's legal name, Christy O'Donoghoe, both Glenthorn's rebirth as an Irish peasant *and* the reinstitution of the rightful earl, who is still identified textually as "Christy" (310), are occluded. This denial continues through the newly recognized earl's refusal to name himself thus—"No name needful, for you will not be astray about the hand" (306)—and by his retention of the erroneous, but familiar, name, Christy (323). Although the original earl is identified as "Irish," that identity is consistently undermined in and by the text. While education serves as the device by which the erstwhile Earl betters his lot and his moral constitution, it is only with the identification and immediate *refusal* of his Irishness that this constitutional change takes place. It is not his Irishness but, rather, the foreclosure *of* Irishness that enables the earl's evolution.

Edgeworth further obscures or complicates Lord Glenthorn's identity through another significant displacement that occurs in the text—namely, the conflation of Anglo-Irish identity with Englishness. Although it is clear that the Glenthorn family is Anglo-Irish, possessing "large estates in England; and in one of the remote maritime counties of Ireland . . . an immense territory," Glenthorn refers to himself as "Milord Anglois" (144–45). By identifying Glenthorn as English, Edgeworth invokes the oppositional relationships of English/Irish that underlie the colonial relationship, again distancing Glenthorn from his own Irish origins.[23]

A similar blurring of identity occurs in relation to Lady Geraldine, an upper-class Irish woman with whom Glenthorn finds himself temporarily enamored. Although she takes great pains to mock English misconceptions of the "Irish," it is clear that she refers to the *Anglo-Irish*: "'what can he see or know of the manners of any rank of people but of the class of gentry, which in England and Ireland is much the same?'" (211). The narrative similarly resists fully admitting Lady Geraldine's difference from English women: "She was not *exactly* cut out according to my English pattern of a woman of fashion . . ." (207, emphasis added). If we accept Lady Geraldine's identification with the Fitzgerald family and its associations with Irish rebellion, then this undermining of her Irish identity becomes particularly problematic. At the same time, the Old English or Anglo-Norman associations of the name "Geraldine" further complicate the portrait of rebellious Irishness underlying her Anglo-Irish and English identifications.[24] Lady Geraldine's multiple associations—Old English (Anglo-Norman), Anglo-Irish, Irish, and English—suggest an elision of Irishness in favor of Anglo-Irish/Englishness akin to that of Lord Glenthorn. Like Glenthorn, in other words, Lady Geraldine's Irishness is undermined even as it is presented. It is all the more ironic, then, when the character declares, "'O! my dear countrywomen . . . Let us dare to be ourselves!'" (225). Her claims of loyalty to one's identity are premised on multiple erasures of Irish identity.

The foreclosure of Glenthorn's Irishness invites a reconsideration of Ellinor's revelation that the Anglo-Irish-turned-English Glenthorns are, in fact, originally Irish. Although Ellinor's genealogy for the Glenthorns can be read as one in a long line of Irish claims to descent from the "kings of Ireland," this claim to descent seems particularly relevant in the context of foreclosed Irishness:[25]

> she had also an excellent memory for all the insults, or traditions of insults, which the Glenthorns had received for many ages back, even to the times of the old kings of Ireland; long and long before they stooped to be *lorded*; when their "names, which it was a pity and a murder, and moreover a burning shame, to change, was O'Shaughnessy." (160)

Like the erstwhile earl's Irishness, the original Irishness of the Glenthorns is practically retracted in its very presentation, here through a series of dependent clauses that render each idea increasingly absurd. The identification of the Glenthorns as O'Shaughnessys renamed follows a humorous and ridiculous string of denunciations, laughable for their hyperbolic and disordered presentation: the name change is both a "pity" and a "murder," which are apparently insufficient as terms of disapprobation, needing the further modification of a "burning shame." Because the tale of the original Irishness of the Glenthorns is presented in the dialect of the native Irish peasant—a notoriously comic and unreliable figure[26]—the significance of Ellinor's tale is diluted even as it is told. Like Glenthorn's identity, then, the Irishness of the Glenthorn line is canceled out in its very presentation. Yet given the restrictions on Irish property-holding and land rights that were current following the Penal Laws, it is literally with the foreclosure of the O'Shaughnessy identity that the Anglo-Irish, land-holding Glenthorns become possible.[27]

By presenting the history of the Glenthorn line in Ellinor's voice, Edgeworth also provides an echo of the symbolic sacrifice of Irish identity that is recreated at other moments in the text. In switching her child at cradle with the true Lord Glenthorn, Ellinor re-enacts for her infant the earlier sacrifice of an Irish identity in favor of an ambiguous English/Anglo-Irish one.[28] Ellinor's narrative itself also reenacts the sacrifice of Irish identity. Just as her narration symbolically repeats the ancestral surrender of Irish identity performed by the O'Shaughnessys by undermining the significance of that disclosure even as it is revealed, Ellinor's revelation of Glenthorn's true identity makes his sacrifice of that identity through education and self-betterment possible. It is the knowledge of his Irishness—and its practical absence—that makes Glenthorn's ascension to "true" Anglo-Irishness possible.

A final sacrificing of Irish identity occurs with Glenthorn's marriage to Miss Delamere and his assumption of an acceptably Anglo-Irish patronymic. Guided by his Anglo-Irish acquaintances, the presumptive earl will recreate the hereditary sacrifice of his Irish identity in order to marry the rather bland Miss Delamere, the object of his devotion and, conveniently, heir to the Glenthorn estate.[29] This final symbolic sacrifice again occurs in the form of a name change: "'I make no doubt that your future son-in-law will have no objection to take and bear the name and arms of Delamere; and I think I can answer for it, that a king's letter may be obtained, empowering him to do so'" (320).[30] Again, while the former earl's Irish identity becomes the condition of possibility for testing his abilities and thus for his eventual betterment, it is the immediate sacrifice of that Irish identity—and its literal disavowal—that makes a happy and productive future plausible.

In each of these instances, Irishness is figured as expendable, what Miranda Burgess calls "a loss to be mourned and . . . a lack to be filled."[31] For prosperity to ensue on this Irish estate, Irishness is a precondition that has to be confronted and simultaneously overcome. In *A Critique of Postcolonial Reason*, Gayatri Spivak argues that the figure of the "autochthone and/or subaltern" is repeatedly offered as a "foreclosed position," a space that is necessary and yet always already foreclosed.[32] I have been suggesting that it is this function which the "Irish national character" or "native Irishness" fulfills in *Ennui*. The sacrifice of Irish identity is repeatedly figured as a necessary rupture that renders movement toward evolution, advancement, or education plausible, as we have seen. For such evolution, particularly through education, to be possible, Irishness must always already have been foreclosed. Its absence is a precondition, not a result. In the process, a class of more sympathetic British subjects is not developed; rather, a group entirely distinct from Irish emerges, "a race of our own training" (216). The fundamental rupture with Irishness is reflected in the creation of a new "race," a race that paradoxically internalizes and yet forecloses Irishness in its very constitution, rupturing the very identification that renders advancement plausible in the first place.

Christy O'Donoghoe, the legitimate Earl of Glenthorn, serves to illustrate the dangers of unforeclosed Irishness in the text. Without the illicit substitution Ellinor perpetrates, the heir-apparent may very well have literally ceased to exist, as Ellinor explains:

> "I got into no trouble at all, for it all fell out just as I had laid it out, except that the real little young lord did not die as I thought; and it was a wonder but he did, for you never saw none so near death, and backwards and forwards, what turns of sickness he took with me for months upon months, and year after year, so that none could think, no more than me, there was any likelihood at all of rearing him to man's estate." (275)

Only with the introduction of Irishness—manifested through Ellinor's constant tending—can the legitimate heir survive. However, the Irishness he learns throughout his lifetime proves to be ultimately detrimental, as Christy is entirely unable to carry out the responsibilities incumbent upon him as the Earl of Glenthorn. Instead, with his Irishness neither foreclosed nor contained, Christy wreaks havoc upon his own estate—financially, physically, and even generationally, with the death of the legitimate Glenthorn heir:

> The castle's burnt down all to the ground, and my Johnny's dead, and I wish I was dead in his place. The occasion of his death was owing to drink, which he fell into from getting too much money, and nothing to do . . . [T]he short of it is, there's nothing remaining of the castle but the stones. (322)

Because it is not contained, the Irishness Christy has learned wreaks havoc on the Anglo-Irish world of Glenthorn Castle. That the destruction comes through those traits stereotypically attributed to the Irish national character—the tendency to excess and the inability to rationally monitor oneself ("too much money"), excessive drinking ("his death was owing to drink"), laziness ("nothing to do")—shows how immutable this Irish national character truly is. Education cannot serve to foreclose Christy's Irishness, and it cannot be used textually to obscure its absence, as in the Earl of Glenthorn's pursuit of betterment. He is simply too Irish. As such, the only textual option is literal foreclosure in the form of death—and this is precisely what occurs, as Christy admits that he will effectively follow his deceased heir: "I write this to beg you . . . will take possession of all immediately, for I am as good as dead" (322). Just as an earlier Irish lord, long ago, surrendered title (and presumably religion) to change into an Anglo-Irish lord, so here must the Glenthorn line literally die again to Irishness to be reborn as an Anglo-Irish line (Delamere).[33]

Not surprisingly, Ellinor meets a similar fate, dying the very night her son leaves, purportedly for England, and thus paving the way for his reincarnation as a gentleman and the legal Earl of Glenthorn. With her son's transformation—ironically, through his very Irishness—into an Anglo-Irish gentleman, Ellinor's words hauntingly echo the literal separation of death that will follow his symbolic break from her: "'I often told Christy I would die before you left this place, dear; and so I will, you will see . . . God bless you, dear; I shall never see you more! The hand of death is upon me—God for ever bless you, dear!'" (288–89). Again, while Ellinor had already experienced a physical separation from Glenthorn by switching him at birth, her anticipation of death seems to intimate an awareness of the more fundamental separation which Glenthorn's transmutation into a "real" Anglo-Irishman represents. It is the foreclosure of his exposed Irishness that makes this fundamental rupture possible. The death of the two characters who embody Irishness—Irishness that is constitutively foreclosed in the reconstitution of Glenthorn-as-Anglo-Irishman—thus brings about a double rupture. Not only is Glenthorn's external link to Irishness eradicated, through the textual eradication of his mother and foster-brother; Christy and Ellinor's deaths also parallel his internal transformation into an Anglo-Irishman. While some would argue that the relationship between Ireland-as-past and Anglo-Ireland-as-future is re-established through this change in Glenthorn, I would insist that this change in Glenthorn—still Irish in origin—reflects the foreclosure of that Irishness and its enabling function in the text. Glenthorn has become Anglo-Irish precisely through the revelation—and immediate disavowal—of his Irishness. It is thus not so much a "past-ing" of Irishness as a constitutive foreclosure of it.[34]

Ennui undoubtedly endorses education over heredity, as so many critics note; however, Edgeworth's representation is not of a society that is premised solely on the goal of reformation and betterment. Rather, the society traced out in *Ennui* is predicated on the constitutive foreclosure of Irishness—a foreclosure that posits the necessary absence of Irishness in order for Anglo-Irishness to thrive. This is a more personal and violent negotiation than questions of "legitimacy," "repression," or reformation can accommodate.[35] Although education is proffered as a means to betterment, Edgeworth's text suggests the underlying belief that Irishness *cannot* be remedied or educated away. Rather, Irishness—whether learnt, as in the case of Christy O'Donoghoe, the legitimate Earl of Glenthorn, or inherent, as in the case of Ellinor—requires erasure or transformation, either through replacement with the characteristics of Anglo-Irishness or, barring that possibility, death. Lord Glenthorn's education is not the *remedy* for Irishness, but rather its result; in his upbringing as an Anglo-Irishman, Glenthorn is already in a position to foreclose his Irish nature, once revealed. Education thus works in *Ennui* as what Spivak terms a "subreptive metalepsis"—a substitution of effect for cause, which suppresses the truth. Here, that truth is that Irishness is already foreclosed in the text in its moment of exposure, and that foreclosure is not the effect, but the cause, of education's success.[36]

This problematic formulation, which Edgeworth's text implies, in many ways replicates the (il)logic of colonialism, in the simultaneous attraction and repulsion toward the colonized, and in the identification with and alienation from the native that it reflects.[37] As Gerry Smyth notes:

> Even when the contemporary Irish writer attempts to refute colonialist stereotypes—by simply ignoring them or by showing the complexity of Irish character—something of the original force of those stereotypes remains, testament to the fact that colonialism is as much a matter of cultural representation and psychological perception as it is of politico-economic organisation.[38]

In spite of the philosophical difference between her view of the flawed Irish character and that of Carlyle, Edgeworth could not embrace her own hypothesis enough to bring it to textual fruition in *Ennui*. Perhaps, this is evidence of the "resistance" to erasing inadvertently "the very identifying features of Irish 'tradition'" that Deane identifies as present within Edgeworth herself.[39]

Critics have variously interpreted the social and even revolutionary implications of Edgeworth's *Ennui*.[40] I read *Ennui* as a tale not of social revolution, peaceful or otherwise, but rather as a lesson in national transformation and cultural stasis. Irishness must give way to Anglo-Irishness in the text, either through foreclosure, as in the case of the original earl, or through death, as for the legitimate Lord Glenthorn; and that Anglo-Irishness is itself shored up by infusions of Englishness that resist the very identification of Irishness the narrative posits. Far from being a novel that encourages a more generous or enlightened interpretation of Irish national character, or a tale that wholeheartedly praises the benefits of education, *Ennui* actually reinforces the concept of an immutable Irishness. That Irishness must be fundamentally divorced for education and "advancement" to take effect. Edgeworth thus emphasizes more than just the insecure positioning of the Anglo-Irish in contemporary Irish society. Her text highlights the colonial attraction and repulsion toward the "native" Irish, a sense of belonging predicated on the impossible absorption and foreclosure of an elemental Irishness. Irishness *is* enabling, but only if it leaves no discernable trace.

Seamus Deane has argued that "the pursuit of modernity" can be conceived of as "dependent for its success on recovery *of* the past, in one light, and recovery *from* the past, in another." Edgeworth's act of cloaking Irishness behind a mantle of educable reform ultimately fails because she cannot negotiate these contradictory drives. The problematic presence of Irishness in all its complexity, and its refusal to be "past-ed," reflects a paradoxical perception of Irishness as an essential yet empty space: filled, but only to be retroactively emptied out.[41]

Notes

1. Carlyle, Thomas. "Chartism," 29: 137. Quoted in Seamus Deane,"Irish National Character 1790–1900," *The Writer as Witness: Literature as Historical Evidence*, ed. Tom Dunne, Historical Studies Series 16 (Cork: Cork University Press, 1987), 90–113, esp. 99, my emphasis.

2. Seamus Deane, *Strange Country: Modernity and Nationhood in Irish Writing Since 1790* (Oxford: Oxford University Press, 1997), 28.

3. Maria Edgeworth and Richard Lovell Edgeworth, quoted in Esther Wohlgemut, "Maria Edgeworth and the Question of National Identity," *SEL: Studies in English Literature* 39, no. 4 (Autumn 1999): 645–58, here 647.

4. In her foundational biography of Edgeworth, Marilyn Butler is equally unforgiving, noting that *Ennui* "has a most improbable plot . . . The earlier part of the tale, while not quite so implausible, is didactic and tiresomely repetitive." She does, however, note the text's "historical importance" in its social commentary. See *Maria Edgeworth: A Literary Biography* (Oxford: Oxford University Press, 1972), 365.

5. In his 1967 study, James Newcomer observes that "*Ennui* is frequently mentioned . . . because the idea has always been current that [Edgeworth's] Irish fiction is her best; *Ennui* is Irish, but its moral is a bore; ergo, the morality of her fiction is boring." See his *Maria Edgeworth the Novelist: 1767–1849, A Bicentennial Study* (Fort Worth: Texas Christian University Press, 1967), 55–56.

6. Although it does not directly engage in a critical reading of *Ennui*, Miranda J. Burgess's impressive article, "Violent Translations: Allegory, Gender, and Cultural Nationalism in Ireland, 1796–1806," reflects the type of sophisticated analysis to which I refer in its suggestion that Anglo-Irish national tales, written after 1796,

separate culture from political history, thereby rendering Irishness "immutable." See *Modern Language Quarterly* 59, no. 1 (Mar. 1998): 33–70.

7. For a reading of Lord Glenthorn's repression of his Irishness in *Ennui*, see Elizabeth Kowaleski-Wallace, *Their Fathers' Daughters: Hannah More, Maria Edgeworth, and Patriarchal Complicity* (New York: Oxford University Press, 1991), 138–72, esp. 163; on Irish and Anglo-Irish relations as "nonblood kinship," see Wohlgemut, "National Identity," 648; on Glenthorn's relationship to Irishness as one of a colonially-paternalistic evolution from child-like Irishness to Anglo-Irish adulthood, see Mitzi Myers, "Canonical 'Orphans' and Critical *Ennui*: Rereading Edgeworth's Cross-Writing," *Children's Literature* 25, eds. Francelia Butler, R. H. W. Dillard, and Elizabeth Lennox Keyser, guest eds. Mitzi Myers and U. C. Knoepflmacher (New Haven: Yale University Press, 1997), 116–36, esp. 125–26; on the "interdependence of Irish identities," see Myers, "'Completing the Union:' Critical *Ennui*, the Politics of Narrative, and the Reformation of Irish Cultural Identity," Special issue on *The Intersections of the Public and Private Spheres* in Early Modern England, eds., Paula R. Backscheider and Timothy Dykstal. *Prose Studies: History, Theory, Criticism* 18, no. 3 (Dec. 1995): 41–77, esp. 55–60.

8. I am suggesting that Irishness is not remedied or "cured" textually but rather is eradicated as a necessary precondition for Anglo-Irishness. I should also note that I am using "Anglo-Irish" here as a social category, to designate those of English descent who inherited or received land through English colonization and dispossession of the "native" Irish. For a definition of Anglo-Irishness as a social category, see Elizabeth Grubgeld, "Class, Gender, and the Forms of Narrative: The Autobiographies of Anglo-Irish Women," *Representing Ireland: Gender, Class, Nationality*, ed. Susan Shaw Sailer (Gainesville: University of Florida Press, 1987), 133–55, esp. 153 n.1. Unlike Myers, who considers the use of terms like "Anglo-Irish" and "Ascendancy" to be potentially homogenizing and reductive, I believe such liminal categories are imperative to understanding Edgeworth's problematic and ambivalent response to Irishness. See Myers, "Canonical Orphans," 118–19, and Myers, "Completing the Union," 69 n.23 and n.26.

9. Gayatri Chakravorty Spivak, *A Critique of Postcolonial Reason: Toward a History of the Vanishing Present* (Cambridge: Harvard University Press, 1999), 70. See also Spivak, 6–9.

10. For the sake of clarity and in an attempt to avoid the inevitable confusion, I will refer to the man who, switched at birth, acquires the title Lord Glenthorn as "the original Lord Glenthorn" or, simply, as "Lord Glenthorn." The man with the original legal right to the name, who was raised as Christy O'Donoghoe, I shall refer to as the "true" or "legitimate" Lord Glenthorn, or, simply, as Christy.

11. Although I recognize the difficulty in the too-ready assignment of the term "colonizer" to a member of the Anglo-Irish Ascendancy, I wish to emphasize the manner in which Edgeworth's representations of the native Irish adhere to the settler colonist's tendency to demonize and degrade the displaced native. For a discussion of settler colonialism—in spite of their exclusion of the Irish example—see Bill Ashcroft et al., *The Empire Writes Back: Theory and Practice in Post-Colonial Literatures*, (London: Routledge, 1989), esp. 25–27.

12. Maria Edgeworth, *Castle Rackrent* and *Ennui*, ed. Marilyn Butler (London: Penguin, 1992), 170. Subsequent references to the text will be cited parenthetically.

13. Deane, *Strange Country*, 32.

14. The body of work tracing the relationship between the colonizer and the colonized is too large to rehearse here. For a representative sampling of texts that consider this topic, see Frantz Fanon, *The Wretched of the Earth* (New York: Grove, 1963); Albert Memmi, *The Colonizer and the Colonized* (Boston: Beacon, 1965); Edward Said, *Orientalism* (New York: Pantheon, 1978); Homi Bhabha, *The Location of Culture*, (New York: Routledge, 1994); Declan Kiberd, *Inventing Ireland: The Literature of the Modern Nation* (London: Jonathan Cape, 1995).

15. That McCleod is Scottish and not English or Anglo-Irish is an interesting caveat. The creation of "a race of our own training" thus becomes more problematic. The re-emergence of McCleod's Scots dialect and familial pride when angered (258–60) suggests the insufficiency of educational reform alone. As I will suggest, it is only with the foreclosure of such Celtic identity that national character can be safely contained.

16. Wohlgemut, "National Identity," 648.

17. Myers, "Completing the Union," 49–50. For a similar point, see Wohlgemut, "National Identity," 649.

18. Robert Tracy, "Maria Edgeworth and Lady Morgan: Legality versus Legitimacy," *Nineteenth-Century Fiction* 40, no. 1 (June 1985): 1–22, here 6. Tracy's excellent article recognizes that this resolution is hardly comfortable for Edgeworth, and that her texts reflect her resistance to the notion that legitimation of Anglo-Irish legal rights through marriage—literal and figurative—to the Irish may be necessary. See Tracy, 19. Terry Eagleton similarly has argued that the great past of the native Irish is only needed for its "symbolic capital" to the present. See his "Form and Ideology in the Anglo-Irish Novel," *Bullán: An Irish Studies Journal* 1, no. 1 (1994): 17–26, esp. 20.

19. The tendency of the colonizer to consign the greatness of the colonized's culture to the past has been well documented by Ashis Nandy, *The Intimate Enemy: Loss and Recovery of Self Under Colonialism* (Delhi: Oxford University Press, 1983), esp. 17, and Said, *Orientalism*, esp. 27. For a discussion of contemporary views of ancient Irish kings, see Sophie Gilmartin, *Ancestry and Narrative in Nineteenth-Century British Literature: Blood Relations from Edgeworth to Hardy*, Cambridge Studies in Nineteenth-Century Literature and Culture 18 (Cambridge: Cambridge University Press, 1998), 24–28. For the discussion of legitimizing Anglo-Irish rule, see Tracy, "Legality Versus Legitimacy."

20. Kowaleski-Wallace, *Their Father's Daughters*, 165. In her feminist reading, Kowaleski-Wallace challenges the assumption that Irish and Anglo-Irish identities are united or negotiated textually in *Ennui*. She suggests that Irishness functions as a grotesque intrusion of physicality in the novel, particularly as it is incarnated in the maternal body through Ellinor, which requires repression and containment for Glenthorn to be "reborn" as an Anglo-Irishman. Glenthorn's (re)ascension to governance thus does not reflect a tempering or negotiation of conflicting identities so much as the *repression* of his Irish identity in favor of a rational, Anglicized one. However, she too sees education as pivotally altering one's relationship to Irishness: "[O]nce Lord Glenthorn learns his true lineage, he will spend the balance of the novel demonstrating that he, unlike Ellinor, has mastered the wayward impulses of his own body" (163). Although Kowaleski-Wallace's reading may arguably be too accepting of one-dimensional representations of Irishness, she hypothesizes a more problematic tension between categories of identity by rejecting the possibility of

reconciliation or negotiation between the Irish and Anglo-Irish identities. For Myers's critique of Kowaleski-Wallace's representation of Irishness, see "Completing the Union," 54, 58–59, 74–75n. 59. While it may be true that Ellinor should not be reduced to the body, Myers's reading is equally problematic, in that it neglects the fact that "to shape Ellinor as an embodiment of the Gaelic past" comes with a price—namely, her own death. I will suggest that Ellinor's death, with the necessity to foreclose Irishness, is inevitable. See Myers, "Completing the Union," 58.

21. For representative examples, see Tracy, "Legality Versus Legitimacy," 5, or Myers, "Completing the Union," 43–49.

22. Myers, "Completing the Union," 59–60. Although Myers notes that "laziness" is "the iconographically 'Irish' trait," Irene A. Beesemyer notes that "ennui [was] the personal, male lacuna of the times." See her "Romantic Masculinity in Edgeworth's *Ennui* and Scott's *Marmion:* In Itself a Border Story," *Papers on Language & Literature: A Journal for Scholars and Critics of Language and Literature* 35, no. 1 (Winter 1999): 74–96, esp. 78–80.

23. For a discussion of the nature of English and Irish relations, see Kiberd, *Inventing Ireland*, esp. 1–25.

24. Tracy, "Legality Versus Legitimacy," 5. See also Myers, "Completing the Union," 60–63. I am grateful to Vera Kreilkamp for helping me to think through this characterization. The Fitzgerald family, earls of Desmond and of Kildare, were "the most long-lived though by no means consistently the most powerful, of the three great dynasties stretching back to the Anglo-Norman conquest." There was additionally the sixteenth-century Geraldine League, "a Gaelic alliance" in opposition to Lord Deputy Grey's repressive policies. See S. J. Connolly, ed. *The Oxford Companion to Irish History* (Oxford: Oxford University Press, 1998). 284, 221.

25. Myers, "Completing the Union," 55. See also Gilmartin, *Ancestry and Narrative*, 23–53.

26. The paradigmatic representation of the laughable and unreliable Irish peasant is, of course, Thady Quirk in Edgeworth's *Castle Rackrent*.

27. For a review of the history of Catholic oppression and the Penal Laws in Ireland, see Thomas Bartlett, *The Fall and Rise of the Irish Nation: The Catholic Question, 1690–1830*, (Dublin: Gill and Macmillan, 1992); Kevin Whelan, *The Tree of Liberty: Radicalism, Catholicism and the Construction of Irish Identity, 1760–1830*, (Cork: Cork University Press in association with Field Day, 1996); and Maureen Wall, *Catholic Ireland in the Eighteenth Century: Collected Essays of Maureen Wall*, ed. Gerard O'Brien, assoc. ed. Tom Dunne (Templeogue, Dublin: Geography Publications, 1989).

28. The destructive influence of the Irish parent exemplified by Ellinor seems to follow a long pattern: one might consider Jonathan Swift's indictment of native Irish parents in "A Modest Proposal," *Swift's Irish Pamphlets: An Introductory Selection*, ed. Joseph McMinn. Ulster Editions and Monographs 2 (Gerards Cross: Colin Smythe, 1991), 141–50; or the social and financial stagnation to which Glorvina is consigned by her loving yet unforgiving and anachronistic father, the Prince of Inismore, in Sydney Owenson's *The Wild Irish Girl: A National Tale*, ed. Kathryn Kirkpatrick (New York: Oxford University Press, 1999). The question of destructive cycles in the Anglo-Irish family is addressed in Margot Backus's recent book, *The Gothic Family Romance: Heterosexuality, Child Sacrifice, and the Anglo-Irish Colonial Order* (Durham: Duke University Press, 1999).

29. Kowaleski-Wallace argues that "his very choice of a marriage partner—Miss

De-la-mere—suggests that he wins for himself a 'new mother,' a new line of maternal inheritance with a different relationship to the body." See *Their Father's Daughters*, 164.

30. This process of renaming smacks of the colonial enterprise by which the English systematically renamed Irish landscape and towns with Anglicized designations to undermine local associations and meanings. For a consideration of this practice and the power of naming, see Brian Friel's play, *Translations* (London: Faber, 1981).

31. Burgess, "Violent Translations," 49.

32. Spivak, *Postcolonial Reason*, 11, 18 n.29.

33. I borrow this idea of Glenthorn as "reborn" from Kowaleski-Wallace, *Their Father's Daughters*, 163–65.

34. Kowaleski-Wallace explores the implications of Ellinor as "embodiment of Ireland" in a different context, *Their Father's Daughters*, 164–66. Burgess notes Terry Eagleton's argument "that national tales are a (failed) attempt to consolidate Anglo-Irish power by defining it as the teleological endpoint of 'ancient' Irish culture." See Burgess "Violent Translations," 36 n.6.

35. The references are to Tracy "Legality Versus Legitimacy," to Kowaleski-Wallace, *Their Father's Daughters*, and to Myers, "Completing the Union," respectively.

36. Spivak, *Postcolonial Reason*, 23.

37. For an analysis of this dynamic, see Bhabha, *Location*, 66–84.

38. Gerry Smyth, *The Novel and the Nation: Studies in the New Irish Fiction* (London: Pluto, 1997), 36.

39. Deane, *Strange Country*, 30.

40. In a recent essay, Clíona Ó Gallchoir reads "[t]he plot of the 'change at nurse' [as] clearly a metaphor for revolution . . .". See Ó Gallchoir, "Maria Edgeworth's Revolutionary Morality and the Limits of Realism," *Colby Quarterly* 36, no. 2 (June 2000): 87–97, here 94.

41. Deane, *Strange Country*, 44, italics in original; the image of "a lack to be filled" I borrow from Burgess, "Violent Translations." See n. 31 above.

Part III
Education, Empire, and the Anglo-Irish Dilemma

"The Fashion Not To Be an Absentee": Fashion and Moral Authority in Edgeworth's Tales

Heidi Thomson

> The secret is, that fashion is imitating in certain things that are in our power and that are nearly indifferent in themselves, those who possess certain other advantages that are not in our power, and which the possessors are as little disposed to part with as they are eager to obtrude them upon the notice of others by every external symbol, at their immediate controul.
> —William Hazlitt, *The Spirit of the Age and Conversations of James Northcote, Esq.,R.A.* [1]

FRANCIS JEFFREY OF *THE EDINBURGH REVIEW* PUT HIS FINGER ON THE PROBlematic definition of an authoritative social identity when he praised Maria Edgeworth's *The Absentee* and her tales of fashionable life in general for exposing "the folly and misery of renouncing the respectable character of country ladies and gentlemen, to push, through intolerable expense, and more intolerable scorn, into the outer circles of fashion in London."[2] The commonplace contrast between country and city is complicated in Jeffrey's statement by the opposition between the wholesomeness of "respectable character" based on a solid sense of identity and the morally objectionable instability associated with the "outer circles of fashion." In the increasingly commercialized world that Edgeworth witnessed during her long life, the language of fashion, as her aptly named *Tales of Fashionable Life* illustrates, became the prime form of expressing not only one's social class and status, but, more importantly, one's desire for and attempts at social emulation. This gradual recognition of the fluidity, however limited, of social status, if not class, is inevitably connected with a sense of threat to the established hierarchies of class. In a master-servant relationship both parties are locked in a mutual relationship that includes the lottery-like possibility of the master acting generously on impulse, and in which the servant may perpetually long for the equally lottery-like chance of preferential treatment. The problems with this kind of regime on Irish estates are explored at length in *Castle Rackrent, Ennui, Ormond,* and *The Absentee*. In contrast to this arbitrary status quo, competitive capitalism enables the enterprising individual to transcend the boundaries of class. The most common expression of success in the capitalist exercise of improvement is the assertion of one's financial creditworthiness by the display of fashionable goods, but, as Edgeworth's fashionable tales and novels illustrate in mordantly comic scenes, the boundaries between the tasteful and the ridiculous are very fragile indeed.

Most critical discussions of Edgeworth's comic scenes, with a few exceptions, involve the Irish novels in which the colonial relationship between the Irish tenant and Anglo-Irish landlord is highlighted from the superior vantage point of the narrative voice.[3] In Edgeworth's fashionable scenes, however, in which equals and near equals mingle and jostle for prominence, relationships are more nebulous and indistinct. The overriding earnestness that Edgeworth displays in scenes where the social or national hierarchy is determined more by manners than by essential characteristics is closely associated with a range of restrictions that authors and audiences then faced and has led to a certain modern neglect of the comic elements in those scenes. With a consummate awareness of the precarious status of the woman novelist, Edgeworth took great care not to use the term "novel" for her own work, as the often quoted "Advertisement" to her popular, fashionable novel *Belinda* indicates. Edgeworth's objection that "so much folly, error, and vice are disseminated in books classed under this denomination" expresses her desire to create virtuous and victorious characters in novels that cannot be condemned for lack of propriety by the powerful magazine critics.[4] Obviously, Edgeworth herself was sometimes exasperated by the solid seriousness of her characters; she rejected her very own Belinda in a comparison with the impetuous Miss Milner of Elizabeth Inchbald's *A Simple Story*: "I really was so provoked with the cold tameness of that stick or stone Belinda, that I could have torn the pages to pieces; and really, I have not the heart or the patience to *correct* her."[5] The idea, however, that Edgeworth's novels are devoid of humor and laughter is a twentieth-century construction in which Edgeworth's erstwhile fame has been completely eclipsed by

Jane Austen, whose novels lend themselves more easily to the character-oriented readings that have become the norm of Romantic and post-Romantic studies.[6] The subversive character sketches of silly characters such as the pompously pious Mr Collins, or the indolently tyrannical Lady Bertram, herself a slave driver of sorts, satisfy our demand for character-based readings of individuals. Jane Austen's novels cause us most problems when a larger set of social values (usually conservative ones) are overtly placed above the individual character. Fanny Price's sisterly marriage to Edmund, Elizabeth Bennett's gratitude to Mr Darcy, Emma's alliance with Mr Knightley, for instance, have all baffled modern readers.[7] In Edgeworth's tales, more often than not, the common good of the society she believes in transcends the importance of the individual character, and in this primarily socially orchestrated world the importance of keeping up fashionable appearances is paramount in maintaining one's authority within the social order. For Anglo-Irish absentees in particular, the attempts at consolidating one's authority in London society come at a very high cost.

In addition to an almost Popean condemnation of the violation of decorum and taste, Edgeworth also alerts her readers to the dangers of debt that accompany her absentees' extravagant lifestyles. Overall, Edgeworth's tales, particularly because of their overtly stated moral intentions and emphasis on enlightened rationalism, have been credited with a wholesale rejection of the world of fashion in favor of a merit-based, professionalized lifestyle. Gary Kelly's fine summary of the main plot in *The Absentee* articulates the most common reading of Edgeworth's tales:

> The plot of "The Absentee" argues for the renewal of gentry hegemony by a particular kind of 'civil courage' in resisting the tyranny of fashion and decadent court culture, a kind of courage no less important in the modern age than the martial courage required by the gentry's medieval ancestors in resisting the tyranny of monarchy or the oppression of barons. But "The Absentee" also deploys a great deal of social description, of fashionable society in London and of lower-class, middle-class, and upper-class society in Ireland. Here Edgeworth employs traditional kinds of social satire, using socially and morally representative characters.[8]

These readings, however justified, do not fully address Edgeworth's ambivalent fascination with the world of fashion and its inevitable, intricate connection with the revival of a professionalized gentry hegemony. In this essay I will explore Edgeworth's uneasy awareness of the inevitable necessity for immersion in and negotiation with the world of fashion. The social satire which Edgeworth uses in her portrayal of the world of fashion does not so much encourage a wholesale rejection of the "tyranny of fashion" as it does a careful manipulation of it.

The worlds of the country gentry and the fashionable metropolitan circles, deemed by Jeffrey in the opening quotation as mutually, essentially exclusive, can no longer be held apart in a world in which the commercial manipulation and industrialization of fashion has become an everyday fact of life.[9] The inevitable social exposure to the world of fashion happened through magazines, fashion plates, and the fashion doll, all transmitted along the rapidly improving transportation systems. In this social context, the journey of enlightenment and self-discovery on which lord Colambre embarks in *The Absentee* cannot be restricted to an affirmation of his supreme lordly rule over the family estate. Just as importantly, his journey involves the recognition that the effective exercise of authority is necessarily a social activity, not conducted in dictatorial isolation on the estate or in the form of absolute tyranny over one's inferiors, but in the manipulation of the elaborate rituals of social encounters across the blurry boundaries of class, status, and perceived merit or moral creditworthiness. Not surprisingly, this process of survival highlights the transient fragility of any standards and the uncertainty of any permanent authority.

Most social encounters in the world of fashion do not really allow for individual heroism because social authority is group-determined, requiring the recognition of one's authority by other people, and involving one's family and a wider circle of acquaintance. Social encounters are often set in crowded, even claustrophobic conditions, such as the crushroom in the opening scene of *The Absentee*, and the pressure to perform gracefully and skillfully overrules the individual assertion of one's moral self-righteousness, as Colambre's impotent anger and Grace Nugent's reported levelheaded resourcefulness at lady Clonbrony's gala illustrates. In the tradition of the bildungsroman it has become commonplace to read a novel in terms of the development of the main character; our attention is focused on the quest for happiness of the hero or heroine. And while this focus is undeniably part of the structure of Edgeworth's novels—Colambre and Grace, Belinda, Helen, Harry Ormond are all on an individual quest of sorts—it ignores Edgeworth's need to affirm the social authority in which she believes within the frame of each novel. The problems of estate management are examples of the social concerns that Edgeworth articulates overtly in *Castle Rackrent, The Absentee, Ennui,* and *Ormond*. In addition, on a less obvious level, Edgeworth also attempts to articulate the shape or appearance of that authority, and this is where "fashion" in its widest dictionary sense of "visible characteristics" enters the picture.

The comic, caricature-like characterization of the power-mongering duchess of Torcaster, lady Langland, and Mrs Dareville in *The Absentee,* however transparent about their moral flaws, does not underestimate the cruel power they exercise over their victims. Similarly, the laughter that is associated with the exposure of distortion or excess in fashionable consumption and estate management, be it in lady Clonbrony's drawing room, Mrs Raffarty's Tusculum villa, or the Killpatricks' Irish inland estate, is uneasy. The rejection of excess emphasizes the need for a carefully balanced order and proportionate standards, but, at the same time, in a commercial world manipulated by manufacturers such as Josiah Wedgwood, a close friend of Richard Edgeworth whose professed emphasis on taste obscured his relentless efforts to bring about fashionable change, it is increasingly obvious that any standards will be transient at best. Stability of any kind, moral, economic, or political, in the *laissez faire* world that Edgeworth favors is an impossibility. The incoherence of Edgeworth's moralizing in her fascination with, and repulsion by, the world of fashion articulates an underlying awareness that the idealized, supposedly pragmatic combination of descent and merit cannot be consolidated on the permanent grounds that the conservative Edgeworth would wish for. Instead, the authority based on this utilitarian combination of descent and merit needs to be constantly negotiated and invigorated. The race, in modern, rational estate management, as in fashion, is endless; like Hazlitt, Edgeworth realized that "fashion is gentility running away from vulgarity, and afraid of being overtaken by it."[10] This fear of being overtaken informs and substantiates the comic scenes in Edgeworth's tales of fashionable life.

The importance of merit, economic individualism, and individual creditworthiness in Edgeworth's tales has been discussed at length.[11] Edgeworth's belief in the principles espoused in Adam Smith's *The Wealth of Nations* (1776) and Arthur Young's *Tour in Ireland* (1780) remained unshaken throughout her writing life, but at the same time her tales belie the uneasy consciousness which Bernard Mandeville articulated earlier and so mordantly in *The Fable of the Bees* (1732), namely that a splendid economy does not equal moral virtue. Edgeworth's tales, for all their emphasis on individual control and moral virtue as befits the model of a bildungsroman, express a fear of the powerfully seductive lure of fashionable luxury which has been made possible by the ethos of a *laissez-faire* economy. The purpose of Mandeville's fable sums up the fear which Edgeworth's tales articulate: "For the main Design of the Fable . . . is to shew the Impossibility of enjoying all the most elegant Comforts of Life that are to be met within an industrious, wealthy and powerful Nation, and at the same time be bless'd with all the Virtue and Innocence that can be wish'd for in a Golden Age."[12] Mandeville's uncomfortable conclusion that private vice and public virtue go together very well goes against the grain of Edgeworth's emphasis on personal creditworthiness, in both the moral and financial sense. Exposure to the fashionable world of consumption and its temptations is an inevitable dimension of an enlightened, civilized existence in which tests of social adaptability are just as important as the imposition of enlightened management principles on the Irish estate.

In accordance with the enlightened, utilitarian principles of the Edgeworths, immersion in the world is a crucial condition for being in charge of it. Complete withdrawal from the fashionable world into a nostalgically antiquated version of a lost Golden Age in *Ormond*, for instance, may be a fictionally desirable plot conclusion, but it is a problematic, incoherent one in terms of the tale's repeated morals of estate management.[13] When the hero, Harry Ormond, has finally become sufficiently socialized and thereby worthy of Florence Annaly's hand, through a course of "improvement" that involves reading *Sir Charles Grandison* and exposure to the temptations of fashionable salon society in France, he chooses to purchase the Black Islands over Castle Hermitage, effectively establishing himself as the successor of King Corny, the proponent of a pre-enlightened Ireland who was described by Edgeworth as "a mixture of the savage virtues & vices of the Czar Peter & the shrewd humor of Sanc[h]o Pansa" (xii). The lesson that "he might do a great deal of good, by carrying on his old friend's improvements, and by farther civilizing the people of the Islands, all of whom were warmly attached to him" (234), resembles the conclusion of *Rasselas* in which the prince wishes for a small realm just for himself, and it is inevitably connected with a farewell to fashionable, civilized society. The consolation that Edgeworth offers in giving Ormond complete authority combined with the affirmation "that the mind is a kingdom of yet more consequence than even that of the Black Islands" and that "Ormond continued to enjoy the empire which he had gained over himself" (234), needs to be read to the exclusion of any larger social context. Another form of retreat from fashionable society is evoked in Edgeworth's anachronistic characters such as King Corny, or more subtly, Count O'Halloran in *The Absentee*. O'Halloran is vital in the plot resolution for Colambre and Grace, but his own status resembles that of a living fossil, a rich repository of valuable antiquarian knowledge for an understanding of past and heritage, but ultimately sterile in his own person. The most complex aspect of the education of Edgeworth's characters, seen perhaps most poignantly in *The Absentee, Belinda, Helen, Harrington,* and *Leonora,* involves the necessary incorporation of fickle fashionable life into their own steady, virtuous course of life. The stiltedness that sometimes accompanies the characterization of the hero or heroine arises from the necessity of maintaining his or her essential virtue in the face of fashionable life, while at the same time affirming that fashionable life is not a force that can be eliminated but one that needs to be accommodated. Total seclusion is not an option for those creditworthy characters: in order for their value to be current, they have to circulate in society.

The characters on whose creditworthiness we are supposed to fasten our attention usually rise above the seduction of fashionable commercialism and its trappings of debt, but their relations or adopted relations do not, thereby endangering the moral credit of the group as a whole and potentially nullifying the main characters' efforts to attain an "improved" society. As a result, we observe Edgeworth's characters in a complicated dance, aiming for fashionable virtue that accommodates circulation in the world of fashion but that is never overtaken by vulgarity. The often comic scenes in which characters are exposed for their failure to be fashionable, decorous, and virtuous at the same time are all characterized by uneasy laughter because of the awareness that the assertion of one character's power on the basis of their fashionable status also reveals the vulnerability and instability of any status based on fashion. Before going into detail about *The Absentee*, it is worthwhile to consider the construction of fashion by Maria Edgeworth and her father in their own social context.

In Edgeworth's lifetime the possibilities and affordability (through a system of credit) of controlling and changing one's appearance increased exponentially, and as a result it became much harder for the upper classes to assert their supposed essential superiority by appearance and dress.[14] Edgeworth's tales are full of anecdotes that illustrate the breakdown of fashion as the sole prerogative of those in power; in *The Absentee*, for instance, tradesmen's wives give vent to fantastic interior decorating fantasies, servants look like their mistresses, and richly decorated carriages can be bought on credit. In other words, the appearance of status is no longer a strict matter of class, and the entries for "fashion" in the *Oxford English Dictionary* illustrate the shift from "being" to "appearance." The definition of fashion as Edgeworth understands it in her title, "Tales of Fashionable Life," means: "of high quality or breeding, of eminent social standing or repute."[15] The same dictionary entry also indicates the shift about which Edgeworth was worried: "This gradually merges into the current sense *b*. That moves in upper-class society, and conforms to its rules with regard to dress, expenditure, and habits." The shift from intrinsic quality to appearance and conformity in material terms indicates the blurring of the essential boundaries of class that Edgeworth affirms in her tales, but that she also fears. The importance of the connection between fashion and superior class, complicated by their uneasy status as Anglo-Irish, cannot be underestimated in the Edgeworth household, as the prominence of the issue in Richard Lovell Edgeworth's *Memoirs* (of which Maria wrote the second volume) indicates.[16]

The desire to stay firmly above the multitudes and not to yield to the excesses of fashion was instilled early into the young Richard Lovell Edgeworth. Among his earliest memories he records this anecdote of his mother reading to him from *Coriolanus*: "The contempt which Coriolanus expresses for the opinion and applause of the vulgar, for 'the voices of the greasy-headed multitude,' suited well with that disdain for low company, with which I had been first inspired by the fable of the lion and the cub" (1: 35–36). His mother also warned him against one of his relatives whose fashionable behavior ultimately led to his downfall (1: 38). From an early age, Richard professed to admire those who did not succumb to the whims of the fashions of the day; for instance, he admired his mother's friend Lady Trimblestone for her beauty and for the fact that her hair was worn in a natural style, "contrary to the fashion of that day" (1: 58). This sense of individual superiority and taste is complicated by young Richard's desire to blend with the socially superior group. When sent to school in England and teased for his Irish accent, he immediately decides to adjust his accent (1: 48). The extent of his desire, even as an adult, not to be mistaken for Irish, his desire to disengage from his group and to be accepted into the English multitude, speaks clearly from this revealing instance of contorted self-distancing:

> Travelling in stage coaches, where people attend much to the idiom of their fellow travellers, I never was taken for an Irishman, though from some organic peculiarity, I believe, in my articulation, or nonarticulation of the letter *r*, I have frequently been thought to be a native of Cumberland, and sometimes I have been mistaken for a German. (1: 63)

The uneasy mixture of class-based superiority and a sense of national inferiority, however disguised in benevolent Irish patriotism, characterizes both Richard Lovell Edgeworth and the enlightened Irish landlords in Maria's novels.

The most striking presence, however, in Richard Edgeworth's life as far as fashion, or the fear of it, is concerned, is his close friend, the eccentric Thomas Day. Edgeworth's portrait of his friend in the *Memoir* is very affectionate and generous, but even so it is hard to ignore Day's narcissistic obsession with his own belief systems as the basis of all his social interactions. Day's controlling habits and antisocial obsessions have been finely described by Mitzi Myers, and this is not the place to dwell on Day's grotesque Pygmalion-like anti-fashion experiment of educating two foundling girls into possible ideal wives for him (an idea that Edgeworth developed in *Belinda*).[17] Suffice it to point out that Day was maniacally opposed to anything fashionable: "Mr. Day had an unconquerable horror of the empire of fashion over the minds of women; simplicity, perfect innocence, and attachment to himself, were at the time the only qualifications which he desired in a wife" (1: 217). In his educational experiment, Day attempted to install anti-fashion ideas into the heads of his two wards: "by continually talking to them, by reasoning, which appeared to me above their comprehension, and by ridicule, the taste for which might afterwards be turned against himself, he endeavoured to imbue them with a deep hatred for dress, and luxury, and fine people, and fashion, and titles" (1: 217). Examples of Day's anti-fashion campaign abound, including his initial dislike of Honora (who became Edgeworth's second and by far most cherished wife) for "too much an air of fashion in her dress and manners" (1: 241). In contrast with Day's obsession about fashionable follies,

Richard Edgeworth, in perfect opposition, is credited by his daughter as "made for society" (2: 144). The contrast between the uncouth Thomas Day and the smooth, companionable Richard Edgeworth, famous for his dancing talent and his ability to charm the ladies, is emphasized by Maria in the second volume; it allows her to emphasize the need for the socialization of domestic and public virtue.

Within the domestic context of her large family, Maria Edgeworth associates "fashion" with her father's meliorist ethos of "improvement," an ethos that underlies her writing at all levels but that always excludes transgression of group boundaries. In the *Memoirs* she selects the concept of "improvement" to characterize her father: "he often assured his children, and more than asserted, demonstrated by his daily practice, that it was his ambition to improve, even to the latest hour of his life" (2: 415). In her educational tales, young children are encouraged to perform beyond their expectations; in the Irish novels, virtuous tenants aim for improved respectability and good landlords are closely involved with the improvement of the estate; in the fashionable tales, young virtuous women improve themselves all the time as opposed to the flighty flirts they are contrasted with. On a more complex level, characters are also portrayed as improving their language toward a universal norm as opposed to the Irish brogue that is associated with inferiority of character. All of these forms of "improvement" suggest an underlying ambivalence about the absolute, enlightened standards that these characters are supposed to attain in a world which, for Edgeworth, remains firmly hierarchical in terms of class, nationality, race, and creed. The rejection of certain forms of consumption, coupled with the desire to promote, manufacture, and distribute other forms congenial to their utilitarian, didactic ethos, is characteristic of the Edgeworths' desire to control their schemes of improvement, to set a fashion of sorts. The ethos of improvement, however, should not be mistaken for pluralism or democratization. Essentially conservative, Maria Edgeworth affirms clear boundaries between groups; indeed, her tales usually focus on the re-affirmation of established groups that have been threatened by infiltration. Children's play, for instance, happens strictly within class boundaries, and Edgeworth proudly points out how the children in her family "naturally" kept away from the company of servants:

> Without any prohibitions, the boys never thought of talking to the menservants, or of making them their play-fellows or companions. The chil-

dren were so completely part of our society, and so much entertained and interested in what was going on among us, so much at ease with us, that there was no temptation for them to go to the servants in search of amusement, or to escape from constraint. (*Memoirs* 2: 398)

Edgeworth's own discomfort with pluralism, her rootedness in conservative standards, is powerfully revealed in her long flirtations with national and religious characteristics that are ultimately rejected in the resolution of plots: Grace Nugent, the epitome of virtuous female Irishness in *The Absentee*, turns out to be not Irish at all. Similarly, Berenice, the virtuous example of Jewishness in *Harrington*, is revealed to be a Christian after all. No matter what pleas for tolerance the novel contains, the "purity" of the segregated groups has not been violated. In the end, all is "stable" for Edgeworth even as the agenda of enlightened rationalism has been served by an extended suggestion of compatibility and understanding. *Harrington*, for instance, allows Edgeworth to flirt with the idea of a mixed marriage between a Christian and a Jew. Berenice's wonderful characteristics are implicitly associated with her Jewishness, but in the end Edgeworth conveniently administers a *coup de grâce* to precisely the characteristic which defines the otherness of Berenice. The union of Harrington and Berenice ultimately depends on the disappearance of Berenice the Jew and the *deus ex machina* invention of Berenice the Christian.[18] In the end, Edgeworth suggests that one's nationality or creed cannot be "improved."

Edgeworth's emphasis on "improvement" in her tales and novels was in itself a fashionable statement, closely connected with the booming commercialization of goods which could be defined in terms of improvement or utility. According to J. H. Plumb, "improvement" was "the most over-used word of eighteenth-century England": "landscapes, gardens, agriculture, science, manufacture, music, art, literature, instruction both secular and religious, were constantly described as improved. Advertisements use the word to the point of boredom; after 'improvement', the phrase in which salesmen put their faith was 'new method', after that 'latest fashion.'"[19] In their attempts to disguise or embellish the capitalist dictum of creating demand, manufacturers took great pains to associate their products with instruction and moral improvement, thereby making the use of the words "fashionable" and "improved" nearly interchangeable. Plumb refers to the Edgeworths' strong disapproval of the commercialization of toys in *Practical Education*

(1798): "Maria denounced dolls and simple action toys, including baa-lambs and squeaky pigs, in favour of pencil, paper, a pair of scissors and small models of instruments used by manufacturers, such as spinning-wheels or water-mills" (311). At the same time, however, the Edgeworths came close to putting their own toys on the market when son-in-law Thomas Beddoes "considered backing a manufacturer in Bristol to make and sell the toys they recommended."[20] The scheme was dropped, but it illustrates how closely bound up the utilitarian Edgeworths were with the contemporary market of supply and demand.

On a social level, particularly within the context of Anglo-Irish estate society, Maria liked to think of her father as a trendsetter of fashionable forms of improvement in polite society, a theme she explored in great detail in *Patronage*. At their initial return to Ireland in 1782, "the fashion for literature had not commenced, and people rather shunned than courted the acquaintance of those, who were suspected to have literary taste or talents" (*Memoirs* 2: 13). However, by 1820, the time of publication of the *Memoirs*: "literature has become, as my father long ago prophesied that it would become, fashionable; so that it is really necessary to all, who would appear to advantage, even in the society of their country neighbours" (2: 376).[21] The importance of "appearing to advantage" on a cultural level is not restricted to subscribing to the right magazines, however; it extends to the entire appearance of one's house and estate. In that respect, the quest for the perfect wallpaper, sought in vain by lady Clonbrony and by Mrs Raffarty in their frustrated attempts to catch up with the fashionable trendsetters, can be read as parodic attempts at improvement.

Closely related to the excesses of interior and exterior decorating and its connection with social emulation in the tales of fashionable life is Richard Edgeworth's friendship with Josiah Wedgwood, the famous potter and member of the Lunar group, an early version of the industrial think tank, into which Edgeworth was introduced by Erasmus Darwin.[22] As the *Memoirs* clearly indicate, Edgeworth maintained close friendships with this group of enterprising intellectuals and industrialists throughout his life, mostly by letter after he moved his family to Ireland in 1782, a move that was partly motivated by his desire to excite the Irish into becoming manufacturers.[23] Richard Edgeworth's interest in the commercial application of industrial improvement, particularly in his schemes with carriages and the telegraph, and Josiah Wedgwood's mastery of that process, touched upon the two worlds that Maria Edgeworth attempts to reconcile in her writing. Those two worlds are the feudal hegemony based on authoritative landownership on the one hand, and the rugged individualism of the newly emerging market economy that requires financial savvy and entrepreneurial skills on the other hand. Wedgwood was a consummate master in the manipulation of his customers' desire for climbing the social ladder and their insecurities about taste and fashion.[24] Endless energy and creativity went into Wedgwood's commercial promotion of his products while the appearance of detached, superior ease was maintained.

Wedgwood, like Maria's father in the *Memoirs*, took great pains not to associate himself with vulgarity, even though in Wedgwood's case it was largely the money of the inevitably vulgar *nouveaux riches* that made him rich. He appealed to the willingness to spend extravagantly in order to keep up with the fashionable set, a necessity that in *The Absentee* ended up almost ruining the Clonbronies. He understood that "*[f]ashion* is infinitely superior to *merit* in many respects, and it is plain from a thousand instances that if you have a favourite child you wish the public to fondle & take notice of, you have only to make choice of proper sponcers."[25] Those proper sponsors, "legislators of taste" as Wedgwood called them, included royalty and the aristocracy whose country houses he portrayed on his pottery, whose advice he sought, and for whom he provided special display rooms and events to show them his wares.[26] At times, Wedgwood's zeal in promoting his wares resembled a full-fledged military campaign, as when he has heard of "a violent *Vase madness*" breaking out among the Irish:

> This disorder sho.d be cherish'd in some way or other, or our rivals may step in before us. We have many Irish friends who are both able & willing to help us, but they must be applied to for that purpose . . . Ld. Bessboro' you know can do a great deal for us with his friends on the other side (of) the Water by a letter of recommendation or otherwise as he may think proper. you are to visit him soon—the rest will occur to you. The Duke of Richmond has many & virtu-ous friends in Ireland. We are looking over the English Peerage to find out *lines, channels & connections*—will you look over the Irish Peerage with the same view—I need not tell you how much will depend upon a *proper & noble* introduction. This, with a fine assortment of Vases & a Trusty & *adequate* Agent will ensure us success in the conquest of our sister kingdom.[27]

The military metaphor of "the conquest of our sister kingdom" captures the assiduous, orderly diligence with which Wedgwood claimed the market for himself. As late as 1792, three years before his death, he managed to slip a focused reference to his own marketing success in a friendly letter to Edgeworth included in the *Memoirs*. The letter is largely an answer to Edgeworth's question about different kinds of clay, but at the end Wedgwood expresses his pleasure at having received young Lovell Edgeworth's poetical description of the Barbarini vase (also known as the Portland vase), probably Wedgwood's most famous reproduction of a classical urn by which he consolidated the new fashion for classically inspired urns and vases. Wedgwood's professed delight in "the perusal of this beautiful description of an unique work of ancient art" celebrates the "improving" exercise of Lovell's poetic skills and the essential beauty of the ancient artifact; it situates the commercial success of the reproduction in a context of domestic taste and improvement (*Memoirs* 2: 147).

Wedgwood successfully promoted the idea that commercially produced fashionable items can be associated with an ethos of domestic stability, taste, and improvement in which children are exposed to the supposedly timeless characteristics of classical art. The display of Wedgwood's vases as background props in fashionable portraits, the depiction of his customers' estates on Wedgwood pottery, all suggest stability and permanence in the social hierarchy.[28] In terms of marketing, however, Wedgwood skillfully manipulated the desire for mobility in the social hierarchy; by providing exclusive first access to his new collections, Wedgwood played exactly on his customers' desire to be first and foremost. Money ensured the possibility of purchase by all, but the system of privilege ensured the inevitable disappointment of belatedness of those who were not on the A-list. The dearly bought classical excesses on Mrs Raffarty's Tusculum estate only serve to illustrate her social inferiority. This emphasis on priority in the social pecking order is exactly what causes lady Clonbrony most grief and what makes her society acquaintances laugh loudest at her expense.

All these factors, the focus on "improvement" within the family, the familial relationships with Thomas Day and Josiah Wedgwood, the contradictory impulses of enlightened rationalism and crass commercialism, the ultimate sense of superiority despite the participation in the open market, serve to illuminate Maria Edgeworth's ambivalence about fashionable life in her tales. Exposure to and participation in the world of fashion is a necessary evil of sorts, but it is also an exciting, challenging opportunity for those characters, on their own or in conjunction with chosen mates, to assert the superiority of their group all the same.

Fashion is a vital instrument to help the ruling classes uphold their authority over the vast majority of society. "Visible characteristics," "appearance," "bearing," and "behaviour" (all *OED* entries for "fashion") are of the utmost importance in visibly maintaining the precarious balance of power. There is humor in the persuasion of lady Clonbrony to return to Ireland by promising her that she can set a match to the despised yellow damasked furniture in order to give her interior decorating mania scope, but the humor highlights the necessary truth that appearances do matter. And having the appearance of an intact corporate family is ultimately the fashion that the Clonbronies stand for.

Anglo-Irish absentees residing in London were particularly vulnerable members of fashionable society, and their predicament was not unlike the one of French vassals under Louis XIV whose fate is described in René König's book on fashion. The pressure to participate in costly festivities, to display solidarity while actually competing within the social hierarchy, puts a great drain on the individual's resources. König's description of the French court under Louis XIV serves as an eerie parallel to the fate of many Anglo-Irish landlords drawn to London like moths to a flame:

> Louis XIV . . . systematically attracted the great nobility to his court at Versailles to promote 'absenteeism'—the absence of the aristocratic families from their estates—and to break the independence of the feudal masters in the provinces. Their functions could then increasingly be taken over by ennobled officials (*noblesse de robe*) and the bourgeoisie, both under obligation to the absolute monarchy. During those festivities, at which the entire upper classes congregated, the originally religious and community-strengthening function of this institution occasionally became very tangibly evident, even if it was aesthetically diluted, as it were. The commensuality of the king and his aristocratic followers created over and over again strengthened a kind of mystical unity. Although the aristocrats were ruined at the end of the festivities, they returned home in heightened splendour. But history decreed that this return became a full retreat: the new forces of the bourgeoisie had meanwhile occupied one economic position after another.[29]

The situation of the Anglo-Irish absentees differed, of course, in quite a number of aspects, but the effects depicted were largely the same: in their efforts to socialize with the group they aspired to identify with (the English aristocracy) the absentees ruined themselves by their absence from the estate. In order to keep up with fashionable life in London, an endless supply of funds was needed, derived from the estate in Ireland by the middleman. Those middlemen or agents, so feared in both the *Memoirs* and the tales, ran the estate for their own profit while the landlord in London was blissfully ignorant of the state of his finances. As a result, the landowner lost his grip over the estate and got embroiled in an intricate system of debts largely incurred by an expensive lifestyle that superficially equated him with the English aristocracy.

In *The Absentee* the social ramifications of financial transactions are primarily explored in the Clonbronies' embarrassing encounters with Mordicai the coachmaker and Soho the interior decorator. At the heart of these embarrassing encounters lies lady Clonbrony's disregard for money matters, her inability to comprehend that she owes the tradesmen and not the other way around. In an economy where financial transactions are based on cash payment (as opposed to feudal service), lady Clonbrony still cherishes the illusion of superior creditworthiness based on her class and status, and on the riches of her long-since exhausted dowry, despite the family's lack of ready money. It is this sense of superiority that characterizes her incomprehension of lord Clonbrony's mortal fear of Mordicai:

> 'Why, he is only a coachmaker, is not he?' said lady Clonbrony: 'I can't think how you can talk, my lord, of dreading such a low man. Tell him, if he's troublesome, we won't bespeak any more carriages; and, I'm sure, I wish you would not be so silly, my lord, to employ him any more, when you know he disappointed me the last birthday about the landau, which I have not got yet. (60)[30]

Edgeworth's professed admiration in her tales for characters who pay off debts honorably, and who are literally and morally not indebted to anybody, jars with her equally strongly held belief that the landowning aristocracy is essentially superior to the trading classes. In her attempt to uphold aristocratic supremacy over the trading classes, Edgeworth partly absolves the Clonbronies' recklessness by characterizing the main tradesman in the book, Mordicai, as an exploitative Shylock. The malicious characterization of Mordicai obscures the volatility of the whole market, in which both debtor and creditor were inextricably connected and in which the tradesmen, more often than not, were the wronged or ruined party.[31]

The first chapters of *The Absentee* focus on the underbelly of fashionable display, the world of debt and consumption, a world whose practices Edgeworth takes great pains to discredit. It introduces the tension between the world of trade and the world of status by juxtaposing the Clonbronies' encounters with Mordicai and with Soho. The exploitative Mordicai, who is portrayed as a monstrous caricature of humanity, "unnatural and shocking," allows Edgeworth to demonize trade based on the essential characteristics of the coachmaker (7). Mordicai's corruption, his unfair refusal to honor a six-month guarantee upon Mr Berryl's curricle, glosses over the gross financial mismanagement of the Berryl family in general and lady Berryl's extravagance in particular. Instead, it prompts us to side against the tradesman, and it smooths the path toward a sympathetic response to Lady Clonbrony in her comically humiliating appointment with Soho in the following chapter. Colambre's encounter with Mordicai is complicated by the introduction of his countryman, the Falstaffian Sir Terence O'Fay, whose familiarity with Mordicai disgusts Colambre, but whose comically reported antics of "evading duns, replevying cattle, fighting sheriffs, bribing *subs*, managing cants, tricking *custodees*" (9) trigger involuntary laughter. While Mordicai is confirmed in his inferiority to Colambre by virtue of being a Jewish tradesman, sir Terence O'Fay, a "man of low extraction" who has been "knighted by an Irish lord lieutenant in some convivial frolic" (21) has managed to become the best friend and a dangerous financial lifeline of Colambre's father by virtue of his indiscriminate access to the great melting pot of Irish absentees in London who, because of their nationality, can never compete with the English aristocracy. Both forms of mingling, with tradesmen and with inferior Irish compatriots, highlight the breakdown of class boundaries in exile and constitute a form of discredit to the Clonbrony family. Colambre, Mordicai, and Terence O'Fay are all linked by Lord Clonbrony's indebted status to Mordicai, a state that ironically gives Colambre, to his horror, creditworthiness on the basis of O'Fay's assertion that the estate can be milked even more. In other words, Colambre's creditworthiness at this point is based on the potential exploitation of his father's estate. Contrary to the situation in the crushroom, when he could choose to ignore Lady Langdale and her entourage, Colambre here has to stoop to interaction with Mordicai in order to settle on a compromised sum. At the end of the chapter, Mordicai makes the most of Colambre's mortification by suggesting equality between the two of them, a suggestion that makes Colambre literally run off: "'Between ourselves, my lord,' continued Mordicai—But the familiarity of the phrase, 'Between ourselves'—this implication of equality—Lord Colambre could not admit: he moved hastily towards the door, and departed" (11).

The difference between the dehumanized, even demonized, Mordicai and the cunning coxcomb trader Soho lies in Colambre's attempted assertion of his authority toward the former and his utter impotence in dealing with the latter. In one of the most hilarious sections of the book, Lord Colambre helplessly witnesses Soho assert all his power with a "conceited, dictatorial tone" and with "condescending superiority" (11) over an entirely compliant Lady Clonbrony whose insecurity is most painfully demonstrated by her inability to exert authority over tradesmen and servants. Like Wedgwood in real life, Soho plays on his customer's sensitivity to status in: supposed exclusive access ("I refused, absolutely refused, the duchess of Torcaster"), previews of new materials ("not a soul has set eye upon the Alhambra hangings except Mrs Dareville, who stole a peep"), and an unapologetic high price tag ("as your la'ship don't value expence") (12). Soho's catalog of fashionable necessities and his torrent of jargon denote the excess of the whole chaotic exercise and the projected lack of any harmonious result.

Lady Clonbrony's gala turns out to be the disaster it has to be: the guests abuse their hostess, ridicule the furnishings, eat, drink, and are merry before absconding to the Duchess of Torcaster's function. Mrs Dareville, herself the lowest in the English pecking order as the opening scene in the crushroom indicates, is most malicious in her satirical imitation of Lady Clonbrony until Grace Nugent's "one glance of indignation" (36) stops her in her tracks. Again, Grace comes to the rescue of the family's appearance while Colambre, forced to act as host in his father's absence, "had not seen—he could not have borne to have beheld—the manner in which his mother had been treated by some of her guests" (38). Instead, Colambre finds out about Grace's sense of social pride by overhearing Lady Salisbury's anecdote about Mrs Dareville's inhospitality after staying with the Clonbronies in Ireland for a whole month. Grace's "civil courage" and "proper pride" in her retort to Mrs Dareville's slight invitation ("A day!—Certainly—to you, who gave us a month" [37]) is the topic for gossip in which her admirable pride, her superiority in the world of fashion, is asserted to the satisfaction of Colambre.

Secure in his Irish heritage, largely, ironically, because of his entirely English upbringing that has forged his confidence as a man of fashion, Colambre is remarkably impatient with, even ignorant of, the amount of manipulative jockeying that regulates the dynamics of the female world of fashion. While the problematic transactions among men are articulated in numerical financial terms of debt and credit, the creditworthiness of women is much harder to gauge, but their interactions are crucial markers of the whole family's social status. Colambre's inability to react subtly to the insulting behavior of Mr Soho toward his own mother, and to the putdowns of Mrs Dareville and Lady Langdale demonstrates his unease with the social flexibility, however distasteful, that has become the norm. No matter how deficient in personal merit or creditworthiness, Lady Clonbrony, as the matriarch of the Clonbrony estate, needs to be protected from upstarts, traders, and condescending English nobility, and Grace manages to do this, not by defensive behavior, but by addressing the enemy with its own weapons of wit and well-timed facial expressions. Unlike Colambre, Grace does not betray her impatience or her emotions; her cool behavior is her most fashionable asset. Nonetheless, Lady Clonbrony is as incapable of keeping her servants in check as she is of refraining from imposing herself upon her fashionable acquaintances. When she fails to bribe Lady St James' servants, she relies on her lowly companion miss Pratt to act as a scout; miss Pratt rather waspishly "suggested that perhaps, though every thing else had failed, dried salmon might be tried with success" (54).

Lady Clonbrony's victory in gaining entrance to Lady St James's party with an Irish gift is pyrrhic, for lady St James had already organized an alternative, select party for the Duchess of Torcaster after it became obvious that it had become "impossible not to *ask the Clonbronies*" (55). Embarrassed by Lady St James's thanks, Lady Clonbrony publicly betrays Ireland once more, which provokes a spirited defense of Ireland by the assertive Lady Oranmore, the sole example in the novel of an Irish landed gentry who exudes authority in both England and Ireland. More mortifyingly, certainly for Grace, if not for Lady Clonbrony, who may be blind to the subtlety of the strategy, the English elite assert their fashionable status by rhetorical exclusion. In contrast to her own display of excess, Lady Clonbrony is kept at a safe distance by a form of rhetorical minimalism, rigid politeness that precludes the intimacy that she craves: "By the most punctilious respect and nice regard to precedency, even by words of courtesy—'Your ladyship does me honour,' &c.—lady St James contrived to mortify and to mark the difference between those with whom she was, and with whom she was not, upon terms of intimacy and equality" (56).

Lady Clonbrony's failure to obtrude into the fashionable elite is matched by her failure to prevent her maidservant from transgressing the barriers that separate them. Mrs Petito's appetite for her mistress's clothes, perhaps the most powerful immediate marker of one's fashionable status, denotes a lust for social climbing that Edgeworth denounces. Having well-dressed servants cuts both ways: they advertise the wealth and fashionable status of their employers, but too close a resemblance between mistress and maid blurs the essential distinction in rank between them. The common practice of giving cast-off clothes to servants, now complemented by the greater ease of access for all to commercially produced fashionable goods, allows servants to participate in the social hierarchy in unprecedented ways. Petito's victorious, threatening ways with Lady Clonbrony are contrasted with her inability to achieve any familiarity with Grace and Miss Broadhurst. Petito leaves the Clonbrony household, and her zenith of fashionable triumph comes in her use of lady Dashfort's "cast barouche" (89) which, like a hand-me-down dress, is kept for use by the maids. Apart from the obvious connotations of Lady Dashfort's ostentatious spending, the use of the carriage by maids also symbolizes the obliteration of the traditional hierarchy of masters and servants who are "as fine ladies, as great dashers too, every bit, as their principals" (89). The carriage as a fashionable asset of splendid mobility allows the maids to circulate with ease and intimacy among the upper classes. In an echo of Colambre's fraught encounter with Mordicai, Mrs Petito's behavior toward Colambre is characterized "with gracious intimacy" (90), and she scores a public victory by forcing an exchange of addresses between them by manipulating him with her knowledge of his affection for Grace:

> Lord Colambre, withdrawing his whip from Mrs Petito, turned his horse away. She, stretching over the back of the barouche as he rode off, bawled to him, 'My lord, we're at Stephen's Green, when we're at Dublin.' But as he did not choose to hear, she raised her voice to its highest pitch, adding, 'And where are you, my lord, to be found?—as I have a parcel of miss Nugent's for you.'
> Lord Colambre instantly turned back, and gave his direction.
> 'Cleverly done, faith!' said the major. (91)

Mrs Petito's double scheme to secure Grace's grandfather for herself and to become "his dear Mrs Reynolds!" while acting as Lady

Dashfort's ambassador comes to nothing, and she has to content herself with the "long looked-for object of her ambition, Lady Dashfort's scarlet velvet gown" (236) as the reward for her disloyal services. The interaction between Petito and Lady Dashfort is purely mercenary and uses fashion (clothes, the use of the carriage) for its currency. The idea of Petito transcending her servant status is unthinkable in Edgeworth's setting, but Lady Dashfort may prove to be a more formidable enemy in the security of her own fashionable status.

In order to justify an interclass marriage, Edgeworth resorts to recasting the desired alliance between money and birth in terms of a union between moral creditworthiness and merit. For the money of the *nouveaux riches* (a phrase for which the *O.E.D.* credits Edgeworth with first recorded usage in English) to be morally acceptable it has to be stripped of its primary connotation as a currency that leads to a leveling in status of the fashionable elite.[32] The marriage of Miss Broadhurst and sir Arthur Berryl is cast in those terms, with both parties diverging considerably from the values of their parents. Arthur Berryl's parents suffer their demise as debtors to Mordicai because of Sir John's financial neglect and Lady Berryl's fashionable extravagance, "especially in equipages" (48). Arthur's efforts to repay his father's debts are rewarded by his marriage to Miss Broadhurst, an heiress who is credited with having turned her father's money-making stratagems into characteristics of merit:

> Her father realised his immense fortune by the power and habit of constant, bold, and just calculation. The power and habit which she had learned from him she applied on a far larger scale: with him, it was confined to speculations for the acquisition of money; with her, it extended to the attainment of happiness. He was calculating and mercenary: she was estimative and generous. (72)

Together, Sir Arthur Berryl and Miss Broadhurst form a new fashionable order in contrast to their parents: she brings the fortune but not the actual acquisition of it, while he brings the title, but not the careless, spendthrift mentality associated with it. Their courtship, tellingly, starts by the mistaken efforts of Mrs Broadhurst and lady Clonbrony to engineer a match by "propinquity" between miss Broadhurst and Colambre. Their marriage consolidates two estates into a larger, more solid one; at the same time, Miss Broadhurst's admiration for Berryl is based not on inherited characteristics but on moral creditworthiness. Proofs of his strength of character include "his refraining from all personal expences, his going without equipage and without horses, that he might do what he felt to be right, whilst it exposed him continually to the ridicule of fashionable young men, or to the charge of avarice" (184).

The Broadhurst-Berryl alliance prefigures the union of Grace and Colambre, a union which is most seriously threatened by the most fashionable character in the book, the seductive, morally bankrupt Lady Dashfort. The fact that Colambre encounters Lady Dashfort in Ireland allows Edgeworth to articulate several concerns about fashionable living in the very setting from which the Clonbronies draw their subsistence and to which Colambre hopes to return. The attraction of Lady Dashfort for Colambre is partly explained by his eagerness to distance himself from the *nouveau riche* Mrs. Raffarty, the wife of a *pro tempore* grocer whose comic attempts at splendid grandeur are an uncomfortable reminder of Colambre's mother's pretensions in London:

> It was the same desire to appear what they were not, the same vain ambition to vie with superior rank or fortune, or fashion, which actuated lady Clonbrony and Mrs Raffarty; and whilst this ridiculous grocer's wife made herself the sport of some of her guests, lord Colambre sighed, from the reflection that what she was to them his mother was to persons in a higher rank of fashion. (88)

In order to appear as she is, Lady Clonbrony needs to be in Ireland, the site where she can appear to fashionable advantage over the likes of Mrs. Raffarty. Her wish to "set the fashion of something better in that country" (195) can be materialized to far greater advantage on the inherited family estate. Despite the obvious parallels between bourgeois upstarts in Dublin and Irish absentees in London, Mrs Raffarty is portrayed more harshly and held more personally accountable for her actions than Lady Clonbrony. Disastrous pronouncements about art and architecture are put directly into her mouth, while Lady Clonbrony's mistakes are partly glossed over by the patronizing statements of Soho, himself exposed for his hauteur, and by the outright nastiness of Mrs Dareville, which softens the reader with a sense of pity for Lady Clonbrony.

In contrast, Lady Dashfort's amoral wit, her intelligence and charm are aspects of her Englishness. The underlying sense in Edgeworth's writings that England is perceived as somehow superior in intellectual and cultural capital, and that emulation on the part of the Irish is inevitable, gives Lady Dashfort an authority beyond her status and morality. Sir James, who previously had instructed Colambre in great detail about the Mrs Raffarties (80–81), exclaims that he hopes the Dashforts may never land in Ireland again: "'One worthless woman, especially one worthless Englishwoman of rank, does incalculable mischief in a country like this, which looks up to the sister country for fashion'" (89). While Lady Clonbrony's and Mrs Raffarty's desperate attempts at fashionable splendor take the form of excessive emulation of a superior set, Lady Dashfort's main strategy is to shun submission to any authority. Lady Dashfort operates outside of authority; instead, she is an English authority in her own right who creates mischief in Ireland by blurring boundaries of decorous behavior and by being the fashionable success of every party. Her attractiveness lies in her perceived superiority to any rank; not only does she consider herself "above the thunder of vulgar censure," but she is treated accordingly, entirely on the grounds of her perceived superior, English rank: "her rank was so high that none could dare to call her vulgar: what would have been gross in any one of meaner note, in her was freedom or originality, or lady Dashfort's way" (96). As a result, Lady Dashfort is fashion incarnate, the arbitrary, fickle code of power in high society: "Lady Dashfort forced her way, and she set the fashion: fashion, which converts the ugliest dress into what is beautiful and charming, governs the public mode in morals and in manners; and thus, when great talents and high rank combine, they can debase or elevate the public taste" (96). In her utter indifference to approval, Lady Dashfort is a formidable enemy to Colambre, whom she perceives as the means which she needs to live in style. Living in style means living in London, hence her plan "to disgust" Colambre "with his native country" so as to "confirm him an absentee" (101). The Dashforts are largely impervious to moral censure imposed from outside, and their destruction is tellingly self-inflicted in the form of Isabel's loose lipped bragging, overheard by Colambre (121).

Lady Dashfort's success in making Colambre laugh despite himself is rooted in her psychological perceptivenes about Colambre's own desire for fashionable superiority, his Darcy-like vanity of perception, and the delight he takes in the fantasy of being the knight in shining armor towards the beautiful, victim-like widowed daughter. Lady Dashfort's zenith of influence over Colambre coincides with the visit to Killpatrickstown, an estate incorporating all the mistakes in outdated estate management that Edgeworth also detailed in *Castle Rackrent, Ennui,* and *Ormond*: spendthrift domestic management based on favor as opposed to merit, inappropriate repairs and alterations, subdivision, bad justice, neglect of the tenants, and excessive, obsequious hospitality. Lady Dashfort does not have to point directly at these problems; instead she comments, cajoles, and imitates a range of Irish brogues (an art in which Edgeworth herself excelled). Her malice goes without saying, but its success, however temporary, is entirely based on Colambre's complicity in perception. Together, Lady Dashfort and Colambre share a sense of humor based on their sense of fashionable superiority.[33] Fashionable superiority is exactly what the Clonbronies will assert on their estate as it will be run by Colambre and Grace.

The conclusion of *The Absentee* sums up the importance of fashion in a seriously humorous way. Larry Brady, in pseudofeudal allegiance to his liege Colambre, writes to his brother Pat to convince him to abandon life in London, where he is employed by Mordicai the coachmaker, and to return to Ireland. Leaving Mordicai is symbolic of leaving the dangerous vortex of consumerism and its moral dangers. The world to which Pat Brady would be returning has been celebrating the return of the Clonbronies with a huge bonfire of the "*ould* yellow damask furniture" (256) that has been replaced by a snow-white set which has been handworked by Grace, the prospective new lady of the manor. Finally, Larry concludes his enthusiastic plea to Pat with "and another thing, Pat, you would not be out of fashion—and you see it's growing the fashion not to be an Absentee" (256). However tongue-in-cheek on Edgeworth's part, Larry's words highlight the importance of "fashion" as a powerful motivator for people's actions and lifestyles. Not only is it, in Edgeworth's sense, politically wise to manage one's own estate, it is also fashionable.

NOTES

1. William Hazlitt, *The Spirit of the Age and Conversations of James Northcote, Esq., R.A.*, vol. 11 of *The Complete Works of William Hazlitt*, ed. P. P. Howe (London: Dent, 1931), 293.

2. Francis Jeffrey, *Contributions to the Edinburgh Review. Complete in One Volume* (London, 1853), 665.

3. See, for instance, Vivian Mercier, *The Irish Comic Tradition* (Oxford: Clarendon, 1972); Eiléan Ní Chuilleanáin, "The Voices of Maria Edgeworth's Comedy,"

in *The Comic Tradition in Irish Women Writers*, ed. Theresa O'Connor (Gainesville: University Press of Florida, 1996), 21–39. For a feminist approach, see Audrey Bilger, *Laughing Feminism: Subversive Comedy in Frances Burney, Maria Edgeworth, and Jane Austen* (Detroit: Wayne State University Press, 1998).

4. Maria Edgeworth, "Advertisement" to *Belinda* (London: J. M. Dent, 1993).

5. Quoted in A. J. C. Hare, ed., *Life and Letters of Maria Edgeworth* (London, 1894), 1: 178.

6. For an excellent assessment of Edgeworth's eclipse from fame, see Mitzi Myers, "Shot From Canons; or, Maria Edgeworth and the Cultural Production and Consumption of the Eighteenth-Century Woman Writer," in *The Consumption of Culture 1600–1800: Image, Object, Text*, eds. Ann Bermingham and John Brewer (London: Routledge, 1995), 193–214.

7. For points of comparison between Edgeworth and Austen, see Marilyn Butler, *Jane Austen and the War of Ideas* (Oxford: Clarendon, 1975). For a recent fine assessment of Austen's relationship to the popular novelists of her time, see Mary Waldron, *Jane Austen and the Fiction of Her Time* (Cambridge: Cambridge University Press, 1999). Paul Delany opens new ways of reading Austen in terms of social stratification in "'A Sort of Notch in the Donwell Estate': Intersections of Status and Class in *Emma*," *Eighteenth-Century Fiction* 12 (2000): 533–48.

8. Gary Kelly, *English Fiction of the Romantic Period 1789–1830* (London: Longman, 1989), 81–82.

9. For a delightful, detailed analysis of the commercialization of fashion in the late eighteenth and early nineteenth century, see Neil McKendrick, John Brewer, and J. H. Plumb, *The Birth of a Consumer Society: The Commercialization of Eighteenth-Century England* (London: Europa Publications, 1982). The essays in the collection of particular interest for this essay are Neil McKendrick's "The Commercialization of Fashion" (34–99) and "Josiah Wedgwood and the Commercialization of the Potteries (100–145), John Brewer's "Commercialization and Politics" (197–262), and J. H. Plumb's "The New World of Children in Eighteenth-Century England" (286–315).

10. Hazlitt, *Spirit of the Age*, 293.

11. See, for instance, Meredith Cary, "Privileged Assimilation: Maria Edgeworth's Hope for the Ascendancy," *Eire-Ireland* 26 (1991): 29–37; Gary Kelly, "Class, Gender, Nation, and Empire: Money and Merit in the Writing of the Edgeworths," *Wordsworth Circle* 25 (1994): 89–93; Teresa Michals, "Commerce and Character in Maria Edgeworth," *Nineteenth-Century Literature* 49 (1994): 1–20.

12. Bernard Mandeville, *The Fable of the Bees: or, Private Vice, Publick Benefits*, ed. F. B. Kaye (Oxford: Clarendon, 1924), 1: 6–7.

13. All references and quotations from *Ormond* are from Maria Edgeworth, *Ormond*, ed. Claire Connolly, vol. 8 of *The Novels and Selected Works of Maria Edgeworth*, ed. Marilyn Butler et al. (London: Pickering and Chatto, 1999). Further references are provided parenthetically in the text.

14. See McKendrick, Brewer, and Plumb, *Consumer Society*, for the state of fashion and consumption at the turn of the eighteenth century. For more details on the actual dress fashions, see Alison Adburgham, *Shops and Shopping, 1800–1914: Where, and in what Manner the Well-dressed Englishwoman Bought her Clothes* (London: Allen and Unwin, 1964).

15. All dictionary quotations are from the *Oxford English Dictionary Online* (Oxford: Oxford University Press, 2000).

16. All references are from Richard Lovell and Maria Edgeworth, *Memoirs of Richard Lovell Edgeworth, begun by himself and concluded by his daughter Maria Edgeworth*, 2 vols., 1820 (Shannon: Irish University Press, 1969).

17. See Mitzi Myers, "My Art Belongs to Daddy? Thomas Day, Maria Edgeworth, and the Pre-Texts of *Belinda*: Women Writers and Patriarchal Authority," *in Revising Women: Eighteenth-Century "Women's Fiction" and Social Engagement*, ed. Paula R. Backscheider (Baltimore: Johns Hopkins University Press, 2000), 104–46. For more about the role of Thomas Day in Maria Edgeworth's life, see Marilyn Butler, *Maria Edgeworth: A Literary Biography* (Oxford: Clarendon, 1972) and Marilyn Butler, "Edgeworth's Stern Father: Escaping Thomas Day, 1795–1801," in *Tradition in Transition: Women Writers, Marginal Texts, and the Eighteenth-Century Canon*, eds. Alvaro Ribeiro and James G. Basker (Oxford: Clarendon, 1996), 75–93.

18. Edgeworth's anti-Semitism and racism extends also to her qualified support of slavery; see for instance George E. Boulukos, "Maria Edgeworth's 'Grateful Negro' and the Sentimental Argument for Slavery," *Eighteenth-Century Life* 23 (1999): 12–29. See also Susan C. Greenfield, "'Abroad and at Home': Sexual Ambiguity, Miscegenation, and Colonial Boundaries in Edgeworth's *Belinda*," *PMLA* 112 (1997): 214–28; Kathryn Kirkpatrick, "'Gentlemen Have Horrors Upon This Subject': West Indian Suitors in Maria Edgeworth's *Belinda*," *Eighteenth-Century Fiction* 5 (1993): 331–48; Edgar E. MacDonald, ed., *The Education of the Heart: The Correspondence of Rachel Mordicai Lazarus and Maria Edgeworth* (Chapel Hill: University of North Carolina Press, 1977); Silvia Mergenthal, "The Shadow of Shylock: Scott's *Ivanhoe* and Edgeworth's *Harrington*" in *Scott in Carnival: Selected Papers from the Fourth International Scott Conference, Edinburgh, 1991*, ed. J. H. Alexander and David Hewitt (Aberdeen: University of Aberdeen Press, 1993), 320–31; Michael Ragussis, "Representation, Conversion, and Literary Form: *Harrington* and the Novel of Jewish Identity," *Critical Inquiry* 16 (1989): 113–43; Sheila A. Spector, "The Other's Other: The Function of the Jew in Maria Edgeworth's Fiction," *European Romantic Review* 10 (1999): 307–40; Heidi Thomson, "Introduction" in Maria Edgeworth, *The Absentee* (Harmondsworth: Penguin, 2000), vii–xviii.

19. See Plumb's essay in McKendrik et al., *Consumer Society*, 332.

20. Butler, *Biography*, 170.

21. Edgeworth substantiates this claim by the tremendous increase in magazine subscriptions: "About the year 1783 or 1784, my father happened to be present in the only great bookseller's shop then in Dublin, when a cargo of new books from London arrived, and among them, the Reviews, or *the Review*, for the Monthly Review was the only one then sufficiently in circulation, to make its way to Ireland. Of these, my father found upon inquiry, that not above a dozen, or twenty at the utmost, were ordered in this island. I am informed, that more than two thousand Reviews are now taken in regularly. This may give some measure of the general increase of our taste for literature. The Edinburgh and Quarterly Reviews are now to be found in the houses of most of our principal farmers: and all therein contained, and the positive, comparative, and superlative merits and demerits of Scott, Campbell, and lord Byron, are now as common table and tea-table talk here, as in any part of the United Empire" (*Memoirs* 2: 377).

22. See Butler, *Biography*, 32–34.

23. See Butler, *Biography*: "In January 1782 he told Wedgwood of his decision to go home, adding that 'if the inhabitants are excited to industry by the present

opportunity of becoming manufacturers,' Ireland could develop into he best remaining British possession [RLE to Jos. Wedgwood, Brereton Green, Cheshire, Jan. 1782]" (77).

24. On Wedgwood, see McKendrick, "Commercialization"; for more information about the Wedgwood firm, see their carefully constructed website (http://www.wedgwood.co.uk) which emphasizes information about history and heritage just as much as on-line sales.

25. Quoted from a 1779 manuscript in McKendrik, "Commercialization," 108.

26. McKendrik, "Commercialization," 110–15.

27. From a letter to Thomas Bentley, written on 2 August 1770, quoted in McKendrik, "Commercialization," 117.

28. See McKendrick, "Commercialization," 110–11.

29. René König, *A la Mode: On the Social Psychology of Fashion*, trans. F. Bradley (New York: Seabury Press, 1973), 109.

30. All references and quotations from *The Absentee* are from Maria Edgeworth, *The Absentee*, eds. Heidi Thomson and Kim Walker (Harmondsworth: Penguin, 2000).

31. For the problems which tradesmen faced, see John Brewer's chapter, "Commercialization and Politics" in McKendrik et al., *Consumer Society*, 192–262.

32. The quotation entry from the *OED* refers to Edgeworth's letter of 6 April 1813: "Larry the footboy and Mrs. Rafferty's dinner are nothing to what has been seen at the dinners of les nouveaux riches at Liverpool and Manchester." The reference is to her own novel *The Absentee* which was actually published a year earlier, in *Tales of Fashionable Life* (1812).

33. Colambre's complicity prevents me from reading lady Dashfort's action as a form of misrepresentation to which Colambre falls victim. For a different view, see Terry Eagleton, *Heathcliff and the Great Hunger* (London: Verso, 1995): "One of the most vigorous characters of *The Absentee* is Lady Dashfort, who maliciously misrepresents Ireland to the young hero Colambre because she has her private reasons for not wishing him to live there" (168).

"Games of Chance": *Belinda,* Education, and Empire

Jessica Richard

NEAR THE HALFWAY POINT OF MARIA EDGEWORTH'S NOVEL *BELINDA* (1801), the eponymous heroine plays jack-straws with Charles Percival, a young boy. Belinda's suitor, Mr. Vincent, quickly wagers "a hundred guineas on the steadiness of Miss Portman's hand." Charles answers with a bet of sixpence:

> "Done! Done!" cried Mr. Vincent.
> "Done! Done!" cried the boy, stretching out his hand, but his father caught it.
> "Softly! softly, Charles! No betting, if you please, my dear. Done! and done!—sometimes ends in—Undone."
> "It was my fault—it was I who was in the wrong," cried Vincent.[1]

This scene brings together seemingly discrete elements of Edgeworth's novel under the aegis of gambling: the incorporation of the Edgeworths' educational theory through the model family, the Percivals, and the presentation, through Vincent, a Creole planter, of new types of British identity that grew out of the expanding empire. As a child and a colonial slave owner lay a wager against each other, the nexus of gambling, education, and empire in this scene draws our attention to the prominence of gaming in Edgeworth's analyses of education and of the expanding British empire in her pedagogical and fictional writing.

Edgeworth's fundamental attitude toward gambling is ambivalent and even contradictory; children should avoid games of chance but parents should use chance as an instructional tool, while the adult gamester's fascination with chance is reprehensible. Edgeworth's equivocal representations of gaming betray her anxiety about her career-long project to constitute the self as a rational being and to portray the social system in which this rational being is a subject as carefully ordered and capable of rational improvement. Richard Lovell and Maria Edgeworth's philosophy of moral action celebrates personal control: both children and adults ought to act from rational principles. Children should be taught that their own actions can bring about their happiness, and adults should make decisions based on reason rather than on emotion. In gaming, however, the rational self risks being undone by passion, by chance, and even by cheaters. Mr. Percival's intervention in his son's jack-straw wager suggests that a carefully supervised exposure to chance, which Vincent never received, could produce properly educated colonial subjects, a population that would allay Edgeworth's fear that British society at the turn of the nineteenth century was not rationally ordered but was itself a game of chance.

The Percivals, *Belinda*'s model Edgeworthian family, teach their children to prefer "game[s] of address, not chance" (249). Throughout her pedagogical and fictional writing, Edgeworth often promotes such "games of address" as billiards, which requires skill and calls for rational analysis, and suggests children avoid "games of chance," thought to encourage indolence. This careful parsing of types of gaming reflects the metamorphosis in the eighteenth century of playing cards and other games from instruments of chance to educational tools used to teach children everything from grammar to morality. By the end of the century, childhood gambling was discouraged by many educational writers, yet even as Edgeworth forbids gambling she remains interested in the pedagogical uses of chance. Thus, she encourages parents to harness its power in the formation of their child subjects.

These children are the subjects of an expanding empire that gives Edgeworth some uneasiness. Drawing on extensive stereotypes of West Indians, Edgeworth identifies Vincent's gambling propensity as a West Indian trait that he has brought to England. In the scene that opens this essay, Vincent blames himself for encouraging Charles Percival to wager, declaring, "It was I who was in the wrong." Because, in Edgeworth's pedagogy, encounters with chance are crucial to the formation of the self, Vincent's childhood gambling among slaves on his father's West Indian plantation molds his character. But even though Vincent's gambling discredits him, the novel is unable to contain the threat to Edgeworthian rational subjectivity he represents. In the preliminary sketch for the novel, Belinda has only one suitor, Clarence Hervey, but in the completed novel she comes close to marrying the Creole planter Vincent.[2] In the sketch, Hervey was a dissipated gamester who gets ill after "drinking for a wager" (483), but in the novel, although he is eccentric and for a time deluded by Rousseauvian educational schemes, he "never play[s]" (419). Instead, gaming is Vincent's fatal flaw, and, though there are other minor, British characters who game, such as Lord Delacour and Mrs. Luttridge, the novel links the passion for play to Vincent's upbringing in the West Indies.

It is difficult to determine, however, whether by using gaming as a convenient plot mechanism, Edgeworth's novel is covertly condemning the speculative imperialist enterprise of the colonies and the slave labor on which they depend, or whether it is hoping to avoid taking a stand on the controversial topic of slavery by vilifying Vincent as a gamester, rather than as a slave owner. In the end, *Belinda* cannot maintain its desired organization of British society into the schema of "Abroad and at Home" (the title of the preliminary sketch for the novel); the gamester's signifying instability is a symptom of the resistance of late eighteenth-century British imperial society to traditional classifications and hierarchies. At the end of the novel, even as the creole gamester Vincent and the gender-bender Harriet Freke are punished, the ex-slave Juba marries a white English servant, the cheating gamestress Mrs. Luttridge goes virtually unpunished, and West Indian slave-based wealth continues to underwrite British society, making the final resolution of the novel possible as Mr. Hartley, a Jamaican planter, and Captain Sunderland, fresh from defeating a slave revolt, are reunited with Virginia St. Pierre. This last is particularly important; despite the gamester's exclusion, English society is unable to isolate itself from West Indians, their wealth, or the sources of that wealth.

Finally, rampant cheating undermines the Edgeworths' careful distinction between games of address and games of chance. Cheating erodes the fair-minded player's ability to play games of address according to principles of reason and thus compromises the Edgeworthian constitution of the self as a rational being. More broadly, cheating undermines the ability of characters to assess each other accurately, while the detection of cheating becomes one of the most valuable skills in the turn-of-the-century fluctuating social system that Edgeworth depicts.

GAMES OF CHANCE: EDUCATION

In *Practical Education* (1798), Edgeworth and her father, Richard Lovell Edgeworth, conclude a discussion of toys by explaining that although they have "recommended all trials of address and dexterity . . . games of chance, we think should be avoided, as they tend to give a taste for gambling."[3] The Edgeworths' theory of the psychology of gaming underwrites their persistent interest in this opposition between games of address and games of chance. Vain people, they believe, develop a taste for gaming because apparent "good luck" (though only a chance outcome) suggests personal merit. Indolent people prefer games of chance either because such play awakens them with little effort from "their habitual state of apathy" or because it makes them equal or superior to their competitors "without any mental exertion" (54). Children who learn, on the other hand, the pleasure of "well-earned praise" will not look "to *chance* for the increase of self approbation" (55). This opposition between games of address and of chance dovetails with a broad goal of *Practical Education*: to help parents teach their children the value of "practice and industry" (28). As in Edgeworth's story "Murad the Unlucky,"[4] where apparent good luck is shown to be the result of prudence and of careful exertion, in *Practical Education* the Edgeworths suggest that when a game seems to depend on "some *knack* or *mystery*," parents should explain to children "how or why . . . they succeed or fail: we may show them, that, in reality, there is no *knack* or *mystery* in any thing, but that from certain causes certain effects will follow" (27).

The Edgeworths' pedagogy means to empower children by showing them how they can learn to control events. This is a scientific process[5]: when learning a game or a skill, "after trying a number of experiments, the circumstances essential to success may be discovered"[6] (27–28). The goals of this educational model are similar to those of probability theory, namely, to increase one's feeling of power in the face of chance by analyzing its operations. The "sober lesson" that outcomes are the consequence of industry rather than luck "may be taught to children without putting it into grave words, or without formal precepts" (28). But even as this educational model demystifies chance in order to promote a scientific analysis of causes and effects that is supposed to develop children's habits of industriousness, Edgeworthian pedagogy depends for its efficacy on chance events, or, more properly, on the parent's manipulation of chance events for educational ends.

The Edgeworths encourage the parent or educator to take advantage of children's inherent love of toys and games, rather than to fight against it. In *Practical Education*, a father explains centrifugal motion after his children happen to see its effects; in *Belinda*, when the Percival children wonder whether their goldfish can hear, Dr. X— tells them the history of a learned dispute on this subject.[7] Education depends on developing the chance occurrence into an instructional occasion. Madame de Rosier, the eponym of Edgeworth's *The Good French Governess*, "knew how much of the art of instruction depends upon seizing the proper moments to introduce new ideas."[8] When Mr. Percival intervenes in Charles's jack-straw wager with Vincent, rather than scold the boy, he uses the occasion to discuss different kinds of games and betting situations. In *Belinda*, the Percival children have been guided toward amusements that give them pleasure but also afford instruction. They collect mineral specimens, look at sulfurs, and visit a bird-seller to see the different breeds they have read about.

Edgeworth's interest in toys that co-opted the engrossing chance event for educational ends can be traced back to John Locke's suggestion, in *Thoughts on Education*, that children wager with a twenty-six-sided alphabetical die in order to learn their letters, "it being as good a sort of play to lay a stake who shall first throw an A or B, as who upon dice shall throw six or seven."[9] Eighteenth-century booksellers issued packs of playing cards that tried, in Locke's words, to "cozen [children] into Knowledge" by turning learning into a game.[10] Playing cards quickly assumed a place in the iconography of childhood; paintings like William Hogarth's "The House of Cards" (1730) and Joseph Francis Nollekens's "The Two Children of the Nollekens Family Playing with a Top and Playing Cards" (1745), suggest both the fragility of childhood and children's inventiveness in images of children building houses of cards. Building on this evident appeal of cards, not just as instruments of chance but as children's toys, card makers issued geographical, alphabetical, grammatical, astronomical, and historical cards, some of which featured both the markings of regular playing cards and instructional material so that children could play card games and learn at the same time, while others abandoned the option of gaming and followed only the size and shape of playing cards. Indeed, an edition of Isaac Watts's *Divine and Moral Songs for Children* takes advantage of the popularity of the playing-card format even though one of the songs, "The Child's Complaint," denounces play with the verse, "Why should I love my sport so well. / So constant at my play; / And loose [*sic*] the thoughts of heav'n and hell / And then forget to pray?"[11]

These educational playing cards illustrated a range of lessons suitable to young subjects of the burgeoning empire. Card packs engraved with the arms of English and Scottish peers[12] instructed children in the order of an aristocratic social and political system, while alphabet cards with proverbs such as "Be learn'd and polite / And quite cleanly be seen / And you'll merit the notice / Of Charlotte our Queen" and "Huzza! For King *George* / How noble he looks! He knows all his Letters / And reads well in Books"[13] promote the monarchs as models of politeness and learning. Even a pack demonstrating Latin grammar featured images of the monarchs of Europe,[14] as if to remind the young scholar that learning did not take place outside of ideology. Geographical card packs taught children to delineate the boundaries of empire, enumerating the counties and products of England and inscribing ethnic difference, as on the eight of spades in a circa 1790 pack where a child could read, among other facts about Turkey, that "The Turks have black hair and black eyes."[15] Dice games, like cards, could also model the values of the society and represent the institutions of punishment for deviance from these values, as is evident in an early board game called "The New Game of Virtue Rewarded and Vice Punished" (1810). Players advanced on a board through symbolic scenes representing "Faith" and "Prudence" if they threw the dice on certain numbers and retreated back to "The Stocks" or "The House of Correction" if they threw other numbers.[16] Games of chance are not thoroughly stable as pedagogical tools, however; this game metes out reward or punishment capriciously, based not on virtue or vice, but on the chance landing of dice. No wonder that even as some educators counseled parents to use chance for instructive ends, most, like the Edgeworths, remained fundamentally suspicious about children's gaming. Mary Wollstonecraft, for example, in her *Thoughts on the Education of Daughters* (1787), warned that "nothing can be more absurd than permitting girls to acquire a fondness for cards."[17]

Alongside these disagreements about the use of games of chance for instruction in virtue, other advisors actually recommended gaming itself as an important component of a child's education. The late seventeenth-century French writers Maréchal de Caillière and the Chevalier de Méré both argued that gaming was an important skill for a gentleman. Gaming could afford an impoverished nobleman the opportunity to replenish his fortune with honor, could cultivate a mastery over passion, and could provide admission to upper-class circles.[18] In England, gaming was not just the high-stakes aristocratic amusement that it was in France; it occupied the disposable income of all levels of society. Some skill in gaming was desirable, therefore, if only as a defense against sharpers. Richard Seymour claimed that his treatise *The Court Gamester* (1718) would help readers detect "Frauds in Play"; although it is dedicated to "the young Princesses," it addresses middle-class aspirations. As Seymour explains in his preface, "Gaming is become so much the fashion among the Beau Monde, that he who in Company should appear ignorant of the games in Vogue, would be reckoned low bred and hardly fit for conversation."[19] Edmond Hoyle was the first to grasp fully the possible market in gaming instruction. In addition to publishing his "Short Treatise on the Game of Whist" (1742), which became the standard rule book for the game until 1869, he tutored would-be players of whist for one guinea a lesson. In 1753, a London newspaper remarked, "[t]here is a new kind of tutor lately introduced into some Families of Fashion in this Kingdom principally to complete the education of the Young Ladies, namely a Gaming Master; who attends his Hour as regularly as the Music, Dancing, and French Master; in order to instruct young Misses in Principles of the fashionable Accomplishment of Card playing."[20] Skill in gaming, then, was part of the display of status for both men and women, an important element in the assemblage of "accomplishments" and leisure occupations that parents hoped might help their children ascend the social hierarchy depicted, for example, in the ranks of peerage on the armorial packs of playing cards described above.

While players might ascend a social ladder via gaming, they could just as easily descend an economic one. The anonymous author of the satirical essay "A Modest Defence of Gaming" (1754) facetiously suggests that gaming is educational because it exposes and inures us to economic flux, "teach[ing] us to bear up against the Charms of Wealth and the Terrors of Poverty" in addition to inculcating a salutary disdain of riches.[21] For the Edgeworths, monetary loss in gaming is inevitable, so "practical education" must involve not only preparation for loss but rational decisions about how much one is willing to lose. In Maria Edgeworth's later novel *Ormond* (1817), the eponymous virtuous character enters enthusiastically into his host's regular gaming parties. When a concerned onlooker warns him to take care, he responds,

> "But there is no danger of my acquiring a taste for play, because I am determined to lose."

"Bon!" said the abbé, "that is the most singular determination I ever heard; explain that to me then, Monsieur."

"I have determined to lose a certain sum—suppose five hundred guineas—I have won and lost backwards and forwards, and have been longer about it than you would conceive to be probable, but it is not yet lost. The moment it is, I shall stop short. By this means I have acquired all the advantages of yielding to the fashionable madness, without risking my future happiness."[22]

Not only does Ormond devise an ingenious way to participate in the gaming culture of France without compromising his virtue or fortune, his exposure to gaming actually helps form his character. His encounter with chance defines who he is both for himself and for those observing him.

Gaming without safeguards such as Ormond's is dangerous precisely because the chance event is so seductive. Throughout *Practical Education,* the Edgeworths advise parents to build on their children's chance impressions because these operate with more force on their minds than irrelevant tasks or lectures. Edgeworth demonstrates the powerful effect of chance events on character formation in the subplot of *Belinda* involving Hervey's attempt to "educate a wife for himself" after reading the works of Jean-Jacques Rousseau (362). Edgeworth critiques book five of Rousseau's *Émile* by having Clarence learn to prefer Belinda's prudence and reason to Virginia's innocence and sentiment. Virginia's own story, however, illustrates the effect of chance on the formation of character. She cannot love Hervey as she feels she ought because her mind has been possessed by the image of a man in a miniature painting she once saw. Because she led a secluded life and was subject to none of the random experiences on which an Edgeworthian education would be based, this one chance sighting has an inordinate influence on her tastes and occupations, leading her to read romances where she can imagine the man in the painting as the hero of her books. Virginia's romance reading is analogous to Vincent's gambling; it creates nonproductive passions, pure emotional expenditure that does not lead to social unions or to virtuous benevolence but to self-absorption. By demonstrating the power of chance events on the mind of the young woman, Edgeworth further critiques Rousseau's proposed method of educating women, for not only is Virginia's unregulated sensibility unsuited for a man of sense, as Clarence learns, but the method of isolation from chance events is foolish, even dangerous.

By secluding Virginia in the New Forest to protect her from preying men, her grandmother only made her more vulnerable, both to those preying men but also to nonproductive self-absorption. By continuing her seclusion at Windsor, Clarence keeps Virginia from the random occurrences that could have prevented her obsession with the man in the miniature and made her more capable of productive love for Hervey himself.

Despite Edgeworth's misgivings about children's participation in games of chance, cards were well established as pedagogical instruments of the expanding empire, gaming was seen as an important component of the accomplished subject of this empire, and even in Edgeworth's works, encounters with chance are crucial to the formation of the self. Ormond and Virginia demonstrate the value of chance events for the constitution of the self, but Vincent's exposure to chance as a child on a West Indian plantation indicates Edgeworth's continuing distrust of childhood gambling as well as her anxiety about the effects of English participation in slavery on those who administer the colonies and then return, tainted by the experience, to England.

GAMES OF CHANCE: EMPIRE

The Edgeworths' educational model, both in their theoretical works and in Maria Edgeworth's fiction, is private and patriarchal. For the most part, they write for parents or tutors educating children within the home—often the home on a landed estate—rather than for schoolteachers.[23] In the West Indies, however, the Edgeworthian ideal of a well-managed home and responsible landowning entailed not only efficient and benevolent management but also the administration of slave labor. If education of Anglo-Irish children in Ireland had to demonstrate the desirability and efficacy of good management that would, among other benefits, keep tenants pacified, education in the West Indies had to teach appropriate personal and public conduct in a slave-holding society. In *Belinda*, Edgeworth is ambivalent about slavery in the colonies and the prominence of slave-derived wealth in England.[24] At the end of *Belinda*, characters are not consistently returned to their supposedly proper geographical locations. Mr. Hartley and Captain Sutherland, both of whose fortunes were made in the West Indies, are allowed to stay in England, as is the former slave Juba. After his gaming proclivity is discovered, however, Vincent goes to Germany where he continues to live as an absentee off the proceeds of his Jamaican slaves' labor.[25]

As Susan Greenfield has argued, Vincent's eventual expulsion helps this novel maintain (however tenuously) the boundaries between "At Home" and "Abroad" that as a Creole slave owner engaged to a British woman he had threatened.[26] Yet the terms of his expulsion—as a gamester, rather than simply as a Creole—need further attention. The novel carefully links Vincent's gaming to his colonial upbringing by drawing on standard stereotypes of West Indians as adventurers who have the gambler's disregard for future events and by explicitly blaming his gaming on the slaves with whom he associated in Jamaica. Giving the Creole the vice of gaming intensifies Vincent's representation of the "Abroad" of Edgeworth's provisional title, the colonial fringe that must not contaminate the metropolis.

To shape Vincent's character, Edgeworth draws on the tendency of contemporary histories of Jamaica to describe white Creoles as a new, mongrelized race and to isolate common English pastimes and concerns, in particular gaming, as endemic to the West Indies. The description of Vincent's childhood gaming condenses these anxieties about Creoles: "The taste for gambling he had acquired whilst he was a child; but as it was then confined to trifles, it had been passed over, as a thing of no consequence, a boyish folly, that would never grow up with him: his father used to see him, day after day, playing with eagerness, at games of chance, with his negroes" (422). We can see the fear that the inheritor of the estate—the ambiguous possessive, "his negroes," reminds us that the father's slaves will some day be the son's—is tainted by engaging in games of chance with slaves, for whom such games carried different moral and educational connotations. At the same time, gaming seems to be a specifically "negro" activity here, like obeah; the passage implicitly blames Vincent's propensity to gamble as an adult on the "negroes" who introduced him to games of chance as a child.

Edgeworth's critique was complicated by the fact that the English colonies in the West Indies were not, in general, settled by aristocrats or gentry. As D. H. Murdoch explains, "plantation agriculture in the West Indies was a high-risk business; it attracted adventurers. The terms of sale [of land] could not exclude speculators determined to circumvent the letter of the law, nor the penalties have any effect on gamblers who had bet everything and lost everything."[27] Nonetheless, as these colonial gamblers became wealthy, they wanted to return to England and to move in the opulent social circles that had once been closed to them. The social-climbing West Indian in London became a stock comic character in English drama alongside his fellow outsiders, the cit, the nabob, and the Irishman, expressing the privileged classes' anxiety that their ranks were being infiltrated. English West Indian landowners, and especially Creoles, were thought to be undeserving not just because they had lower-class antecedents, but because their proximity to, and involvement with, slaves seemed to compromise not just their social standing but their very racial identity. The word "creole," meaning a person born in the West Indies, whether of European or African descent, suggests a concern with the fluidity of national and racial identities engendered by imperial ambitions.[28] Discussing white Creoles in his *New History of Jamaica* (1740), Vice Admiral Edward Vernon claimed, "their Complection is muddy."[29] Edward Long, in his *History of Jamaica* (1774), describes the supposedly racial traits of white Creoles in minute detail:

> The native white men, or Creoles, of Jamaica are in general tall and well shaped . . . Their cheeks are remarkable high-boned, and the sockets of their eyes deeper than is commonly observed among the natives of England . . . a light grey, and black, or deep hazel, are the more common colours of the pupil. The effect of climate is not only remarkable in the structure of their eyes, but likewise in the extraordinary freedom and suppleness of their joints, which enable them to move with ease, and give them a surprising agility.[30]

In addition to physical descriptions, such pseudo-anthropological accounts of this new race also listed Creoles' social occupations as if they were specifically determined by their birth and residence in slave colonies. Gaming was chief among these occupations. "They live well . . . make Money, and are quite careless of Futurity," according to Vernon.[31] Long claims, "they affect gaiety and diversions, which in general are cards, billiards, backgammon, chess, horse-racing . . . They are too much addicted to expensive living, costly entertainments, dress, and equipage." To finance such tastes, planters would buy up new tracts of land to mortgage, thus "plung[ing] deeper and deeper into debt and distress."[32] This supposed West Indian addiction to gaming and high living and the unconcern for the future on which it is based are described as if the English had never confronted these problems in their own country.

Carefully supervising children's education in such an environment was crucial. Belinda blames Vincent's father for passing over Vincent's gambling as "a thing of no consequence." While Mr. Percival quickly intervened in little Charles's jack-straw wager, Vincent's father "was never alarmed" by his son's gambling; "he was too intent upon making a fortune for his family, to consider how they would spend it" (422–23). Here too Edgeworth draws on a standard concern in fiction about the West Indies: the supposed neglect of Creole children's education because of parents' overwhelming concern with getting rich quickly. Most wealthy planters in the West Indies hoped eventually to return to England to live off the revenue of their estates as absentees;[33] while in residence in the West Indies, however, they faced the problem of educating their children for the exalted class position they hoped one day to assume. The didactic novel *Sanford and Merton* (1783–1789), by the Edgeworths' friend Thomas Day, notes the difficulty of raising children in an atmosphere of slavery that was detrimental even to adults, whose character was supposed to be already formed. Merton, the wealthy owner of a large slave estate in Jamaica, moves back to England to educate his only son properly, that is, out of the slave environment. Tommy Merton is indolent and tyrannical because, though very young, he is used to commanding slaves to do everything for him. "While he lived in Jamaica, he had several black servants to wait upon him, who were forbidden upon any account to contradict him. If he walked, there always went two negroes with him; one of whom carried a large umbrella to keep the sun from him, and the other was to carry him in his arms whenever he was tired."[34] The slaveholding hero of Sarah Scott's novel *The History of Sir George Ellison* (1766) took the unusual step of hiring a tutor to come from England to instruct "all the children of his negro slaves," but his own son had to be sent to England at six years of age to counteract his Creole mother's unthinking overindulgence.[35] As Constantia remarks in Helena Wells's *Constantia Neville; or the West Indian* (1800), "Except where an uncommon degree of attention is paid by parents, young persons of both sexes, who continue there after seven years old, run great risk of contamination of the negroes."[36] English stereotypes of Creole adults reflected the supposed neglect of their education. Creole women were almost universally described as indolent, lascivious, and cruel.[37] Creole men were described as debased and cruel, tyrants and keepers of black concubines, or as morally weak and excessively sentimental, with an overdeveloped sense of chivalry and honor, or as a paradoxical combination of both types.

Edgeworth casts Vincent in the sentimental Creole mode, the most famous literary example of which is the hero of Richard Cumberland's play, *The West Indian* (1771). Such a person was, in Long's words, "sensible, of quick apprehension, brave, good-natured, affable, generous . . . unsuspicious, [a] lover of freedom, fond of social enjoyments . . . liable to sudden transports of anger; but these fits . . . though violent while they last, are soon over."[38] Vincent is handsome and expressive, sun-burnt and foreign-seeming. His repeated gesticulations during conversation indicate his emotionalism. "He had a frank ardent temper, incapable of art or dissimulation, and so unsuspicious of all mankind, that he could scarcely believe falsehood existed in the world" (217). He was "totally deficient" in the "power and habit of reasoning" (217). Perhaps most important, like the adventurer-planters of the West Indian colonies who, in Vernon's words, were "quite careless of Futurity," Vincent "enjoyed the present, undisturbed by any unavailing regret for the past, or troublesome solicitude about the future" (218).

Edgeworth frequently calls Vincent a "man of feeling," and even "our man of feeling" (427), blending the Creole stereotype with that other literary type made famous by Henry Mackenzie and Laurence Sterne. Markman Ellis has shown that sentimentality and slavery are far from antithetical, and the "man of feeling" trope is in many ways coterminous with the West Indian stereotype;[39] indeed, Vincent demonstrates his sensibility by way of his sympathy for a slave, in a dramatic reading of Thomas Day's poem, "The Dying Negro,"[40] a performance enacted to distract Belinda from her fears about his gaming. When Belinda discovers that Vincent is a frequent gambler at Mrs. Luttridge's E O table,[41] Lady Delacour praises his generosity on the occasion of his former slave Juba's marriage to an English servant, hoping to "drive the E O table from Belinda's thoughts . . . From thence she went on to the African slave trade, by way of contrast, and she finished precisely where she had intended, and where Mr. Vincent could have wished, by praising a poem called 'The Dying Negro,' which he had, the preceding evening, brought to read to Belinda" (347). Belinda's anxiety about Vincent's gaming is to be calmed by evidence that he is a man of feeling, though a slave owner. His generosity to Juba is remarkable precisely because Juba had been his slave, and, given the notoriously inconsistent application of the Mansfield Judgement,[42] Vincent could have refused him his freedom. The tantalizing account of Lady Delacour's segue ("From thence she went on to the African slave trade") is similar to the unspecified question on the slave trade that Fanny Price asked Sir Thomas in *Mansfield Park*.[43] What, one wonders, did Lady Delacour say about the slave trade? What did Vincent think about or say in response to Lady Delacour's remarks? Whatever this conversation may have been, Vincent's apparent sympathy for slaves on English soil—indicated by his appreciation for the poem and by his benevolent treatment of his former slave Juba—effaces his slave-owning in the colonies. It is suggestive of Edgeworth's ambivalence about slavery in this novel that although Belinda is very upset by the possibility that Vincent gambles, she never expresses concern that her fiancé's wealth is built on slave labor.

When Vincent came to England as Percival's ward at age eighteen, his guardian, before he discovered Vincent's taste for gambling, noticed he had "that presumptuous belief in his special good fortune, which naturally leads to the love of gambling" (423). Demonstrating the method the Edgeworths recommend in *Practical Education*, Percival does not lecture his ward, but "appealed to his understanding, and took opportunities of showing him the ruinous effects of high play in real life" (423). Vincent's response is, in keeping with his character, emotional rather than reasoned. He expresses his "detestation of the selfish character of a gamester" with vehemence and indignantly rejects the suggestion that he has this propensity. When the opportunity to game arises, therefore, Vincent is "eager, rather than averse, to expose himself to the danger, that he might prove his superiority to the temptation" (423). He purposely maintains his acquaintance with Mrs. Luttridge even though he knows she is a "professed gambler" in order to demonstrate to Percival that his worry was needless. This exposure to gaming would not necessarily be dangerous if, consistent with Edgeworthian pedagogy, it was carefully regulated, perhaps according to a plan like Ormond's. Instead, of course, Vincent overestimates his own invincibility because his "detestation" of gaming was based on his feelings rather than his reason, and he is drawn into high-stakes play at Mrs. Luttridge's.

Because Vincent "disdain[s] reason as a moral guide" and instead "[thinks], act[s], and suffer[s] as a man of feeling," he needs constant emotional stimulation. While Belinda is at Oakly-park, the Percivals' country estate, his love for her occupies him, but when she goes back to London for a short time his *ennui* becomes unbearable: "Emotion of some kind or another was become necessary to him;

he said that not to feel, was not to live; and soon the suspense, the anxiety, the hopes, the fears, the perpetual vicissitudes of a gamester's life, appeared almost as delightful as those of a lover" (424). Lady Delacour assures Belinda that Vincent's gambling does not represent "any serious, *improper* attachment to the E O table; only a little flirtation, perhaps, to which his passion for you has, doubtless, put to a stop" (346–47). As Virginia St. Pierre's nonproductive absorption in romance reading competed with Hervey's attempts to inspire her affection, so Vincent's nonproductive gambling competes with his love for Belinda, preventing it from proceeding to productive marriage.

Vincent justifies his initial gaming with the Luttridges by invoking the Percivals' distinction between games of address and games of chance:

> Billiards, however, was a game of address, not chance; there was [a] billiard-table at Oakly-park, as well as at Mr. Luttridge's and he had played with his guardian. Why then, should he not play with Mr. Luttridge? He did play: his skill was admired; he betted, and his bets were successful: but he did not call this gaming, for the bets were not to any great amount, and it was only playing at billiards. (424)

The distinction made so much of in the novel between games of chance and of address is, however, more problematic than Vincent realizes. In the scene with which I opened this essay, Percival warns his son Charles against wagering on his game of jack-straws, but when Vincent suggests his bet would have been bad because "chances were . . . against me," Percival replies, "It does not appear to me to be a matter of chance . . . This is a game of address, and that is the reason I like it" (249). Vincent allows himself to play, and to wager on, billiards because it is game of skill, but he forgets that in Percival's view, though one can *play* a game of address, it is still dangerous to *wager* on it. Lady Delacour points this out to Belinda. Discussing the possibility that Vincent is a gamester, Belinda remarks, "I know he used to play at billiards at Oakly-park, but merely as an amusement. Games of address, however, as Mr. Percival says, are not to be put on a footing with games of hazard." To which Lady Delacour dryly answers, "A man may, however, contrive to lose a good deal of money at billiards, as poor lord Delacour can tell you" (347).

Finally, though, the distinction between games of address and of chance proves untenable because the cheaters in this novel manipulate games for their own profit. Lord Delacour and Vincent lose at their game of skill, billiards, because the Luttridges' table is "not perfectly even"; Vincent loses at E O, a game of chance, because the table had been "constructed for purposes of fraud" (421). Playing with cheaters, there is no such thing as a game of address or a game of chance. In fact, Vincent is ultimately excluded from the novel's happy resolution not just because he games, but because he is dishonest with Belinda about his gaming, becoming a kind of cheater himself: "His former nice sense of honor had been considerably deadened at the gaming-table; and he could *now* stoop to that dissimulation, at which he would have shuddered but a few months before" (442). After Hervey saves Vincent from financial ruin by revealing that Mrs. Luttridge's E O table was rigged, Vincent cannot bring himself to confess to Belinda as promised.

When Belinda discovers the truth, her farewell letter expresses as much disappointment in having been deceived as in his actual gaming: "The hopes of enjoying domestic happiness with a person whose manners, temper, and tastes, were suited to my own, induced me to listen to your address. Your unfortunate propensity to a dangerous amusement, which is now, for the first time, made known to me, puts an end to these hopes for ever" (448). The discovery of Vincent's gaming hits Belinda in a vulnerable spot, for after trying to understand Hervey's confusing behavior earlier in the novel, Belinda had lamented to Lady Anne Percival that it was very difficult for women to bestow their affections where they were deserved since "men have it in their power to assume the appearance of every thing that is amiable and estimable, and women have scarcely any opportunities of detecting the counterfeit" (240). Both Hervey and Vincent cheated Belinda by appearing to be what they were not; Vincent's fall shows Belinda's system of rational esteem to be inadequate in the face of deceptive appearances. Belinda's experience with Hervey and Vincent belies Lady Anne's assurance that in "private society" a woman could discern a man's "real character" (240).

Clarence Hervey is reinstated as Belinda's lover in no small part because he is able to detect cheaters. Though Edgeworth critiqued Rousseau via Hervey's wife-education project, in other ways Hervey models the Edgeworths' educational theory both in his practice and in his pedagogy. He approaches problems with the Edgeworthian scientific method; faced with the suggestion that Mrs. Luttridge wins her money unfairly, "it occurred to him that, perhaps, the E O table might be so contrived, as to put the fortunes of all who played at it in the power of the proprietor. Clarence had sufficient ingenuity to invent the method by which this might be done" (421) and he has sufficient intrepidity to sneak into the Luttridges' drawing room and inspect the table on the sly. Proceeding from the principle laid out in *Practical Education* "that, in reality, there is no *knack* or *mystery* in any thing, but that from certain causes certain effects will follow" (27), Hervey easily discovers the fraud that is posing as chance. Then, following Edgeworth's appreciation of the educative power of chance events rather than imposed tasks and lectures, Hervey allows Vincent to game at the fixed table and (seemingly) lose his whole fortune so that he will "feel all the horrours of a gamester's fate" (421) and vow to reform.

The Edgeworths' educational theory is aimed at producing inquiring and industrious young citizens. Their system, in which children are encouraged to query how the world works, could be turned to radical ends, but characters such as Belinda, the Earl of Glenthorn in *Ennui*, and Lord Colambre in *The Absentee* suggest that the properly rational Edgeworthian character will work to maintain the established social order. But it seems that Belinda's rationality is not enough to help her negotiate this novel's constantly fluctuating world of money lending, cross-dressing, gambling, dueling, and slave rebellions. In a world where virtue and vice are rewarded or punished inconsistently, seemingly at random, a world that is, in short, a game of chance, the ability to detect fraud, to save oneself from cheaters, may be the most important skill to learn.

Notes

1. Maria Edgeworth, *Belinda*, ed. Kathryn J. Kirkpatrick (New York: Oxford University Press, 1995), 248. Subsequent quotations from this text will be cited parenthetically. This text and my argument here are based on the first edition of the novel. For discussions of Edgeworth's changes to the novel, especially to Juba and Vincent, when *Belinda* was included in Anna Barbauld's *British Novelists* collection (1810), see Kathryn J. Kirkpatrick, "'Gentlemen Have Horrors Upon This Subject': West Indian Suitors in Maria Edgeworth's *Belinda*," *Eighteenth-Century Fiction* 5, no. 4 (1993): 331–48; and Suvendrini Perera, *Reaches of Empire: The English Novel from Edgeworth to Dickens* (New York: Columbia University Press, 1991), 16–17, 27–29.

2. Kirkpatrick includes this sketch, which was printed in Frances Edgeworth's *A Memoir of Maria Edgeworth* (London, 1867) in her edition of *Belinda*, 479–83.

3. Maria and R. L. Edgeworth, *Practical Education* (London, 1801 [2d ed.]), 53. Subsequent quotations from this text will be cited parenthetically.

4. Maria Edgeworth, *Popular Tales* (London, 1804). Reprinted in Robert L. Mack, ed., *Oriental Tales* (New York: Oxford University Press, 1992), 215–56.

5. See Julia Douthwaite, "Experimental Child-Rearing After Rousseau: Maria Edgeworth, *Practical Education*, and *Belinda*," *Irish Journal of Feminist Studies* 2, no. 2 (1997): 35–56, for a discussion of the influence of scientific experimentalism on the Edgeworths' educational model.

6. Marjory Lang, "Maria Edgeworth's *The Parent's Assistant* (1796): A Document of Social Education," *History of Education* 7, no. 1 (1978): 21–33, argues that "since the enlightened eighteenth-century image of reality included an orderly rational universe that functioned predictably according to scientific laws, [Edgeworth's] stories must demonstrate that the actions of the present lead to predictable consequences."

7. Clarence Hervey's ability to follow Dr X——'s lead by regaling the children with tales of animals in different cultures is supposed to be a sign of his good character, though his pride in this ability (he "piqued himself in being able always to suit his conversation to his companions" [*Belinda*, 99]) marks his relative immaturity in the first half of the novel. Perera, *Reaches of Empire*, examines how Hervey's most sparkling conversations, both with children and with adults, draw on the resources of the expanding British empire (27).

8. Maria Edgeworth, *Moral Tales* (London, 1801), 305.

9. John Locke, *Some Thoughts Concerning Education*, ed. John W. Yolton and Jean S. Yolton (Oxford: Clarendon, 1989), 209.

10. Locke, *Some Thoughts*, 208.

11. "Divine and Moral Songs for Children by Isaac Watts, D. D.," (London, 1816). Victoria and Albert Museum, E2556–1953.

12. Roger Tilley, *A History of Playing Cards* (London: Studio Vista, 1973), 74.

13. "Alphabet Cards with Figures of Fun and Humorous Verses. A Reward for the Good," (undated [late eighteenth century]). Victoria and Albert Museum, 27896.

14. Tilley, *Playing Cards*, 75.

15. Untitled, undated pack, Victoria and Albert Museum, E821.1939. See also Tilley, *Playing Cards*, 75–76.

16. F. J. Harvey Darton, *Children's Books in England: Five Centuries of Social Life* (Cambridge: Cambridge University Press, 1966), 153.

17. Mary Wollstonecraft, *The Works of Mary Wollstonecraft*, ed. Janet Todd and Marilyn Butler, vol. 4 (London: William Pickering, 1989), 45.

18. Philippe Ariès, *Centuries of Childhood*, trans. Robert Baldick (London: Pimlico, 1962), 80–81.

19. Catherine Perry Hargrave, *A History of Playing Cards and a Bibliography of Cards and Gaming* (New York: Dover, 1966), 205.

20. Hargrave, *History and Bibliography*, 206.

21. Anon., *A Modest Defence of Gaming* (London, 1754), 28.

22. Maria Edgeworth, *Ormond, A Tale* (New York, 1895), 302.

23. Some of Edgeworth's stories, such as "The Orphans" and "Simple Susan" (*The Parent's Assistant*, [London, 1796–1800]), feature lower-class, even impoverished children. Their admirable industriousness, however, is always ultimately in service of, rather than a threat to, paternalistic society. And their industriousness does not seem to be enough to support them, but it brings them to the attention

of local benevolent landowners, who give the hard-working children pecuniary assistance.

24. Edgeworth glances at, but does not develop, the analogy between Irish and West Indian absenteeism when a village innkeeper in *The Absentee* tells Lord Colambre that Lord Clonbrony "knows nothing of his property, nor of us. Never set foot among us, to my knowledge, since I was as high as the table. He might as well be a West India planter, and we negroes, for any thing he knows to the contrary—has no more care, nor thought about us, than if he were in Jamaica, or the other world" (125). The innkeeper's implication, of course, is not that West Indian absenteeism is wrong, but that a landowner should pay more attention to his Irish tenants than to his slaves. In her story "The Grateful Negro," Edgeworth argues for ameliorative treatment of slaves (rather than abolition of slavery) by narrating the bonds of sympathy that tie a grateful slave to his master (*Popular Tales*, 289–326). See George E. Boulukos, "Maria Edgeworth's 'Grateful Negro' and the Sentimental Argument for Slavery," *Eighteenth-Century Life* 23, no. 1 (1999): 12–29.

25. For an early fictionalized argument against West Indian absenteeism, see Sarah Scott, *The History of Sir George Ellison*, ed. Betty Rizzo, *Eighteenth-Century Novels by Women* (Lexington: University Presses of Kentucky, 1996).

26. Susan C. Greenfield, "'Abroad and at Home': Sexual Ambiguity, Miscegenation, and Colonial Boundaries in Edgeworth's *Belinda*," *PMLA* 112, no. 2 (1997): 214–28.

27. D. H. Murdoch, "Land Policy in the Eighteenth-Century Empire: The Sale of Crown Lands in the Ceded Islands, 1763–1783," *The Historical Journal* 27, no. 3 (1984): 573. For the history of British involvement in the West Indies through the eighteenth century, see Peter Hulme, *Colonial Encounters: Europe and the Native Caribbean, 1492–1797* (London: Methuen, 1986); Richard S. Dunn, *Sugar and Slaves: The Rise of the Planter Class in the English West Indies, 1624–1713* (Chapel Hill: University of North Carolina Press, 1972); Sidney W. Mintz, *Sweetness and Power: The Place of Sugar in Modern History* (New York: Viking, 1985); and Lowell Joseph Ragatz, *The Fall of the Planter Class in the British Caribbean, 1763–1833* (New York: The Century Company, 1928).

28. The *OED* defines "creole" as "a person born and naturalized in the country, but of European (usually Spanish or French) or of African Negro race: the name having no connotation of colour, and in its reference to origin being distinguished on the one hand from born in Europe (or Africa), and on the other hand from aboriginal."

29. Quoted in Wylie Sypher, "The West-Indian as a 'Character' in the Eighteenth Century," *Studies in Philology* 36 (1939): 505.

30. Edward Long, *The History of Jamaica, or General Survey of the Antient and Modern State of that Island*, ed. George Metcalf, 1774 ed., 3 vols. (London: Frank Cass, 1970), 2: 261–62.

31. Sypher, "West Indian," 505.

32. Long, *History of Jamaica*, 2: 262, 265, 266.

33. *Mansfield Park*'s Sir Thomas Bertram is perhaps the best-known fictional example of such absentee West Indian planters.

34. Thomas Day, *The History of Sanford and Merton* (New York, 1857), 9. The Mertons' return to England in order to educate their child without the taint of slavery suggests a hope, evident in *Belinda* as well, that even as an increasing portion of the

domestic economy derived from slave labor, the West Indies bore the moral weight of slavery and England itself was untainted. Day, by calling the slaves that care for Tommy his "servants," shields his English child readers from confronting the difficult issue of slavery.

35. Scott, *Sir George Ellison*, 17.

36. Quoted in Sypher, "West Indian," 515.

37. See Sypher, "West Indian"; Barbara Bush, "White 'Ladies,' Coloured 'Favourites,' and Black 'Wenches': Some Considerations on Sex, Race and Class Factors in Social Relations in White Creole Society in the British Caribbean," *Slavery and Abolition* 2, no. 1 (1982): 245–62; and the extensive critical discussions of *Jane Eyre*'s Bertha Mason for the history of the female West Indian stereotype.

38. Long, *History of Jamaica*, 2: 261.

39. Markman Ellis, *The Politics of Sensibility: Race, Gender and Commerce in the Sentimental Novel* (Cambridge: Cambridge University Press, 1996) explores the extensive links between sensibility and slavery.

40. Perera, *Reaches of Empire*, 30–31 and Greenfield, "Abroad and at Home," 220.

41. E O is a game of chance similar to roulette, in which players wager on whether a ball will fall "into one of several niches marked E [Even] or O [Odd]" *OED*, 2d ed. "E O." Incidentally, the *OED* quotes from *Belinda* to exemplify this definition: "He likes the lady's E O table better than the lady" (*Belinda* 346).

42. Ellis, *The Politics of Sensibility*, notes that "The test case of slavery in England was prosecuted by Granville Sharp in 1771, against Charles Stewart, a customs official from Boston, Massachusetts, who had brought with him from America, a slave, James Somerset . . . [Lord Mansfield's] decision was held by some to abolish slavery in England, although its practical force was limited" (117).

43. "Did not you hear me ask him about the slave trade last night?" Jane Austen, *Mansfield Park*, ed. Claudia L. Johnson (New York: Norton, 1998), 136.

Control Experiment: Edgeworth's Critique of Rousseau's Educational Theory

CATHERINE TOAL

"PEOPLE ARE ALWAYS TELLING ME TO MAKE *PRACTICABLE* SUGGESTIONS. You might as well tell me to suggest what people are doing already."[1] This is Rousseau's complaint in the preface to *Émile*, his opus on education of 1762. *Practical Education* (1798),[2] the title of Maria Edgeworth's educational treatise, written in collaboration with her father who had witnessed disastrous effects in applying Rousseau's theories to the tutelage of his eldest son,[3] seems indirectly to rebuke the radicalism of *Émile*. Opinion continues to be divided however on the degree to which the Edgeworths' project, in foregrounding the "practical," represents a return to established norms and traditions or "what people are doing already." On the one hand, because of its promotion of "the merits of experimentation" and its "encouragement of rational inquiry," the work is deemed "a challenge to the Burkean respect for precedents, 'wise prejudice' and the sanctity of custom."[4] On the other, critics of the Edgeworths' treatment of gender allege that they "proclaimed as advances" ideas that were in fact reactionary and regressive.[5] The controversy is complicated by the notorious elements of traditionalism in Rousseau's own position. As enlightenment feminists knew, his revolutionary stance did not encompass a support for gender-blind education, instead relegating women to a domestic role and predicating their formation on criteria shaped by male interests and desires.[6]

The difficulty of clarifying the Edgeworths' text as "conservative" or innovative can be summed up in the paradoxes of its relationship to Rousseau's thesis. Unlike *Émile*, *Practical Education* does not scrutinize and challenge the fundamental ordering of social, economic, and political arrangements or explore the intricacies of human estrangement from "nature," focusing instead on knowledge and skills useful for entry into an already constituted public or domestic sphere. Yet in juxtaposing Rousseau's philosophical probings with a British tradition of scientific investigation, the Edgeworths make available, for both male and female children, an ideal of curiosity and independent reasoning.[7] The two tendencies conjoined facilitate the Edgeworths' transcendence of Rousseau's objectifying view of female identity, while allowing them to preserve an unquestioning acceptance of women's confinement to domestic life, and an expectation that female education should be adapted to the requirements of that realm.[8]

This essay argues that *Practical Education*'s dialogue with *Émile*, and its implications for the politics of the Edgeworths' educational system, can clarify the terms of an ongoing debate concerning the relative levels of "conservatism" and "subversiveness" in Maria Edgeworth's fiction.[9] I examine the novel containing a subplot that parodies the scheme concocted by the enthusiastic devotee of Rousseau (and close friend of Richard Lovell Edgeworth) Thomas Day, to educate a wife for himself on the model of *Émile*'s "Sophy": *Belinda* (1801).[10] Marilyn Butler contends that Edgeworth's educational writings carry on a sustained antagonistic engagement and struggle with Day.[11] But in criticizing her father's friend's assumptions, Edgeworth simultaneously grapples with the theories of Rousseau underpinning them. The critique of *Émile* that appears in *Belinda*'s parody of Day, when read in conjunction with *Practical Education*, reveals the nature and foundations of the kind of political and educational authority the novel claims, as well as the tensions and stratagems concealed within it.

Like the affiliations of *Practical Education*, the issue of *Belinda*'s alignment with radicalism or traditionalism has provoked considerable dispute.[12] Ostensibly, the narrative offers a "moral tale"[13] of a young lady's introduction to society and acquisition of the lessons needed to avoid its perils and achieve "domestic happiness." Nevertheless, in charting the heroine's progress, it devotes prominent attention to a variety of other, disruptive strands: the story of Lady Delacour, the dissolute aristocrat temporarily alienated from home and motherhood; the antics of Harriot Freke, a cross-dressing mischief maker who encourages Delacour's truancy from domestic life; and a series of references to an unstable colonial space, evoked by the bad habits and unruly passions of the Creole Mr. Vincent and the "obeah" Ashanti religious beliefs of his servant Juba, associated with slave insurrection.[14] Critics come to very different decisions about whether such "subversive" elements eventually succumb to a pervading "domestic ideology" (and imposition of imperial-colonial hierarchy), or surreptitiously succeed in upsetting the compromises and resolutions of *Belinda.*

With its strong focus on gender transgression and on colonialism, the debate over the novel frequently neglects the unfolding of the narrative interlude describing Clarence Hervey's adoption of an orphan called Rachel whom he renames (combining the protagonist and author of another Rousseau-influenced text)[15] Virginia St. Pierre, hiding her away from society to preserve her "natural" sensibility. *Belinda*'s interpreters either dismiss the episode as "somewhat silly,"[16] regard it as Edgeworth's Wollstonecraftian defense of a female right to rational education,[17] or note Virginia's integration, along with other anomalous presences in the plot, into a regime of domesticity and loyal usefulness to the imperial enterprise.[18] But the reasons for the failure of Hervey's plan, and the way in which Virginia evades and escapes her Rousseauvian sequestration, show how the precepts of *Practical Education* (most visible in its quarrels with Rousseau) provide a comfortable conservative framework for the novel, one so sturdy that it permits the broad inclusion and indulgence of apparently extreme, lawless perspectives and behaviors.

A reading of the treatise and its departures from Rousseau recasts the "carnivalesque" qualities of *Belinda* as side effects or epiphenomena of its underlying confidence in a "natural" order shaping individual development and its social and domestic locations. At the same time, and as the diversity, and very presence, of potentially insubordinate elements in the narrative suggest, *Belinda*'s faith in *Practical Education* goes far beyond a simple reiteration of its principles. The refutation of Rousseau in the subplot elevates the self-assurance of the Edgeworthian educational credo into a kind of wish fulfillment, or utopian fantasy. As a result, Edgeworth produces an unexpected "subversion" of Rousseau in the matter of gender—not in keeping with the typical preoccupations of *Practical Education*—while also indirectly highlighting the preconceptions that govern the treatise's critique of *Émile*, and their unacknowledged dependency on contrivance and control.

Recent analyses of *Belinda*, exploring the political meanings lurking in the seemingly innocuous title originally conceived for it, "Abroad and at Home,"[19]—empire and England, fashionable life and domesticity—have overlooked its relevance to the Virginia subplot, and the girl's imprisonment in an isolated domestic space. Edgeworth's parodic critique of Hervey's plan to hide Virginia from the world, has for its subtext a strong divergence of emphasis, between *Émile* and *Practical Education*, on the relationship between education and spatial demarcation, or the question of how pedagogy, centered on the familiar, delimited space of "home," should mediate external forces or influences from "abroad."

Émile gives such prominence to the theme of geographical space, that geographical contractions and enlargements become almost synonymous with the tactics of the educational process itself. The tutor takes care to decide what climatic zone of the world his imaginary charge should be born in, choosing the temperate regions because that will—it is assumed—make him most adaptable to other conditions in other places (22).[20] Once underway, Émile's education bears out this anticipation of flexibility, moving from a rural life to encounters with Parisian society and exposure to the workings of governments and empires (70, 496–522).[21] The trajectory of the scheme, however, is intended to inculcate a preference for the rural, the local, and the confined; Émile favors country over urban living (184);[22] he returns from traveling, having witnessed the depredations of colonialism, convinced of the virtues of self-sufficiency (523).[23] We are to understand that the young man's affiliations and commitments spring from the tutor's early and strategically repeated use of a limited environment to filter and orchestrate the influences upon him: he brings Émile up in the country, where the pedagogue will be a person of consequence: "you will not be master of the child unless you can control everyone about him" (69),[24] and transports him back to that home in the phase where "the passions" develop, so that he will have no distractions to "inflame" his imagination (230, 217).[25]

As the above stipulation makes clear, Émile's tutor strives to narrow his pupil's physical space in order to contain the destabilizing power of desire. He likens the first appearance of sexual feelings to the experience of a hazardous, storm-tossed, sea voyage, implying the prospect of a total loss of self-identity (207).[26] More generally, he argues that when human beings fixate on a cherished aim or object beyond their reach, they become fatally drawn away from the fitting physical, and psychological frontiers of their immediate domain: "the object which seemed within our grasp flies quicker than we follow, when we think we have grasped it, it transforms itself and is again far ahead of us. We no longer perceive the country we have traversed and think nothing of it, that which lies before us becomes vaster and stretches still before us" (52).[27] In each of these unsettling visions, enthrallment to desire, identified with straying too far from a recognizable home, produces an enfeebled, vulnerable self: "we spread ourselves, so to speak, over the whole world, and all this vast expanse becomes sensitive" (55).[28] Rousseau's warnings that desire may draw the individual out of the familiar and appropriate proportions of his immediate world into a chaos of nonidentity convey his perception of a disjunction between an underlying "good," "natural" order and superimposed, man-made distortions of it.[29] The tutor's role consists, paradoxically, in the artful fashioning of carefully calculated techniques for conserving the space of natural development and warding off socially generated customs and prejudices. It is this paradox—the use of art to bring forth "nature"—that shapes the Edgeworths' objections to and departure from Rousseau, and glosses the preconditions of their own educational system.

The very tone of *Practical Education* discloses its contrasting treatment of the themes raised by *Émile*. Though the text disavows any claim to be a primer for the formation of worthy and useful imperial or colonial subjects, its preface evinces a contented attachment to an imperial context for education (notwithstanding the Edgeworths' criticisms of aspects of the colonial endeavor in Ireland and elsewhere),[30] and its chapters betray no anxiety comparable in fervency to Rousseau's, concerning the controlled management of environmental influence. The Edgeworths' stable, untroubled perspective is epitomized in their description of the ideal tutor, who, far from seeking to narrow his pupil's world, must compensate for its minuteness, by becoming in a way symbolic of spatial vastness himself: "He must be acquainted not only with the local topography of his own district but he must have the whole map of human knowledge before him; and whilst he dwells most upon his own province he must yet be free from local prejudice and must consider himself as a citizen of the world" (*PE* 3, 40). *Émile*'s tutor, with his encyclopedic knowledge of systems of government and his interest in introducing these (at the right time) to his pupil, embodies similar traits, but his awareness of different cultures works largely to ratify an unbending ideological commitment to the local and the confined. For the Edgeworths, the master's knowledge, rather than being disturbed and threatened by the existence of a vast beyond, makes consciousness of the unknown a central aspect of his own wisdom: "those who have a general view of human knowledge perceive how many unexplored regions are yet to be cultivated by future industry" (3, 121). Forming a tacit alignment between knowledge and imperial expansion and renovation, these spatial metaphors express the ease and equanimity with which the Edgeworthian paradigm contemplates the absorption of influences from "abroad" into the confined space of "home," eschewing any ultimate antithesis, practical or theoretical, between the two.

Practical Education's more serene conception of the educational space and its links to external experiences and knowledge, derives from a view of the relationship between imagination, desire, and surrounding conditions diametrically opposed to that outlined in *Émile*. While Rousseau insists on the unnerving susceptibility of the developing mind to dangerous, unfamiliar attractions, the Edgeworths consider the child's imagination safely and inevitably compassed by fixed borders and concrete impressions of its encircling world. A key passage sketches the precise terms and implications of the disagreement:

> Rousseau advises, that children should be governed solely by the necessity of circumstances; but when he had the management of a refractory child, he found himself obliged to invent and arrange a whole drama, by artificial experience to convince his little pupil, that he had better not walk out in the streets of Paris alone; and that therefore, he should wait till his tutor could conveniently accompany him. Rousseau had prepared the neighbours on each side of the street to make proper speeches as his pupil passed by their doors, which alarmed and piqued the boy effectually. At length the child was met, at a proper time, by a friend who had been appointed to watch him; and thus he was brought home submissive. This scene, as Rousseau observes, was admirably well performed, but what occasion could there be for so much contrivance and deceit? If his pupil had not been uncommonly deficient in penetration, he would soon have discovered his preceptor in some of his artifices; then adieu both to obedience and confidence. A false idea of the pleasures of liberty misled Rousseau. Children have not our abstract ideas of the pleasures of liberty; they do not, until they have suffered from ill-judged restraints, feel any strong desire to exercise what we call free will; liberty is, with them the liberty of doing certain specific things which they have found to be agreeable; liberty is not the general idea of pleasure, in doing whatever they WILL to do" (1, 272–74).[31]

Unimpressed by Rousseau's recourse to ingenuities of invention and artifice, the Edgeworths make evident their lack of anxiety about the conventional hierarchical structure of pedagogy, seeing no reason why parental or tutorly authority must be disguised as objective "necessity." Their unworried sense of the legitimacy of such authority rests on a fundamental belief in the inherently restricted character of the child's world: his longings are grounded in proximate, visible, physical objects or previous experiences of enjoyment, and he cannot therefore be subject to abstract temptations, unpredictable, phantasmal desires. Consequently, all efforts to discipline the effects of the surrounding environment—especially by the convoluted theatrical, means disparaged here—will prove at once impossible and superfluous.

The assumptions underlying the Edgeworths' argument receive further crucial illustration in a contrast between *Practical Education* and *Émile*'s views on childhood artistic experimentation. Whereas Rousseau distrusts any departure from mimesis in his pupil's attempt at drawing—"lest he should substitute absurd and fantastic forms for the real truth of things" (129)[32]—the Edgeworths quote approvingly the opinion of Joshua Reynolds that too much realism in art diminishes aesthetic stimulation in the viewer (3, 151). Seemingly radical in its endorsement of inventiveness, the Edgeworths' approach rests on similar grounds to their anti-Rouseauvian theory of childhood desire: the pupil may be allowed to abandon mimesis because he will never be able to produce anything that lies outside previously experienced impressions and associations. He or she may indulge creative impulses because imagination "herself" is not an anti-mimetic artist: "we argue about imagination as if she were actually a paintress who has colours at her command, and who, upon some invisible canvas in the soul, pourtrays the likeness of all earthly and celestial objects" (3, 131–32). The unshakeable self-assurance of the Edgeworths' belief in the moderateness of the imagination attains its zenith in a statement about that most overpowering and indeterminate of eighteenth-century aesthetic categories, the sublime. Announcing the meaninglessness, for children, of its usual connotations, immensity and mystery, the Edgeworths tie sublimity inextricably to the logic of association: the pleasure of the sublime is produced, they staunchly maintain, "by suggesting certain ideas, those who have not the previous ideas will not feel the pleasure" (3, 147).

Practical Education's divergences from *Emile* then, are defined by its authors' persuasion of the intrinsically limited reach both of the educational space and the child's imagination, and their resulting rejection of any rigid or complex schemes to dictate or regulate its effects. Their unambivalent estimation of the correctness and justice of their educational theory, as well as the facility with which it allows them to banish the anxieties—over mastery, proscription, desire—driving Rousseau's, is intimated by one fleeting but telling moment in the text. Having enthusiastically approved Rousseau's suggestion that "the senses of children must be cultivated with the utmost care" by encouraging them "to judge of distances and weight" and compare "the observations of their sense of feeling and sight" the Edgeworths tersely remark: "Rousseau rewards Emilius with cakes when he judges rightly; success we think, is a better reward; Rousseau was himself childishly fond of cakes and cream" (3, 195–97). Though their jibe appears trivial, it stealthily nullifies the significance of Rousseau's dedication to molding and constricting the child's environment, by ascribing a lack of self-command to the person of the *philosophe* himself. The issue of circumscription and restraint is thereby shifted away from discussion of the child's development and the educational procedure, and rendered a problem that afflicts only the misguided pedagogue.

Belinda, published within a few years of *Practical Education*, continues to expound the unfaltering convictions of the treatise, and to accentuate their contrast—by means of the parodic subplot—with those of Rousseau's *Émile*. Transposing the domestic context of the Edgeworthian project to the vicissitudes of the fashionable aristocratic world, the novel preserves its unflagging confidence in the positive contribution of surrounding influences to improvement and development, and its disapproval of theoretical schemes and techniques for containing or channeling their effect. Yet in assembling a fictionalized defense and glorification of *Practical Education's* ideas, *Belinda* gives them a strikingly optimistic, even extravagant coloring. The transformation signals the secure authority that the treatise and its precepts lend to the fiction; the way in which the Edgeworthian model of a naturally bounded educational environment allows many diverse elements to be accommodated within the essentially safe landscape that *Belinda* describes. In appropriating and highlighting the prior text's foundations, however, (by applying them to a whole social landscape) the novel lays bare the structure of its presuppositions, and the frameworks of regulation on which they constantly rely.

Belinda's "Virginia" subplot, when read in the light of the Edgeworths' educational theories, appears to formulate a methodical exposition both of *Practical Education's* critique of *Émile* and the principles it opposes to Rousseau's system. At the outset of her account of Hervey's plan, Edgeworth repeats the treatise's insinuation that Rousseau may be less interested in recovering "natural learning" than he is in exercising absolute, factitious control over it. She constructs the Rousseauvian educational program as dependent on the illusion of a previously formed, archetypally perfect subject: "[Hervey] was some time delayed, by the difficulty of finding a proper object for his purpose . . . it was difficult to find simplicity without vulgarity, ingenuity without cunning, or even ignorance without prejudice . . . a heart wholly unpracticed, yet full of sensibility" (373). The obstacle Hervey encounters, and the impossible antitheses he prizes, parody Rousseau's eulogy for the wonderful balance in Sophy's disposition: "she has taste without deep study, talent without art, judgement without learning" (446).[33] Indeed Virginia is not a blank slate, but the marks of her childhood carry very different valences to those that Hervey (unconsciously) expects or initially wants.

Despite being renamed, relocated, and secluded from society by Hervey, exposed to no other male company than his, and encouraged by her governess (who knows Hervey's intentions) to read novels and intensify supposed romantic feelings for her guardian, Virginia's imagination wanders to another object. The girl idolizes the image of an anonymous man in a picture (who is the son of a neighbor of her grandmother's), identifying the stranger with the heroes of the novels she reads. He turns out to be a real-life "hero"—Captain Sunderland—who rescued Virginia's father during a "rebellion of the negroes" on the latter's Jamaican plantation (476). Early associations (the picture from the first home) infiltrate and overturn the purpose of the fabricated, claustrophobic environment, just as the revival of Virginia's "real" name, Rachel Hartley, heralds the triumph of British empiricism over French Rousseauvianism. The two efficiently pertinent rhetorical questions that Virginia eventually throws at her kindly captor: "is it my fault, that I cannot forget?" (referring to her childhood memories) and, more philosophically, "do you think I cannot feel without being taught?" assert her unbreakable bond with a prior existence, and its resistance to the new circumstances in which she has been placed (400).

Importantly, the associations in themselves—in a glance at Rousseau's concern with determining and orchestrating the effects of the childhood space—are neither dangerous nor threatening; precipitating distress and confusion at first, they have a wholly felicitous result, uniting Virginia with an appropriate husband, and reintegrating her with her family's social milieu and economic interests. By means of the manner in which it fashions the groundwork for this conclusion, Virginia's imagination produces a miraculous reiteration of *Practical Education*'s rudimentary aesthetic theory. Though she fixates on mental portraits without knowing the real persons they depict ("Only a picture!—but have you never seen the original?" cries Hervey in astonishment at his ward's romantic obsession (468)—Virginia's fancy does not stray perilously into the unknown: far from sketching the likeness of "all earthly and celestial objects"[34] it faithfully reproduces the outline of familiarity and home.

On one level, therefore, the Virginia subplot dramatizes the Edgeworths' argument, in *Practical Education*, against Rousseau's elaborately theatrical struggle to redirect and alter Émile's desires: tutorly domination of the child's surrounding world will always prove unworkable and unnecessary because the subtle operation of childhood impressions both evades manipulation and contributes usefully to development. But as the improbably mimetic yield of Rachel's imagination demonstrates, her case brings about a fantastically fortuitous return to a conformist order of things, transforming malaise into health, estrangement into intimacy, and most bizarrely, fantasy into reality. Critical commentary on the subplot—stating that it upholds, against Rousseau, the Wollstonecraftian ideal of a rational education for women, or ridicules the "absurdity" "in a practical world" of Rousseau's interest in preserving women's "'natural' ignorance and innocence"—while warranted by the terms of the Edgeworthian instructional project as a whole, does not ask what inference we should draw from the miraculous realization of "Virginia's dearest romantic wishes."[35] The girl's experience fails, contrary to the claims of one critic, even really to serve as a "warning" against the hazards of an addiction to novels, since her notions of actuality are no more thwarted than those of the exemplary reader (Belinda).[36]

Edgeworth's leniency with Virginia, her insertion of the girl into the tableau of domestic bliss, could be read simply as a further burlesque of Rousseau's vision, and of the generic demands of the "happy ending." I would propose, however, that the subplot miniaturizes the novel's strikingly idealized, "utopian" version of *Practical Education*'s premises, figuring early imprints on the imagination as innately wholesome, and implying that individual formation will self-sufficiently, organically progress toward "normal" outcomes.

The episode also alerts us to the fact that *Belinda*'s redeployment of *Practical Education*'s doctrines nurtures deeply ambitious political ends, retrospectively illuminating the unspoken political parameters of the treatise itself. Virginia's picture conjures up someone who, as well as being a family friend, is a "heroic" guardian of the imperial status quo. Her marriage, in addition to reconciling the "home" space of education with the "abroad" of "the [social] world," thereby countering the fears expressed in *Émile* about the snares of an unknown spatial beyond, positions Virginia within a colonial economy—in decisive contrast to Rousseau's excoriation of empire—as a "reward" for Sunderland's defense of the Jamaican plantocracy.[37] Pointing out the thoroughness with which *Belinda* renews and reconstitutes imperial power by reinscribing it within a domestic ideology, Andrew McCann contends that the coming-to-life, in Sunderland's person, of Rachel's romantic dreams, discloses the ideology's "fictionality."[38] Reconnecting *Belinda* with its predecessor text, we might say that the principles of *Practical Education* lie behind the victory of this "fiction" and indeed the fictional strategies of *Belinda* as a whole. Duplicating (and inflating) the treatise's unruffled preconceptions and worldviews, the novel turns them into the basis for an expansive authority, which enables the consolidation of a carefully designed, hierarchical, conservative political and social settlement, and, simultaneously, a flirtation with "subversions" of imperial-colonial alliance and conjugal happiness. Nonetheless, in making "fiction" of *Practical Education*, *Belinda* obliquely casts an unrealistic, far-fetched aura over the solid domestic, civic, and economic interdependencies that it takes for granted, and exposes the ideological mechanisms safeguarding these.

Belinda's triumphant, wish-fulfilling affirmation of *Practical Education*'s theories goes some way to explaining peculiarities in the narrative that have continually perplexed its interpreters. Critics often observe that the heroine's educational advancement toward domesticity and conjugal love involves much exposure to persons who flout and spurn this norm, Harriot Freke but more particularly Lady Delacour, whose history is "perhaps inadvertently" "privileged" over Belinda's own.[39] In granting substantial latitude to such characters, Edgeworth formulates an exorbitant version of *Practical Education*'s opposition to strict control of the pedagogical environment, by proclaiming even the most "harmful" phenomena helpful to the consolidation of conventional mores: "Mrs Freke's conversation, though at the time it confounded Belinda, roused her, upon reflection, to examine by her reason the habits and principles which guided her conduct. She had a general feeling that they were right and necessary; but now . . . she established in her own understanding the exact boundaries of right and wrong. . . . [and] felt a species of satisfaction and security" (232). Just as it converts Harriot Freke into a profitable reflection, the novel's "satisfaction" with and "security" in its educational postulates facilitates the near-effortless incorporation of Lady Delacour into its domestic idyll. Susan Greenfield argues that the wound in lady Delacour's breast—which signifies rejection of maternity and domesticity—turns out to be curable because "the breast stands for women's natural difference," a value *Belinda* zealously seeks to enforce.[40] Taking her point further, the absence, all along, of any disease in the breast, figures the sanguinity with which the narrative contemplates deviations from domestic conformity, envisaging their easy re-assimilation to its standards.

Belinda's exaggerated adoption of *Practical Education*'s trust in the good offices of environmental influence, affects its treatment of exemplary as well as refractory characters. Readers cannot fail to discern a contrast between the liveliness of Delacour and Freke and the vacuity of Belinda herself, who is, as Annette Wheeler Cafarelli points out, just as "insipid" as Rachel/Virginia.[41] Lacking background as well as substance, Belinda seems, as Caroline Gonda notes, "to have come absolutely from nowhere" since readers receive no information about her parents and only a very vague account of her education, stating that it took place "chiefly in the country" and endowed her with "a taste for domestic pleasures" (7).[42] The indistinctness of Belinda's origins and personality might be judged to represent the homogenizing quality of the domestic ideal the narrative promotes. Considered within the frame of the novel's relation to *Practical Education*, however, it is more precisely the symptom of a refusal to define or interrogate the preconditions of the Edgeworthian system, and of a determination to celebrate and defend (without acknowledging their structure, or the problems they might present) its treasured protocols. Belinda's lack of individualized characteristics stands for Edgeworth's reluctance to acknowledge that particular circumstances and horizons (social, political, and ideological) are required by "practical" pedagogy. The heroine's emptiness decrees her function as a cipher for the repeated confirmation of the preordained boundaries and happy results of "experimental" learning since she behaves like an automaton of exemplarity, systematically treating all experiences as sources of wisdom and improvement.

In magnifying *Practical Education*'s proposals to create its own reliable domestic and political arrangements, the narrative not only dissolves the main object of Edgeworthian training (Belinda), but marginalizes its chief practitioners and proponents, the Percivals. As Lady Delacour comments, the Percivals are saved from the "odium" of perfection through their error concerning Mr. Vincent, whom they recommend as a husband for Belinda, unaware that he has a taste for gambling (451). Like Hervey in his dealings with "Virginia," the Percivals' judgment and good intentions are subverted by aspects of their ward's childhood: "when Mr. Hervey asked himself, how it was possible that the pupil of Mr. Percival could become a gamester, he forgot that Mr. Vincent had not been educated by his guardian, that he had lived in the West Indies till he was eighteen; [where] his character was in a great measure formed" (422). Superficially, Mr. Vincent's case reminds Edgeworthian educators that they exercise no more comprehensive a dominion over environmental influences than their Rousseauvian counterparts. But a comparison between Virginia's story and Vincent's unveils an inconsistency in the novel's evocation of *Practical Education*: for Virginia, romance reading and fantasizing indirectly produce "domestic happiness," while Vincent's addiction precipitates the dissolution of his betrothal, and leads almost to his suicide. Taken together, the two plot strands uncover the wider political agenda fulfilled by *Belinda*'s use of the treatise's assessments: "to serve England's colonial interests in Jamaica but protect against the development of a Jamaican presence in England."[43] The broadening of Edgeworthian educational theory to meet these global ends accounts for the sacrifice of the Percivals' centrality—since they are primarily identified with the space of "home"—to one of its defining tenets.

Belinda's ending sums up the freedom, flexibility, and ambitiousness granted to the novel by its antecedent text, as well as the contradictions that its ostentatiously comfortable authority contains. The Percivals' exclusion from the concluding tableau, rather than underlining their superior "perfection,"[44] reconfirms the application of *Practical Education*'s ideas to legitimizing a far-reaching blueprint for the structure of "home" and its links with "abroad." Their absence also fits with the carnivalesque license sanctioned by the novel's inflation of the treatise's self-assured creed. Lady Anne labels Lady Delacour as "*la femme comme il y en a peu*" from Marmontel's moral tale

(105), confining her within a grid of generic conventions. Exploding this imposition, it is Lady Delacour who chooses the genre of the finale; a theatrical tableau, which emphasizes the artificiality of the characters' situations while simultaneously assigning them to their proper places (478). Greenfield has speculated that the overt artificiality in Lady Delacour's design weakens the novel's propagation of an inborn femininity, conjugal domesticity, or imperial ascendancy,[45] but, throughout, the articles of faith borrowed from *Practical Education* let the narrative entertain, without undoing its stability, a close proximity between the natural and the artificial, the subversive and the normative.

After all *Belinda*'s apparently commodious and auspicious reconciliations, one figure remains more resolutely and conspicuously excluded than any other: Harriot Freke, the outspoken, cross-dressing advocate for the "rights of woman," who is repudiated by Lady Delacour in favor of domestic life, and who exits from the plot after being caught in a man-trap when she trespasses on the Delacour estate (309). The trap's injury to Harriot's leg both punishes her for her transvestitism and returns her to conventional femininity, since she will "never more be able to appear to advantage in man's apparel" (312). Seeking to explain Harriot's role in the narrative, Colin and Jo Atkinson argue that her treatment accords with Maria Edgeworth's overall "paternalistic" political philosophy, which cultivates a concern with "duty" over a demand for "rights."[46] Yet the lavish excesses of caricature devoted to Freke's portrayal, her reduction to a mere collection of signifiers,[47] and the abruptness of her dismissal from a text so actively interested in taming refractory characters, manifests a more multi-layered and conflicted purpose. Eleanor Ty points out that through the creation of Freke, Edgeworth endeavors to protect her own advocacy of women's education from association with the notoriety attached to "enlightenment feminists" such as May Wollstonecraft and Mary Hays.[48] Harriot Freke echoes Hays in insisting that when a woman "likes" a man she should "go and tell him so at once honestly" (230).[49] By heaping ridicule on the notion of women's freedom of sexual expression then, Edgeworth offers a token of her own moral conservatism, insulating her educational theories from the potential objections of traditionalists.

But as we have seen, the Virginia subplot, where Edgeworth supposedly pits Wollstonecraftian rationality against Rousseauvian "absurdity," principally achieves the fulfillment of fantasy and romantic longing. The invention (and destruction) of Harriot Freke may therefore constitute an attempt to validate the legitimacy of female desire without endorsing the freedom of expression proposed by Mary Hays and reputedly practiced by Wollstonecraft.[50] Rousseau's *Émile*, and his wider politics, play a complex role in this dynamic. Though taken to ventriloquize the social attitudes of the conservatives Shaftsbury and Burke,[51] Mr. Percival's reply to Harriot Freke's defense of a woman's right to make her preferences clear—"if she be a woman of sense, she knows that by such a step she would disgust the object of her affection" (230)—also resonates with *Émile*'s view that women's articulation of their desires induces "disgust" in men (528).[52] The ironic connection traces the contradictory nature of Rousseau's place in late eighteenth-century British political and cultural debate. Synonymous with the discourse of natural rights cursorily trumpeted by Freke, he was at the same time known to have opposed women's education, and to have identified their essence and value with their appeal as sources of sexual pleasure.[53] The reversals that occur in *Belinda*'s rewriting of the "Sophy" section of *Émile* show Edgeworth countering Rousseau's neutralization of a separate, self-determining female desire, even as she stigmatizes (in the person of Freke) the British feminist inheritors of his radical politics who are most critical of his pronouncements on women's social, educational, and sexual status.

By having "Virginia" fall in love with a picture, overturning Hervey's amorous inclinations and arrogant ruses thereby, Edgeworth, while purveying a version of *Practical Education*'s conception of development, literalizes and mocks the gender politics of *Émile*'s use of images to mold and check otherwise tumultuous passions. The tutor concentrates his pupil's emergent sexual longings on a fictitious ideal, "Sophy" an abstract embodiment of appropriate female attributes: "whether or no he personifies the model I have contrived to make so attractive to him, this model, if well done, will attach him nonetheless to everything that resembles itself and will give him a taste for all that is unlike it as if Sophy really existed" (352).[54] According to him, the fictitious Sophy is so powerfully compelling that it does eventually bring a "real" Sophy into being: "there were many charming girls in the town, is it chance that his choice is discovered in a country retreat?" (475).[55] This fortunate translation of a set of immaterial attributes into physical reality, and the actualization of desire that it accomplishes, forms a sharp contrast to Rousseau's history of the Sophy figure herself. Digressing into an abrupt, hypothetical ending to her story, Rousseau has Sophy fall in love with a fictional hero, Telemachus, leading her to cherish an ideal which no real-life suitor can match, which arouses her parents' anger, and causes her own death from a broken heart when she is forced into a marriage of their making (440–41).[56] Charting the life of a Sophy who never meets Émile (a man who would embody Telemachus's qualities) and still remains faithful to her inner, imaginary standard of virtue and merit, the fable declares its moral to be that "enthusiasm for the good and the beautiful is no more foreign to women than to men" (441).[57]

Although Rousseau seems to use the fable to give Sophy equality with Émile, and to predicate their projected union on her aspirations as much as on his, it is noteworthy that the false ending furnishes the only sustained reflection on Sophy's experience of longing and desire. Her demise, her surrender to the spell of Telemachus's image, bespeaks Rousseau's resistance to the idea of an independent, desiring female will. A resolution he makes for the portrayal of the revived Sophy—"let us . . . provide her with a less vivid imagination" (441)[58]—hints at the decision to turn away from such a prospect, and foreground the realization of Émile's hopes, relegating Sophy to the position of desired object. In the Rousseau subplot of *Belinda*, Edgeworth reverses Rousseau's cancellation of Sophy's dreams and his prioritization of Émile's: Virginia's beloved picture takes human form, while Hervey's loses all substantiality; instead of killing off Sophy, Edgeworth chides Rousseau by bringing Telemachus to life.

With the device of giving concrete embodiment to Virginia's romantic desires and fictional fantasies, the novel provides an apt condensation of the species of authority enjoyed by its own "fiction," one that gestures toward its limits and points of destabilization. Edgeworth gives fictional embodiment to *Practical Education*'s stress on the lack of need for carefully planned regulation of the educational environment, and its emphasis on the inevitably favorable coalescence of diverse influences into a felicitous formation. These underlying hypotheses make possible her wish-fulfilling and inclusive staging of the developmental process, to the point where she extols autonomous female desire against the most reactionary prejudices of the otherwise radical Rousseau. At the same time, the ending of Virginia's story, along with the treatment of Harriot Freke, underscores an important political point: that the apparently free-ranging, carnivalesque quality of Edgeworthian novelistic "practical education" rests on a secure trust in the underpinnings of conventional institutions and values, in the "proper" ordering of family and imperium, "home" and "abroad." Consequently, Edgeworth's fiction takes care to dominate forces and competing perspectives that would threaten both its sanguine celebration of uncontrived beneficence and its confident, comfortable preservation of "natural" constraint. As *Belinda*'s intricate narrative strategies attest, the forms of control to which the Edgeworthian system resorts are no less calculated and complex than those for which it criticizes Rousseau.

NOTES

1. Jean-Jacques Rousseau, *Émile*, trans. Barbara Foxley (London: Dent, 1993), 2. "Proposez ce qui est faisable, ne cesse-t-on de me répéter. C'est comme si l'on me disait: Proposez de faire ce qu'on fait..." Jean-Jacques Rousseau. *Émile ou de l'Éducation* (Paris: Flammarion, 1966), 33. All citations from *Émile* will be from these editions. Contrary to the remark in Rousseau's Preface, and to the Edgeworths' implicit comment on his system, Rousseau does exhibit a concern with fidelity to the "practical." His invention of an imaginary pupil is, he claims, designed to ensure that his theories are properly tested: "cette méthode me paraît utile pour empêcher un auteur qui se défie de s'égarer dans des visions; car, dès qu'il s'écarte de la pratique ordinaire, il n'a qu'à faire l'épreuve de la sienne sur son élève, il sentira bientôt, ou le lecteur sentira pour lui, s'il suit le progrès de l'enfance et la marche naturelle au cœur humain." Rousseau (1966), 54.

2. All citations from *Practical Education* in this essay are from the 1801 edition: Maria Edgeworth, and Richard Lovell Edgeworth *Practical Education*, ed. Jonathan Wordsworth (repr. New York: Woodstock Books, 1996).

3. Marilyn Butler. *Maria Edgeworth: A Literary Biography* (Oxford: Clarendon Press, 1972), 37–38.

4. Susan Manly, "Introductory Note," *Practical Education*, ed. Susan Manly, vol. 11 in *The Novels and Selected Works of Maria Edgeworth*, ed. Marilyn Butler and Mitzi Myers 12 vols. (London: Pickering and Chatto, 1999; 2003), 3. Many thanks to Susan Manly for allowing me to see a pre-publication copy of her introduction. Catherine Gallagher also describes the Edgeworths' educational system as progressive: "the Edgeworths were certainly not traditionalists; indeed, they famously advocated an educational system that stressed individual liberty, regardless of the child's gender." Catherine Gallagher, *Nobody's Story: The Disappearing Acts of Women Writers in the Marketplace, 1670–1820* (Berkeley: University of California Press, 1997) 267.

5. Annette Wheeler Cafarelli, "Rousseau and British Romanticism: Women and British Romanticism," in *Cultural Interactions in the Romantic Age: Critical Essays in Comparative Literature* ed. Gregory Maertz, (Albany: State University of New York Press, 1998), 145. Cafarelli's skepticism about the Edgeworths' progressivism is echoed by Julia Douthwaite, "Experimental Child-Rearing After Rousseau: Maria Edgeworth, *Practical Education* and *Belinda*," *Irish Journal of Feminist Studies* 2, no. 2 (Dec. 1997): 51.

6. Cafarelli, "Rousseau and British Romanticism," 126–29.

7. Jonathan Wordsworth, "Introduction," *Practical Education* (1996). Manly, "Introductory Note," 8.

8. This stance is seen most clearly in *Practical Education*'s recommendation that girls should be habituated to their future situation in life by means of "slight reproofs" and a general "restraint" which will assist in the cultivation of an accommodating temper (*PE* 1, 258–59).

9. Gary Kelly remarks that Edgeworth "was both a conservative and a progressive," Gary Kelly, "Amelia Opie, Lady Caroline Lamb, and Maria Edgeworth: Official and Unofficial Ideology," *Ariel: A Review of International English Literature*, 12, no. 4 (October 1981): 20. Placing Edgeworth in the Jacobin and anti-Jacobin "war of ideas," Marilyn Butler has proposed that Edgeworth's novels "do not belong unequivocally to one side," Marilyn Butler, *Jane Austen and the War of Ideas* (Oxford: Clarendon Press, 1975), 124. The problem of classifying Edgeworth politically forms the central theme of criticism of *Belinda*, with some readings drawing attention to the "carnivalesque" playfulness of the text while others emphasize the rigidity of its "domestic ideology."

10. Maria Edgeworth, *Belinda*, ed. Kathryn J. Kirkpatrick (Oxford: Oxford World's Classics, 1994). All quotations from *Belinda* will be from this edition. Day's scheme for educating a wife is cited as a source for *Belinda* in Marilyn Butler *Maria Edgeworth: A Literary Biography* (Oxford: Oxford University Press, 1972) 243.

11. Marilyn Butler, "Edgeworth's Stern Father: Escaping Thomas Day, 1795–1801," ed. Alvaro Ribeiro and James G. Basker, *Tradition in Transition: Women Writers, Marginal Texts, and the Eighteenth-Century Canon* (Oxford: Clarendon Press, 1996).

12. Key arguments in favor of *Belinda*'s radicalism include Eleanor Ty's contention that Edgeworth explores and interrogates "the boundaries of gender," Eleanor Ty, "Freke in Men's Clothes: Transgression and the Carnivalesque in Edgeworth's *Belinda*," ed. Jessica Munns, Penny Richards *The Clothes That Wear Us* (Newark: University of Delaware Press: 1999), Marjorie Lightfoot, "'Morals For Those That Like Them': The Satire of Edgeworth's *Belinda*, 1801" *Eire/Ireland: A Journal of Irish Studies* 29, no. 4 (1994): 117–31, and Audrey Bilger's *Laughing Feminism: Subversive Comedy in Frances Burney, Maria Edgeworth and Jane Austen* (Detroit: Wayne State University Press, 1998). Andrew McCann, "Conjugal Love and the Enlightenment Subject: The Colonial Contest of Non-Identity in Maria Edgeworth's *Belinda*," *Novel: A Forum on Fiction* 30, no. 1 (1996): 56–77, delineates the thoroughness of *Belinda*'s conservatism. Susan Greenfield also analyses the novel's conservative arrangement of domestic and imperial affairs, while noting ways in which it undermines the "naturalness" of its own schemes. Susan Greenfield, "'Abroad and at Home': Sexual Ambiguity, Miscegenation and Colonial Boundaries in Maria Edgeworth's *Belinda*," *PMLA* 122, no. 2 (1997): 214–28. Similarly, Elizabeth Kowaleski-Wallace shows the stridency of the novel's insistence on an ideology of motherhood and domesticity, but also observes moments where this agenda is modified or betrays the silencing of alternative perspectives. Beth Kowaleski-Wallace, "Home Economics: Domestic Ideology in Maria Edgeworth's *Belinda*," *The Eighteenth-Century: Theory and Interpretation* 29, no. 3 (1988): 242–63.

13. "The following work is offered to the public as a Moral Tale—the author not wishing to acknowledge a novel," "Advertisement," in Maria Edgeworth, *Belinda*.

Belinda is thereby placed in the same genre as the Marmontel story identified as the master narrative for Lady Delacour's reform (105), but other elements of the work are at odds with such a structure, most notably the pointedly artificial, theatrical conclusion, fashioned by Lady Delacour herself (478).

14. The political meanings of obeah are pointed out by McCann, "Conjugal Love" 66.

15. Bernardin de St Pierre's *Paul et Virginie* (1787).

16. Colin and Jo Atkinson, "Maria Edgeworth, *Belinda* and Women's Rights" in *Éire/Ireland* 19, no. 4 (1984): 115. This judgment of the subplot is also offered by Iain Topliss, "Mary Wollstonecraft and Maria Edgeworth's Modern Ladies," *Études Irlandaises* 6 (1981): 26.

17. Colin and Jo Atkinson, "Maria Edgeworth," 115. Ty, "Freke in Men's Clothes," 163.

18. McCann,"Conjugal Love and the Enlightenment Subject," 73. Greenfield, "'Abroad and at Home,'" 219.

19. Greenfield, "'Abroad and at Home,'" 214. See also McCann, "Conjugal Love and the Enlightenment Subject."

20. Rousseau, *Émile ou de l'Éducation*, 56.

21. Ibid., 115, 590–618.

22. Ibid., 247.

23. Ibid., 618.

24. "Vous ne serez point maître de l'enfant si vous ne l'êtes de tout ce qui l'entoure." *Émile*, 115.

25. *Émile*, 300, 284.

26. Ibid., 274.

27. "Mais l'objet qui paraissait d'abord sous la main fuit plus vite qu'on ne peut le poursuivre; quand on croit l'attendre, il se transforme et se montre au loin devant nous." *Émile*, 94.

28. "Chacun s'étend, pour ainsi dire, sur la terre entière, et devient sensible sur cette grande surface." *Émile*, 97.

29. This is the opening premise, and repeated argument of *Émile*. Rousseau, *Émile*, 5, Rousseau, *Émile ou de l'Éducation*, 35.

30. The Edgeworths' preface states: "to pretend to teach courage to Britons would be as ridiculous as it is unnecessary." They also praise "the superior delicacy of our fair countrywomen" (*PE* 1, ix).

31. The incident to which *Practical Education* refers is described in Rousseau, *Émile*, 104–5; Rousseau, *Émile ou de l'Éducation*, 154–55.

32. "Je veux qu'il ait sous les yeux l'original même et non pas le papier qui le représente ... afin qu'il s'accoutume à bien observer les corps et leurs apparences, et non pas à prendre des imitations fausses et conventionelles pour de véritables imitations." Rousseau, *Émile ou de l'Éducation*, 183.

33. "Elle a du goût sans étude, des talents sans art, du jugement sans connaissances." Rousseau *Émile ou de l'Éducation*, 538.

34. Edgeworth, *Practical Education*, 132.

35. See notes 16 and 17 above.

36. Heather MacFadyen, "Lady Delacour's Library: Maria Edgeworth's *Belinda* and Fashionable Reading," *Nineteenth-Century Literature* 48, no. 4 (1994): 427–28.

37. Greenfield, "'Abroad and at Home,'" 222.

38. Andrew McCann, *Cultural Politics in the 1790s: Literature, Radicalism and the Public Sphere* (London: Macmillan, 1999), 204.
39. Kowaleski-Wallace, "Domestic Ideology in Maria Edgeworth's *Belinda*," 243.
40. Greenfield, "'Abroad and at Home,'" 218.
41. Cafarelli, "Rousseau and British Romanticism," 156.
42. Caroline Gonda, *Reading Daughter's Fictions 1709–1834* (Cambridge: Cambridge University Press, 1996), 211.
43. Greenfield, "'Abroad and at Home,'" 219.
44. Douthwaite, "Experimental Child-Rearing After Rousseau," 51.
45. Greenfield, "'Abroad and at Home,'" 224.
46. Colin and Jo Atkinson, "Maria Edgeworth," 115.
47. McCann, *Cultural Politics,* 62–63.
48. Ty, "Freke in Men's Clothes," 167.
49. Colin and Jo Atkinson note Freke's allusion to Mary Hays's *Memoirs of Emma Courtney* (1796). Colin and Jo Atkinson, "Maria Edgeworth," 110.
50. Cafarelli describes the public perception of the "immorality" of radical female critics of Rousseau, as well as the challenge their own lives and reflections posed to existing sexual mores. Cafarelli, "Rousseau and British Romanticism," 132.
51. Colin and Jo Atkinson, "Maria Edgeworth" 109, 113.
52. "Women, faithful but foolish, importune men with their desires and only disgust them." Rousseau *Émile,* 528. "Les femmes, fidèles, mais indiscrètes, en les importunant de leurs désirs, les dégoûtent d'elles." Rousseau, *Émile ou de l'Éducation,* 623.
53. Cafarelli's essay identifies these pivotal contradictions and the problems they posed for radical British women writers. Cafarelli, "Rousseau and British Romanticism," 127.
54. "Mais, soit qu'il personnifie ou non le modèle que j'aurai su lui rendre amiable, ce modèle, s'il est bien fait, ne l'attachera pas moins a tout ce qui lui ressemble, et ne lui donera pas moins d'éloignement pour tout ce qui ne lui ressemble pas, que s'il avait un objet réel." Rousseau, *Émile ou de l'Éducation,* 431.
55. "Est-ce par hasard que, les villes fournissant tant de filles amiables, celle qui lui plaît ne se trouve qu'au fond d'une retraite éloignée?" Rousseau, *Émile ou de l'Éducation,* 568.
56. Rousseau, *Émile ou de l'Éducation,* 530–31.
57. "L'enthousiasme de l'honnête et du beau n'est pas plus étranger aux femmes qu'aux hommes." Rousseau, *Émile ou de l'Éducation,* 531.
58. "Ressuscitons cette amiable fille pour lui donner une imagination moins vive." Rousseau, *Émile ou de l'Éducation,* 532.

Part IV
Edgeworth's Influences

Harrington and Anti-Semitism: Mendelssohn's Invisible Agency

SUSAN MANLY

'AND WHY NOT A GOOD JEW?'[1] THE FINAL WORDS OF EDGEWORTH'S 1817 novel, *Harrington*, pose a question that is left to send its uncomfortable reverberations back through a narrative that many find comes perilously close to the anti-Semitic philo-Semitism of early nineteenth-century London's conversionist Protestant societies. Michael Ragussis and Peter Melville Logan, two of the best recent critics of *Harrington*, have, for instance, persuasively argued that the novel ends by enacting what it purports to protest against: the irrational prejudice against, and fear of, Jews. Catherine Gallagher, criticizing the psychologizing of antipathy by which Edgeworth explores anti-Jewishness, remarks that the tale "all too often makes the Jewish Question seem like a private obsession." Logan too interprets Harrington's telling of his story in terms of a continuing neurosis, the sociopathology identified early on in the fiction as "party spirit," while Ragussis claims that Harrington's superficial conversion from anti-Semitism is in reality never effected, as demonstrated in the compulsion to end the narrative with his marriage to the daughter of the Jewish hero, Montenero—a daughter who turns out to have been raised as a Protestant, for all her loyalty to her father.[2] These are strong readings, and I shall want to return to some of them later in this essay to examine them more fully, but I want to suggest that these readings in some measure misrepresent Edgeworth's novel.

Harrington sets out to examine how anti-Semitic bigotry is sustained by imaginary representations of Jews, notably by Shakespeare's Shylock, as well as by unfair legislation and xenophobia. At its simplest, the novel is the personal narrative of a recovering anti-Semite, a young man whose phobia of Jews is instilled by an unscrupulous nurse in early childhood and who has to unlearn his irrational prejudice through contact with various Jewish mentors, and through his love for the young lady, apparently Jewish, whom he first encounters at a performance of *The Merchant of Venice*.

However, the novel is much more than a simple love story or a bildungsroman, although the psychological portrait Edgeworth creates of the inception of bigotry and its hard-won defeat is fascinating and acute. *Harrington* is also a highly political work, drawing subtle but hard-hitting parallels between the legislation underpinning the social exclusion of Jews in England and the discriminatory penal laws affecting Catholics in Ireland at the time of writing. Edgeworth gives added emphasis to these political themes by setting the action of the novel between the Jewish Naturalization Act fracas of 1753–54 and the ultra-Protestant Gordon Riots, which shocked polite London in June 1780. Seamus Deane accuses Edgeworth of propagating, through her fictions, "Enlightenment values [that] are specifically 'Protestant'" and British.[3] In contrast to this view, I would argue that Edgeworth's fictional examination of religious intolerance in *Harrington* hits out at English ruling-class complacency—highlighted by the fact that the principal plotters against Harrington's struggle to throw off the remaining vestiges of his childhood anti-Jewish phobia and to reassert rationality turn out to be a family of aristocrats, the De Brantefield Mowbrays, who are deeply proud of their staunchly Protestant and Royalist ancestral history.

David Hume, one of Edgeworth's most important historical sources, in the twelfth of his *Political Essays* argued that England's mixed constitution had bred a freer spirit among the English, who gloried more than other nations in eccentricity and difference.[4] But Edgeworth's exposure of illiberality, hysterical xenophobia, and sheer mean-mindedness among the English upper middle classes and aristocracy depicts an inflexible hostility to otherness and exposes the lie of "English liberties" so frequently asserted as fact in late eighteenth-century print and popular culture. Instead it is *Harrington*'s foreign interloper, the idealized Jewish hero, Mr. Montenero, who displays the supposedly English virtues of self-restraint, generosity, toleration, kindness, civility, and loyalty. Edgeworth thus uses her novel, and the conversion of the title character Harrington, to question both nascent nationalist myths about England's exceptional liberalism and democracy, and to interrogate established sectarianism, by which Protestantism was identified with legitimate government and authority and adherents of other religions identified with despotism, subversion, and hostile intelligence. In the remainder of this essay I will show how Edgeworth allies herself in *Harrington* with European, non-Protestant opponents of the idea of state religion, as I uncover the influence of one of the most prominent of these opponents—Moses Mendelssohn.

While Michael Ragussis sees Edgeworth as the founder of the "revisionist novel of Jewish identity" (8) and as a writer who was seeking to "reinvent the representation of Jewish identity by calling into question the ideology of conversion" (7), he ultimately suggests that "Berenice's 'conversion' [in the form of her marriage to the Christian hero] in *Harrington* may be a sign of Edgeworth's submission to the ruling ideology," a "figurative banishment of the Jew" (79). Edgeworth has, if we attend to this interpretation of the novel's *dénouement*, betrayed the promise her novel seems initially to hold out in its exposure of the predominance of anti-Semitism and intolerance afflicting the educated and wealthy no less than the uninstructed.

But in mitigation of Edgeworth's failure at the close of the novel, Ragussis is struck by the way in which Montenero is used to bring to light the significance of Shylock in creating the stereotype of the Jew, particularly by the passage in which Montenero historicizes Shakespeare's play and traces the figure of Shylock back to a Christian merchant in the original source. Montenero thereby suggests, argues Ragussis, that the genealogy of anti-Semitic prejudice is a specifically textual genealogy, that literary representations feed into and confirm political and social perceptions, and that this can be undone if we are willing to read interrogatively.[5]

In highlighting this moment in Edgeworth's novel, Ragussis is able to show that *Harrington* is subverting one of the most consistent tropes of the genre of conversionist memoirs, a trope he himself identifies in his first chapter, where the memoirist discovers the truth of Christianity in one or more scenes of reading, often performed in secret.[6] In this scene, Montenero reads an influential public text demonizing Jews and shows that in fact the Christian author and his credulous audience are dupes of a lie, a distorted true source. But there is an earlier act of reading which interrogates the notion that Jews are inevitably alien, inhuman, and malign: Harrington's textual encounter, as a young man on his way to university in Cambridge, with Moses Mendelssohn. I would argue that as much as Berenice's hidden Protestantism and absorption into the Harrington family at the close of the novel disappoints, the influence of Mendelssohn continues to make itself felt, not only in Harrington's sense of connection with his fatherly mentor, Mr. Montenero—whose character is arguably based upon Mendelssohn—in preference to his own absurd and occasionally offensive father, but also in the question with which the novel concludes: "And why not a good Jew?" Significantly, this influence within the novel of cosmopolitan, liberal, European Jewish values was probably passed on to Edgeworth through her own version of Montenero, the Swiss translator of Jeremy Bentham and associate of Comte de Mirabeau, Pierre Étienne Dumont, who wrote the Edgeworths a long series of informative letters between 1805 and 1811, and who sought to promote equal rights for Jews in his home country in the wake of the Napoleonic Wars.

Dumont in fact seems, as Marilyn Butler notices, to have been partly responsible for making Edgeworth "tackle subjects on which ... she had previously never had opinions worth repeating" and for prompting her to think about anti-Semitism in relation to unfounded antipathy in general.[7] In 1811 Dumont wrote to her proposing that she write a moral tale with serious intent: "J'aurais voulu faire un conte sur chacun des fausses manières de raisonner en morale et en legislature sur les causes d'antipathie etc. Les gens du monde ont besoin d'être instruits comme des enfants."[8] We might link this suggestion by Dumont that apparent sophisticates are as much in need of re-examining their prejudices as the ignorant to Harrington's observation in the opening pages of his narrative that "[w]e must be content to begin at the beginning, if we would learn the history of our own minds; we must condescend to be even as little children, if we would discover, or recollect those small causes, which early influence the imagination, and afterwards become strong habits, prejudices, and passions."[9]

It was probably also indirectly through Dumont that Edgeworth herself first encountered Moses Mendelssohn, since Mirabeau, for whom Dumont worked as speechwriter in the late 1780s, and with whom he produced the French revolutionary *Courrier de Provence* in the early 1790s, is the source for her outline of the life of Mendelssohn.[10] It is, as I shall explain, the biographical details that are drawn from Mirabeau's memoir, *Sur Moses Mendelssohn*, which help to effect Harrington's first conversion from anti-Semite to philo-Semite, and it is Mendelssohn's fictional facsimile, Mr. Montenero, who extends and deepens this emotional and intellectual conversion as the narrative draws toward its conclusion.

It is worth noting here that much of the influence of Mendelssohn in the novel becomes invisible after the first edition, and indeed much of the effectiveness of Edgeworth's narrative as an investigation of conversionism is lost if we read it in its 1825 or 1833 version, in which it is substantially revised and, indeed, bowdlerized. When the novel appears in its revised form in the first collected Edgeworth, the 1825 *Tales and Miscellaneous Pieces*, its whole tone is changed by the cumulative effect of many fairly small alterations.[11] There is a strong possibility that these changes were not carried out by Edgeworth herself: written during her father's last illness in late 1816 to early 1817, the novel had painful associations for her, as she indicates in a letter to Harriet Edgeworth in 1824, when the latter seems to have been preparing the texts of *Harrington* and *Ormond* for a new edition: "Thank you my dear kind Harriet for all you have done about Harrington and Ormond—I . . . would willingly trust every thing I have in this world to your judgment and your friendship—I am glad you like it—But I have no stomach for it."[12]

The modern reader may wonder whether this trust was misplaced, since the alterations made for the 1825 edition of *Harrington* radically change the tone of the novel. Excisions and alterations of passages relating to Jewishness are particularly noticeable. Quite often the cutting of allusions to Jewishness is effected by removing the word "Jew," "Jewish," or "Jews" and substituting for it a less loaded term—man, Simon, the Hebrew nation, Israelite—or else omitting it altogether. These are changes which may seem small-scale taken singly but which over the course of an entire novel about conversion from anti-Semitism effect, ironically enough, an erasure of the very difference Edgeworth sets out to foreground.[13]

Thus, in the later editions of *Harrington*, the discomfort which might arise in the nineteenth-century reader from the foregrounding of the Jewishness of some of the principal characters is avoided by its linguistic removal. Significantly, this eradication of Jewishness is not a feature of Mirabeau's short biography of Moses Mendelssohn, written just six years after Christian Wilhelm von Dohm's essay, "On the Civic Improvement of the Jews," and in part responding to it. Mirabeau indeed begins his celebration of Mendelssohn's life by announcing that his intention is to make Mendelssohn—that "estimable citoyen du monde"[14]—more widely known in France so as to dismantle the prejudice which ensures that Jews are represented as incapable of being morally admirable or sound political thinkers.[15] Mirabeau's point is precisely to establish that Mendelssohn's Jewishness, far from being incidental or subsidiary to his moral virtue and intellectual giftedness, was the basis upon which he founded all the principles informing his exemplary life. As part of this objective, Mirabeau looks in detail at Mendelssohn's early friends and mentors, recognizing the vibrant Jewish intellectual culture in the midst of which the philosopher, by sheer hard work and the encouragement of these scholars and companions, learnt his rigorous thinking and moral integrity. He praises the commitment of Mendelssohn, which led him to study even when he had to forego food and other necessities in order to buy the books he needed, and observes that many of Mendelssohn's mentors such as Israel Moyse and Salomon Gumperz were notable themselves for their "manière de penser libre, fiere, & dégagée de préjugés."[16]

At this point, I want to turn back to Edgeworth's *Harrington* and look closely at just one of the passages substantially modified in 1825, where the transformative textual encounter of the fictional narrator with Mendelssohn is described. In a kind of reverse "road to Damascus" incident, Harrington is at this juncture in the novel recounting how, as he journeyed to Cambridge to begin his first term as an undergraduate, he caught sight of Jacob, a Jewish pedlar whom he had defended against an anti-Semitic campaign by fellow schoolmates when a boy. Falling into conversation with him, Harrington is given a copy of a life of Moses Mendelssohn, which he finds unexpectedly engrossing:

> I soon perceived why the life of Mendelssohn had so deeply interested poor Jacob. Mendelssohn, a Jew, born like himself in abject poverty, who, by vigorous perseverance, made his way through incredible difficulties to the highest literary reputation among the most eminent men of his country, and of his age. In consequence of his early, intense, and misapplied application in his first Jewish school, he was seized at ten years old with some dreadful nervous disease; this interested me, and I went on with his history; when he got over that, he traveled on foot from Anhalt to Berlin, to work for his bread, and to obtain instruction. He there met with a young Jew, as poor, as ardently fond of literature, and better informed than himself, who undertook to instruct him; and the two friends, sitting in a corner of a retired street in Berlin, used to study together a Hebrew Euclid. With this unpropitious place for study, and this low beginning, still he worked on, and in time he compassed learning Latin. With infinite labour, spending sometimes hours over one page, he read Locke in a Latin version. And under and through all these obstacles, he thought and suffered, and suffered and thought, and persevered, till at last he made himself one of the first philosophical writers of his country, attained the highest reputation among the most eminent

men of his time, and obtained the title of the Jewish Socrates, or the Jewish Plato; and then he was seized again with a nervous disease, and his physicians insisted upon it, that he must leave off thinking, whenever he felt an attack coming on; and to stop or prevent himself from thinking, he used to go to his window, and count the tiles on the roof of his opposite neighbours' houses. Of all these particulars I should probably have remembered none, except what related to the nervous disorder, but that it happened soon after I had read this life, that I had occasion to speak of it, and that it was of considerable advantage to me, in introducing me to good company at Cambridge.[17]

In 1825, the passage is substantially cut:

I soon perceived why the life of Mendelssohn had so deeply interested poor Jacob. Mendelssohn was a Jew, born like himself in abject poverty, but, by perseverance he made his way through incredible difficulties to the highest literary reputation among the most eminent men of his country, and of his age, and obtained the name of the Jewish Socrates. In consequence of his early, intense, and misapplied application in his first Jewish school, he was seized at ten years old with some dreadful nervous disease; this interested me, and I went on with his history. Of his life I should probably have remembered nothing, except what related to the nervous disorder, but it so happened, that soon after I had read this life, I had occasion to speak of it, and it was of considerable advantage in introducing me to good company at Cambridge.[18]

The first point to notice here is that most of the details about Mendelssohn's life are omitted in 1825: the references to his determination to learn, his intriguing alliance of "thinking" and "suffering," and the recurrence of his childhood nervous disorder—all are weakened or removed altogether in the 1825 version. Why is this important? The answer is that much of *Harrington*'s impact is located in subtle, seemingly insignificant details, as the eponymous narrator himself points out at the close of the first chapter, most of which is devoted to a painstaking reconstruction of the exact circumstances and words which gave rise to his deep-rooted phobia of Jews. Having told us of the "apparently puerile details" that constitute the "history of the mental and corporeal ills of [his] childhood" Harrington suggests that the better-informed among his readers will quickly see the vital connection between such details and "subjects of higher importance," and he links his personal enquiry into irrational prejudice with Bacon's stated intention in *Sylva Sylvarum* to examine "[t]he history of the power and influence of the imagination, not only upon the mind and body of the imaginant, but upon those of other people"—a history Harrington regards as long overdue.[19]

In other words, Harrington is suggesting, as he reflects on his early upbringing, that there is a clear link between the private dysfunctional imagination, tortured and terrified by its own fearful fantasies, and society at large—that the details of a life can be projected into the forms of an apparently rational public imagination; for instance, one that endorses adherence to established religion but penalizes adherence to dissident belief systems. So by examining these seemingly "puerile details" we can, Harrington argues, produce a "philosophical history" which can help us analyze and thus understand and combat the irrational associations that underlie bigotry.[20] A similar imaginative dysfunction is described by Hume in the ninth of his *Political Essays*:

> In such a state of mind, infinite unknown evils are dreaded from unknown agents; and where real objects of terror are wanting, the soul, active to its own prejudice, and fostering its predominant inclination, finds imaginary ones, to whose power and malevolence it sets no limits.[21]

Hume is here discussing superstition, which he tendentiously links to Catholicism; extreme Protestantism, on the other hand, which can manifest as "enthusiasm" gives rise, argues Hume, to "raptures, transports, and surprising flights of fancy."[22] Interestingly, it is Harrington's identifiably Christian maladies of superstition and enthusiasm that Montenero remedies by teaching him "philosophic calm and moderation"—an outlook that Montenero himself has had to learn, as Edgeworth tells us, by the strenuous application of his "reason" against the "great natural sensibility, perhaps susceptibility" with which he has struggled in the past.[23] This is strongly reminiscent of Mirabeau's depiction of Mendelssohn, who is described in the memoir as having "un tempérament foible et même infirme, un caractère timide," and "une sensibilité fort active," but who, Mirabeau shows, conquered this natural emotional vulnerability to become a figure of tremendous moral and intellectual force, always tolerant, calm, and possessed of "une raison très messurée."[24]

Montenero, continuing Mendelssohn's transformative textual agency, is the mentor who educates Harrington to see the irrationality not only of his "superstition" about Jews, instilled in early childhood and returning at times of stress even in adulthood, but also of his more mature "enthusiasm," displays of which alarm Berenice and her father to such an extent that for a time they fear that he is prey to some hereditary insanity.[25] If Harrington is suffering from a form of madness, it is not the "Jewish insanity" that his mother imputes to him,[26] but a specifically English and Christian mental affliction that his European and Jewish mentor alone can bring him to face, as it is his parents' erroneous and irrational attitudes that have fostered it.

The real Moses Mendelssohn's life in all its detail, then, anticipates the fictional Montenero's influence on Harrington's necessary psychological and moral reformation. The "vigorous perseverance" that Mendelssohn is said to have displayed as he "thought and suffered, suffered and thought," and his recurrent nervous disorder, the result of an overtired mind, which he had to fight to overcome, strike a chord with Harrington as he reads—his interest is stirred.[27] Just as the noxious infantile imagining of Jewish monsters may, if left unexamined, still exert its influence in the supposedly rational adult mind and affect or infect, by a kind of contagion, the whole of society, so the imaginative and emotional sympathetic identification that Harrington undergoes as he reads of Mendelssohn's nervous affliction and successful self-mastery is the beginning of his recovery from the psychopathological condition he has been tracing until this point in his story.

A few days after this textual encounter with the first of a series of Jewish mentors, Harrington returns the biography to Jacob, "assuring him that it had interested [him] very much," at which Jacob offers, since Harrington is evidently "so kind to the Jews," to introduce him to the man who will become his second Jewish mentor.[28] Harrington's recovery is thus at its inception a re-education of the heart—a recognition of a shared vulnerability that cuts across differences of race, class, and religion, and that causes him to recognize himself as he has been—nervous, debilitated—and as he could be, if he follows Mendelssohn's example. At the beginning of the passage, it is noticeable that it is the Jewish pedlar Jacob to whom Harrington attributes the interest that stems from identification with the subject of the biography, since both are Jews from a poor family background—but by the close of the summary of Mendelssohn's life, it is clear that Harrington too feels a strong kinship to the delicately framed Jewish philosopher—he is, as Jacob suggests, of Mendelssohn's kind—and, more importantly, his own life history, as recounted in his narrative, shows that he bears a kinship to Mendelssohn's struggle to overcome nervous infirmity and achieve wisdom.

For, as Peter Melville Logan has noted, the themes of gaining rational control over strong feelings, and the public benefit such individual efforts at self-mastery bring, are central to Edgeworth's novel.[29] We can relate this preoccupation in *Harrington* to the rationale behind Edgeworth's suggestive use of Mendelssohn, whose more obvious textual presence in the earlier edition begins to undo the neurotic fears aroused by the terrifying folk tales about murderous Jews with which the six-year-old Harrington's phobia had been fed by his unscrupulous nurse.

Although, as we have seen, most of the details of Mendelssohn's life mentioned by Harrington appear to have come directly from Mirabeau's celebratory memoir, there is one significant absence in Edgeworth's summary of the philosopher's life history. Edgeworth does not reproduce the circumstances that caused the nervous illness that recurred in Mendelssohn's later life. As I have already noted, one of the mentors of the younger Mendelssohn cited in Mirabeau's memoir was Israel Moyse, a Polish-Jewish scholar from a similarly impoverished background whose freethinking—"sa manière de penser libre, fiere, et dégagée des préjugés"[30]—led to his suffering continual persecution from orthodox leaders. The result was, Mirabeau notes, a severe melancholy from which he died while still young. In this we see prefigured the link between thinking and suffering, suffering and thinking that so impresses Harrington as he reads Mendelssohn's life. Moyse's suffering for his freethinking was also something that Mendelssohn had experienced in 1769, when Johann Lavater—the physiognomist and Protestant minister—attempted to engage him in a public debate on the claims of Judaism versus those of Christianity.

Unwilling to jeopardize the focus on "des vérités également importantes à tous les hommes"[31] by which he was working to improve the civil status of Jews in Prussia, and reluctant to engage in religious dispute that might damage this process of *rapprochement*, Mendelssohn refused to take up Lavater's challenge, but the stress that he suffered as a result of Lavater's efforts to force his hand caused a recurrence of the nervous crisis he had known as a child. Edgeworth is, then, in alluding to the recurrence of Mendelssohn's nervous susceptibility, also making an allusion to Lavater's infamous public conversion attempt, and the suffering this action inflicted on a man famous for his adherence to the cause of individual liberty of conscience. In contrast to Lavater's aggressive public proselytism, Mendelssohn's conversion of Harrington from his former phobic anti-Semitism is gradual and inward and works by combining an appeal to his heart as well as to his reason.

Since Mirabeau's account would have provided Edgeworth with knowledge of the circumstances surrounding Mendelssohn's second breakdown, we might conjecture that the naming of her protagonist is a further deliberate attempt to emphasize the extent to which Mendelssohn is being held up as an exemplary forerunner for Harrington. I have explored this elsewhere in more detail, but it seems very likely that Edgeworth's hero is named after James Harrington (1611–77), political philosopher and author of *The Commonwealth of Oceana* (1656).[32] There are many points of connection between James Harrington and his fictional namesake. The fictional Harrington, for instance, must consciously struggle to reconcile his familial and religious loyalties, which tie him to English Protestantism, with his sense of justice and loyalty to newer, freely chosen attachments, which draw him toward cosmopolitanism, Jews, and Judaism. James Harrington experienced a similar ambivalence in his struggle to reconcile his personal regard for King Charles I with his republican convictions. Harrington is said to have suffered so acutely at Charles's death that for a long time he lived in withdrawal and melancholy, until he turned to studying and writing, and eventually emerged with his theory of political justice, *The Commonwealth of Oceana*, which took the ancient Israelite state as one of its models and thus drew on Jewish learning to urge the republican conversion of the English state.[33] So in some senses, James Harrington's life and Mendelssohn's experiences bear similarities to one another, which the fictional Harrington's struggles echo.

As Edgeworth would have known, Mendelssohn was famous not only for his political role in advancing the cause of the Jews in Prussia, but also for his political philosophy in the form of his definitive statement on the relationship between personal religious belief and government, as explained in *Jerusalem* (1783). He emphasizes the social function of religion: its role in making good citizens. For Mendelssohn, the way we act—how we live out our feelings and thoughts—is more significant than what we think, feel, or believe. Liberty of conscience is, for him, fundamental to the good of society. Judaism was, Mendelssohn argued, nondogmatic and rational: "Faith accepts no commands: it accepts only what comes to it by way of reasoned conviction."[34] Mendelssohn also asserted that no religion—not even Judaism—could be the sole instrument through which God discloses his truth, and therefore it was of prime importance that freedom of thought should be protected by the granting of equal respect for all religious ideas. As Alfred Jospe notes, this stance is "in harmony with Judaism's persistent aversion to the formulation of creeds and its insistence that man wins merit primarily by his affirmation of God through conduct, not creed."[35]

I would suggest that the transformation Harrington undergoes, and that draws in his entire family, is very much in the spirit of the kind of Judaism Mendelssohn espoused, and which is echoed in a letter by Abraham Geiger, one of the founders of Reform Judaism, written in 1830. Complaining that "[m]ost rabbis apply all the authority vested in them to the indiscriminate preservation of whatever has been handed down to them by tradition," Geiger instead proposed a more flexible definition of tradition in which it could be seen as

> the developing power which continues in Judaism as an invisible agent, as a certain ennobling essence that never obtains its full expression, but ever continues to work, transform and create . . . Tradition, like revelation, is a spiritual energy that ever continues to work, a higher power that does not proceed from man, but is an emanation from the Divine Spirit, a power that works in the community, chooses its own ministers, manifests itself by its ever purer and riper fruits, and thus preserves vitality and existence itself.[36]

Harrington's progress toward an acceptance of religious diversity and a conquering of his irrational fears about Jews and Jewishness is similarly effected by a transformation from within as he meets and forms an attachment to the third and most important of his Jewish mentors, Mr. Montenero, whose name is immediately associated with a horror of tyranny and persecution and with America, where he has spent some years and where he had enjoyed perfect toleration and freedom of religious opinion. Interestingly, Mirabeau notes the resemblance between Mendelssohn's analysis of institutionalized intolerance and liberty of conscience in *Jerusalem* and the opening of the declaration of the republic of Virginia, which legislated for absolute religious freedom. Depicted as cosmopolitan, learned, cultivated, and with "a thorough knowledge of mankind and of the world"[37] Montenero is clearly based on Mendelssohn and the values Mendelssohn held most dear. Like his real-life model,

Montenero is a man committed to the faith of his fathers but willing to engage with a changing world of enlightened rationality. Harrington first loves and respects Montenero, then strives to emulate his mentor's self-command and his perseveringly rational response to intolerance and incivility. Harrington's kinship with Montenero is clinched by his betrothal to Berenice, Montenero's daughter, the event on which the novel closes and that brings together both Harrington's birth heritage, and the adopted inheritance he has succeeded to via his emulation of Montenero and his values of tolerance, integrity, and patient endurance of others' hostile plots, an endurance that finally results in a moral victory.

In conclusion, then, the passage cut in 1825 that relates to the details of Mendelssohn's life, his suffering, his determination to remain rational and fair, his perseverance, and his eventual achievement of famed wisdom, encodes the kind of unobtrusive agency by which Harrington himself will subsequently be converted from irrational phobia to rational self-command and recover from mental suffering, caused by imaginary dysfunctions, to a state where his ideas are broadened and function to make difference fruitful rather than fearsome. Where later editions of the novel literally made Mendelssohn less visible as an agent of change and progress, they did Edgeworth a disservice: her vision of race and religion is much more nuanced, much more pluralist, than it has hitherto been thought.

Notes

1. All references and quotations from *Harrington* are from Maria Edgeworth, *Harrington*, ed. Marilyn Butler and Susan Manly, vol 3 of *The Novels and Selected Works of Maria Edgeworth*, ed. Marilyn Butler et al. (London: Pickering and Chatto, 1999), 178.

2. See Michael Ragussis, *Figures of Conversion: "The Jewish Question" & English National Identity* (Durham: Duke University Press, 1995), chapter 2, "Writing English Comedy: Patronizing Shylock," 57–88; Peter Melville Logan, *Nerves and Narratives: A Cultural History of Hysteria in Nineteenth-Century English Prose* (Berkeley: University of California Press, 1997), chapter 5, "Harrington's Last Shudder: Maria Edgeworth and the Popular Fear of the Nervous Body," 109–39; Catherine Gallagher, *Nobody's Story: The Vanishing Acts of Women Writers in the Marketplace, 1670–1820* (Berkeley: University of California Press, 1994), 311.

3. Seamus Deane, *Strange Country: Modernity and Nationhood in Irish Writing Since 1790* (Oxford: Clarendon Press, 1997), 31.

4. David Hume, *Political Essays*, ed. Knud Haakonssen (Cambridge: Cambridge University Press, 1994), 85–86.

5. See Ragussis, *Figures of Conversion*, 83–84.

6. Ibid., 31.

7. Marilyn Butler, *Maria Edgeworth: A Literary Biography* (Oxford: Clarendon Press, 1972), 221–22.

8. "I would have liked a story on each of the false ways of arguing in morals and law about the causes of antipathy etc. People in high society need to be instructed just as much as children." All translations from the French are mine.

9. Edgeworth, *Harrington*, 173.

10. James Schmidt, editor of *Moses Mendelssohn: The First English Biography and Translations*, (Bristol: Thoemmes Press, 2002), has suggested in correspondence that Edgeworth might have been alerted to Mirabeau's essay by a reference in an anonymously published article in the *Monthly Magazine* of 1798 (VI: 38–44), entitled "A Biographical Sketch of the Jewish Socrates," and that this may be the magazine article lent by Jacob to Harrington in the novel. Isaac D'Israeli later claimed that the article was his, a plausible assertion, as its assimilationist argument, into which Mendelssohn's biography is woven, is strongly prefigured in D'Israeli's 1797 novel, *Vaurien*. Here, the eponymous protagonist meets a Jewish philosopher, discovered reading "Mendelsohn's [sic] Phaedon" and eating pork. He laments the iniquities suffered by the Jews of Europe, but declares that this is partly the fault of Jews themselves, mired in superstitious and backward-looking rabbinical learning (*Vaurien: or, Sketches of the Times: Exhibiting Views of the Philosophies, Religions, Politics, Literature, and Manners of the Age*, 2 vols. (London, 1797), vol. 2, ch. 28). In the *Monthly Magazine* article published the following year, D'Israeli draws heavily on Mirabeau's essay on Mendelssohn, but uses the biographical details of Mendelssohn's life to suggest the latter's untypically Jewish genius, which flourished despite the "defects derived from . . . his jewish education" (40). Despite this bias, however, D'Israeli's article begins by commenting that the suffering of Jews has in some measure deepened their potential for thought and original writing: "Whenever a nation suffers, it thinks . . ." (38)—a phrase perhaps picked up by Edgeworth in the connection she draws between thinking and suffering, both in the life of Mendelssohn and the character of Montenero.

11. It is also worth noting that Michael Ragussis takes the title of the chapter on *Harrington* in his *Figures of Conversion* from the 1825 text: in 1817, the playgoers do not go to "patronize Shylock," but to see *The Merchant of Venice* "whenever Macklin should act Shylock." The original phrasing foregrounds that this is a performance of a fictional character by a non-Jewish actor, and carries no hint of patronage (Edgeworth, *Harrington*, 210).

12. Letter to Harriet Edgeworth, Maria Edgeworth's stepsister, 21 May 1824.

13. These alterations may be seen in the textual variants appended to *Harrington*, 375–88.

14. "A great citizen of the world."

15. Comte de Mirabeau, *Sur Moses Mendelssohn, sur la réforme politique des juifs: et en particulier sur la révolution tentée en leur faveur en 1753 dans la grande Bretagne* (London, 1787; Paris: Éditions d'Histoire Sociale 1968), 14.

16. "Way of thinking, which was free, proud and without prejudice." Mirabeau, *Sur Moses Mendelssohn*, 5. All diacritics are given as in Mirabeau.

17. Edgeworth, *Harrington*, 190–91.

18. Edgeworth, *Tales and Miscellaneous Pieces*, 14 vols (London, 1825), 13: 44–45.

19. Edgeworth, *Harrington*, 172–73.

20. Ibid., 173.
21. Hume, *Political Essays*, 46.
22. Ibid., 47.
23. Edgeworth, *Harrington*, 232.
24. "A susceptible, even fragile temperament, a timid character; a highly active sensibility; a most measured reason." Mirabeau, *Sur Moses Mendelssohn*, 1, 56, 40, 39, 56. Again, the spelling is Mirabeau's.
25. See, for instance, the fit of "enthusiasm" to which Harrington gives way during the visit to the Tower; Edgeworth, *Harrington*, 240–41.
26. Edgeworth, *Harrington*, 201.
27. Ibid., 191.
28. Ibid.
29. Logan, *Nerves*, 109 ff.
30. Mirabeau, *Sur Moses Mendelssohn*, 5.
31. "Truths which are equally important to all mankind." Mirabeau, *Sur Moses Mendelssohn*, 31.
32. For more details, see my "Jews, Jubilee and Harringtonianism in Coleridge and Maria Edgeworth: Republican Conversions" in Nicholas Roe, ed., *Samuel Taylor Coleridge and the Sciences of Life* (Oxford: Oxford University Press, 2001).
33. See J. G. A. Pocock ed., *The Political Works of James Harrington* (Cambridge: Cambridge University Press, 1977), Introduction, 5.
34. See Jospe and Yahil's summary of Jerusalem's argument, *Encyclopedia Judaica*, 11: 1335–38.
35. Moses Mendelssohn, *Jerusalem and other Jewish Writings*, trans. and ed. Alfred Jospe (Paris: Schocken, 1969), 5.
36. Abraham Geiger, *Judaism and its History*, trans. Maurice Mayer (1866), cited in Nicholas de Lange, *Judaism*, chapter 2, "Torah and Tradition" (Oxford: Oxford University Press, 1986), 29.
37. Edgeworth, *Harrington*, 220.

A Whillaluh for Ireland: *Castle Rackrent* and Edgeworth's Influence on Sir Walter Scott

KIT KINCADE

TO ENDEAR HERSELF TO HER NOVEL-READING AUDIENCE, MARIA EDGEworth opens her preface to *Castle Rackrent* by explaining that popular taste for "anecdote"[1] proves that readers have more sense than those critics who rely on history as their measuring stick for wisdom: "The heroes of history are so decked out by the fine fancy of the professed historian; they talk in such measured prose, and act from such sublime or such diabolical motives, that few have sufficient taste, wickedness, or heroism, to sympathize in their fate" (61). On the most literal level, Edgeworth is preparing the reader for an antihistory told by a narrator with so little understanding of the events he recalls, and with no ability at all to see any perspective but the narrowly defined, ill-informed viewpoint from which he interprets these events, that he cannot fathom the irony the reader elicits from the text his words create. But Edgeworth's prefatory position is more than a defense of the validity of a biographical narrative from one who, at best, is dim-witted and stubborn; it is a defense of the validity of narratives of "real" people. And not just of any real people, but of real people who have never had an opportunity to be judged by the way they behave on an everyday scale. Edgeworth suggests in fact that "We cannot judge either of the feelings or of the characters of men with perfect accuracy, from their actions or their appearance in public; it is from their careless conversations, their half-finished sentences, that we may hope with the greatest probability of success to discover their real characters" (61).

Maria Edgeworth presents the Rackrent family from the perspective of a loyal, longtime servant who has seen them at their best and at their worst. Edgeworth's preface implicitly suggests that the servant always knows more about the "careless conversations" of his master than anyone else. When using this family history as a microcosm of national history, who better to represent the various barbarities and failings of the Anglo-Irish Ascendancy than the one who will be, and has been, most affected by these deeds? Indeed, Thady is an Irish everyman.

Maria Edgeworth's attitude toward Irish politics stems from a complex combination of her own Anglo-Irish and family history and from a keen awareness of what political unification with England would do to the Irish as a people, not merely to the province as a governable colony. Her awareness of the cultural differences between Ireland and England and the threat of the subsumation of Ireland into English culture spurred her to create *Castle Rackrent*, a document satirically critical of both the Anglo-Irish rule already established in Ireland and of England's goal of dismissing or overtaking Irish culture. England simply did not understand and, in fact, could not recognize that between the two cultures there stood an enormous gulf of difference. This was a cultural arrogance other writers, influenced by Edgeworth, would elaborate on, among them Sir Walter Scott in his nationally aware novels of similar cultural dilemmas in Scotland.

Castle Rackrent was released simultaneously in London and Dublin,[2] an apparently obvious response to the proposed Act of Union that was being so heatedly debated and which was soon to be passed. As Brian Hollingworth so succinctly puts it, "To publish an Irish story in January 1800 was a political act."[3] The fact that Edgeworth began writing the story almost ten years earlier, with the 1799 addition of a glossary, indicates that rushing *Castle Rackrent* into publication was no mere coincidence. Edgeworth was highly conscious of what she was doing:[4]

> *Castle Rackrent*, then, is no innocent text . . . it broadcast manifestly Edgeworthian ideas and attitudes towards the forthcoming Union. One strong political purpose of *Castle Rackrent* is that of all Edgeworth's Irish writing. She intends to combat English prejudices against the Irish and to increase understanding between the two kingdoms. In January 1800 it seemed imperative to do so since the two countries were now heading inexorably towards union—a union which, as the text reveals, the Edgeworths viewed with considerable unease.[5]

Marilyn Butler, too, recognizes that Edgeworth's

> goal is to gain for her Irish characters, regardless of their religion, the rights enjoyed by their English counter parts. And so her strategy is not

to prove that the Irish are unique, and therefore worthy of nationhood, but to show them the same, and therefore worthy of equality.[6]

Edgeworth lulls her English readers into a certain level of security so that the Irish may seem familiar enough that the English are not reductive and overpowering when dealing with them. Simultaneously, Edgeworth is situating Ireland as "other" in order to mislead the English into thinking that they understand a nation and a people whom they do not, thereby turning the humor onto the unsuspecting reader.

A metaphorical example of Edgeworth's act of turning her reader into the real subject of the tale appears at the beginning pages of Thady's narrative. Thady has begun his history with a description of the first lord who legally takes the surname Rackrent, Sir Patrick O'Shaughlin. Sir Patrick dies an alcoholic in debt. The irony of this situation turns on the futility of the law to dun a corpse for debts, particularly a corpse that could not pay his bills when alive, and the subsequent question of his heir's honorable promise to discharge these debts. Sir Patrick's funeral becomes a parody of the takeover of the English legal system:

> But who'd have thought it? just as all was going on right, through his own town they were passing, when the body was seized for debt—a rescue was apprehended from the mob; but the heir who attended the funeral was against that, for fear of consequences, seeing that those villains who came to serve acted under the disguise of the law: so, to be sure, the law must take its course, and little gain had the creditors for their pains. First and foremost, they had the curses of the country: and Sir Murtagh Rackrent, the new heir, in the next place, on account of this affront to the body, refused to pay a shilling of the debts, in which he was countenanced by all the best gentlemen of property, and others of his acquaintance; Sir Murtagh alleging in all companies, that he all along meant to pay his father's debts of honour, but the moment the law was taken of him, there was an end of honour to be sure. It was whispered (but none but the enemies of the family believe it), that this was all a sham seizure to get quit of the debts, which he had bound himself to pay in honour. (68)

Place England in the position of the law, and Ireland in the oppositional position of honor and the ironic parody takes explicit shape. Ireland owes England a "debt" (in England's opinion anyway) and the country is too poor to pay it, so England seizes the body of Ireland itself, represented by an Irishman subsumed by England in the assumption of the Anglo-Irish title Rackrent. Law overrides honor, and honor/Ireland is at an end. Finally, the enemies of the family, such as France and the Irish who want to remain independent, believe that the act of seizure/union was a sham: nothing more than a means to an end. Adding a further layer to the allegory is Sir Murtagh, representative of the Anglo-Irish landlords, who rides on the back of the mob representing the Irish, and who, in doing so, creates diametric opposition by juxtaposing law (England) and honor (Ireland). While claiming to embody both, he violates both.

The most apparent use of Edgeworth's obfuscatory technique is demonstrated in the narrator himself. If readers think that they understand Ireland because they understand the kind of person they believe Thady M'Quirk to be, then they are sorely mistaken. Thady is the epitome of that literary device, the unreliable narrator, who in this case turns out to be uncomfortably situated as well. The reader can only trust Thady so far, not because of any outright duplicity, but because it is obvious that he does not know all of the facts and is prone to misinterpretation of the facts to which he is privy. Maria Edgeworth, to a great extent, believes England to be much like Thady, a country of people who are willing to see and hear what they want to believe to justify their ends. In the voice of "the Editor," Edgeworth points out how little the English know about Ireland, and, as a consequence of this ignorance, has decided not to embellish Thady's narrative for greater entertainment value:

> The Editor could have readily made the catastrophe of Sir Condy's history more dramatic and more pathetic, if he thought it allowable to varnish the plain round tale of faithful Thady. He lays it before the English reader as a specimen of manners and characters, which are, perhaps, unknown in England. Indeed, the domestic habits of no nation in Europe were less known to the English than those of their sister country, till within these few years. (121)

The English might wish to believe that Thady's story is simple and true, but any careful reader should see Thady's propensity for misunderstanding as a sign that there is nothing simple about his tale. What is the true history of the Rackrents? What is the true situation of Ireland? And how much does England really know about either? There have been more interventions into the "real" Rackrent history than merely Thady's perspective on it.

The final irony of this text rests in the historic reception of the novel. A perfect example comes from a letter written by Richard Lovell Edgeworth to his friend Dr. Beaumont on the response of George III to *Castle Rackrent*, "We hear from good authority that the King was much pleased with Castle Rackrent—he rubbed his hands and said—what-what—I know something now of my Irish subjects."[7] Given the historical character of the king, it seems doubtful that he was being ironic. The odds are equally good that many English readers missed Edgeworth's commentary as well, and the fact of the matter is that *Castle Rackrent* was a huge best-seller in England.[8]

Little to nothing has been recorded of the reception of *Castle Rackrent* by the Irish. Some assumptions can be made, however. The Irish readership would have understood several things: that Thady was unreliable (based on their knowledge of their own culture); that the English would not be "in on the jokes," (based on the Editor's comments to that effect) and would, by extension, become the butt of those jokes; and that the Anglo-Irish depicted were somehow separate from both cultures yet evolving from both (based on each Rackrent's personal behavior). Maria Edgeworth attempts to overlap ends in her novel. She wants to introduce the English to an Ireland that is docile, one that proves no threat to England, and that is laughable, disarming the potentially hostile audience with the kind of stock comic characters they had come to expect in novels in general. However, setting the novel a century in the past enables Edgeworth to comment satirically not only on the political machinery and historical circumstances that permitted the fall of the Rackrent estate, but also on the present tension between the Catholic populous and the Protestant aristocracy. Edgeworth satirically encourages her audience to view the setting in anachronistic terms:

> The Editor hopes his readers will observe, that these are 'tales of other times;' that the manners depicted in the following pages are not those of the present age: the race of the Rackrents has long since been extinct in Ireland; and the drunken Sir Patrick, the litigious Sir Murtagh, the fighting Sir Kit, and the slovenly Sir Condy, are characters which could no more be met with at present in Ireland, than Squire Western or Parson Trulliber in England. There is a time, when individuals can bear to be rallied for their past follies and absurdities, after they have acquired new habits, and a new consciousness. (63)

Edgeworth is not only winking at the reader when she tells us that these characters could have only existed in the past, but she is also expressing the hope that the new generation really is more responsible, suggesting that a qualitative change is inherent in their ability to recognize their difference from their ancestors. Her final comment about becoming detached from national identity is a complex satirical jab at her English readers who, on the one hand, would believe it possible for an entire country such as Ireland to simply let its identity slip away from its national consciousness, as would happen with the union of Ireland with Britain, and, on the other, would find it the most offensive moral outrage to be asked to give up their English identity. The irony of the situation is enhanced by the novel's apparently English editor. Even this editor (a person who, by definition, is more attuned to the author's position and, by implication, to the reader's understanding) has missed what is really happening. There is an inherent appearance of innocence, and, as Hollingworth posits, "the organization of the narrative, despite its claims to naivety, is no more innocent than its purposes."[9]

A literary critic's inability to pigeonhole the text can be seen in microcosm by examining the full title of the novel: *Castle Rackrent: an Hibernian Tale taken from facts and from the manners of the Irish squires before the year 1782.* This title is packed with implicit meaning. The fact that the building on which the title is centered is a "castle" places it in the category of "Big House" fiction, which would become an Anglo-Irish tradition. The term "rackrent" described the widespread but not universal rent system that abused tenants and, therefore, the term had come to mean extortion. And the date 1782 has a double meaning. It was in that year that the British parliament repealed the Declaratory Act, thereby restoring Irish legislative sovereignty and causing a short-lived period of political independence under the parliamentary leadership of Henry Grattan. Personally, it was the year that Edgeworth's father, Richard Lovell Edgeworth, relocated his family from England to his familial estate, Edgeworthstown, County Longford, when Maria was approximately fourteen.[10] The words "tale," "facts," and "manners" work to establish the context of a fictional story told by a single narrator ("tale"), then reverse the context by introducing provable details ("facts"), and then mute the reversal by indicating influence by a social condition that is simultaneously provable and based on personal interpretation of a specific social group ("manners"). All of these words destabilize the story before it has even begun and leave the reader slightly off balance. This is the perfect position for Edgeworth to begin to undermine the English reader's assumptions about Irish national identity, without openly politicizing the events of the recent past.[11]

Often, the debate over authorial intention is one in which scholars shake their fingers in your face and say, without hesitation, that you can never know what the author's intent really was. And authors, of course, have been known to obscure their intentions, as Edgeworth did. One of her successors, however, Sir Walter Scott, alleviates this scholarly discomfort by coming right out and saying that he intended to copy Maria Edgeworth:

> Without being so presumptuous as to hope to emulate the rich humour, pathetic tenderness, and admirable tact which pervade the works of my accomplished friend, I felt that something might be attempted for my own country, of the same kind with that which Miss Edgeworth did fortunately achieve for Ireland—something which might introduce her natives to those of the sister kingdom in a more favourable light than they had been placed hitherto, and tend to procure sympathy for their virtues and indulgence for their foibles.[12]

This passage comes from the opening preface to the Waverley novels, of which *The Heart of Mid-Lothian* is perhaps Scott's most beloved. In fact, the Waverley novels might not even exist were it not for Edgeworth's favorable impression on Scott: "Two circumstances in particular recalled my recollection of my mislaid manuscript. The first was the extended and well-merited fame of Miss Edgeworth."[13] We also have his confession in a private letter to Edgeworth, written under the pretense that he was communicating on behalf of the author of the Waverley novels:

> *I know* that the exquisite truth and power of your characters operated on his mind at once to excite and subdue it. He felt that the success of his book was to depend upon the characters, much more than upon the story; and he entertained so just and so high an opinion of your eminence in the management of both, as to have strong apprehensions of any comparison which might be instituted betwixt his picture and story and yours . . . "If I could but hit Miss Edgeworth's wonderful power of vivifying all her persons, and making them live as real *beings* in your mind, I should not be afraid."[14]

These are merely two excerpts among many. Scott carried on a fruitful correspondence and maintained a very long friendship with

Maria Edgeworth, so it is not to go very far out on a limb to state that her "fingerprints" are all over his work.

Scott obviously did not copy Edgeworth outright; he had his own style and material. Edgeworth, in writing *Castle Rackrent*, was distinguishing Ireland from England in many more ways than any writer had previously done. William Molyneaux, Charles Lucas and others had identified Ireland as a political entity, but Edgeworth showed the Irish as a separate people with their own language and customs about which, in essence, the English were ignorant. Scott wanted to do for the Scottish what Edgeworth had done for the Irish. Although Scott may be most indebted to her novel *The Absentee* (1812), W. J. McCormack rightly notes that "the entire canon of Scott's fiction might legitimately claim a relationship to the little anonymous fiction of 1800."[15] In fact, I would venture one step further by saying that Scott's fiction would not exist in the form that it does presently, that is, there would not be any Waverley novels, if not for *Castle Rackrent*.

The first, and most important, contribution Edgeworth can claim to have made to Scott's idea is the idiom—the nationalistic historical novel itself. Scott took from her not only the pretext of a novel about his homeland, rather than England, but also the novel's historical quality. Both authors combined historical fact and regional folklore into a believable matrix. This verisimilitude that enriches the story of the Rackrent family and of Jeanie Deans also provides for a type of reflection upon a "simpler" age. Edgeworth and Scott play on the notion of the past as less tumultuous. On the surface, both novels appear to be a kind of Romantic nostalgia; however, it is this patina that disarms the reader and makes way for sharper political allegory. Both novels function through the contemporary reader's ability to refer to the past as either a golden age or as one similar to a dark age. Ina Ferris notes that "*Castle Rackrent*, notoriously, has yielded to contradictory readings, as a nostalgic lament for and as a devastating critique of the world it represents."[16] Scott's critics point out similar attempts in his novels in general and specifically in *The Heart of Mid-Lothian*:

> The conscious focus of *The Heart of Mid-Lothian* is mainly on the reform of the existing social and political order. While the novel contains the rudiments of a moral and psychological study, it is also unabashedly topical. Scott is concerned here with the issue of the Union, with the troubled relationship between England and her Scottish subjects, and with

the necessity of preserving Scotland's national identity within what he perceives as the essential beneficial strictures of the Union settlement. The novel's generic tensions must be understood as a product of Scott's effort to write an ambitious political fable. Scott's resolution to the social and political conflicts he describes in *Mid-Lothian* is to return the Scottish nation to the footing of a simple morality, founded on the social structure of the old peasantry. His solution of the formal and thematic dislocations which so many critics have hit upon is to write an extended piece of pastoral embellished with historical detail.[17]

Duncan Forbes compares Scott's use of history to the eighteenth-century rationalist historians as both a means to reconcile dissension and as a beacon for the political future: "Scott's purpose was never merely entertainment. An element of conscious stagecraft underlies his work . . . besides promoting sound morality, [Scott's work] was to do for England and Scotland what Maria Edgeworth's Irish Tales had done for England and Ireland."[18] Ferris acknowledges that Scott's purpose, like Edgeworth's, was to show difference between the two nations:

> Even as Scott supported the Union between Scotland and England, even as he affirmed the centralizing drive of British history, he sought through this fiction to counteract the erasure of difference that they implied . . . For Scottish readers, Scott . . . engages in an act of recovery, while for English readers he seeks to counteract stereotypes of Scotland, citing as an analogue for his effort Maria Edgeworth's undermining of English images of the Irish.[19]

By setting their novels in the past, both Edgeworth and Scott were able to be severe in their critique of the current political situations and to show the difference in their cultures in relation to England.

Both use a separate narrator to tell a tale framed by the "authorial" voice. This narrative technique has a twofold function. On the outside of the actual story is the question of authority. In fiction, a specific narrator, as opposed to an omniscient one, is supposedly a part of the story, and, therefore, not always to be taken too literally. The narrator of a memoir generally has a certain amount of assumed authority. When the two are mixed they provide the text with the possibility of historical accuracy: "Interpretive authority in both texts is finally granted through a nonfictional voice that identifies the aim and referent of the fiction as historical."[20] With this pattern established, it is easy for both authors to refer to actual historical events in their stories in order to anchor their tale, for example the riots against "Unionification" in Ireland and the Porteuos Incident in Scotland. Edgeworth ends *Castle Rackrent* with the editor's reflecting that:

> It is a problem of difficult solution to determine, whether an Union will hasten or retard the melioration of this country. The few gentlemen of education, who now reside in this country, will resort to England: they are few, but they are in nothing inferior to men of the same rank in Great Britain. The best that can happen will be the introduction of British manufacture in their places.
> Did the Warwickshire militia, who were chiefly artisans, teach the Irish to drink beer? or did they learn from the Irish to drink whiskey? (122)

The Porteous Incident in Scotland is the frame on which *Heart of Mid-Lothian*'s entire story hangs. In 1725, the British Parliament imposed a tax on malt, the basic ingredient of Scotland's national drink, causing a national uproar and an outburst of smuggling.[21] Scott's novel begins with Andrew Wilson, a baker turned beer smuggler, who is the victim of repeated seizures by the King's revenue officers. He and an accomplice, George Robertson, robbed a collector and, as a result, both he and Wilson are arrested. Wilson bungles their first attempt at escape, and, as a point of honor, facilitate Robertson's escape:

> The generous intrepidity which Wilson had displayed on the occasion augmented the feeling of compassion which attended his fate. The public, where their own prejudices are not concerned, are easily engaged on the side of disinterestedness and humanity, admired Wilson's behavior, and rejoiced at Robertson's escape. This general feeling was so great, that it excited a vague report that Wilson would be rescued at the place of execution, either by the mon or by some of his old associates, or by some extraordinary and unexpected exertion of strength and courage on his own part. The magistrates thought it their duty to provide against the possibility of disturbance. They ordered out, for protection of the execution of the sentence, the greater part of their own City Guard, under the command of Captain Porteous, a man whose name became too memorable from the melancholy circumstances of the day, and subsequent events. (33)

The point of overlap between fiction and history begins with Robertson, who is the father of Effie Dean's illegitimate child.

Another shared trait of Edgeworth's and Scott's narrators is that both offer insights into the stories which the characters do not see and to which the "authorial" voices are not privy. Thady Quirk is a character and a narrator. He is directly involved with the events by virtue of his position and the history of his family's position as upper servants to the Rackrent family; however, he is not omniscient. In fact, Thady is barely reliable, but he is the link for the reader and he can only be understood within the context of the story.

> Having, out of friendship for the family, upon whose estate, praised be Heaven! I and mine have lived rent-free, time out of mind, voluntarily undertaken to publish the MEMOIRS of the RACKRENT FAMILY, I think it my duty to say a few words, in the first place, concerning myself. My real name is Thady Quirk, though in the family I have always been known by no other than "*honest Thady,*"—afterwards, in the time of Sir Murtagh, deceased, I remember to hear them calling me "*old Thady,*" and now I'm come to "poor Thady"; for I wear a long great coat winter and summer, which is very handy, as I never put my arms into the sleeves; they are as good as new, though come Holantide next I've had it these seven years; it holds on by a single button round my neck, cloak fashion. To look at me, you would hardly think "poor Thady" was the father of attorney Quirk; he is a high gentleman, and never minds what poor Thady says, and having better than fifteen hundred a year, landed estate, looks down upon honest Thady; but I wash my hands of his doings, and as I have lived so will I die, true and loyal to the family. The family of the Rackrents is, I am proud to say, one of the most ancient in the kingdom. (65–66)

Thady is more a part of the Rackrent family and their history than of his own family. The evolution of his epithets and his great coat are both ironic and symbolic of the Rackrents. Also, ironically, he is the only one left to tell their story. Jedediah Cleishbotham, on the other hand, is a narrator who is not present in the story except as a narrative voice. He is committed to telling the "Tales of my Landlord" (8), just as Thady is. Both record the generosity of their landlords and both associate protection with outer wear: "Nor has it been without delectation, that I have endued a new coat, (snuff-brown, and with metal buttons)" (8). Both narrators associate their refusal to own part of the landlord's land as a sign of fealty, Thady by disassociating himself from his son Jason's buy-out of the Rackrent estate, and Cleishbotham by refusing to purchase a piece of the estate adjacent to his garden. Both proclaim their adherence to the truth of narrative, Thady by his nickname "honest Thady" and Cleishbotham by instance of his veracity in the face of accusation.

These cavillers have not only doubted mine identity, although thus plainly proved, but they have impeached my veracity and the authenticity of my historical narratives! verily, I can only say in answer, that I have been cautelous in quoting mine authorities. It is true, indeed, that if I had harkened with only one ear, I might have rehearsed my tale with more acceptation from those who love to hear but half the truth. (9)

The only real difference between them is that although Cleishbotham has a very Scottish name, he does not, unlike Thady, speak (or write) in Scots during the narrative intervention, except to, as they both do, record the dialogue in dialect.

This use of dialect has not only the effect of reinforcing the differences between both the Irish and the Scottish and the English languages, but also of privileging the speakers of the dialect over English readers. Clearly, the English could not understand the character and dialect as a native would. As Ferris puts it, "The definition of the role of 'vernacular idiom' in [Scott's novels], and the admission that to 'the *ignorant* English reader' the memoirs may be unintelligible" establishes this separate and superior position.[22] In many ways, Scott takes Edgeworth's idea to its natural conclusion. Where Edgeworth has to an extent "Anglo-phoned" her Irish, Scott goes out of his way to present the dialect to the reader as he believes it should be pronounced. Edgeworth privileges the speaker by means of regional clichés and folklore-based phrases: "Is the large room damp, Thady? said his honor. 'Oh, damp, your honor! how should it be but dry as a bone,' says I, 'after all the fires we should have kept in it day and night? it's the barrack-room your honor's talking on" (77). Scott advances this to the next level by taking great pains to make his Scottish characters not only sound Scottish in general, but to have each conform to his or her social classes in terms of both idiom and expression. Madge Wildfire's mother, for instance, sounds like the villagers: "It's my bairn!—it's Magdalene Murdockson I'm wantin' . . . havena I been tellin' ye sae this half-hour? And if ye are deaf, what needs ye sit cockit up there, and keep folk scraughin's t'ye this gate" (189); whereas the Duke of Argyle sounds like an aristocrat but still maintains his touch of Scottish: "Did you wish to speak with me, my bonny lass? . . . Never mind grace, lassie; just speak out a plain tale, and show you have a Scotch tongue in your head" (345–46). The Duke does not speak that way in front of Queen Caroline, so Scott is able to show varying degrees of dialect and how and when it is useful. The Duke is able to converse on the level that the company and situation demand at that time, thus showing his ability to move between worlds. The irony inherent in Edgeworth's use of dialect comes through as an "in joke" between her and her audience, at the expense of Thady.

Scott's irony, on the other hand, is contained within the story; he does not share the joke with the reader. An example of this is Jeanie's audience with the Queen. The Duke has primed her for this meeting, instructing Jeanie on how and what to say. When Jeanie converses with the Queen, she, in her attempts to speak plainly, says things that in the context of the company present mean more than Jeanie intends or understands. James Kerr looks at this situation from the different perspectives of the court (the Queen and the Duke) and Jeanie's: "Jeanie's language is not simply an expression of truth, but an instrument for saying one thing and meaning another."[23]

> "Stand up, young woman," said the Queen, but in a kind tone, "and tell me what sort of a barbarous people your country folk are, where child-murder is become so common as to require the restraint of laws like yours?"
>
> "If your Leddyship pleases," answered Jeanie, "there are many places besides Scotland where mothers are unkind to their ain flesh and blood."
>
> It must be observed, that the disputes between George the Second, and Frederick, Prince of Wales, were then at the highest, and that the good-natured part of the public lays the blame on the Queen. She coloured highly, and darted a glance of a most penetrating character first at Jeanie, and then at the Duke. (363)

Although we are allowed to witness the humor, we are never permitted to laugh at Jeanie. The reader understands the joke in the same way as the Duke does, from the position of insider in both worlds; indeed, the Duke is a metaphor for Scott's ideal English reader; one who understands a bit of both countries. This is the exact position Edgeworth's framing editor seems to be in.

The use of dialect in both novels requires a glossary for English readers. Edgeworth used this device and Scott copied it. Maria Edgeworth's glossary is less geared toward general vocabulary and is more a lexicon of folkloric and regional clichés; a typical entry reads:

> *Monday Morning.*—Thady begins his memoirs of the Rackrent Family by dating *Monday Morning*, because no great undertaking can be auspi-

ciously commenced in Ireland on any morning but *Monday Morning.* (123)

She goes on to expand on the original cliché and explains how the phrase was shortened and why it came about. Edgeworth was concerned about the preservation of the Irish people's national heritage of folklore and dialect, and she felt that this glossary, which later led her to write a collection of folklore, *Popular Tales,* would catalog Irish phrases and folkloric traditions. This is not to say that she does not define any single words, but such definitions are in the minority. The glossary is inconsistent and paradoxical. Its intrusion on Ireland is almost rude. Although it claims to understand and interpret Ireland, the glossary weakens its own logic by its use of internal conflicts and paradoxes. In the process, however, the glossary represents a microcosm of English attempts to subsume Ireland into the Union. The glossary stands as part of the work as a whole and not simply as a reference tool. Edgeworth's glossary can be read as a demonstration of her sense that it is the established Anglo-Irish who can best mediate Ireland's political and social conflicts with Britain, even as the glossary's author's attempt to undertake such mediation is demonstrably undermined by the inherent self-contradictions required by the task.

Scott uses his glossary, which many modern critics have claimed to be questionable at best, to define words almost exclusively in their contexts. On rare occasion he defines phrases, but he never gives origins or etymological background. Yet, why would Scott be so scant in the potentially rich element that a glossary could yield for enriching understanding of Scottish culture? I believe the answer is that Scott wanted his reader, in keeping with Edgeworth's plan to render Thady as an Irish "everyman," to concentrate on Jeanie Deans as an embodiment of a Scottish "everywoman," and to spend a great deal of time on the glossary would detract from Jeanie's draw as Scottish folklore.

Folklore and tradition are inextricably mixed into both novels, and they are two of the primary self-defining tools of any nation or group of people. Along with her glossary, Maria Edgeworth incorporated Irish folklore and customs into the matrix of her, and Thady's, story. Dáithí Ó hÓgáin describes Edgeworth's use of folklore as amazingly thorough and accurate:

> In approaching *Castle Rackrent* as a folklorist, one is impressed by the authenticity, accuracy, and originality of Maria Edgeworth's observations

of the life of the common people of Ireland at the end of the eighteenth century. In these respects, since the interest in folk customs and beliefs had not yet developed as a discipline, the author of *Castle Rackrent* is ahead of her time. Moreover, as an accomplished maker of fiction, she invests these cultural circumstances with persuasive character and social elements to render a powerful portrayal of Irish country life before the Union.[24]

One of Edgeworth's driving forces is didactic in nature. In a Swiftian mode of political allegory, Edgeworth shows the Irish trapped in an extremely hostile class system and details its impact on the morals and attitudes of both master and servant. This novel is about the feudal tradition in Ireland and appropriate folklore touches are tied in. The Irish tradition of recounting genealogy from time immemorial is part of the backdrop of Thady's narrative. In the opening sentence of *Castle Rackrent*, Thady draws on this tradition by indicating that his family have been servants to the Rackrents since "time out of mind" (65). Thady's genealogy is intermixed with the Rackrents', and he is proud of this relationship. As Ó hÓgáin indicates, "one notices running throughout Thady's narrative, not the servile attitude which the Big House might have expected from a servant, but a feeling of identity and pride which springs from a mutually respected tradition."[25] Thady has also explained that the Rackrent family assumed that surname in his grandfather's generation. Sir Patrick Rackrent came into his estate by changing his name from O'Shaughlin in order to inherit from a distant cousin, Sir Tallyhoo Rackrent. Thady points out that O'Shaughlin was "related to the kings of Ireland" (66). Ó hÓgáin explains that "The reference here seems to the name of the famous High King of Ireland at the turn of the eleventh century, Maoilsheachlainn, and we doubtless have an instance of the folk tendency to assume proof from facile etymological evidence."[26] Thady's bragging about the Rackrent family raises his family's position from mere servants to country squires to that of servants to descendants of a great king. This technique also references a folkloric tendency to establish, without actually dating, the "Irishness" of a family.

Scott adopts and adapts the use of folklore and customs for his romantic tale. We see the characters' use of folklore as a natural part of their lives and as a further class distinction between social groups. Incorporating levels of it into his characters and their speech helps define not only characters' social positions, but also helps to measure reason and intelligence. Because Scott's purpose is different, there is no intrusive editor to detail and describe what the folklore and customs are. He is not writing a biting satire about a failed political system, but a moral story about the failure of English law and justice. Law and justice function as a subversive metaphor for the English similarly in *Castle Rackrent*. Scott's use of folklore is usually connected to the development of specific characters or threads in the plot. All of Scott's Scottish characters incorporate folklore into their lives. It is part of what makes them inherently Scottish, from the Duke of Argyle down to the lowest criminal. The amount and the circumstances in which it is used are what differentiate class distinctions.

The Duke uses traditional clichés in conversation with his countrymen and women, such as in conversation with Jeanie: "'I do not know that,' replied the Duke; 'ilka man buckles his belt his ain gate—you know our old Scotch proverb?'" (349). Jeanie's folk beliefs surface in only the most grave of circumstances, such as when she is about to take her leave of Reuben Butler to walk to London to beg a pardon from the King for Effie. She asks Reuben to comfort and care for her sister while she is gone:

> And O, Reuben, the poor lassie in yon dungeon!—but I needna bid your kind heart—gie her what comfort ye can as soon as they will let you see her—tell her—But I maunna speak mair about her, for I maunna take leave o' ye wi' the tear in my ee, for that wadna be canny—God bless ye, Reuben!"
>
> To avoid so ill an omen she let the room hastily, while her features yet retained the mournful and affectionate smile which she had compelled them to wear, in order to support Butler's spirits. (273)

Madge Wildfire, representing the lowest wrung of society, sprinkles her conversation, in Ophelia-like fashion, with bits of songs. She wanders around, almost half dazed, after her lover, George Staunton, has rejected her. Her mother kills the child who is the result of this affair, and because of the combination of being jilted by her lover and losing her child, Madge is deemed crazy. Her songs, which she interjects throughout her conversation, tell her story in bits and pieces. The songs are generally old folk ballads:

> What did ye wi' the bridal ring-bridal ring-bridal ring?
> What did ye wi' your wedding ring, ye little cutty quean, O?
> I gied it till a sodger, a sodger, a sodger,
> I gied it till a sodger, an auld true love o' mine, O. (172)

The "bridal ring" that she gave to George Staunton was her innocence. Although he was not a soldier, he was an "old true love" of hers who had probably wooed her with promises of marriage. Madge will even respond to direct questions with lyrics from folk songs:

> Good even, good fair moon, good even to thee:
> I prithee, dear moon, now show to me
> The form and the features, the speech and degree,
> Of the man that true lover of mine shall be. (179)

In this particular scene, Madge is being interrogated by Ratcliff as to George Staunton's location. It is almost midnight and the authorities are looking for Jeanie, whom they think can lead them to George (known as Robertson to them). Madge is wandering outside at night, hoping to find her lover. To the other characters her songs seem the ravings of a madwoman, but they are, perhaps, the last vestige of her sanity. Through these songs it is clear she has some grasp at some level of what is happening. She even communicates that she understands her life is over through the three songs she sings (one about work being over, one about being reborn into heaven, and one about a false lover) before she dies.

Folklore and traditions play the most curious role in the development of the character of Effie Deans. At the beginning of the novel, she is more like Madge, especially because of her love for George, and her character displays this. When Jeanie is looking for Effie because she is late, she sees two figures out by the road. It seems that the figures have seen Jeanie spotting them, and while one turns away the other turns and walks toward her. It turns out to be Effie:

> She met her sister with that affected liveliness of manner, which in her rank, and sometimes in those above it, females occasionally assume to hide their surprise or confusion: and she carolled as she came—
> "The eflin knight sate on the brae,
> The broom grows bonny, the broom grows fair;
> And by there came lilting a lady so gay,
> And we daurna gang down to the broom nae mair." (104)

The song describes Effie's state of mind. She is the "lilting" lady.

As Effie's character develops from a young, impressionable Scottish girl to the sophisticated affected English gentlewoman, she loses her former traditions, customs, and folkloric touches. As Lady Staunton, Effie no longer talks with a broad brogue, nor does she use any traditional linguistic devices that identify her with ever having been in Scotland. When she meets Jeanie again after years of being in exile, Jeanie does not recognize her. When Effie reveals her identity to Jeanie, and the two are interrupted by the local captain, Effie refers to him as "that tiresome Highland fool" (468). When Jeanie begs her not to affront the Captain, Effie responds, "Affront? ... nobody is ever affronted at what I do or say, my dear. However, I will endure him, since you think it proper" (468). Effie's English facade shields her from her past and her true self, but she has become so good at "lying" (as she puts it) that she has lost the true Scottish nature of her character.

Maria Edgeworth was writing a satirical political allegory with a framework constructed as an historical and nationalistic novel, but she drew on her own family's and on Ireland's history without blatant England-bashing to comment on the proposed Act of Union between the two countries and to alert both countries to adjustment difficulties they may not have bargained for, either because of misunderstanding or because of ignorance.

Scott's stylistic departure comes from the notion of the romance novel. Lest it be forgotten, however, *The Heart of Mid-Lothian* is still a political satire:

> England has been much longer a highly civilized country: her subjects have been very strictly amenable to laws administered without fear or favour, a complete division of labour has taken place among her subjects, and the very thieves and robbers form a distinct class in society, subdivided among themselves according to the subject of their depredations, and the mode in which they carry them on, acting upon regular habits and principles, which can be calculated and anticipated at Bow Street, Hatton garden, or the Old Bailey. Our sister kingdom is like a cultivated field,—the farmer expects that, in spite of all his care, a certain a number of weeds will rise with the corn, and can tell you beforehand their names and appearance. But Scotland is like one of her own Highland glens, and the moralist who reads the records of her criminal jurisprudence, will find as many curious anomalous facts in the history of mind, as the botanist will detect rare specimens among her dingles and cliffs. (24)

Both novelists seek to establish their countries as distinctive cultural entities from England. Scott takes many techniques, as well as basic ideas on how to write a historical novel, from Edgeworth. Perhaps Maria Edgeworth's greatest gift to Scott was the inspiration and determination to continue a project that he had once considered not worthy of his time: the Waverley novels.

Notes

1. Maria Edgeworth, *Castle Rackrent and Ennui*, ed. Marilyn Butler (New York: Penguin, 1992), 61. All subsequent references are to this edition.
2. Cóilín Owens, ed. *Family Chronicles: Maria Edgeworth's* Castle Rackrent (Dublin: Wolfhound, 1987), 7.
3. Brian Hollingworth, *Maria Edgeworth's Writing: Language, History, Politics* (New York: St Martin's, 1997), 73.
4. Marilyn Butler, introduction to *Castle Rackrent and Ennui*, by Maria Edgeworth (New York: Penguin, 1992), 4.
5. Hollingsworth, *Maria Edgeworth's Writing*, 75.
6. Marilyn Butler, *Maria Edgeworth: A Literary Biography* (Oxford: Clarendon Press, 1972), 391.
7. Kathryn Kirkpatrick, ed. *Castle Rackrent* (Oxford: Oxford University Press, 1995), ix.
8. "*Castle Rackrent* saw three editions in London and Dublin (1800) before appearing with the author's name in the London edition of 1801. Between then and Maria Edgeworth's death, it ran through seven editions and a German translation (1802), including publications in North Carolina (c. 1802), Boston (1814), and Paris (1841). It was also included in two collected editions (1825, 1832–33) reprinted several times in the nineteenth century" (Owens, *Family Chronicles*, 8).
9. Hollingworth, *Maria Edgeworth's Writing*, 75.
10. "Maria Edgeworth's date of birth used to be given as 1 January 1767, but she herself seems to have considered 1768 correct." John Cronin, "Maria Edgeworth 1768–1849" in Owens, *Family* Chronicles, 14.
11. "Saddened by the increasing alienation of tenants and landlords, Edgeworth wrote: 'It is impossible to draw Ireland as she now is in a book of fiction—realities are to strong, party passions too violent to bear to see, or care to look at their faces in a looking-glass.'" Ann Owen Weeks, *Irish Women Writers: An Unchartered Tradition* (Lexington: University Presses of Kentucky, 1990), 20.
12. Sir Walter Scott, *On Novelists and Fiction*, ed. Ioan Williams (New York: Barnes and Noble, 1968), 413.
13. Ibid.
14. Walter Scott, *Memoirs of the Life of Sir Walter Scott*, vol. 3, ed. Robert Cadell (Edinburgh, 1838), 304.
15. W. J. McCormack, *Ascendancy and Tradition in Anglo-Irish Literary History from 1789 to 1939* (Oxford: Clarendon, 1985), 97–98.
16. Ina Ferris, *The Achievement of Literary Authority: Gender, History, and the Waverley Novels* (Ithaca: Cornell University Press, 1991), 114.
17. James Kerr, *Fiction Against History: Scott as Story-Teller* (Cambridge: Cambridge University Press, 1989), 62.
18. Duncan Forbes, "The Rationalism of Sir Walter Scott," in *Critical Essays on Sir Walter Scott: The Waverley Novels*, ed. Harry E. Shaw (New York: G. K. Hall, 1996), 88.

19. Ina Ferris, "Story-Telling and the Subversion of Literary Form in Walter Scott's Fiction," in J. H. Alexander and David Hewitt, eds., *Scott in Carnival: Selected Papers from the Fourth International Scott Conference, Edinburgh, 1991* (Aberdeen : Association for Scottish Literary Studies, University of Aberdeen, 1993), 105.
20. Ferris, *Literary Authority*, 111.
21. Walter Scott, *The Heart of Mid-Lothian*, ed. John Henry Raleigh (Boston: Houghton Mifflin, 1966), xiii. All subsequent quotations from the novel are from this edition.
22. Ferris, *Literary Authority*, 115.
23. Kerr, *Fiction Against History*, 74.
24. Dáithí Ó hÓgáin, "'Said an Elderly Man . . .': Maria Edgeworth's Use of Folklore in *Castle Rackrent*," in Owens *Family Chronicles*, 62.
25. Ó hÓgáin, "'Said an Elderly Man,'" 64.
26. Ibid., 63.

Bibliography

Adams, James. *The Pronunciation of the English Language . . . with an Appendix on Dialect . . . and Vindication of the Dialect of Scotland.* Edinburgh, 1799.

Adburgham, Alison. *Shops and Shopping, 1800–1914: Where, and in what Manner the Well-dressed Englishwoman Bought her Clothes.* London: Allen and Unwin, 1964.

Agnew, Jean, ed. *The Drennan-McTier Letters.* 3 vols. Dublin: The Women's History Project / Irish Manuscripts Commission, 1998–9.

Anon., *A Modest Defence of Gaming.* London, 1754.

Ariès, Phillipe. *Centuries of Childhood.* Trans. Robert Baldick. London: Pimlico, 1962.

Ashcroft, Bill, Gareth Griffiths, and Helen Tiffin, eds. *The Empire Writes Back: Theory and Practice in Post-Colonial Literatures.* London: Routledge, 1989.

Atkinson, Colin and Jo Atkinson. "Maria Edgeworth, *Belinda* and Women's Rights" *Éire/Ireland* 19, no. 4 1984: 94–118.

Austen, Jane. *Mansfield Park.* Ed. Claudia L. Johnson New York: Norton, 1998.

———. *Northanger Abbey.* Ed. Anne H. Ehrenpreis. London: Penguin, 1972.

Backus, Margot. *The Gothic Family Romance: Heterosexuality, Child Sacrifice, and the Anglo-Irish Colonial Order,* Post-Contemporary Interventions Series. Durham: Duke University Press, 1999.

Barrington, Jonah. *Personal Sketches and Reminiscences of His Own Time.* Dublin: Ashfield, 1997.

Bartlett, Thomas. *Acts of Union,* Inaugural lecture delivered at University College Dublin 24 February 2000.

———. "Defenders and Defenderism in 1795," *Irish Historical Studies* 24 1984–85: 373–94.

———. *The Fall and Rise of the Irish Nation: The Catholic Question, 1690–1830.* Savage, MD: Barnes & Noble, 1992.

Beddoes, Thomas. "Alternatives Compared: or what shall the Rich Do in Order to be Safe?" London, 1797.

Beesemyer, Irene A. "Romantic Masculinity in Edgeworth's *Ennui* and Scott's *Marmion:* In Itself a Border Story." *Papers on Language & Literature: A Journal for Scholars and Critics of Language and Literature* 35, no. 1 (Winter 1999): 74–96.

Bhabha, Homi. *The Location of Culture.* New York: Routledge, 1994.

———. "Representation and the Colonial Text: A Critical Exploration of Some Forms of Mimeticism." In *The Theory of Reading,* ed. Frank Gloversmith, 93–122. Sussex: Harvester, 1984.

Bianchi, Tony. "Aztecs in Troedrhiwgwair." In *Peripheral Visions: Images of Nationhood in Contemporary British Fiction*, ed. Ian A. Bell, 44–76. Cardiff: University of Wales Press, 1995.

Bilger, Audrey. *Laughing Feminism: Subversive Comedy in Frances Burney, Maria Edgeworth, and Jane Austen.* Detroit: Wayne State University Press, 1998.

Boswell, James. *Boswell's Life of Johnson*, ed. R. W. Chapman. Oxford: Oxford University Press, 1904.

Botkin, Frances. "Edgeworth and Wordsworth: Plain Unvarnished Tales." In *Ireland in the Nineteenth Century: Regional Identity*, ed. Leon Litvack and Glenn Hooper, 140–55. Dublin: Four Courts Press, 1999.

Boulukos, George E. "Maria Edgeworth's 'Grateful Negro' and the Sentimental Argument for Slavery." *Eighteenth-Century Life* 23, no. 1 (1999): 12–29.

Brewer, John. "Commercialization and Politics." In *The Birth of a Consumer Society: The Commercialization of Eighteenth-Century England*, eds. Neil McKendrick, John Brewer, and J. H. Plumb, 197–262. London: Europa Publications, 1982.

Brook, Peter. *The Melodramatic Imagination: Balzac, Henry James, Melodrama and the Mode of Excess.* New Haven: Yale University Press, 1976.

Burke, Edmund. *Reflections on the Revolution in France.* Ed. L. G. Mitchell. Oxford: Oxford University Press, 1999.

Burgess, Miranda J. "Violent Translations: Allegory, Gender, and Cultural Nationalism in Ireland, 1796–1806." *Modern Language Quarterly* 59, no. 1 (Mar. 1998): 33–70.

Burns, Robert. "On the late Captain Grose's peregrinations thro' Scotland collecting the antiquities of that kingdom," *Collected Poems*, The Official Robert Burns Site, 22 May 02 http://www.robertburns.org/works/275.html ll 1–30.

Bush, Barbara. "White 'Ladies,' Coloured 'Favourites,' and Black 'Wenches': Some Considerations on Sex, Race and Class Factors in Social Relations in White Creole Society in the British Caribbean." *Slavery and Abolition* 2, no. 1 (1982): 245–62.

Butler, Marilyn. "Edgeworth's Stern Father: Escaping Thomas Day, 1795–1801." In *Tradition in Transition: Women Writers, Marginal Texts, and the Eighteenth-Century Canon*, eds. Alvaro Ribeiro and James G. Basker, 75–93. Oxford: Clarendon Press, 1996.

———. "Introduction." In Maria Edgeworth's *Castle Rackrent* and *Ennui*, ed. Marilyn Butler, 1–54. London: Penguin, 1992.

———. "Irish Culture and Scottish Enlightenment." In *Economy, Polity and Society*, S. Collini, R. Whatmore, B. Young, 160–66. Cambridge: Cambridge University Press, 2000.

———. *Jane Austen and the War of Ideas.* Oxford: Clarendon Press, 1975.

———. *Maria Edgeworth: A Literary Biography.* Oxford: Oxford University Press, 1972.

———. *Romantics, Rebels and Reactionaries.* Oxford: Oxford University Press, 1981.

Cafarelli, Annette Wheeler. "Rousseau and British Romanticism: Women and British Romanticism." In *Cultural Interactions in the Romantic Age: Critical Essays in Comparative Literature*, ed. Gregory Maertz, 125–55. Albany: State University of New York Press, 1998.

Carlyle, Thomas. "Chartism," *The Works of Thomas Carlyle, 30 vols.* London: 1898–99.

Cary, Meredith. "Privileged Assimilation: Maria Edgeworth's Hope for the Ascendancy." *Eire-Ireland* 26 (1991): 29–37.

Connolly, Claire. "'I accuse Miss Owenson': *The Wild Irish Girl* as Media Event." *Colby Quarterly* 36, no. 2 (June 2000): 98–115.

Connolly, S. J., ed. *The Oxford Companion to Irish History.* Oxford: Oxford University Press, 1998.

Corbett, Mary Jean. "Another Tale To Tell: Postcolonial Theory And The Case of *Castle Rackrent.*" *Criticism* 36, no. 3 (Summer 1994): 383–400.

———. "Public Affections and Familial Politics: Burke, Edgeworth, and the 'Common Naturalization' of Great Britain." *ELH* 61, no. 4 (Winter 1994): 877–99.

Croker, John Wilson. [Unsigned rev. of second series of *Tales of Fashionable Life*]. *Quarterly Review* 7 (June 1812): 336.

[———.] Unsigned rev. of *Memoirs of Richard Lovell Edgeworth. Quarterly Review* 23 (May 1820): 511.

Cullen, L. M. *The Emergence of Modern Ireland, 1600–1900.* New York: Holmes and Meier, 1981.

Curtin, Nancy J. *The United Irishmen: Popular Politics in Ulster and Dublin, 1791–1798.* Oxford: Clarendon Press, 1994.

Darton, F. J. Harvey. *Children's Books in England: Five Centuries of Social Life.* Cambridge: Cambridge University Press, 1966.

Davies, John, Sir. "A Discoverie of the True Causes why Ireland was never entirely subdued" [1612]. Vol. II of *Complete Works in Verse and Prose of Sir John Davies,* ed. Chertsy Worthies Library, Alexander B. Grosart. 3 vols London, 1878. Vol. 2.

Day, Thomas. *The History of Sanford and Merton.* New York, 1857.

Deane, Seamus, gen. ed. *The Field Day Anthology of Irish Writing* 3 vols. Derry: Field Day, 1991.

———. "Irish National Character 1790–1900." In *The Writer as Witness: Literature as Historical Evidence,* ed. Tom Dunne, 90–113. Historical Studies Series 16. Cork: Cork University Press, 1987.

———. "The Production of Cultural Space in Irish Writing." *Boundary* 2, no. 21 (1994): 117–44.

———. *A Short History of Irish Literature.* South Bend: University of Notre Dame Press, 1994.

———. *Strange Country.* Oxford: Clarendon Press, 1997.

Delany, Paul. "'A Sort of Notch in the Donwell Estate': Intersections of Status and Class in Emma." *Eighteenth-Century Fiction* 12 (2000): 533–48.

D'Israeli, Isaac. *Vaurien: or, Sketches of the Times: Exhibiting Views of the Philosophies, Religions, Politics, Literature, and Manners of the Age.* 2 vols. London, 1797.

Dinwiddy, J. R. "Bentham as a Pupil of Miss Edgeworth's." *Notes and Queries* 29 (June 1982): 208–10.

Douthwaite, Julia. "Experimental Child-rearing After Rousseau: Maria Edgeworth, *Practical Education,* and *Belinda.*" *Irish Journal of Feminist Studies* 2, no. 2 (1997): 35–56.

Drennan, William. *Orellana* or *Letters of an Irish Helot*. Dublin, 1785.

———. "Protest against an Union with Great Britain," *The Microscope; or Minute Observer*, 1800.

Dunn, Richard S. *Sugar and Slaves: The Rise of the Planter Class in the English West Indies, 1624–1713*. Chapel Hill: University of North Carolina Press, 1972.

Dunne, Tom. "'A gentleman's estate should be a moral school': Edgeworthstown in Fact and Fiction, 1760–1840," in *Longford: Essays in County History*, eds. Raymond Gillespie and Gerard Moran. Dublin: Lilliput, 1991.

———. "Haunted by History: Irish Romantic Writing, 1800–1850." In *Romanticism in a National Context*, eds. Roy Porter and Miklas Teich, 68–91. Cambridge: Cambridge University Press, 1988.

———. "The Scullabogue Massacre," paper delivered at the Royal Irish Academy Conference, Dublin, Apr. 1998.

Eagleton, Terry. "Form and Ideology in the Anglo-Irish Novel." *Bullán: An Irish Studies Journal* 1, no. 1 (1994): 17–26.

———. *Heathcliff and the Great Hunger*. London: Verso, 1995.

Edgeworth, Frances. *A Memoir of Maria Edgeworth*. London, 1867.

Edgeworth, Maria. *The Absentee*. Ed. W. J. McCormack and Kim Walker. Oxford: Oxford University Press, 1988.

———. *The Absentee*. Eds. Heidi Thomson and Kim Walker. London: Penguin, 2000.

———. "Advertisement" to *Belinda*. Ed. Eiléan Ní Chuilleanáin London: J. M. Dent, 1993.

———. *Belinda*. Ed. George Watson. New York: Oxford University Press, 1995.

———. *Castle Rackrent* and *Ennui*. Ed. Marilyn Butler. London: Penguin, 1992.

———. *Harrington*. Ed. Marilyn Butler and Susan Manly. Vol 3 of *The Novels and Selected Works of Maria Edgeworth*, ed. Marilyn Butler et al. London: Pickering and Chatto, 1999.

———. *Ormond*. Ed. Claire Connolly. London: Penguin, 2000.

———. *Tales and Miscellaneous Pieces*. 14 vols. London, 1825.

Edgeworth, Richard Lovell and Maria Edgeworth. *Essay on Irish Bulls*. 2^d ed., corrected. London, 1803.

———. *An Essay on Irish Bulls*. In *Castle Rackrent, Irish Bulls and Ennui*, eds. Jane Desmarais, Tim McLoughlin, and Marilyn Butler, 69–154. London: Pickering and Chatto, 1999.

———. *Memoirs of Richard Lovell Edgeworth, Esq. Begun by Himself and Concluded by his Daughter, Maria Edgeworth*. 2 vols. London, 1820. Introd. Desmond J. Clarke. Shannon: Irish University Press, 1969.

———. Edgeworth, Maria. *Popular Tales* London, 1804. Reprinted in Robert L. Mack, ed., *Oriental Tales*. New York: Oxford University Press, 1992.

Edgeworth, Maria and R. L. Edgeworth. *Practical Education*. [2nd ed.] London, 1801. Repr. New York: Woodstock Books, 1996.

[———]. Unsigned rev. of John Carr's *The Stranger in Ireland*. *Edinburgh Review* 10 (Apr. 1807): 42–43.

Elliott, Marianne. *Partners in Revolution: The United Irishmen and France.* New Haven: Yale University Press, 1982.
———. *Wolfe Tone, Prophet of Irish Independence.* New Haven: Yale University Press, 1989.
Ellis, Markman. *The Politics of Sensibility: Race, Gender and Commerce in the Sentimental Novel.* Cambridge: Cambridge University Press, 1996.
Fanon, Frantz. *The Wretched of the Earth.* New York: Grove, 1963.
Fénelon, François de Salignac de Mothe. *Les Aventures de Télémaque.* Ed. J. L. Goré Paris: Éditions Garnier, 1987.
Ferris, Ina. *The Achievement of Literary Authority: Gender, History, and the Waverley Novels.* Ithaca: Cornell University Press, 1991.
———. "Narrating Cultural Encounter: Lady Morgan and the Irish National Tale." *Nineteenth-Century Literature* 51, no. 3 (Dec. 1996): 287–303.
———. "Story-Telling and the Subversion of Literary Form in Walter Scott's Fiction," in *Scott in Carnival: Selected Papers from the Fourth International Scott Conference, Edinburgh, 1991,* eds. J. H. Alexander and David Hewitt, 98–108. Aberdeen: Association for Scottish Literary Studies, University of Aberdeen, 1993.
Forbes, Duncan. "The Rationalism of Sir Walter Scott." In *Critical Essays on Sir Walter Scott: The Waverley Novels,* ed. Harry E. Shaw, 83–97. New York: G.K. Hall, 1996.
Foster, R. F. "Protestant Magic: W. B. Yeats and the Spell of History." *Proceedings of the British Academy,* 75 (1989): 243–66.
France, Peter, ed. *Thomas Bentley, Journal of a Visit to Paris (1776).* Brighton: University of Sussex Library, 1977.
Friel, Brian. *Translations.* London: Faber, 1981.
Frye, Northrop. *Anatomy of Criticism.* Princeton: Princeton University Press, 1957.
Frye, Northrop. "Conclusion to *A Literary History of Canada.*" In *The Stubborn Structure: Essays on Criticism and Society.* London: Methuen, 1970.
Gallagher, Catherine. *Nobody's Story: The Vanishing Acts of Women Writers in the Marketplace, 1670–1820.* Berkeley: University of California Press, 1994.
Geiger, Abraham. *Judaism and its History.* Trans. Maurice Mayer (1866). Cited in Nicholas de Lange, *Judaism,* chapter 2, "Torah and Tradition." Oxford: Oxford University Press, 1986.
Gilbert, Sandra and Susan Gubar. *The Madwoman in the Attic: The Woman Writer and the Nineteenth-Century Literary Imagination.* New Haven: Yale University Press, 1979.
Gillespie, Raymond. "A Question of Survival: The O'Farrells and Longford in the Seventeenth Century." In *Longford: Essays in County History,* eds. Raymond Gillespie and Gerard Moran, 13–29. Dublin: Lilliput, 1991.
Gilmartin, Sophie. *Ancestry and Narrative in Nineteenth-Century British Literature: Blood Relations from Edgeworth to Hardy.* Cambridge Studies in Nineteenth-Century Literature and Culture 18. Cambridge: Cambridge University Press, 1998.
Gonda, Caroline. *Reading Daughter's Fictions 1709–1834: Novels and Society from Manley to Edgeworth.* Cambridge: Cambridge University Press, 1996.
Greenfield, Susan C. "'Abroad and at Home': Sexual Ambiguity, Miscegenation, and Colonial Boundaries in Edgeworth's *Belinda.*" *PMLA* 112, no. 2 (1997): 214–28.

Grose, Francis. *A Classical Dictionary of the Vulgar Tongue*, ed. Eric Partridge. New York: Barnes and Noble, 1963.

Grubgeld, Elizabeth. "Class, Gender, and the Forms of Narrative: The Autobiographies of Anglo-Irish Women," In *Representing Ireland: Gender, Class, Nationality*, ed. Susan Shaw Sailer, 133–55. Gainesville: Florida University Press, 1987.

Gwynn, Stephen. *Experiences of a Literary Man*. London: Butterworth, 1926.

Harden, Elizabeth. "Transparent Thady Quirk." In *Family Chronicles: Maria Edgeworth's Castle Rackrent*, ed. Cóilín Owens, 86–96. Dublin: Wolfhound, 1987.

Hare, Augustus J. C., ed. *Life and Letters of Maria Edgeworth*. 2 vols. London, 1894.

Hargrave, Catherine Perry. *A History of Playing Cards and a Bibliography of Cards and Gaming*. New York: Dover, 1966.

Harlow, Ilana. "Creating Situations: Practical Jokes and the Revival of the Dead in Irish Tradition." *Journal of American Folklore* 110, no. 436 (Spring 1997): 140–68.

Hawthorne, Mark. *Doubt and Dogma in Maria Edgeworth*. Gainesville: University of Florida Press, 1967.

Hayden, John O., ed. *Scott: The Critical Heritage*. London: Routledge and Kegan Paul, 1970.

Hazlitt, William. *The Spirit of the Age and Conversations of James Northcote, Esq., R.A.* Vol. 11 of *The Complete Works of William Hazlitt*, ed. P. P. Howe. London: Dent, 1931.

Hollingworth, Brian. *Maria Edgeworth's Irish Writing: Language, History, Politics*. London: Macmillan, 1997.

Hooper, Glenn. "Stranger in Ireland: The Problematics of the Post-Union Travelogue." *Mosaic* 28, no. 1 (Mar. 1995): 25–47.

Hulme, Peter. *Colonial Encounters: Europe and the Native Caribbean, 1492–1797*. London: Methuen, 1986.

Hultin, Neil C. "Mrs. Harrington, Mrs. Leary, Mr. Croker, and the 'Irish Howl.'" *Eire-Ireland* 20, no. 4 (Winter, 1985): 43–64.

Hume, David. *Political Essays*, ed. Knud Haakonssen. Cambridge: Cambridge University Press, 1994.

James, Francis Godwin. "The Church of Ireland in the Early 18th Century." *Historical Magazine of the Protestant Episcopal Church* 48, no. 4 (Dec. 1979).

———. *Lords of the Ascendancy: The Irish House of Lords and its Members, 1600–1800*. Washington, D.C.: The Catholic University of America Press, 1995.

Jeffrey, Francis. *Contributions to the Edinburgh Review. Complete in One Volume*. London, 1853.

Johnston, Joseph, ed. "Archbishop King's Diagnosis." In *Bishop Berkeley's Querist in Historical Perspective*, 20–35. Dundalk: Dundalgan, 1970.

Joyce, James. *Ulysses: The Corrected Text*. Ed. Hans Walter Gabler. 2 vols. New York: Vintage, 1986.

Kelly, Gary. "Amelia Opie, Lady Caroline Lamb, and Maria Edgeworth: Official and Unofficial Ideology." *Ariel: A Review of International English Literature*, 12, no. 4 (Oct. 1981): 3–24.

———. "Class, Gender, Nation, and Empire: Money and Merit in the Writing of the Edgeworths." *Wordsworth Circle* 25 (1994): 89–93.

———. *English Fiction of the Romantic Period 1789–1830*. London: Longman, 1989.

Kerr, James. *Fiction Against History: Scott as Story-Teller*. Cambridge: Cambridge University Press, 1989.

Kestner, Joseph. "Defamiliarization in the Romantic Regional Novel: Maria Edgeworth, Walter Scott, John Gibson Lockhart, Susan Ferrier, and John Galt." *The Wordsworth Circle*, 10, no. 4 (Autumn, 1979): 326–31.

Kiberd, Declan. *Inventing Ireland: The Literature of the Modern Nation*. London: Jonathan Cape, 1995.

———. "Ireland—England's Unconscious." in *Inventing Ireland: The Literature of a Modern Nation*, 29–32. London: Jonathan Cape, 1995.

Kirkpatrick, Kathryn. "'Gentlemen Have Horrors Upon This Subject': West Indian Suitors in Maria Edgeworth's Belinda." *Eighteenth-Century Fiction* 5 (1993): 331–48.

———. "Introduction." In Maria Edgeworth, *Castle Rackrent*, ed. George Watson, vii–xxxvi. The World's Classics. Oxford: Oxford University Press, 1995.

———. "Putting Down the Rebellion: Notes and Glosses on *Castle Rackrent*." *Eire-Ireland* 30:1 (Spring 1995): 77–90.

König, René. *A la Mode: On the Social Psychology of Fashion*. Trans. F. Bradley. New York: Seabury Press, 1973.

Kowaleski-Wallace, Elizabeth. "Domestic Ideology in Maria Edgeworth's *Belinda*." *The Eighteenth-Century: Theory and Interpretation* 29, no. 3 (1988) 242–63.

———. *Their Father's Daughters: Hannah More, Maria Edgeworth, and Patriarchal Complicity*. Oxford: Oxford University Press, 1991.

Lang, Marjory. "Maria Edgeworth's *The Parent's Assistant* (1796): A Document of Social Education." *History of Education* 7, no. 1 (1978): 21–33.

Leadbeater, Mary. *Cottage Dialogues Among the Irish Peasantry*. Ed. Maria Edgeworth. London, 1811.

Leerssen, Joep. "Anglo-Irish Patriotism and its European Context: Notes Towards a Reassessment." *Eighteenth-Century Ireland* 3 (1988): 7–24.

———. *Remembrance and Imagination: Patterns in the Historical and Literary Representation of Ireland in the Nineteenth Century*. Cork: Cork University Press, 1996; South Bend: University of Notre Dame Press, 1997.

———. *Mere Irish and Fíor-Ghael: Studies in the Idea of Irish Nationality, Its Development and Literary Expression Prior to the Nineteenth Century*. Cork: Cork University Press, 1996.

Lightfoot, Marjorie. "'Morals For Those That Like Them': The Satire of Edgeworth's *Belinda*, 1801." *Eire/Ireland: A Journal of Irish Studies* 29, no. 4 (1994): 117–31.

Lister, T. H. [Unsigned rev. of *The Croppy, The Denounced, Yesterday in Ireland, The Collegians*, and *The Rivals*]. *Edinburgh Review* 52 (Jan. 1831): 411–12.

Locke, John. *Some Thoughts Concerning Education*, eds. John W. Yolton and Jean S. Yolton. Oxford: Clarendon Press, 1989.

Logan, Peter Melville. *Nerves and Narratives: A Cultural History of Hysteria in Nineteenth-Century English Prose*. Berkeley: University of California Press, 1997.

Long, Edward. *The History of Jamaica; or, General Survey of the Antient and Modern State of that Island.* Ed. George Metcalf, 1774 ed., 3 vols. London: Frank Cass, 1970.

Lovecraft, H. P. "The Call of Cthulhu." In *The H. P. Lovecraft Omnibus 3: The Haunter in the Dark*, 61–98. London: Panther, 1985.

Lukacs, Georg. *The Theory of the Novel.* Trans. Anna Bostock. Cambridge, Mass.: MIT Press, rpt. 1973.

Mabey, Richard. "Landscape: Terra Firma?" In *Towards a New Landscape*, ed. Bernard Jacobson, 62–68. London: Bernard Jacobson, 1993.

MacDonald, Edgar E., ed. *The Education of the Heart: The Correspondence of Rachel Mordicai Lazarus and Maria Edgeworth.* Chapel Hill: University of North Carolina Press, 1977.

Macintosh, Fiona. *Dying Acts: Death in Ancient Greek and Modern Tragic Drama.* Cork: Cork University Press, 1994.

Mandeville, Bernard. *The Fable of the Bees: or, Private Vice, Publick Benefits.* Ed. F. B. Kaye. 2 vols. Oxford: Clarendon Press, 1924.

Manly, Susan. "Introductory Note." *Practical Education*, ed. Susan Manly. Vol. 11 in *The Novels and Selected Works of Maria Edgeworth*. 12 vols. London: Pickering and Chatto, 2003.

———. "Jews, Jubilee and Harringtonianism in Coleridge and Maria Edgeworth: Republican Conversions." In *Samuel Taylor Coleridge and the Sciences of Life*, ed. Nicholas Roe, 69–87. Oxford: Oxford University Press, 2001.

McBride, I. R. *Scripture Politics.* Oxford: Oxford University Press, 1998.

McCann, Andrew. "Conjugal Love and the Enlightenment Subject: The Colonial Contest of Non-Identity in Maria Edgeworth's *Belinda*." *Novel: A Forum on Fiction* 30, no. 1 (1996) 56–77.

———. *Cultural Politics in the 1790s: Literature, Radicalism and the Public Sphere.* London: Macmillan, 1999.

McCormack, W. J. *Ascendancy and Tradition in Anglo-Irish Literary History from 1789 to 1939.* Oxford: Clarendon, 1985.

———. "Introduction" in "Irish Gothic and After, 1820–1945." In *The Field Day Anthology of Irish Writing*, gen. ed. Seamus Deane. 3 vols., 2:831–53. Derry: Field Day, 1991.

McFadyen, Heather. "Lady Delacour's Library: Maria Edgeworth's *Belinda* and Fashionable Reading." *Nineteenth-Century Literature* 48, no. 4 (1994) 423–39.

McKendrick, Neil, John Brewer, and J. H. Plumb, eds. *The Birth of a Consumer Society: The Commercialization of Eighteenth-Century England.* London: Europa Publications, 1982.

McKendrick, Neil. "The Commercialization of Fashion." In *The Birth of a Consumer Society: The Commercialization of Eighteenth-Century England*, eds. Neil McKendrick, John Brewer, and J. H. Plumb, 34–99. London: Europa Publications, 1982.

———. "Josiah Wedgwood and the Commercialization of the Potteries." In *The Birth of a Consumer Society: The Commercialization of Eighteenth-Century England*, eds. Neil McKendrick, John Brewer, and J. H. Plumb, 100–145. London: Europa Publications, 1982.

McMillan, Dorothy. "Constructed Out of Bewilderment: Stories of Scotland." In

Peripheral Visions: Images of Nationhood in Contemporary British Fiction, ed. Ian A. Bell, 80–102. Cardiff: University of Wales Press, 1995.

McMinn, Joseph. Ed. *Swift's Irish Pamphlets: An Introductory Selection*, Ulster Editions and Monographs 2. Gerards Cross: Colin Smythe, 1991.

MacNeice, Louis "Selva Oscura." In *The Collected Poems of Louis MacNeice*, ed. E. R. Dodds, 512–13. Rev. ed. London: Faber, 1979.

Mellor, Anne K. "A Novel Of Their Own: Romantic Women's Fiction, 1790–1830." In John Richetti, ed., 327–351. *The Columbia History of the British Novel*. New York: Columbia University Press, 1994.

Memmi, Albert. *The Colonizer and the Colonized*. Boston: Beacon, 1965.

Mendelssohn, Moses. *Jerusalem and other Jewish Writings*. Trans. and ed. Alfred Jospe. Paris: Schocken, 1969.

Mercier, Vivian. *The Irish Comic Tradition*. Oxford: Clarendon, 1972.

Mergenthal, Silvia. "The Shadow of Shylock: Scott's *Ivanhoe* and Edgeworth's *Harrington*." In *Scott in Carnival: Selected Papers from the Fourth International Scott Conference, Edinburgh, 1991*, eds. J. H. Alexander and David Hewitt, 320–321. Aberdeen: University of Aberdeen Press, 1993.

Michals, Teresa. "Commerce and Character in Maria Edgeworth." *Nineteenth-Century Literature* 49 (1994): 1–20.

Mintz, Sidney W. *Sweetness and Power: the Place of Sugar in Modern History*. New York: Viking, 1985.

Mirabeau, le Comte de. *Sur Moses Mendelssohn, sur la réforme politique des juifs: et en particulier sur la révolution tentée en leur faveur en 1753 dans la grande Bretagne*. London, 1787; Paris: Éditions d'histoir Sociale 1968.

Morash, Christopher. "The Time is Out of Joint (O Cursèd Spite): Towards a Definition of Supernatural Narrative." In *That Other World: The Supernatural and Fantastic in Irish Literature and its Contexts*, ed. Bruce Stewart, 2 vols. 1:123–42. Gerrards Cross: Colin Smythe, 1998.

Mowittt, John. *Text: The Genealogy of an Antidisciplinary Object*. Durham: Duke University Press, 1992.

Moynahan, Julian. *Anglo-Irish: The Literary Imagination in a Hyphenated Culture*. Princeton: Princeton University Press, 1995.

Murdoch, D. H. "Land Policy in the Eighteenth-Century Empire: The Sale of Crown Lands in the Ceded Islands, 1763–1783." *The Historical Journal* 27, no. 3 (1984): 549–74.

Musgrave, Richard, Sir, Bart. *Memoirs of the Different Rebellions in Ireland*, eds. Steven W. Myers and Dolores E. McKnight. Fort Wayne, Indiana: Round Tower Books, 1995.

Myers, Mitzi. "Canonical 'Orphans' and Critical *Ennui*: Rereading Edgeworth's Cross-Writing." *Children's Literature* 25 (1997): 116–36.

———. "'Completing the Union': Critical *Ennui*, the Politics of Narrative, and the Reformation of Irish Cultural Identity." In *The Intersections of the Public and the Private Spheres*, eds. Paula R. Backscheider and Timothy Dykstal. *Prose Studies: History, Theory, Criticism* 18, no. 3 (Dec. 1995): 41–77.

———. "The Dilemmas of Gender as Double-Voiced Narrative; or Maria Edgeworth Mothers the Bildungsroman." In *The Idea of the Novel in the Eighteenth Century*, ed. Robert W. Uphaus, 67–96. East Lansing: Colleagues Press, 1988.

———. "My Art Belongs to Daddy? Thomas Day, Maria Edgeworth, and the Pre-Texts of *Belinda*: Women Writers and Patriarchal Authority." In *Revising Women: Eighteenth-Century "Women's Fiction" and Social Engagement*, ed. Paula R. Backscheider, 104–46. Baltimore: Johns Hopkins University Press, 2000.

———. "Shot From Canons; or, Maria Edgeworth and the Cultural Production and Consumption of the Eighteenth-Century Woman Writer." In *The Consumption of Culture 1600–1800: Image, Object, Text*, eds. Ann Bermingham and John Brewer, 193–214. London: Routledge, 1995.

Nandy, Ashis. *The Intimate Enemy: Loss and Recovery of Self Under Colonialism*. Delhi: Oxford University Press, 1983.

Newcomer, James. "The Disingenuous Thady Quirk." In *Family Chronicles: Maria Edgeworth's Castle Rackrent*, ed. Cóilín Owens, 79–86. Dublin: Wolfhound, 1987.

———. *Maria Edgeworth the Novelist: 1767–1849, A Bicentennial Study*. Fort Worth: Texas Christian University Press, 1967.

Ní Chuilleanáin, Eiléan. "The Voices of Maria Edgeworth's Comedy." In *The Comic Tradition in Irish Women Writers*, ed. Theresa O'Connor, 21–39. Gainesville: University Press of Florida, 1996.

O'Flanagan, J. Roderick. *Lives of the Lord Chancellors of Ireland*. 2 vols. London, 1875.

Ó Gallchoir, Clíona. "Maria Edgeworth's Revolutionary Morality and the Limits of Realism." *Colby Quarterly* 36, no. 2 (June 2000): 87–97.

Ó hÓgáin, Dáithí. "'Said an Elderly Man . . .': Maria Edgeworth's Use of Folklore in *Castle Rackrent*." In *Family Chronicles: Maria Edgeworth's* Castle Rackrent, ed. Cóilín Owens, 62–70. Dublin: Wolfhound, 1987.

O'Regan, Philip. *Archbishop William King of Dublin (1650–1729) and the Constitution in Church and State*. Dublin: Four Courts Press, 2000.

Owens, Cóilín, ed. *Family Chronicles: Maria Edgeworth's* Castle Rackrent. Dublin: Wolfhound, 1987.

Owenson, Sydney. *The Wild Irish Girl*. New York: Oxford University Press, 1999.

Perera, Suvendrini *Reaches of Empire: The English Novel from Edgeworth to Dickens*. New York: Columbia University Press, 1991.

Plumb, J. H. "The New World of Children in Eighteenth-Century England." In *The Birth of a Consumer Society: The Commercialization of Eighteenth-Century England*, eds. Neil McKendrick, John Brewer, and J. H. Plumb, 286–315. London: Europa Publications, 1982.

Pocock, J. G. A. ed., *The Political Works of James Harrington*. Cambridge: Cambridge University Press, 1977.

Porter, James. *Billy Bluff and the Squire*. Belfast: *The Northern Star*, serialized NS May–Nov. 1796.

Ragatz, Lowell Joseph. *The Fall of the Planter Class in the British Caribbean, 1763–1833*. New York: The Century Company, 1928.

Ragussis, Michael. *Figures of Conversion: "The Jewish Question" & English National Identity*. Durham: Duke University Press, 1995.

———. "Representation, Conversion, and Literary Form: *Harrington* and the Novel of Jewish Identity," *Critical Inquiry* 16 (1989): 113–43.

Rahill, Frank. *The World of Melodrama*. University Park: Pennsylvania State University Press, 1967.

[Rev. of *The Anonymous*]. *British Critic* 42 (Nov. 1813): 534–35.

[Rev. of *Castle Rackrent*]. *Imperial Review* 1 (Apr. 1804): 550.

[Rev. of *Castle Rackrent*]. *Monthly Review* 32 (May 1800): 91–92.

[Rev. of first series of *Tales of Fashionable Life*]. *Christian Observer* 8 (Dec. 1809): 786.

[Rev. of first series of *Tales of Fashionable Life*]. *Edinburgh Review* 14 (July 1809): 379.

[Rev. of first series of *Tales of Fashionable Life*]. *Monthly Review* 62 (May 1810): 96–97.

[Rev. of *Harrington* and *Ormond*]. *Blackwood's Edinburgh Magazine* 1, no. 6 (Sept. 1817): 632.

[Rev. of *Harrington and Ormond*]. *British Review* 11 (Feb. 1818): 51–52.

[Rev. of *Popular Tales*]. *Edinburgh Review* 4 (July 1804): 330.

[Rev. of second series of *Tales of Fashionable Life*]. *Christian Observer* 11 (Dec. 1812): 793.

[Rev. of second series of *Tales of Fashionable Life*]. *Critical Review*, 4th ser., 2 (Aug. 1812): 122–23.

[Rev. of second series of *Tales of Fashionable Life*]. *Edinburgh Review* 20 (July 1812), 126.

[Rev. of *To-Day in Ireland, Tales of the O'Hara Family, O'Hara, or 1798,* and *The Adventurers*]. *Edinburgh Review* 43 (Feb. 1826): 358.

[Rev. of *To-day in Ireland, Tales by the O'Hara Family, The O'Briens and The O'Flahertys, Tales of the Munster Festivals,* and *The Croppy*]. *Westminster Review* 9 (Apr. 1828): 423.

Roberts, Warren. *Jane Austen and the French Revolution*. Basingstoke: Macmillan, 1979.

Rothschild, Emma. "Condorcet and Adam Smith on Education and Instruction." In *Philosophers on Education: Historical Perspectives*, ed. Amélie Oksenberg Rorty, 209–26. London: Routledge, 1998.

Rousseau, Jean-Jacques. *Émile*. Trans. Barbara Foxley. Everyman's Library. London: Dent, 1974, repr. 1993.

Rowan, P & B. [Catalogue Description.] Prior, Thomas. *A List of the Absentees of Ireland, and the Yearly Value of their Estates and Incomes spent abroad. With Observations on the Present State and Condition of that Kingdom* Dublin 1729 *Books and Periodicals of Irish Interest* . . . Catalogue 56: Part B, Belfast: P & B Rowan [2002].

Sacks, Sheldon. *Fiction and the Shape of Belief: A Study of Fielding with Glances at Swift, Johnson and Richardson*. Berkeley: University of California Press, 1964.

Sage, Victor. *Horror Fiction in the Protestant Tradition*. Basingstoke: Macmillan, 1988.

Said, Edward. *Orientalism*. New York: Pantheon, 1978.

Sampson, William. *A Faithful Report on the Trial of Hurdy Gurdy*. Belfast: *The Northern Star*, serialized NS July–Aug. 1794.

——— and Thomas Russell, *Review of the Lion of Old England*. Belfast: *The Northern Star*, serialized NS, Sept.–Dec. 1793.

Schmidt, James. Ed. *Moses Mendelssohn: The First English Biography and Translations.* Bristol: Thoemmes Press, 2002.

Scott, Sarah. *The History of Sir George Ellison.* Ed. Betty Rizzo. *Eighteenth-Century Novels by Women.* Lexington: University Presses of Kentucky, 1996.

Scott, Walter, Sir. *The Heart of Mid-Lothian.* Ed. John Henry Raleigh. Boston: Houghton Mifflin, 1966.

———. *Memoirs of the Life of Sir Walter Scott.* Ed. Robert Cadell. 3 vols. Edinburgh, 1838.

Senior, Nassau. [Unsigned review of *Rob Roy, The Heart of Midlothian, The Bride of Lammermoor, Ivanhoe,* and *Kenilworth* by Walter Scott]. *Quarterly Review* 26 (Dec. 1821) 109–48.

Smollett, Tobias, trans. *The Adventures of Telemachus, the Son of Ulysses.* Intro. Leslie A. Chilton, ed. O. M. Brack, Jr. Athens: University of Georgia Press, 1997.

Smyth, Gerry. *The Novel and the Nation: Studies in New Irish Fiction.* Contemporary Irish Studies Series. London: Pluto Press, 1997.

Smyth, Jim. *The Men of No Property: Irish Radicals and Popular Politics in the Late 18th Century.* London: Macmillan, 1992.

———. "An End to Moral Economy: The Irish Militia Disturbances of 1793." *Past and Present* 99 (1983): 41–64.

Spector, Sheila A. "The Other's Other: The Function of the Jew in Maria Edgeworth's Fiction." *European Romantic Review* 10 (1999): 307–40.

Spivak, Gayatri Chakravorty. *A Critique of Postcolonial Reason: Toward a History of the Vanishing Present.* Cambridge: Harvard University Press, 1999.

St Pierre, Bernardin de. *Paul et Virginie* (Paris, 1787).

Sullivan, C. W. "A Wizard Behind Every Bush." *Planet* 64 (Aug./Sept. 1987): 48–51.

Swift, Jonathan. *Poems of Swift.* Ed. Harold Williams, 3 vols. Oxford: Oxford University Press, 1958.

Sypher, Wylie "The West-Indian as a 'Character' in the Eighteenth Century." *Studies in Philology* 36 (1939): 503–20.

Thomson, Heidi. "Introduction." In Maria Edgeworth, *The Absentee,* vii–xviii. London: Penguin, 1999.

Thuente, Mary Helen. *The Harp Restrung.* Syracuse: Syracuse University Press, 1994.

Tracy, Robert. "Maria Edgeworth and Lady Morgan: Legality versus Legitimacy." *Nineteenth-Century Fiction* 40, no. 1 (June 1985): 1–22.

Tilley, Roger. *A History of Playing Cards.* London: Studio Vista, 1973.

Topliss, Ian. "Mary Wollstonecraft and Maria Edgeworth's Modern Ladies." *Études Irlandaises,* 6 (1981):3–31.

Trumpener, Katie. *Bardic Nationalism: The Romantic Novel and the British Empire.* Princeton: Princeton University Press, 1997.

Ty, Eleanor. "Freke in Men's Clothes: Transgression and the Carnivalesque in Edgeworth's *Belinda.*" In *The Clothes That Wear Us,* eds. Jessica Munns and Penny Richards, 157–73. Newark: University of Delaware Press, 1999.

Vance, Norman. *Irish Literature: A Social History* Dublin: Four Courts Press, 1990.

Vuaflart, Albert and Henri Bourin. *Les Portraits de Marie-Antoinette: Étude d'Iconographie Critique*. 2 vols. Paris: André Maty, 1910.

Waldron, Mary. *Jane Austen and the Fiction of Her Time*. Cambridge: Cambridge University Press, 1999.

Wall, Maureen. *Catholic Ireland in the Eighteenth Century: Collected Essays of Maureen Wall*. Ed. Gerard O'Brien, assoc. ed. Tom Dunne. Templeogue, Dublin: Geography Publications, 1989.

Ward, John. [unsigned rev. of *Patronage*]. *Quarterly Review* 11 (Jan. 1814): 309.

Wedde, Ian. "Introduction." In *The Penguin Book of New Zealand Verse*, ed. Ian Wedde and Harvey McQueen, 123–52. Auckland: Penguin, 1985.

Weeks, Ann Owen. *Irish Women Writers: An Unchartered Tradition*. Lexington: University Presses of Kentucky, 1990.

Whelan, Kevin. Foreword to "Writing Ireland, Reading England." In *Wild Irish Girl: a National Tale*, eds. Claire Connolly and Stephen Copley, ix–xxiv. London: Pickering and Chatto, 2000.

———. "Politicisation Co Wexford." In *Ireland and the French Revolution*, ed. Hugh Gough and D. Dickson, 156–70. Dublin: Dublin University Press, 1990.

———. *The Tree of Liberty: Radicalism, Catholicism and the Construction of Irish Identity, 1760–1830*. Cork: Cork University Press, 1996.

Williams, Aubrey, ed. *Poetry and Prose of Alexander Pope*. Boston: Houghton Mifflin, 1969.

Williams, David. *Incidents in my Own Life*. Brighton: University of Sussex Press, 1980.

———. *Liturgy on the Universal Principles of Religion and Morality*. London, 1776.

Williams, Harold, ed. *Swift's Correspondence* 5 vols. Oxford: Clarendon, 1963.

Williams, Ioan, ed. *Sir Walter Scott On Novelists and Fiction*. London: Routledge and K. Paul, 1968.

Williams, Raymond. *The County and the City*. London: Hogarth, 1993.

Wilson, Colin. Introduction to *H.P. Lovecraft, Crawling Chaos: Selected Works 1920–1935*. London: Creation, 1992.

Wohlgemut, Esther. "Maria Edgeworth and the Question of National Identity." *SEL: Studies in English Literature* 39:4 (Autumn 1999): 645–58.

Wollstonecraft, Mary. *The Works of Mary Wollstonecraft*. Eds. Janet Todd and Marilyn Butler, vol. 4. London: William Pickering, 1989.

Wordsworth, Jonathan. Introduction to Maria Edgeworth and Richard Lovell Edgeworth, *Practical Education*.1801 repr. New York: Woodstock Books, 1996.

Contributors

JACQUELINE BELANGER is a Research Associate at Cardiff University. She has published articles and essays on nineteenth-century Irish literature and Romantic-era fiction.

FRANCES BOTKIN is an Assistant Professor at Towson University where she teaches British Romantic Literature and Women's Studies. She has published on Maria Edgeworth, Lady Morgan, William Wordsworth, and Walter Scott. Professor Botkin is currently working on a book-length project on female witches, religious leaders, and political figures in nineteenth-century British and Colonial literature.

MARILYN BUTLER, Rector (Head) of Exeter College, Oxford, is the author of books on Romantic-period literature, such as *Jane Austen and the War of Ideas* and *Romantics, Rebels and Reactionaries*. She is currently working on the last volume of a twelve-volume edition of Edgeworth's works.

PETER COSGROVE teaches eighteenth-century British literature at Dartmouth College where he is an Associate Professor of English. His book *Impartial Stranger: History and Intertextuality in Gibbon's Decline and Fall of the Roman Empire*, was published by the University of Delaware Press, 1999. He has also published articles on Handel's oratorios, the photographs of Walker Evans, and historical films, as well as a consideration of Burke's theory of the sublime.

KATHLEEN COSTELLO-SULLIVAN is completing a Ph.D. at Boston College in the English Department, Irish Studies Program. Her dissertation considers nineteenth-century English and Irish novels' varied reflections of modernity. Kate has published articles on Swift, Kipling, and contemporary Irish art and has work forthcoming on Emily Lawless and Somerville and Ross.

CHRIS FAUSKE is Assistant Dean, School of Arts & Science at Salem State College in Salem, Massachusetts. He has published work on subjects ranging from Jonathan Swift and archbishop William King to bishop John Frederick MacNeice and Louis MacNeice.

DARRYL JONES is Lecturer in English, Trinity College, Dublin. He is the author of *Studying Poetry* (2000) [with Stephen Matterson], *Horror: A Thematic History in Fiction and Film* (2002), and is currently completing a monograph on Jane Austen, to be published in 2004. He has also written a number of articles on eighteenth-century and Romantic literature.

HEIDI KAUFMAN is an Assistant Professor of English at the University of Delaware. She is completing a book project on representations of Jewish history and culture in nineteenth-century British fiction. She has forthcoming articles on the intersections of British Imperial culture and Jewish cultural studies.

KIT KINCADE is an Assistant Professor at Indiana State University. She is the editor of the forthcoming *Essay on the History and Reality of Apparitions* by Daniel Defoe. She is also actively involved in *The Eighteenth Century: A Current Bibliography*, serving as both an editor and a reviewer.

SUSAN MANLY is a Lecturer in the School of English at the University of St Andrews. She is the editor of Maria Edgeworth's *Harrington* (1817) and *Practical Education* (1798), and the co-editor of Edgeworth's *Leonora* (1806) and *Helen* (1834), all published as part of the *Novels and Selected Works of Maria Edgeworth*, twelve vols. (1999/2003). Her paperback edition of *Harrington*, with an expanded introductory essay and contextual material, will be published in 2004.

JESSICA RICHARD is an Assistant Professor of English at Wake Forest University. She is completing a book about gambling in eighteenth-century British culture and has forthcoming articles on women writers' responses to *Rasselas* and *Frankenstein* and polar exploration. She is also editing *Rasselas*.

HEIDI THOMSON is Senior Lecturer in English at Victoria University of Wellington, New Zealand. She has edited *The Absentee* for Penguin Classics (2000). Together with Kim Walker she edited volume five of

Edgeworth's Tales (1999). She has published articles and reviews in *Journal of English and Germanic Philology, Studies in Romanticism, Yearbook of English Studies, Modern Language Review,* and *Criticism.*

CATHERINE TOAL is Research Fellow at Emmanuel College, Cambridge. She is currently completing a book project on cruelty and form in nineteenth-century French and American literature.

Index

Note: Novels are not indexed for pages in chapters where they appear in the title of that chapter. References to the notes are provided only when something substantive is to be found there. References to authors of essays in this collection refer to sections other than their own essays. Characters in novels are not indexed.

Abbott, Charles, 108, 110, 112
Absentee Anglo-Irish landlords: their fate in London, 179
Act of Union, 13, 45, 66, 96
Anti-Jacobin, The, 140
Arnold, Matthew, 131–32
Association for Preserving Liberty and Property . . . , 129
Atkinson, Colin and Jo, 225
Austen, Jane, 131, 167; *Mansfield Park*, Fanny Price discusses slavery in, 205; *Northanger Abbey*, 129

Bacon, Francis: *Sylva Sylvarum*, 241
Banim, John and Michael, 121–22
Batchelor, The: or Speculations of Jeoffry Wagstaffe, Esq., 141–42
Beaufort, Daniel, 114
Beddoes, Thomas: (RLE's son-in-law), 42, 176
Bedford, Duke of: protest against French War, 40
Belanger, Jacqueline, 21, 127
Bentham, Jeremy, 49, 238
Bentley, Thomas, 35
Bhabha, Homi, 118
Black book of Edgeworthstown, The, 95
Boileau, Nicolas: *Art Poetique*, 127
Botkin, Frances, 20
Boulton, Matthew, 35
Brooke, Charlotte, 34
Burgess, Miranda, 153, 158
Burke, Edmund: family as paradigm of government, 19, 76; lobbies parliament with Robert Nugent, 54; organic definition of society, 86; *Reflections on the Revolution in France*, 67
Burns, Robert, 34, 38; *Poems*, 38; "Tam o' Shanter," 39
Butler, Marilyn, 15, 19–20, 88, 128, 135, 138, 251

Caillière, Maréchal de, 197
Campbell, Thomas: "The Exile of Erin," 55
Caoinan, 87, 93
Carleton, William, 121–22
Carlyle, Thomas: on the "Irish national character" in "Chartism," 146, 147
Chesterfield, Lord: *Letters to His Son*, 63, 71–72, 78
Corbett, Mary Jean, 16, 75
Cosgrove, Peter, 20
Costello-Sullivan, Kathleen, 22
Courier de Provence, 238
Creoles: character of, 201–4
Croker, John Wilson, 47, 116; *An Intercepted Letter from J—— T—— Esq . . .* , 114
Croker, Thomas Crofton, 88
Cullen, L.M., 67
Cumberland, Richard: *The West Indian*, 204

Darwin, Erasmus, 35, 176
Davies, Sir John, 50, 114
Day, Thomas, 24, 35, 173, 178; "The

Dying Negro," 204; his manners compared to RLE's, 174; *Sanford and Merton*, 203; his scheme to eduacte a wife parodied in *Belinda*, 213
Deane, Seamus, 47, 105, 122, 148
Declaratory Act, repeal of, 255
D'Israel, Isaac: "Biographical Sketch . . ." and ME, 248
Dohm, Christian Wilhelm von: "On the Civic Improvement of the Jews," 239
Don Quixote, 140
Drennan, William: on Act of Union, 13; and evocation of Ireland, 42; and founding of United Irishmen, 34; on "Irish" rights, 18; *Letters from an Irish Helot*, 35; meets RLE at Volunteer congress, 35, 135
Dumont, Pierre Étienne, 238. *See also* Mirabeau, le Comte de
Dunne, Tom, 47, 132, 135

Eagleton, Terry, 47, 56, 130–31, 132
Edgeworth, Maria: *The Absentee*, 15, 16, 49, 50, 52, 62, 75, 85, 106, 120, 140, 166, 257; *Belinda*, 16, 23–24, 50, 56, 166, 171, 173, 208, 213; *Castle Rackrent*, 15, 16, 20, 33, 40, 48, 49, 62, 63, 106, 118, 121, 127, 138, 166, 188; *Ennui*, 22, 47, 62, 85, 100, 106, 118, 120, 127, 128, 130, 133, 135, 140, 166, 169, 188, 208; *An Essay on Irish Bulls*, 15, 19, 22, 33, 38, 108, 121, 137: "Bath Coach Conversation," 109–10; "Little Dominick," 46; "The Hibernian Mendicant," 46, 139; "The Irish Incognito," 46; *Harrington*, 24, 116, 119, 125, 171, 175; in *Tales and Miscellaneous Pieces*, 239; *Helen*, 127, 171; *Leonora*, 128, 171; *Moral Tales*: *The Good French Governess*, 196; *Ormond*, 20, 50, 55, 56, 85, 100, 116, 130, 166, 169, 170, 188, 198, 239; *Patronage*, 49, 55, 105; *Popular Tales*, 116, 263: "The Grateful Negro," 210; "The Purple Jar," 55; *Tales of Fashionable Life*, 49, 116–18, 165; *Vivian*, 49; *Whim for Whim*, 42
Edgeworth, M. Pakenham, 11, 13, 22, 127

Edgeworth, Richard Lovell: and Act of Union, 85–86; attempts to create "religion of nature," 35; contacts with United Irishmen, 35, 42; and his Irish accent, 172–73; his manners compared to Thomas Day's, 174; and Jacobinism, 138; on magazine subscriptions in Ireland, 190; *Memoirs*, 23, 134, 135, 146, 172, 176; *Memoirs* and avoidance of "vulgarity," 177; and rebellion of 1798, 133, 134
Edgeworth, Richard Lovell and Maria: *Practical Education*, 24, 36–37, 175–76, 194, 195, 198, 205, 208, 212; Rev. of *The Stranger in Ireland* by John Carr, 111, 115–16
Elers, Anna Maria: (first wife of RLE), 35
Elizabeth I, 42, 56
Emmet, Robert: "London Pride and the Shamrock," 45; rebellion of (1803), 51; "The Two Ships," 45
Erin, or Ierne: appearance of, 42

"Fashion": *OED* definitions of, 172, 179
Fénelon, François de la Salignac de la Mothe: *Les Aventures de Télémaque*, 56, 65, 81
Fenwick, Eliza: *Secresy, or The Ruin on the Rock*, 130
Ferrier, Mrs., 85
Ferris, Ina, 47, 257, 261
Fielding, Henry, 63
Fitzgerald, family, 51; Lord Edward, 42–43
Fitzgibbon, Charles, Lord Chancellor for Ireland, 43
Fontaine, Jean de la, 49
Forbes, Duncan: on Scott's use of history, 258
Foster, John, 47
Foster, Roy, 131
Foy, Nathaniel, 27
Franklin, Benjamin: "religion of nature," 35
Frye, Northrop, 22, 74

Gagoty, Jean Baptiste André: *La Benefaisance de la Dauphine*, 83

INDEX

Gallagher, Catherine, 47, 235
Geiger, Abraham, 246
George III: his reaction to *Castel Rackrent*, 107, 254
Gillespie, Raymond: on the O'Farrell family, 48
Godwin, William, 138; *Caleb Williams*, 130; *Political Justice*, 50
Gonda, Caroline: and Belinda's provenance, 223
Gordon Riots, 236
Gough, John: *A Tour in Ireland in 1813 and 1814 . . .* , 123
Grace O'Malley, 42
Granard, Earl of, 134
Granard, Lady, 128
Granu, or Granuweal, 42, 51
Grattan, Henry, 255
Greenfield, Susan, 201, 223, 225
Grose, Francis, 34, 38; *Antiquities of Scotland*, 39; *A Classical Dictionary of the Vulgar Tongue*, 39; *A Provincial Dictionary*, 39; death of, 40
Gumperz, Salomon, 240
Gwynn, Stephen: his definition of "Anglo-Irish," 16

Hamilton, Mrs. (Emma), 85
Harrington, James: *The Commonwealth of Oceana*, 245; and sentiment about Charles I, 245
Hawthorne, Mark, 64
Hays, Mary, 225
Hazlitt, William: *The Spirit of the Age . . .* , 165
Herbert, Edward (Lord Cherbury), 56; *Arcadian Autobiography*, 56; *De Veritate*, 36
Hogarth, William: "The House of Cards," 196
Holcroft, Thomas, 138
Hollingworth, Brian, 64, 65, 110, 137, 251
Hooper, Glenn, 123
Hoyle, Edmond: "Short Treatise on the Game of Whist," 198
Hultin, Neil, 88
Hume, David: *Political Essays*, 236, 242

Hunter, R., 138
Hutcheson, Francis, 34

Inchbald, Elizabeth: *A Simple Story*, 166

James I, 56
James II, 27
Jeffrey, Francis, 52, 116, 118; Rev. of *The Absentee*, 165
Jewish Naturalization Act, 236
Johnson, Joseph, 137, 138
Johnson, Samuel, 39, 71
Jones, Darryl, 21–22
Jones, Todd, 135
Jospe, Alfred, 246

Keir, James, 35
Kelly, Gary, 167
Kerr, James, 262
Kestner, Joseph, 67
Kiberd, Declan, 132
Kincade, Kit, 25
King, William, 16, 27
Kirkpatrick, Kathryn, 96–97
König, René, 179
Kowaleski-Wallace, Elizabeth, 18, 150

Lavater, Johann Caspar: attempt to debate Mendelssohn, 244–45
Leadbeater, Mary: *Cottage Dialogues Among the Irish Peasantry*, 100
Leerssen, Joep, 17, 33, 80, 86
LeFanu, Sheridan, 131
Limerick, Treaty of, 27
Locke, John, 140
Logan, Peter Melville, 235, 244
London Corresponding Society, 129
Long, Edward: *History of Jamaica*, 202
Louis XIV, 179
Louis XV, 66
Lovecraft, H.P.: "The Call of Cthulhu," 143
Lucas, Charles, 15, 257
Lukács, Georg, 68–69
Lunar Society (of Birmingham), 35, 138, 176
Lynch, Patrick: *Bolg an Tsolar*, 34

INDEX

Mabey, Richard: provides definition of "landscape," 12
Macintosh, Fiona: *Dying Acts: Death in Ancient Greece* . . . , 86
MacNeice, Louis, 14
MacPherson, James, 34
Maginn, William, 131
Mandeville, Bernard: *The Fable of the Bees*, 169–70
Manly, Susan, 24–25
Maturin, Charles, 131; *Melmoth the Wanderer*, 129, 131
McCann, Andrew, 222
McCormack, W.J., 16, 131; on Scott's debt to M.E., 257
McCormack, W.J. and Kim Walker, 114
McCracken, Henry Joy: "The Thistle and the Shamrock," 41
McTier, Martha, 13
Mendelssohn, Moses, 24, 237; *Jerusalem*, 245
Méré, Chevalier de, 197
Mirabeau, le Comte de, 238; of the republic of Virginia , 246; *Sur Moses Mendelssohn*, 238
"Modest Defence of Gaming, A," 198
Moira, 3rd Earl of (Francis Rawdon-Hastings), 128, 132
Moira, Lady, 128
Molière, 49, 140
Molyneaux, William, 15, 257
Moore, Tom, 33
Morellet, Abbé, 78
Mowitt, John, 63
Moynahan, Julian: his definition of "Anglo-Irish," 16, 95
Moyse, Israel, 240, 244
Murdoch, D.H., 201
Musgrave, Sir Richard: *History of the Irish Rebellions of 1641, 1688* . . . , 45; *Memoirs of the Different Rebellions in Ireland* . . . , 132–33
Myers, Mitzi, 64, 173

Neilson, Samuel: *Northern Star*, 34–35, 38
"New Game of Virtue Rewarded and Vice Punished, The," 197

Nollekens, Joseph Francis: "The Two Children of the Nollekens Family . . . ," 196
Nugent, Grace, 52
Nugent, Robert, 54

Oates, Titus, 45
O'Brien, FitzJames, 131
O'Connor, Arthur and Thomas Addis Emmet: *The Press*, 41
Ó Gallchoir, Clíona, 125
O'Halloran, Sylvester, 34, 51
Ó hÓgáin, Dáithí: on ME's use of folklore, 263; on Thady Quirk's narrative, 264
Orangemen, Loyal Order of, 136
Otaheite, 106
Owenson, Sydney (Lady Morgan), 50, 85, 116; *The O'Briens and the O'Flaherties*, 56; *The Wild Irish Girl*, 34, 85, 86

Paddy's Resource, 41
Paine, Tom, 36
Percy, Thomas, 34
Perera, Suvendrini, 15
Petty, William, 27
Plowden, Francis, 51
Plumb, J.H.: on "improvement," 175; on *Practical Education* as example of above, 175–76
Pope, Alexander, 63, 76; "Epistle to Cobham," 77; "Epistle to Dr. Arbuthnot," 76; *An Essay on Man, Epistle II*, 77
Porteous Incident, 259
Priestley, Joseph, 35
Prior, Thomas: *A List of the Absentees of Ireland* . . . , 27

Ragussis, Michael, 235, 237
Rawdon-Hastings, Francis (2nd Earl of Moira), 128. *See also* Moira, Third Earl of
Reeves, John, 129
Reynolds, George Nugent: death of at Stowe, 55; "The Exiled Irishman's Lament," 54; "Green were the fields where my forefathers . . .," 54–55

Reynolds, Joshua: on realism and aestheticism in art, 218
Richardson, Samuel, 63
Rochefoucault, Adélaïde de la, 49
Rowan, Hamilton, 135
Royal Irish Academy, the, 40
Richard, Jessica, 23–24
Ritson, Joseph, 34
Rousseau, Jean-Jacques, 44, 212; *Émile*, 24, 35, 198, 212; *Julie ou la Nouvelle Héloise*, 35

Sacks, Sheldon, 64
Sampson, William: Society for Obtaining Authentic Information . . . , 132
Satyrical and Burlesque Dictionary of M Le Roux, 39
Scott, Sarah: *The History of Sir George Ellison*, 203
Scott, Sir Walter, 13, 25, 250; Waverly novels: *Heart of Mid-Lothian*, 256
Sévigné, Marquis de, 49
Seymour, Richard: *The Court Gamester*, 198
Shakespeare, William: *I Henry IV*, 65
Shylock: his role in *Harrington*, 235
Sidney, Sir Philip: *Arcadia*, 56
Sir Charles Grandison, 170
Smith, Adam: *The Wealth of Nations*, 169
Sovereignty queen, 51; Florence Annaly as exemplar of, 52; Grace Nugent as exemplar of, 52
Spenser, Edmund, 55, 114, 137; *The Færie Queene*, 56; *View of the Present State of Ireland, A*, 110, 136
Spivak, Gayatri: *A Critique of Postcolonial Reason*, 147, 153
Stoker, Bram, 131
Swift, Jonathan, 43, 56; "The Injured Lady," 46; "Verses said to be written on the Union," 46

Talbot, Richard, Earl of Tyrconnell: relationship to Grace Nugent and "Lillibulero," 53

Tandy, Napper, 135
Toal, Catherine, 24
Toland, John, 36
Thomson, Heidi, 15, 22–23
Thuente, Mary Helen, 33
Trumpener, Katie, 33, 47, 56
Ty, Eleanor, 225

United Irishmen (Society of), 13, 19, 33, 34, 37, 132, 134, 139

Vance, Norman, 33
Vattel, Emerich de, 63
Vernon, Vice Admiral Edward: *New History of Jamaica*, 202
Voltaire, 49

Ward, John: Rev. of *Patronage* in *Quarterly Review*, 106
Watt, James, 35
Watts, Isaac: *Divine and Moral Songs for Children*; "The Child's Complaint," 196
Wedgwood, Josiah, 35, 176
Wells, Helena: *Constantina Neville; or the West Indian*, 203
Whelan, Kevin, 47, 132
Whillaluh, 87, 250
Wilde, Oscar, 131
Williams, David: *Liturgy on the Universal Principles of Religion* . . . , 58
Williams, Raymond, 131
Wollstonecraft, Mary, 225; *Thoughts on the Education of Daughters*, 197; "A Vindication of the Rights of Women," 18, 36

Yorke, Philip, Third Earl of Hardwicke, 108, 112
Young, Arthur, 114; *Tour of Ireland*, 110, 169
Young, Edward: *Conjectures on Original Composition*, 73